In the Anglo-Arab Labyrinth

Cambridge Studies in the History and Theory of Politics

EDITORS

MAURICE COWLING
G. R. ELTON
E. KEDOURIE
J. G. A. POCOCK
J. R. POLE
WALTER ULLMANN

In the Anglo-Arab Labyrinth

The
McMahon–Husayn Correspondence
and its Interpretations
1914–1939

ELIE KEDOURIE

Professor of Politics in the University of London

Cambridge University Press

Cambridge

London · New York · Melbourne

Published by the Syndics of the Cambridge University Press
The Pitt Building, Trumpington Street, Cambridge CB2 1RP
Bentley House, 200 Euston Road, London NW1 2DB
32 East 57th Street, New York, NY 10022, USA
296 Beaconsfield Parade, Middle Park, Melbourne 3206, Australia

Library of Congress Cataloguing in Publication Data

Kedourie, Elie.

In the Anglo-Arab labyrinth.

(Cambridge studies in the history and theory of politics)

Bibliography: p.

Includes index.

1. Great Britain – Foreign relations – Near East.
2. Near East – Foreign relations – Great Britain.
I. Title.
DS63.2.G7K4   327.41'017'4927   75-3975
ISBN 0-521-20826-2

First published 1976

Printed in Great Britain
at the
University Printing House, Cambridge
(Euan Phillips, University Printer)

Philochorus says the Cretans...will not allow the Labyrinth to have been anything but a prison, which had no other inconvenience than this, that those who were confined there could not escape.

PLUTARCH

...diplomatic history...the record of what one clerk said to another clerk.

G. M. YOUNG

Contents

vii

Maps

Preface

The genesis, and the subsequent official interpretations, of the
McMahon–Husayn correspondence are essential to the understanding of a great deal of Middle-Eastern diplomatic history during and
after the first world war, as well as of the Palestine dispute in the
1920s and 30s. But the history of the correspondence and its
interpretations is so long and complicated that its inclusion in a
general narrative raises great difficulties: either such a narrative is
broken by inordinately long digressions, or the various episodes
connected with the correspondence and its historiography become
well-nigh unintelligible. I have therefore thought it best to set out
the history of the correspondence in one consecutive account. A
consecutive story has the additional advantage of bringing out the
great intrinsic interest of the correspondence and its fortunes over
the years. For the story, as the reader will discover, is essentially
a drama: it is as though, over the years, the telegrams, despatches,
memoranda and minutes – the *personae* of this book – have managed to perform a ghostly comedy of errors, intricate in plot, rich
in surprises, and abounding in curious – sometimes even farcical –
situations.

This study, as will quickly become apparent, would not have been
possible without the wealth of documents which have become
available in the course of the last decade at the Public Record Office
and the India Office Records in London, and at the Archives du
Ministère des Affaires Etrangères in Paris. I am very much in the
debt of their staffs for their constant and ready helpfulness. I am
also very grateful to the Service historique de l'Armée, Paris; the
Cambridge University Library; the Bodleian Library, Oxford; the
Middle East Centre, St Antony's College, Oxford; Rhodes House
Library, Oxford; Pembroke College, Cambridge; the Library of the
School of Oriental Studies, Durham University; the Beaverbrook
Library, London; and the Israel State Archives, Jerusalem, for
access to documents in their possession. I would also like to renew
my thanks to New College, Oxford, and to Yale University Library
for having made available, some twenty-five years ago, papers which

I used in the main in an earlier book, *England and the Middle East*, but to which I have also referred in this work.

In the footnotes, the customary abbreviations indicate the provenance of the documents. P.R.O., F.O., C.O. and Cab. refer to papers in the Public Record Office, while L/P & S refers to papers in the India Office Records.

Crown Copyright records appear by permission of the Controller, Her Majesty's Stationery Office. I am most grateful to Mr R. D. Chancellor for permission to quote a passage from a draft letter written by his father, Sir John Chancellor; and to Mr Stewart Perowne, o.b.e., for permission to quote a passage from one of his letters.

I would like to thank the Government Research Division, London School of Economics, for valuable help, and Mrs Denise Angus for research assistance, expertly given, at a time when illness made such assistance very welcome.

I would also like to thank my colleague, Professor Emrys Jones, for his help in connection with the maps included in this book, and the Drawing Office of the Department of Geography at the School for producing them.

I am most obliged to Dr J. B. Kelly for the great care with which he read this book in typescript, and for the many valuable suggestions he has made. I am also grateful to Professor B. Lewis for many useful comments.

E.K.

The London School of Economics and Political Science
July 1975

PART I
THE QUICKSAND

This Arab question is a regular quicksand.
SIR EDWARD GREY

1. Cairo, London and the Sharif of Mecca

Between July 1915 and March 1916, the British high commissioner in Egypt and the Sharif of Mecca exchanged a number of letters now generally known as the McMahon–Husayn correspondence. Almost from the start, the correspondence became the subject of conflicting interpretations, and the passage of time did not diminish – indeed sharpened – the controversy. It is perhaps not too much to say that for half a century the correspondence haunted Anglo-Arab relations. Less than a year after the end of the war, details of the correspondence were disclosed in a long article in *The Daily Telegraph* signed by the journalist Perceval Landon, but in reality written by Colonel T. E. Lawrence. By 1923 English readers had at their disposal in chapter 1 of J. de V. Loder's book *The Truth about Mesopotamia, Palestine and Syria*, an accurate and reasonably full account of these exchanges, and by 1934 readers of Arabic had available to them, in a well-known work by Amin Sa'id, a more or less complete text of the letters. Finally, in 1938 most of the letters were printed in an English version by George Antonius as an appendix to his book *The Arab Awakening*. But it was not until 1939 that the British government at last officially published the correspondence in a white paper.[1]

Official publication of the letters was at the request of the Arab delegations to the Palestine conferences of 1938–9. The delegations believed that the correspondence showed that Sir Henry McMahon had promised Palestine to the Sharif in 1915, and that its publication therefore would strengthen the Arab case against Zionism. Such belief was indeed widely prevalent in the Arab world, and it had been greatly strengthened over the years by the refusal of successive British governments to disclose officially the text of these letters. The correspondence thus became part of the Palestine dispute, and it was in the light of this dispute that it has been generally

[1] Cmd. 5957, 1939 (*Accounts and Papers* 1938–9, vol. XXVII). Amin Sa'id's work is *al-Thawra al-'arabiyya al-kubra* [The Great Arab Revolt], 3 vols., Cairo [1934]; the correspondence is in vol. I, pp. 130–44. Lawrence's authorship of the article in *The Daily Telegraph* of 11 Sept. 1919 is affirmed in a minute by H. W. Young, 12 Sept., in F.O. 371/4182, 128367/2117.

read, scrutinized, and argued over as lawyers, say, would argue over the wording of a contract or the proper construction of a statute. But when McMahon and Husayn were secretly writing to one another in 1915–16, the Balfour declaration had not been written, there was no British mandate in Palestine and no dispute between Zionists, Arabs and British over the control of Palestine. When they were written, the letters had formed part of quite a different history, that of British and of Sharifian war-time diplomacy.

In order fully to understand the meaning of these documents, which are at once deliberately vague and unwittingly obscure, and to account for the remarkably divergent interpretations to which they have given rise, we must see them then as belonging to two different histories: that of Anglo-Sharifian negotiations during 1914–16, and that of the Palestine dispute which began with the British conquest of Palestine and the Balfour declaration. We must also form some idea of the character and aims of those who wrote them, and of the misunderstandings, the divergent preoccupations, the conflicting ambitions which in later years led to such confusion and contention.

I

The first letter in the correspondence came from Mecca, but it was not written by Husayn or addressed to McMahon. Dated 14 July 1915 and received in Egypt on 18 August, it was addressed to Ronald Storrs, oriental secretary at the British residency in Cairo, and it came from Abdullah, second son of the Sharif. The letter asked for British acknowledgement of Arab independence in an extensive territory comprising the Levant, Mesopotamia and Arabia, for a treaty making Great Britain responsible for the defence of this independent state, and for British approval of the proclamation of 'an Arab Khalifate of Islam'. The letter did not come out of the blue, for writer and recipient had met and corresponded intermittently on political questions since February 1914. The original contact was sought by Abdullah who, while on a visit to Cairo, saw Kitchener and represented to him that affairs in the Hijaz were not going well 'owing to the recent appointment of a new Turkish Vali who combined civil and military functions...and does not act harmoniously with his father'. In case matters got worse, and an attempt was made to depose his father, would the British government, Abdullah asked, use its 'good offices' with the Sublime Porte to prevent this? If Istanbul embarked on such a design 'the tribes of the Hejaz would fight for the Sharif and a state of war against the Turkish troops would ensue'. The British government could surely not remain indifferent to disturbances in the holy places which so many of its subjects visited yearly? If disturbances did ensue Abdullah hoped that 'the British Government would not allow reinforcements to be sent by sea for the purpose of preventing the Arabs from exercising the rights which they have enjoyed from time immemorial in their own country round the holy places.'[1]

Abdullah's move was audacious. It was nothing less than an attempt to recruit the British government as an auxiliary in his father's quarrel with the Porte. The quarrel was between a centralizing government intent on extending the Hijaz railway from Medina to Mecca, and an over-mighty subject who had no desire to give up his quasi-independent status, his armed following, or his autocratic powers over the population of the Hijaz. The clash between Husayn and the Porte – a clash between a traditional despotism and a modernizing absolutism – is well described by acting consul Abdurrahman, whose despatch, sent from Jeddah a month or so after Abdullah's visit to Cairo, supplies the context in which the latter's overtures to Kitchener have to be seen. The consul described the insecurity which had been lately reigning in the Hijaz: armed robberies and plundering of shops by beduins in Jeddah, telegraph and telephone wires between Mecca and Jeddah cut almost daily, the mails and the caravans robbed and escort soldiers murdered, kidnapping of women, and an Afghan, 'a very respectable resident of Mecca in the bad books of the Grand Shereef for his outspokenness', murdered on the latter's orders together with seven soldiers of his escort while travelling to Ta'if. 'It is an open secret', affirmed the consul, 'that the cause of all this disturbance is the Grand Shereef himself. He was, up to the arrival of the New Vali, the sole monarch of the Hedjaz and his word was law in this country. The Grand Shereef is naturally opposed to any reform and wants that everything should run in ancient rut. All departments in Mecca and Jeddah were under the authoritative guidance of the Shereef and the Turkish Government was only in name. Every Vali who came here during the last five years had to be either slave of the Grand Shereef or be summarily dismissed'.[2] Devey, the British consul in

[1] F.O. 371/2130, 6672, Kitchener to Grey, no. 22 Secret, Cairo 6 Feb. 1914.
[2] F.O. 371/2130, 15057/6672, acting consul S. Abdurrahman despatch no. 16, Jeddah 11 Mar. 1914 enclosed with Mallet's despatch no. 219, Constantinople 2 Apr.

Damascus (who had served in Jeddah) supplemented the information in Abdurrahman's despatch: 'The Vali of Mecca Wahab Bey', he wrote in a memorandum of 30 March, 'is on bad terms with the Shereef: on his arrival in Mecca the Shereef turned out all his Bisha force of Police to meet him with honour, but soon afterwards the Vali ordered these native "Bisha" police to be deprived of their government rifles which were at once handed over to the Turkish Government uniformed police. He also told the Shereef not to inflict punishment on Arabs. Consequently the Shereef is inciting the Arabs round about Mecca to insurrection on the pretext of protesting that they will allow no railway to be made to Mecca because it will lessen their camel transport profits. The Union and Progress are striving to bring the Arabs to consent to this project, and the chief representative of their party in Mecca, a Circassian Bey or colonel, who was visiting round the Arabs for this purpose, was lately killed and hacked to pieces.'[1]

The Vali's determination to assert his authority crumbled very quickly. He had no forces to oppose to the Sharif and was obliged to sue for peace. In a despatch of 19 March, the acting British consul reported that the Sharif's conditions for calling off the disturbance were that the government should abandon the idea of extending the railway to Mecca, that the Hijaz should remain free from conscription as hitherto, and most significantly, that the court of justice in Jeddah should deal only with foreigners' cases, presumably abandoning the Ottoman inhabitants of the Hijaz and their interests to his unfettered discretion.[2] This was a mere reversion to what used to obtain under the Hamidian regime, when the Sharif of Mecca, in return for abstaining from meddling in imperial politics, from intriguing with foreign powers, and threatening the Sultan's title to the caliphate, was allowed to oppress the Hijazis and fleece the pilgrims with impunity. But the privileges which Abd al-Hamid bestowed amicably, and not under duress, the zealous and clumsy Young Turks had now to concede under threat, at a heavy cost to the prestige and authority of the Porte.

The Sharif, then, won his skirmish with the Porte without the British aid which Abdullah had been sent to solicit. From Cairo the latter had gone to Constantinople in order to negotiate on the spot with the Ottoman ministers. On his way back to the Hijaz, he stopped in Cairo once more where, as on the previous occasion, he

[1] F.O. 371/2130, 18245/7772, enclosed with Mallet's despatch no. 258, 27 Apr. 1914.
[2] F.O. 371/2130, 15057/6672.

stayed in Abdin Palace as the Khedive's guest. Storrs went to see him there on 18 April. Abdullah declared himself dissatisfied with the result of his negotiations at Constantinople, and he disclosed that his father had instructed him, Storrs recorded in a note dated the following day, to approach Kitchener 'with a view to obtaining with [sic] the British Government an agreement similar to that existing between the Amir of Afghanistan and the Government of India, in order to maintain the status quo in the Arabian peninsula and to do away with the danger of wanton Turkish aggression. He assured me', Storrs went on, 'that the Arabs were concentrating and solidifying, that Ibn Saud, the Idrissi, and even the Imam Yehia would before long be in complete unity with each other and with the Sherifate.' On the morrow Storrs returned and, under instruction, informed Abdullah 'that he should not expect any encouragement from the British Government; that it was more than possible that the Porte did not really intend to carry out their threat [to extend the railway to Mecca]; that in any case we should wait to hear how the latest developments were received at Mecca before communicating the Sherif's desire to the Foreign Office; that we had in principle not the smallest wish to interfere in the government or the administration of the Holy Cities, which only concerned us in so far as they affected the safety and comfort of British pilgrims.'[1] Kitchener, writing to Sir William Tyrell, Sir Edward Grey's private secretary, a few days later may have been correct in saying that Abdullah was told that 'the Arabs of the Hejaz could expect no encouragement from us and that our only interest in Arabia was the safety and comfort of Indian pilgrims',[2] but the language recorded in Storrs's note (which was not sent to the foreign office until the following December) is clearly less categorical than Kitchener made out. For by saying that British interest in the Hijaz was only 'in principle' solely directed to the welfare of the pilgrims, and by suggesting that reactions in Mecca to Ottoman policies should be awaited before anything further was done, Storrs hinted that the rejection of Abdullah's approach was not as final or irrevocable as it, at first sight, seemed to be.

Again, one wonders whether the note which Storrs composed for the record in fact contains all that passed between him and Abdullah. In his memoirs he mentions one other episode which does not figure

[1] F.O. 371/1973, 87396, 'Note' by R. Storrs, 19 Apr. 1914, enclosure no. 1 in Cheetham's despatch no. 204, Cairo 13 Dec. 1914.
[2] G. P. Gooch and H. W. V. Temperley (eds.), *British Documents on the Origins of the War*, vol. x pt 2, p. 831, Kitchener by Tyrrell, Cairo 26 Apr. 1914.

in the note. Here, he describes the charm of Abdullah's conversation and he goes on: 'Travelling by a series of delicately inclined planes, from a warrior past I found myself in the defenceless Arab present, being asked categorically whether Great Britain would present the Grand Sharif with a dozen, or even a half-dozen machine guns. When I enquired what could possibly be their purpose, he replied (like all re-armers) "for defence"; and, pressed further, added that the defence would be against attack from the Turks. I needed no special instructions to inform him that we could never entertain the idea of supplying arms to be used against a Friendly Power. Abdullah can have expected no other reply, and we parted on the best of terms'.[1]

We may better appreciate this delicate ironizing about Friendly Powers and the like by referring once more to Storrs's note which confirms that the two interlocutors found each other congenial. Abdullah confided in Storrs the 'poor opinion' he had formed of the Sultan and the other Princes, who, he said, 'had their hands tied behind their backs, and recorded like phonographs the thoughts of the Jews.' Abdullah was here repeating the widespread accusations made against the Committee of Union and Progress by their Ottoman rivals and by British embassy circles at Constantinople.[2] Abdullah may indeed have sensed that retailing gossip of this kind would please his interlocutor, who seems, in fact, to have shared this belief in the occult and nefarious influence of the Jews over the Young Turks. Thus, in 1916 he was still speaking of 'Jews now reigning in the Bosphorus'. Earlier, in a letter of December 1914 to Colonel O. A. G. Fitzgerald, Kitchener's personal military secretary, in which he discussed various plans for the future control of Palestine, Storrs referred to 'a section [of the Jews] which has undoubtedly helped to thrust the Turks over the precipice' and thought it worth while to enclose with his letter a report on

[1] Ronald Storrs, *Orientations*, definitive ed., 1943, pp. 122–3. On the basis of a report written by Abdullah for his father which he was able to see in the papers of Zayd, the youngest of Husayn's sons, Sulayman Musa declares, *al-Haraka al-'arabiyya* [The Arab Movement], Beirut, 1970, p. 72, that this conversation with Storrs took place not in April, but in February during Abdullah's first visit to Cairo. But the text of Abdullah's letter, as Sulayman Musa subsequently published it, has no reference to arms; see Sulayman Musa (ed.), *al-Murasalat al-tarikhiyya 1914–1918* [Historical Correspondence], vol. 1, Amman, 1973, pp. 21–2, undated letter from Abdullah in Cairo to Husayn (which Sulayman Musa tentatively dates 15 Feb. 1914). The text of the letter shows that in citing Husayn's words in The Arab Movement Sulayman Musa somewhat prettified them by ironing out colloquialisms and ungrammatical expressions.

[2] See Elie Kedourie, 'Young Turks, Freemasons and Jews' in *Arabic Political Memoirs and Other Studies*, 1974, pp. 243–62.

Palestine and Jerusalem submitted by an unnamed Syrian to the British military authorities in Egypt, in which it was declared that 'the only thing that filled the inhabitants with hatred against the [Ottoman] Government is the fact that the Zionists are supported by the Government and the Union and Progress party, and the lands of the natives are taken away by force to be sold to the Zionists. These Zionists are closely connected with Berlin and Constantinople and are the most important factor in the policy of Palestine'.[1]

The friendliness which their interview established between Abdullah and Storrs appears from other remarks which the latter's note records. Abdullah reported that the Grand Vizier had insisted on extending the railway to Mecca because he was afraid of the ambitions of a Power which he refused to name, and that he, Abdullah, then said to the Grand Vizier that it must be Great Britain which he was suspecting. For a prominent Ottoman subject to report such an exchange to an official of the very Power which his government held in suspicion was already to create a certain friendly complicity between them. This complicity must have been confirmed by Abdullah's parting words: he told Storrs 'with a smile that he had received instructions not to return to Arabia via Egypt or, if that route was inevitable, at least not to see Lord Kitchener or any representative of his. He also told me that as he embarked Enver Pasha [the minister of war] sent him a pair of pistols and he left me in very little doubt as to the direction in which he would like to discharge these pieces should the occasion arise'.

But between Abdullah and Storrs, was it only a matter of hints and intimations, of delicate allusions and barely expressed suggestions? From Abdullah's contemporary report to his father, it would seem that what passed between him and Storrs was sensibly more explicit, and this as early as the February visit. As has been seen, Kitchener's despatch to Grey gave an account of his conversation with Abdullah on this occasion, but mentioned no other encounter. According to Abdullah, however, some days after his conversation with Kitchener he asked Storrs to go and see him at Abdin Palace and put to him the following proposal: 'If the C.U.P. compel us to fight in defence of our country, and if you will prevent them from bombarding our coasts and landing troops, and allow us to use Port-Sudan for transport and communications, we would facilitate

[1] Storrs, *Orientations*, p. 162; P.R.O. 30 57/45, Kitchener Papers, Storrs to Fitzgerald, Cairo 28 Dec. 1914.

your trade and give you preference over all Powers'. As may be seen, this is the same proposal, couched in more far-reaching and less reticent terms, as Abdullah had put before Kitchener a few days before. Storrs's response to this, if Abdullah is to be believed, was: 'Yes, this is my idea, which I have been trying to realize for ten years. But what would we do if the Turks say that you have to re-establish public security?'[1] This exchange is at first sight astonishing, but on reflection one may come to think that it is not inherently improbable. After all, there was no conceivable advantage for Abdullah, who was writing a confidential report for his father's eyes, to invent it *de toutes pièces*. The report, again, was written very shortly after the conversation was said to have taken place. And as will be seen, there is no doubt at all that Storrs did have very grandiose ideas about extending British power and influence in the Middle East. Another point which speaks in favour of Abdullah's account is the *quid pro quo* which he says he offered to Storrs and on which Kitchener's despatch of 6 February is silent. It may well be that in a formal interview with the British agent and consul-general this delicate point was not broached, but it is highly unlikely that Abdullah would expect the British government to take the serious step of denying the Suez Canal to Ottoman transports merely out of solicitude for the welfare of Indian pilgrims. The interview with Storrs was a good opportunity to spell out the advantages he was offering. And in fact we do know that at his April interview with Storrs, Abdullah did propose that the Hijaz should become a client state of Britain's.

Another circumstance attending Abdullah's visit to Cairo deserves to be noticed. On both of his visits, he stayed at Abdin Palace as the guest of Khedive Abbas. This was by no means devoid of political significance. Relations between Abdullah's branch of the Hashemite family and the Khedives were close. It was Muhammad Ali who, during his conquest of the Hijaz, had raised Abdullah's great-grandfather from obscurity and made him amir of Mecca. More recently, Abbas himself had nursed ambitions in the Levant and in Arabia and had perhaps even dreamed – however vaguely – of superseding the Ottomans in the caliphate.[2] According to Abdullah, during his February visit, Abbas had asked the Ottoman high commissioner to warn his government against alienating Husayn.

[1] Sulayman Musa, The Arab Movement, p. 71, and Historical Correspondence, vol. I, pp. 21–2.
[2] For Abbas's ambitions in the Arab world at the turn of the century, see Elie Kedourie, 'The Politics of Political Literature: Kawakibi, Azoury and Jung' in *Arabic Political Memoirs*, pp. 107–23.

It was he also who encouraged Abdullah to approach Kitchener and Storrs. Abdullah reports him as saying: 'I do not trust them [the British] in my country, but I trust them in the Arab countries, and particularly in your area. They would not think of occupying your country, being afraid of the anger of their Muslim subjects. They can therefore serve us without our having to be apprehensive of them. We have established the basis [of our relationship] with them, we should now press towards a conclusion and obtain the necessary undertaking from them.'[1] When Husayn rose against the Ottomans in 1916, Abbas, then an exile in Europe, spoke to his intimates of his involvement with the Sharif, how he had hoped to establish an Arab caliphate controlled by an Egyptian sultanate, how he supplied arms to Husayn, and how he concerted with Abdullah what demands the Sharif should present to the Ottoman government.[2] Again, according to Abdullah, when Abbas made him approach Storrs, the Khedive instructed him what offer to make, and told him, 'Do not go into the question of expenses and the like, these will be found by us.'[3]

Abbas's involvement with the Sharif was undoubtedly known to Storrs. Thus, after Abdullah had left for Constantinople following his February visit, we see the residency reporting by telegram on 21 March the arrival of a messenger from the Sharif to the Khedive with a message that the Sharif and the Vali had fallen out over the extension of the railway and that the road from Jeddah to Mecca was closed by the tribesmen who were demanding the Vali's recall.[4]

Abass's ambition to become Caliph – which may have become more lively after the Young Turk *coup d'état* and Abd al-Hamid's deposition – was also known to Storrs, and we may safely assume it to form the background or context of Storrs's conversations with Abdullah. A memorandum by Storrs on the caliphate written in May 1915 is significant here. It shows not only his view of what it was possible for Britain to do in the Middle East following the break with the Ottoman empire, but also how such possibilities had

[1] Sulayman Musa, The Arab Movement, pp. 70–1; and Historical Correspondence, vol. I, pp. 18–20, Abdullah's undated letter to Husayn from Cairo which Sulayman Musa dates 7 Feb. 1914, and pp. 21–2, Abdullah's letter of 15 Feb. cited above.
[2] See 'Mudhakkirat' [Memoirs], the memoirs of the Egyptian nationalist leader, Muhammad Farid, himself then also an exile in Europe, printed in the Cairo periodical *al-Katib*, and particularly in the instalment published in the Oct. 1970 no., pp. 168–9. Another relevant passage occurs in the July 1970 no., p. 177.
[3] Sulayman Musa, Historical Correspondence, vol. I, p. 21.
[4] F.O. 371/2130, 12652/6672, Kitchener's telegram no. 20 secret, 21 Mar. 1914.

come to be present to his mind. He argues that it would be to British advantage if Husayn were to become Caliph. Such a prospect, moreover, might now be quite acceptable to the Muslim and the Arab world. 'In Egypt', he wrote, 'opinion has for the last five years been veering, owing to the detestation caused in religious circles by Young Turkish methods and character, towards the idea of the Arab Khalifate, and it was only the de facto supremacy of the Turks and their possession of Constantinople which prevented this idea from being more loudly voiced. It will be remembered,' he went on, 'that the ex-Khedive took care to stand in with the Sharif even when he was on ostentatiously good relations with the Porte, and although there is no doubt this His Highness cherished vague personal ambitions in the same direction, it is equally clear that he would not have dared to espouse the Arab cause so openly in Egypt unless he had been well assured of its popularity with the Egyptians'.[1] This last assertion was wrong. Arab nationalism and an Arab caliphate were certainly not popular among Egyptians, as the oriental secretary of the residency should have known. But what his language perhaps indicates is Storrs's partiality to such schemes, and the eagerness with which he took them up and pressed them on his colleagues and superiors: what Abbas was ambitious, but unable, to effect the British empire could, with advantage, surely bring to pass.

Storrs, as will be seen, was not the only British official in the Middle East to entertain such ideas. Sir Reginald Wingate, the governor-general of the Sudan, also was very keen on an Arab caliphate patronized and controlled by Britain. And he too, it is significant to note, took his cue from Abbas's dreams and ambitions. 'I had long been cognizant', he wrote to Lord Hardinge in December 1918, 'of the machinations of the ex-Khedive who...was for many years an ardent anti-Turk in so far as he entertained hopes that with the disappearance of Sultan Abdel Hamid, he might, in certain circumstances, aspire to taking his place – not as Sultan of Turkey – but as Khalif of Islam – and with this idea in his mind he had for years conducted secret propaganda both in Arabia, Syria and Tripoli in order to gain the goodwill of the Arabs – his machinery was fairly elaborate and he had some success – until circumstances threw him into the hands of the C.U.P.

[1] F.O. 141/587, 545/2, memorandum by Storrs, 'The Khalifate', 2 May 1915. In a later memorandum, F.O. 141/471, 1731/14, Storrs gives further details of Abbas's relations with Arabia and with Arab secret societies. His intermediaries were Ali Yusuf, the well-known journalist, and Hasan Himada, a Syrian Shari'a lawyer resident in Egypt.

'It was due to some extent to my knowledge of his methods', Wingate went on, 'that I was able to get into touch with the Sharif – and in doing so made use of some of the groundwork already prepared by the ex-Khedive.'[1]

II

It is this groundwork of which we must be aware, as Storrs, Wingate and Kitchener were aware of it, if we are to measure the full significance of Abdullah's conversations during his February and April visits. That these conversations made a deep impression on Kitchener's imagination is startlingly indicated by what followed the outbreak of war in Europe in August and Kitchener's appointment as secretary of state for war. The possibility of the Ottomans joining the Central Powers, had, of course, now to be reckoned with and, likewise, the possibilities open to Britain in countering Ottoman hostility. In this connexion the intelligence department of the Egyptian war office in Cairo produced a paper dated 6 September, entitled 'Appreciation of Situation in Arabia'. The paper, it is curious to note, opens by reiterating a point which, as has been seen, Abdullah had made in his interview with Storrs the previous April when he affirmed that 'the Arabs were concentrating and solidifying, that Ibn Saud, the Idrissi, and even the Imam Yehia would before long be in complete unity with each other and with the Sharifate.' In his report, Storrs had not commented on these assertions which were simply untrue: Ibn Sa'ud and the Idrisi were the bitter enemies of Husayn who had waged war on them ostensibly on behalf of his Ottoman suzerains, but in reality in order to aggrandize himself, while the Imam Yahia was the Idrisi's friend and unlikely to look upon Husayn as a confederate or an ally. The intelligence department paper now took up this assertion and affirmed its truth. 'For some years past', the paper begins, 'the Turkish Government in Arabia has had great difficulty in keeping the country quiet, and Turkish authority has been steadily on the decline.

'There seems little doubt that there has been a distinct tendency towards combination on the part of the more powerful chiefs such as: Ibn Sa'ud of Nejd, the Idrisi of Asir, the Sherif of Mecca, and possibly also Ibn Rashid, with a view to throwing off the Turkish domination and working towards an Arabia for the Arabs'. These statements are immediately followed by a paragraph which recalls

[1] Hardinge Papers, Cambridge University Library, vol. 39, Wingate to Hardinge, Cairo 28 Dec. 1918, fo. 255.

the political context which, for Kitchener and Storrs, lent such significance to Abdullah's approach earlier in the year. This paragraph declares: 'There has been every indication that H. H. The Khedive has interested himself to a considerable extent in fostering this movement by means of money and secret emissaries, with a view to eventually securing the Khalifate in the event of the Turks being expelled from Arabia.' The paper, however, went on to sound an alarm about the possibility of these Arabian chiefs rallying to the Ottoman government. The latter, it seemed, 'has made great efforts to come to an arrangement with the principal Chiefs in Arabia in order to secure, if not their active assistance, at least their friendly neutrality, and it appears probable that considerable success is attending their efforts. In any case it seems almost certain,' the paper somewhat inconsistently went on, 'that the Sherif of Mecca has now definitely thrown in his lot with Turkey'. We may legitimately suspect that this paper was designed not so much to convey intelligence – the information it contains being worthless and seemingly based on nothing substantial – as obliquely to urge a policy by simultaneously hinting at possibilities of anti-Ottoman action and sounding the alarm over Ottoman activities in Arabia.[1]

The paper was sent to Kitchener. It was accompanied, or followed, by a private letter from Captain G. F. Clayton, Sudan agent in Cairo and director of the intelligence department, to Kitchener, urging an immediate approach to Husayn. The letter was sent to London by Storrs who had in fact initiated the whole course of events some time previously by submitting a note, presumably to Sir Milne Cheetham then in charge at the residency, 'suggesting that by timely consultation with Mecca we might secure not only the neutrality but the alliance of Arabia in the event of Ottoman aggression.' When Storrs saw his suggestion forgotten or neglected, he consulted Clayton who approved his thesis and presumably prepared the paper of 6 September and, as Storrs writes in his memoirs, 'actively condoned my proposed irregularity of urging it upon Lord Kitchener in a private letter.'[2] Storrs's later account is confirmed by a contemporary letter of his to Fitzgerald, Kitchener's personal secretary. In this letter, dated 10 November 1914, Storrs, discussing the character of the Egyptian regime which was to follow Abbas's deposition, stated: 'I urge haste because it took me, with Clayton's help, three weeks to get the first telegram suggesting action

[1] A copy of the paper was enclosed with Cheetham's despatch no. 149 Confidential, Cairo 7 Sept. (received 21 Sept.), F.O. 371/2140, 51344/46261.

[2] Storrs, *Orientations*, pp. 148–9. Clayton's letter to Kitchener cannot now be traced.

in Mecca and Arabia, sent off.'[1] Again, many years later, in 1935, he noted on the margin of an Arab Bureau history of British negotiations with the Sharif that Kitchener's first message to Mecca 'was in fact an answer to a private appeal from Sir R. Storrs in the sense of the reply'.[2] Kitchener responded immediately to the intelligence department paper and to Storrs's urging. He drafted in his own hand a telegram as follows:

> Telegram for Cheetham to be submitted to Sir E. Grey before being sent
>
> Intelligence report 6th September statement regarding attitude of Sharif of Mecca. Tell Storrs to send secret and carefully chosen messenger from me to Sherif Abdullah to ascertain whether 'should present armed German influence at Constantinople coerce Sultan against his will and Sublime Porte to acts of aggression and war against Great Britain, he and his father and Arabs of Hejaz would be with us or against us.'
>
> Kitchener.

The draft was submitted to Grey who sanctioned its despatch.[3]

Kitchener, it is interesting to note, was responsible shortly afterwards for another initiative in the Arabic-speaking areas of the Ottoman empire. On 17 October, i.e. before the Ottomans joined the war, Cheetham reported from Cairo that two Muslim Syrians 'of good standing' who had connexions in southern Palestine, one of them being an influential Beduin shaykh, had arrived in Egypt and got in touch with the intelligence department. They confirmed that Ottoman military preparations were going on in Syria and that belief in an impending attack on Egypt was general among the Beduins. 'In view of the efforts of German and Turkish agents to stir up religious feeling against Great Britain,' Cheetham suggested, 'it might be desirable to give some indication to ruling chiefs of Arabia, such as Ibn Rashid, Idrisi, of attitude of British Government in case of attack by Turkey. I am told that Arabs are apprehensive of a Turkish crisis and anxious as to British intentions, so that even some expression of friendship for them would do something to counteract pressure which is being exercised. State of feeling in Arabia,' Cheetham added, 'would have great effect on Egyptian and Senussi Arabs.'[4] A reply was sent the following day from the

---

[1] P.R.O. 30, 57/45, Kitchener Papers.
[2] F.O. 882/5, fo. 142, marginal note signed RS 19.XII.35. In his article on T. E. Lawrence for the *Dictionary of National Biography* Storrs again states that he 'had initiated the negotiations which culminated in the Arab Revolt'.
[3] F.O. 371/2139, 52598/44923, telegram to Cheetham no. 219 Secret, 24 Sept. 1914.
[4] The context clearly shows that by Egyptian 'Arabs', Cheetham meant the beduins of Egypt.

foreign office, but it was Kitchener again who drafted it. 'You should', it said, 'inform the Arabs that England has always supported the Arabs, and will continue to do so. Great Britain has no quarrel with the Arabs, and even if Turkish Government, forced by Germany, commits acts of aggression against us which necessitate acts of war, England will not consider that the Arabs are involved in this war, unless they by overt acts take part in assisting German–Turkish forces which we have the utmost confidence they will not do even under coercion.'[1] A few days later Cheetham reported that the intelligence department had received enquiries about the British attitude in case of war breaking out with the Ottomans 'from responsible adherents of the Pan-Arab movement living in Cairo' that an answer had been given them in the sense of Grey's telegram of 18 October, and that they had sent reliable agents of theirs to Arabia, Syria and Palestine to communicate the message verbally to the Arab chiefs in those countries 'and a considerable sum of money has been placed at the disposal of the promoters of the movement for their use.' Letters were also being sent by 'prominent local Arabs' to influential friends in these areas 'urging them to do their best to dissuade the Arabs from joining Turkey against their own interests.'[2]

Following the instructions contained in the telegram of 24 September, a messenger was sent to Mecca. He was called Ali Asghar, from his name a Persian, most probably a Baha'i like his son-in-law Husayn Ruhi whom Storrs used as an agent and an Arabic secretary.[3]

[1] F.O. 371/2140, 60661/46756, Cheetham's telegram no. 202, Cairo 17 Oct. and Grey's telegram no. 269, London 18 Oct. 1914.

[2] F.O. 371/2140, 63581/46261, Cheetham's telegram no. 223, Cairo 26 Oct. 1914. On these emissaries, see Elie Kedourie, *England and the Middle East: The Destruction of the Ottoman Empire 1914–1921*, 1956, p. 62. Sulayman Musa, The Arab Movement, p. 159n1, chooses for some reason to deny the connexion of one of these emissaries, Muhibb al-Din al-Khatib, with the British, but the above telegram is clear in stating that the emissaries were being financed by the British, and another telegram of Cheetham's, no. 228 dated 28 Oct. (F.O. 371/2140, 64467/46261) declares: 'The agents destined for the Persian Gulf sailed on the 26th October in an Italian steamer from Suez for Bombay; from there they intend to go to Koweit.

'I think the Indian Government should be warned of the coming of these men, whose names are Moheb-ed-Din-el-Khatib and Abd-ul-Aziz-el-Atiki. They could then instruct the authorities at Bombay and Koweit to give them all assistance.

'At Koweit they will go to see our Resident, and they will then be able to arrange to work in unison with him as regards any instructions he may have received in this connection.'

[3] Storrs, *Orientations*, pp. 149 and 159; Sulayman Musa, The Arab Movement p. 142.

That Ali Asghar was a Baha'i, or at any rate a sceptic so far as Islam was concerned, appears from the report of his journey printed in Storrs, *Orientations*, pp. 150–2. According to his statement, on reaching Mecca he 'performed the necessary rites of the pilgrimage which he considered very ridiculous but, from the physical point of view "*Wahid gymnastic kwayis*" – "a good gymnastic"'.

What exactly was said in the Arabic letter we do not know. A marginal note in the Arab Bureau history of the negotiations, made in 1921, records that Storrs had kept no copy of the letter and Arabic sources are equally uninformative. The point is of some importance because, as will be seen, Storrs was sometimes liable to embroider on his superiors' instructions.[1] The messenger left on 5 October, reached Jeddah on 8 October, and was back in Cairo with Abdullah's answer on 30 October. Abdullah declared that 'the people of the Hedjaz will accept and be well satisfied with more close union with Great Britain and its Government, owing to the notorious neglect by Constantinople of religion and its rights;...and Great Britain will take the first place in their eyes so long as she protects the rights of our country and the rights of the person of His Highness our present Emir and Lord and the rights of his Emirate and its independence, in all respects without any exceptions or restrictions, and so long as it supports us against any foreign aggression, and in particular against the Ottomans, especially if they wish to set up anyone else as Emir...and provided that the Government of Great Britain would guarantee these fundamental principles clearly and in writing.'[2] The gist of Abdullah's letter was immediately telegraphed to London: 'Communication,' said the telegram, 'is guarded, but friendly and favourable.' Husayn, in a conversation with the messenger, it went on, had declared: 'Stretch out to us a helping hand and we will never aid these oppressors'. Abdullah's answer, the telegram rightly pointed out, was only repeating what he had proposed on his visit to Kitchener the previous February. The telegram concluded by asking for immediate instructions; a reply in any case was being prepared 'disclaiming all intention of internal intervention and guaranteeing, against external aggression only, independence of Shereefate.'[3]

A reply arrived the same day. A telegram of 31 October (the day of the formal declaration of war between Britain and the Ottoman empire), drafted by Kitchener and approved by Grey, directed that a message from the former to Abdullah be sent as follows:

> Germany has bought the Turkish Government with gold, notwithstanding that England, France and Russia guaranteed the integrity of the Ottoman Empire if the Turks remained neutral in this war. The Turkish Government

[1] F.O. 371/6237, E155/4/91, p. 8. A minute by H. W. Young recorded Storrs as saying that his letter was 'merely a paraphrase of Lord Kitchener's message'. Considering the usual character of Storrs's paraphrases, it would be dangerous to take this remark at face value.

[2] F.O. 371/1973, 87396 enclosed with Cheetham's no. 204, Cairo 13 Dec. 1914, previously cited.

[3] F.O. 371/2139, 52598/44923, cited above, Cheetham's telegram no. 233, Cairo 31 Oct. 1914.

have, against the will of the Sultan, through German pressure, committed acts of aggression by invading the frontiers of Egypt with armed bands of Turkish soldiers.

If the Arab nation assist England in this war that has been forced upon us by Turkey, England will guarantee that no internal intervention takes place in Arabia, and will give Arabs every assistance against external foreign aggression.

It may be that an Arab of true race will assume the Khalifate at Mecca or Medina, and so good may come by the help of God out of all the evil that is now occurring.[1]

Two features of this message are worth noting. The first is the ambiguity of its references (in the second paragraph) to the Arab nation and the Arabs. The context clearly shows that this passage was meant to be a response to Abdullah's request for British protection, and that by the terms Arab nation and Arabs Kitchener meant the inhabitants of Arabia, a loose and careless way (the result no doubt of haste and stress) of referring to the Hijaz which, indeed, was the subject of Abdullah's negotiation. But the terms could be understood or interpreted to have a wider, more far-reaching meaning. However, what was merely ambiguous in Kitchener's message was made pointed and clear by the manner in which Cairo chose to transmit the message. The other feature of Kitchener's message is the reference, in the last paragraph, to the caliphate. This was a subject which had not been overtly broached either on Abdullah's visits to Cairo earlier in the year, or in Kitchener's first message. That it should now suddenly be introduced into the discussion shows what an impression Abbas's abortive schemes had made on Kitchener, and what wide-ranging possibilities war with the Ottoman empire was now conjuring up in his mind. The effect of such an unsolicited reference to the caliphate on Husayn may be imagined. And again it was made even more powerful by the wording of the message as it reached him from Cairo.

This wording was almost certainly that of Storrs. It was Storrs who had from the start urged an approach to the Sharif. The conduct of the negotiations in Cairo, the drafting and translation of letters to the Sharif were in his hands, and likewise the choice and the despatch of messengers. Furthermore, a copy of this second message to Abdullah in the Storrs Papers is initialled by him and headed: 'Translation of my 2nd letter.'[2] The letter, then, trans-

---

[1] F.O. 371/2139, 65589/44923, Grey's telegram no. 303, 31 Oct. 1914. The last two paragraphs of this message are suppressed by Storrs in his *Orientations*, p. 152. His account of the subsequent negotiations as will be seen is also both cursory and garbled.

[2] Storrs Papers, Pembroke College, Cambridge, box II/4.

mitting Kitchener's message of 31 October to Abdullah was dated
1 November and read as follows:

> We have understood your reasons and acknowledge the justice of your
> request. So we have reported to Lord Kitchener, who has replied as follows:
> Salaams to the Sherif Abdullah.
> That which we foresaw has come to pass. Germany has bought the
> Turkish Government with gold, notwithstanding that Great Britain, France
> and Russia guaranteed the integrity of the Ottoman Empire if Turkey
> remained neutral in this war. The Turkish Government have, against the
> wishes of the Sultan and through German pressure, committed acts of war
> by invading without provocation the frontiers of Egypt with armed bands
> followed by Turkish soldiers who are now massed at Akaba to invade Egypt,
> so that the cause of the Arabs, which is the cause of freedom, has become
> the cause also of Great Britain.
> If the Amir and Arabs in general assist Great Britain in this conflict that
> has been forced upon us by Turkey, Great Britain will promise not to
> intervene in any manner whatsoever, whether in things religious or otherwise.
> Moreover, recognizing and respecting the sacred and unique office of the
> Amir Hussein, Great Britain will guarantee the independence, rights and
> privileges of the Sherifate against all external foreign aggression, in particular
> that of the Ottomans. Till now we have defended and befriended Islam in
> the person of the Turks; henceforward it shall be in that of the noble Arab.
> It may be that an Arab of true race will assume the Caliphate at Mecca
> or Medina, and so good may come, by the help of God, out of all the evil
> which is now occurring.
> It would be well if Your Highness could convey to your followers
> and devotees, who are found throughout the world, in every country, the
> good tidings of the freedom of the Arabs, and the rising of the sun over
> Arabia.[1]

What is most remarkable in this document is its stress (absent in
Kitchener's message) on a wide and general Arab movement of
which, it was hinted, the Sharif was the head: 'the cause of the
Arabs, which is the cause of freedom, has become the cause also
of Great Britain', 'Till now we have defended and befriended Islam
in the person of the Turks; henceforward it shall be in that of the
noble Arab', and 'the good tidings of the freedom of the Arabs, and
the rising of the sun over Arabia' which Husayn was bidden to
convey 'to your followers and devotees, who are found throughout
the world, in every country'. Further, the Arabic version whether
intentionally or through inexpert translation, heightened even further the effect produced by these fulsome declarations. The English
text spoke of 'the Amir and the Arabs in general' assisting Great
Britain; the Arabic version rendered 'Arabs in general' as 'kāffat
al-'urbān' which, properly translated, signifies 'all the beduins'. But

[1] F.O. 371/1973, 87396, annex to Cheetham's no. 204, 13 Dec. 1914, cited above.

elsewhere the word 'Arab' of the English text was rendered simply as "*arab*', a collective noun which in this context, could not fail to have a clear political connotation.[1] Someone who read the letter in Arabic, therefore, would understand that in return not only for guaranteeing the 'independence, rights and privileges of the Sherifate against all external foreign aggression' – in itself a wide undertaking – but also for supporting an Arab movement and an Arab caliphate – an unqualified and general commitment – Britain merely expected unspecified help from the Sharif of Mecca and 'all the beduins'.

It is clear that in sending this letter Storrs and Cheetham – who was in charge of the residency – greatly exceeded their instructions. Some light on an otherwise inexplicable and anomalous action may perhaps be thrown by the reports of the intelligence department which were reaching the residency about the Pan-Arab movement. It will be recalled that on 26 October, five days before this letter was sent, Cheetham telegraphed a report about the Pan-Arab movement in Cairo, its contacts with the intelligence department and the emissaries being sent to various parts of the Ottoman empire. The leaders of this movement, Cheetham further said in his telegram, 'have given us to understand that for the moment the Arabs do not expect more from Great Britain than a benevolent attitude towards their aspirations for self-government and an assurance of her moral support, should the time come for putting their plans in execution.'[2] It is therefore likely that in embellishing Kitchener's message with such profuse magniloquence Storrs and Cheetham thought they were merely giving expression to vague sentiments, devoid of any binding character, which might be useful in attracting and enticing the Sharif. They may also have thought that this was in line with Kitchener's wishes, since the reference to the Arab caliphate in his message itself opened up such wide prospects and possibilities.

No wonder that Storrs's messenger when he returned to Cairo on 8 December reported that Husayn had strongly and repeatedly emphasized that the friendliness he felt towards Great Britain was greater than appeared in the letter he was sending in answer to the message of 1 November. His position in the world of Islam and the present political situation in the Hijaz, however, did not allow him to break immediately with the Turks, though he assured Storrs that

---

[1] The Arabic version of the letter is printed in Sulayman Musa, The Arab Movement, pp. 145–6, copied from the papers of Amir Zayd.

[2] F.O. 371/2140, 63581/46261, Cheetham's telegram no. 223, Cairo 26 Oct., cited above.

he was only waiting for a colourable pretext. He also now openly said that the Ottoman caliphate no longer existed.[1]

In his written answer Abdullah informed Storrs that he was taking the letter of 1 November 'as a basis for action and a reference for the present and the future. In accordance with it, and in view of its fidelity and accord, our country has come to hold most conscientiously to your suggestions, and has undertaken to carry out faithfully what we said in our previous letter and confirm in our present one.' The future was to show that Abdullah meant these words seriously, to the extent at any rate, of endeavouring tirelessly to persuade the British to hold conscientiously to the promises which they had so unexpectedly and so gratuitously made. His sententious conclusion takes on, in retrospect, the aspect of a well-deserved rebuke to those who, like Kitchener and Storrs, assumed that the high-flown rhetoric they affected would be as harmless as they imagined, and as meaningless to its recipients as it was to them. In his last paragraph, then, Abdullah affirmed 'that we act upon the words of him who said, Perform ye the promise ye make to God when ye pledge yourselves.'[2]

A month or so later another document issued from the residency, which again was almost certainly composed by Storrs. Dated 4 December 1914, this was 'An official Proclamation from the Government of Great Britain to the natives of Arabia and the Arab provinces'. Again, its language does not seem to have been authorized from London, nor does it seem that the foreign office was informed of its publication.[3] Indeed, if a copy had not survived in the archives of the Cairo embassy, its existence would have remained

---

[1] F.O. 371/2139, 81133/44923, Cheetham's telegram no. 310, Cairo, 10 Dec. 1914. The messenger's note of his interview may be seen in F.O. 371/2768, 69301/38, on p. 3 of an India office print of the correspondence with Husayn.

[2] F.O. 371/1973, 87396, enclosed with Cheetham's despatch no. 204, Cairo 13 Dec., cited above.

[3] Unless a telegram of Grey's (no. 347 of 14 Nov. 1914) be taken as authorization. This telegram was in answer to one from Cheetham (no. 264 of 13 Nov.), in which the latter stated that leaders of the Arab movement in Cairo suggested that the Arabs [of the Hijaz] might be suspicious of the intentions of Great Britain to annex territory and more especially to occupy Red Sea ports. Cheetham went on to say that an excellent effect would be produced by a definite statement on the part of the British government 'that there was no intention to undertake any military or naval operations in Arabia, except for the protection of Arab interests or in support of attempt by Arabs to free themselves from Turkish rule'. In his reply, drawn up together with Kitchener, Grey said: 'You can give the assurances you suggest in the name of the British Government.

'The Arab movement should be encouraged in every way possible'. On Cheetham's suggestion in his telegram no. 269 of 15 Nov. it was arranged for Reuters to publish a statement to the effect that the government had no intention of undertaking any military or naval operations except to protect Arab interests against Turkish and other aggression or to support attempts by Arabs to free themselves of Turkish rule. F.O. 371/2140, 70884, and 71282/4626.

unknown. 'This', the proclamation began, 'is a message of peace and consolation from the Empire of Great Britain to the natives of Arabia, Palestine, Syria and Mesopotamia – the countries lying between the Red Sea, Bahr El Arab, Persian Gulf, frontiers of Persia and Anatoli[a] and the Mediterranean Sea.

'The Government of Great Britain informs you hereby that she has decided not to attack you nor initiate war against any of you – nor', the proclamation went on in its most startling passage, 'does she intend to possess any part of your country neither in the form of conquest and possession nor in the form of protection or occupation. She also guarantees to you that her allies in the present war will follow the same policy.' If the Arabs were to get rid of the Turks 'and take the reins of the Government of their country into their hands, we will', the proclamation promised, 'give up those places to them at once'. If the Arabs were to unite their forces, declare independence and drive out the Turks and their allies, 'then Great Britain and her allies will recognize your perfect independence and will moreover guarantee to defend you if the Turks or others wish to transgress against you and will help you to establish your independence with all her might and influence without any inter- ference in your internal affairs.' The other main theme of the proclamation was that the caliphate belonged to the Arabs. Great Britain had always defended the caliphate 'even if it was a Khaliphate of conquest and necessity as the Turkish Khaliphate.' But Great Britain and the Muslims knew that 'the Islamic Khalifate is a right to the Koreish the tribe of the Great Prophet of Islam and that the Arabs are more powerful than the Turks in the administration of the government and are better prepared to uphold the elements of progress and civilisation – also that the Arabs have a better claim to England's goodwill and assistance'. No nation, this document insisted, was better fitted than the Arab nation for the caliphate and no country more fitted to be its seat than the Arab countries: 'The Government of Great Britain therefore promises you help if you help yourselves and take steps to establish an Empire for the Khalifate to administer your vast countries and she would not require of you, in return, to help in fighting the Turks or others but she wishes you to work for yourselves and unite in serving your cause and interests.

'Do not allow the varieties of tribes or localities or sects to break your union to this end – but be constructive and just the same as your predecessors the four Khalifs and the Abbasides'.[1]

---

[1] F.O. 141/710, file 3156, copy of proclamation marked 'Translation' forwarded under brief covering letter from Hogarth to Storrs, Cairo 19 June 1916.

A second proclamation, less sweeping in its promises, but still couched in imprudently vague and wide terms was issued a few months later. Its history is instructive in showing how confusion and lack of precision on the part of Grey combined with the eagerness to attract the Sharif which was prevalent in Cairo to produce engagements which no one had weighed or properly considered, still less intended. At the time of the Constantinople agreement in March 1915 Grey had, following a decision of the war council,[1] announced to the Russian government that when the agreement became known the British government would state that throughout the negotiations they had stipulated that in all circumstances 'Arabia and the Moslem holy places should remain under independent Moslem rule'. This, as Sir Arthur Hirtzel, secretary of the political department at the India office, explained in a lucid and comprehensive minute, 'was comparatively harmless, though the words "independent Moslem rule" perhaps imply more than was intended – "rulers" would have been nearer the mark.' Shortly afterwards, Wingate sent from Khartoum the copy of a letter from the grand qadi of the Sudan, Muhammad Mustafa al-Maraghi, which advocated an Arab caliphate with Sharif Husayn as Caliph.[2] On 14 April Grey sent a telegram to McMahon (seen and approved by Asquith) which referred to Maraghi's letter and went on to say: 'You should inform Wingate that I authorize him to let it be known, if he thinks it desirable, that His Majesty's Government will make it an essential condition of any terms of peace that the Arabian Peninsula and its Moslem Holy Places should remain in the hands of an independent sovereign Moslem State.' This telegram Hirtzel described as 'a fatal document', for in it 'Arabia' became 'the Arabian Peninsula', and 'independent Moslem rule' became 'an independent sovereign Moslem State'. On 14 May McMahon informed Grey that the purport of Grey's message of 14 April had been communicated where desirable in the Sudan and to certain quarters within Egypt. He went on to argue that if the Sharif were to become Caliph this would be in the British interest, but that the attempt to influence Muslim opinion would be obviously harmful; all that could usefully be done was 'to increase public confidence in our determination to safeguard welfare of independence and integrity of the Hedjaz.' On 19 May Grey therefore authorized

---

[1] Cab. 42/2/14, meeting of war council, 19 Mar. 1915, which discussed French demands for territory in the Ottoman empire following the Constantinople agreement.

[2] Very shortly afterwards he changed his mind; see Elie Kedourie, *The Chatham House Version and Other Middle-Eastern Studies*, 1970, pp. 179–81 and 208–10.

McMahon and Wingate if they thought it opportune to make a public announcement about the Arabian peninsula, the holy places and the caliphate in the terms of his telegram of 14 April.

Following this exchange a leaflet was widely disseminated on the coasts of the Hijaz which declared: 'The Government of His Majesty the King of England and Emperor of India has declared when this war ends it shall be laid down in the terms of peace, as a necessary condition, that Arabian peninsula and its Mahommedan holy places shall remain independent. We shall not annex one foot of land in it, nor suffer any other Power to do so. Your independence of all foreign control is thus assured, and with such guarantees the lands of Arabia will, please God, return along the paths of freedom to their ancient prosperity.'

The text of this leaflet, composed in Cairo and published on the high commissioner's authority, was not sent to London until 30 June 1915, and then only in response to an enquiry instigated by the government of India. It created a bad impression at the foreign office. Clerk minuted that the passage quoted above was 'unfortunately open to a wide interpretation and certainly goes further than anything we have authorized' and Sir Arthur Nicolson, the permanent under-secretary wrote: 'The proclamation or leaflet is not a happy production and might even infer that we might cede Aden.' Justified as the strictures were, yet the proclamation was only an embroidery on Grey's instructions of 14 April. And Grey's attention was in fact drawn to the wide construction of which his words were capable. In a letter of 18 May, Lord Crewe, the secretary of state for India showed himself to be in two minds over the desirability of publishing the substance of the telegram of 14 April, as he feared that 'the impression produced on the mind of hearers might be that of a Great Arabian Sultanate', which might not be practical politics.

Both McMahon and Storrs, it is significant to observe, had a comment to make on Grey's language in this telegram of 14 April. McMahon told Grey, in his telegram of 14 May, that when communicating privately the purport of Grey's message in the Sudan and in Egypt, 'Term "independent sovereign State" has been interpreted in a generic sense because idea of an Arab unity under one ruler recognized as supreme by other Arab chiefs is as yet inconceivable to Arab mind.' While it is by no means certain what interpreting such expressions 'in a generic sense' exactly means or entails, it seems that both McMahon and Storrs believed that these expressions, when used to their Arab interlocutors, did not bear their ordinary or literal meaning but were at best only a kind of metaphor. This emerges with a startling clarity from a note addressed by Storrs to McMahon. The note is undated, but is attached to the residency copy of McMahon's telegram of 14 May, and seems to have been written when the query regarding the Arabic leaflet from which a passage has been quoted above reached Cairo towards the end of June. Storrs wrote:

> The expression 'Arab Empire', 'Kingdom', 'Government', 'Possessions' etc. is used throughout the Sherifial correspondence, on both sides, in a general and undefined sense: and is variously rendered by the words Hukuma (Government) Mamlaka (Possessions) and Dawla (Power, Dynasty, Kingdom).
> Neither from these terms, nor from any phrase employed by H.M.G. throughout the negotiations, is it possible to elaborate any theory as to the precise nature of this vaguely adumbrated body.
> ...Y[our] E[xcellency]'s tel. of May 14, 1915 clearly shews this.[1]

This note of Storrs's provides us with a valuable clue as to the reason why he was so blithely liberal in his use of rhetoric. But what he does not seem to have considered is the possibility that his interlocutors might take, or affect to take, his words in their accepted, literal sense.

These reckless proclamations, then, and the letter of 1 November sent to Abdullah embodying Kitchener's second message enlarged both by their hints and their outright engagements the scope of British promises far beyond what Kitchener had authorized in his telegram of 31 October. And that telegram itself had opened the door to prospects far more alluring than Abdullah had dared mention either during his Cairo visits or in his answer to Kitchener's first message. Kitchener's messages, as has been seen, were transmitted to Cairo through the foreign office, and had the approval of the foreign secretary. This approval was no doubt the outcome of Kitchener's persuasions. Thus we see Grey minuting on 24 September – the date of the telegram embodying Kitchener's first message – the intelligence department paper of 6 September (the role of which in triggering off the whole sequence of events has been described above) as follows: 'This paper is very important: it should

[1] F.O. 141/461, file 1198. Hirtzel's minute is in L/P & S/10/466, p. 2315/15. Grey's telegram no. 173, 14 Apr. 1915, McMahon's no. 188, Cairo 14 May, Grey's no. 262, 19 May, Crewe's private letter of 18 May, and Clerk's and Nicolson's minutes on McMahon's telegram no. 306, Cairo 30 June are all in F.O. 371/2486, file 34982. According to Sulayman Musa, The Arab Movement, p. 154, copies of the Arabic leaflet found their way to Syria, while the Viceroy in a telegram of 23 June (copy in F.O. 371/2846, *ibid.*) stated that it was also distributed in the Western Desert.

have been sent to me as well as to Lord Kitchener. I have only seen it now because Lord Kitchener has sent it me.'[1] The significance of this minute arises from the fact that the other available evidence strongly suggests that, left to themselves, the foreign office would have been very reluctant to approach the Sharif, let alone themselves raise the issue of the caliphate. Shortly after the outbreak of war in Europe Cheetham reported that Aziz Ali al-Misri, the Ottoman officer of Egyptian origin who had earlier that year been accused by the Ottoman government of organizing anti-Ottoman activity among the Arabs, had informed Clayton of approaches from Enver Pasha for him to go to Constantinople and help to mobilize the Arabs in a war against Britain. Aziz declared that he refused to have anything to do with the plan, and that he inclined to an 'Arab Empire under British suzerainty', and asked for British help in leading the tribes of Iraq and Syria against the Turks. The answer from the foreign office on 11 August, authorized by Sir Eyre Crowe, was: 'It is very desirable that you should again impress on El Mazri the need for him to keep quiet and to leave the Arabs alone.'[2] Aziz was again seen on 16 August, by Captain R. E. M. Russell of the intelligence department. He once again mooted the project of an Arab revolt, claiming to be the mandatory of a 'Central Committee' at Baghdad, and asking for money and armaments. Captain Russell pointed out that he was asking Britain to stake a lot in return for very problematical benefits, and 'told him definitely and repeated several times that I had the highest authority for informing him that England regarded the present time most inopportune to raise such a question.'[3]

The same attitude was adopted when the Basra magnate, Sayyid Talib, made advances at the beginning of October. A message, drafted by the embassy at Constantinople and amended by George Clerk, head of the newly set-up war department at the foreign office, was sent to him in reply. The acting consul at Basra was told to inform Talib that 'His Majesty's Government have no designs against Turkey', and that they were 'sincerely friendly to all Mahommedans and consider that their best interests are safeguarded by the maintenance of the integrity of the Turkish Empire.' Talib was further to be told that the government 'have every sympathy with the Arabs, and they have always hoped, and indeed still hope,

[1] F.O. 371/2140, 51344/46261, cited above.
[2] F.O. 371/1968, 37584, Cheetham's telegram no. 76, Cairo 9 Aug. 1914 and telegram to Cheetham no. 87, London 11 Aug.
[3] F.O. 371/2140, 46261, 'Precis of conversation with Abd El Aziz El Masri, on 16 August, 1914' enclosed with Cheetham's despatch no. 143 Secret, Cairo 24 Aug.

to see Arabs forming an integral part of the Turkish Empire under a tolerant and intelligent central government. If, however, the Sublime Porte force a war...on His Majesty's Government, it will be evident that they are blind to the interests of the inhabitants of the Ottoman Empire, including the Arabs, and His Majesty's Government will remember that it is the Turkish Government and not the Arabs, with whom they are at war.'[1] This message was much more careful and non-commital than Kitchener's request to Abdullah, approved by Grey on 24 September, to indicate whether in the event of war with the Ottomans, 'his father and the Arabs of Hedjaz would be with us or against us.'

Such information as was available to the foreign office directly from the Arab parts of the Ottoman empire indicated, contrary to what Cairo was reporting, that feeling among the Muslims was pro-German. This, in particular, was what acting consul Abdur-rahman was reporting from Jeddah.[2] But, in any case, the idea of intervening in the issue of the caliphate, or of encouraging the Sharif to dream of succeeding to such an office was very remote from Grey's mind. A fortnight before Kitchener's second message with its hint about the caliphate, Grey sent to the India office the copy of a memorandum by G. H. Fitzmaurice, in which the ex-dragoman of the British embassy at Constantinople discussed the transfer of the caliphate from the Turks to the Arabs, and the separation of the spiritual from the temporal hitherto united in the person of the Sultan. The covering letter stated that 'Sir E. Grey agrees with Mr. Fitzmaurice's view regarding the advisability of a separation of the Khaliphate from the Sultanate and shares his opinion that such a change must be brought about, if at all, by the Moslems themselves.'[3] But an expression of Grey's view which came after the outbreak of war with the Ottomans is most startling, because it is at complete variance with Kitchener's advances to Husayn which the foreign secretary had twice approved. On 16 December 1914 the Paris embassy sent a report of an approach which had been made to them by E. Jung involving an Arab revolt and the proclamation of an Arab

[1] F.O. 371/2140, 57090/46261, Mallet's telegram no. 942, Constantinople 7 Oct. and Grey's telegram no. 655, London 10 Oct. 1914. On Sayyid Talib's pre-war activities in Basra see Kedourie, *England and the Middle East*, pp. 204–5.

[2] F.O. 371/2140, 66662/46261, Jeddah despatch no. 43, 12 Sept. enclosed with Mallet's despatch no. 635, Constantinople 9 Oct. 1914. Interestingly enough Storrs's agent, Ali Asghar, found when he was in Mecca in the first half of October that Husayn's deputy there (Husayn being away in Ta'if), Sharif Sharaf, had the same political ideas as the Egyptians, i.e. pro-Ottoman and pro-German, and that he did not bother to hide them; Storrs, *Orientations*, p. 150.

[3] F.O. 371/2140, 57234/46261, foreign office to India office, 16 Oct. 1914.

caliphate. On this report, Grey minuted: 'We must not stir the dangerous question of the Caliphate.'[1]

The question, therefore, arises whether Grey knew what he was doing or realized that his various decisions were incoherent and indeed contradictory. Another episode to be noticed intensifies these doubts. The Damascene Izzet Pasha al-Abid, Abd al-Hamid's influential and well-known second secretary, had been living in exile in Paris since the Young Turk *coup d'état*. In December 1914 he approached the foreign office, advocating that the Sharif of Mecca should be, with British help and encouragement, proclaimed Caliph. Grey minuted that he was disposed to authorize that Izzet be officially informed that 'HMG would willingly[2] give their support, if desired,[3] to an Arab Caliphate of the true race.' But before doing so, he asked that the India office be consulted. A letter based on his minute was therefore sent to them, the text of which Kitchener saw and approved. But the India office declared that they had grave objections to such an official statement being made. Thereupon, notwithstanding the declaration he had been so recently ready to make, Grey telegraphed to McMahon at Cairo (without, it would seem, asking Kitchener's advice on this occasion) that he was not in favour of acting on Izzet's suggestion, and that indeed he was 'strongly opposed to any interference in religious question and fear disquieting effect which Sherif's ambitions might have on other Arab rulers.'[4]

The explanation of Grey's incoherent views may lie in the fact that, as Lord Esher put it, he 'was never intended for the service of Mars.' His biographer observes that during his last period in office, from the outbreak of war until December 1916, there was 'a certain lethargy' in Grey's behaviour, and that he was ready to defer to the views of his colleagues in matters relating to the conduct of the war. A good example of this tendency is precisely the manner in which Grey reacted to Cheetham's telegram of 31 October 1914, reporting the return of the messenger who had taken Kitchener's first message to the Sharif. As will be recalled, Cheetham reported that the Sharif wanted a promise that Britain would abstain from intervention in the Hijaz and a guarantee against 'Ottoman aggres-

[1] F.O. 371/2147, 87764. On Jung's scheme see Kedourie, 'The Politics of Political Literature' in *Arabic Political Memoirs*.
[2] He had originally written 'gladly'.
[3] 'By whom?' Hirtzel queried in a minute commenting on Grey's suggestion, L/P & S/10/523/53/15.
[4] F.O. 371/2479, file 1286 for the correspondence relating to Izzet's suggestion; Grey's telegram to McMahon no. 19, 12 Jan. 1915, is in 2154/1286.

sion'. On this telegram, Grey minuted: 'Does Lord Kitchener agree? If so I will approve.'[1] This passivity may perhaps explain why he oscillated between acquiescence in Kitchener's views, and agreement with the different views of his own department and of the India office. This diffidence about his own ability to conduct a diplomacy geared to the necessities of war was aggravated by his own personal circumstances. The outbreak of war was a great disaster, as well as a great personal defeat, and put in doubt the bases and methods of the policy which he had himself conducted for well-nigh eight years. This demoralization and the low spirits it induced were accompanied by physical and mental tiredness, and by failing eyesight which made the concentrated and continuous reading of documents very painful. To his colleague Runciman Grey confessed in March 1915 that he had been 'inhumanly busy and tired. I dozed this morning in intervals of work'. And about the same time Asquith described him as 'most dolorous and despondent'. It must therefore remain an open question how much he was in control of the policies for which he was nominally responsible.[2]

Grey's decision to consult the India office on Izzet's proposal was natural. The India office had a substantial claim to be consulted over policy towards the Arab provinces of the Ottoman empire. Its interest naturally arose out of the control of Aden by the government of India, the paramountcy that it had established in the Persian Gulf, and its great influence in Eastern Arabia, Southern Persia and Lower Mesopotamia. Thus, Talib's ambitions also came to the notice of the authorities at Delhi. Just before the outbreak of war with the Ottomans, the British consul at Mohammerah informed them that the Sayyid wanted to be recognized as shaykh or amir of Basra under British protection. He was instructed to tell Talib that this could not be agreed, 'but you may tell him informally that his eventual position in the event of war will depend on degree of his influence and extent to which he uses it in our interests'. After the outbreak of war, and the landing of the Indian Expeditionary Force in Mesopotamia, Talib again approached the British through the political agent at Kuwait. Sir Percy Cox, chief political officer of the Force to whom the matter was referred, replied 'that as Talib had refused our friendly offer when it was open, he could now offer him no terms whatever'.[3]

[1] F.O. 800/48, Grey Papers.
[2] Keith Robbins, *Sir Edward Grey*, 1971, to which the above paragraph is much indebted; see particularly pp. 301, 303, 321-2, 325 and 333.
[3] F.O. 371/2140, 64904 and 77724/46261, copies of telegrams from viceroy to India office, 28 Oct. and 30 Nov. 1914.

The Quicksand

These exchanges bring out very clearly the stance which the government of India (and the India office) were inclined to adopt in Arab affairs. It had many similarities to the attitude of the foreign office, but was at the opposite pole from the policy favoured by Kitchener, Storrs and Clayton. The India office were therefore taken aback to receive from the foreign office, after a considerable interval, news of Kitchener's approaches to the Sharif. For it was not until 12 December 1914 that they received a copy of Kitchener's two messages. Hirtzel minuted on this letter:

> The F.O. have apologized for the oversight by which the earlier stages of what seems a very dangerous correspondence have only now been communicated to us.[1] Whether such a correspondence ought to have taken place without the concurrence of the S[ecretary] of S[tate] for I[ndia] is a matter for H[is] L[ordship] [i.e. Lord Crewe].
>   The assurance to the Grand Sharif that we 'will give the Arabs every assistance against external foreign aggression' seems to me very difficult of fulfilment; and the hint to the Arabs to assume the Caliphate at Mecca and Medina does the very thing which this Office has always understood that H.M.G. would *not* do.

When Hirtzel saw the text of Storrs's embellished version of Kitchener's second message to Abdullah which reached the India office on 4 January 1915,[2] he described it in a minute, rightly, as 'a guarantee given to the Grand Sherif in writing without the authority of H.M.G., and', he added, 'it is a startling document.'

That a document as far-reaching as Kitchener's second message could be issued without the authority of the government seemed to Sir Thomas Holderness, the permanent under-secretary at the India office, to be simply incredible. Commenting on Hirtzel's minute of 12 December, he opined that 'Lord Kitchener's action was probably taken with the knowledge of the Cabinet.' But the secretary of state, Lord Crewe, set out the true position when Hirtzel's and Holderness's minutes reached him. He minuted, 'No this was a private communication of Lord Kitchener's, though HMG were aware that he has friendly relations with the Sherif's family'. And, he put the matter on record in an official telegram of 14 December to the viceroy which said, 'His Majesty's Government as a whole was unaware of this correspondence.' When a copy

---

[1] The file contains nothing about an apology, and it must have been a verbal one.
[2] Cheetham's despatch no. 204 of 13 Dec. with which it was enclosed arrived in London on 28 Dec. F.O. 371/1973, 87396, cited above.

of this telegram reached the foreign office, Grey simply initialled it without comment.[1]

Izzet's suggestion and Kitchener's second message elicited two comments in the India office by Holderness and Crewe respectively. These minutes bring out with utter clarity the equivocal situation which Kitchener's initiative brought about, and point out its likely dangers. Holderness wrote:

> I doubt if the Foreign Office quite realises wherein the Caliphate consists and what it implies. Unlike the Papacy it must, if it is to be more than a mere empty claim, have the substance of an extensive temporal empire. The Sherif of Mecca could not, I imagine, make good a title to the Caliphate unless he established temporal ascendancy over the states and chiefdoms of Arabia and could enforce his will and exercise political sovereignty over Arabia. The guarantee given by Lord Kitchener was a guarantee to the Sheik of the *status-quo* – 'the independence, rights and privileges of the Sherifate.' But the *status quo* will not carry him to the Caliphate of Arabia, much less of the Moslem world. If we are to hold out hopes of the latter, we should have to help him in a career of conquest: and I am sure that this is not intended.

With this view, the secretary of state agreed entirely. 'It is dangerous', Crewe observed, 'to mix up the Khalifate and the Sherifate, or to suppose that the latter can easily be transformed into the former.'[2]

[1] India Office Records, L/P & S/10/523, pp. 4854–5/14 and 54/15. Copy of Crewe's telegram of the 14 Dec. in F.O. 371/2139, 83620/44923.
[2] L/P & S/10/523 p. 53/15, cited above; minutes dated 5 Jan. 1915.

2. Kitchener, Grey and the Arab Question

The secret messages to the Sharif instigated by Storrs and Kitchener and the various proclamations which followed them were of course immediately occasioned by apprehended, and later on, by actual hostilities with the Ottoman empire. The hostilities were bound to force a reconsideration of traditional British policy towards the Ottoman empire. This policy had been formulated when the empire was being threatened by the Pasha of Egypt, Muhammad Ali, in the fourth decade of the nineteenth century. It aimed to preserve the integrity and independence of the Ottoman empire. But by 1914 this traditional policy had lost most of its meaning and it was more of a slogan than a guide to diplomacy. Most eager for the formulation of a new policy were Kitchener and the British officials in Cairo and Khartoum, and their approach to Husayn is to be seen not only as a war-time tactic, but as part of a wider and more far-sighted strategy.

This was early made unmistakably clear by Kitchener in a private letter to Grey sent shortly after his second message to Abdullah. Kitchener wrote on 11 November 1914:

> Supposing that the Arabs took up arms against the Turks I think it would be our policy to recognise a new Khalif at Mecca or Medina of the proper race; and guarantee the Holy Places from foreign aggression as well as from all internal interference. If this were done there appears to me to be a possibility for allowing Syria to be organised as an Arab state under the Khalif but also under European consular control and European guidance as regards Government.
>
> France would be greatly weakened by having Syria which is not a remunerative possession and which from its geographical position must lead France astray from her real objective Tunis Algeria Morocco.
>
> I believe it is more sentiment than anything else which induces France to keep up her influence in Syria and if we frankly said, we do not want Syria, they would probably say the same and allow the formation of an Arab state that would enable the new Khalifate to have sufficient revenue to exist on.
>
> I think we might tell the Arabs now that this is what we hope for. When there are signs of its realisation it will be time enough to recommend the matter to France and induce her to accept the situation.[1]

[1] F.O. 800/102, Grey Papers.

32

Kitchener, Grey and the Arab Question

Kitchener's aims – a British-sponsored caliph governing a British-protected Syria – sketched out in this letter, are asserted much more emphatically in the private correspondence of his erstwhile subordinate in Cairo, Ronald Storrs. Storrs, who inclined to flatter his superiors, in a letter to Kitchener's private military secretary evoked the splendid vision of a North African or Near Eastern vice-royalty to be presided over by Kitchener and to include Egypt and the Sudan and stretch all the way from Aden to Alexandretta.[1] In a letter to his parents at about the same time he described the settlement he would like to see. Syria would be incorporated into the Egyptian sultanate, as was the wish of all Muslims and most Christians in Syria. He was aware of French claims, but hoped that France might be diverted into 'channels of profit and consolidation in West Africa'. He went on, giving a more pointed and detailed version of the scheme Kitchener had put before Grey the previous November:

> Syria is not only a goal per se but also a necessity both with regard to Irak and the Arabian peninsula. If, as would seem the ideal solution, we could make this latter into a sort of Afghanistan uncontrolled and independent within, but carrying on its foreign relations through us, we should be giving a maximum of satisfaction and assuming a minimum of responsibility; but the plan is not feasible unless we hold Syria.

The caliphate would in the end devolve on the Sharif and 'we should do our all to help it in that direction.' 'A hereditary spiritual Pope with no temporal power – his allegiance to us inspired, as his revenues derived, from annual subventions and the proceeds of an annual pilgrimage' was the ideal to be worked for, and by fortunate chance the Sharif, an 'enlightened and ambitious man' also shared it: 'I had it last spring from the lips of his favourite son Abdullah, that the State of Afghanistan is always before their eyes as an attainable summum bonum.'[2] The letter strikingly shows how deep an impression Abdullah's blandishments in the spring of 1914 had left on Storrs.

It is not clear what either Kitchener or Storrs understood by Syria. It is most likely that they included in the term the whole of the

---

[1] Kedourie, *The Chatham House Version*, p. 17, Storrs's letter of 8 Mar. 1915.

[2] Storrs Papers, Pembroke College, Cambridge, box II/3, letter of 22 Feb. 1915.

In the Cairo embassy archive (F.O. 141/587, file 546/1) there is an undated memorandum by Lieutenant H. Pirie Gordon, RNVR, Intelligence Officer, HMS *Doris*, on 'The Historical Connexion between Egypt and Syria', which must have been written about this time. The paper argues that Egypt and Syria have been historically united by foreign conquest, that the defeat of Muhammad Ali's plans has had 'disastrous effects' on Syria, and that this policy should be reversed by the restoration of Egyptian rule to that country.

territory stretching from Rafah in the south to Alexandretta in the north. But in view of later controversies, it is interesting to note that within the larger territory, Storrs at any rate distinguished a smaller one which he called Palestine. Thus, in a letter to Fitzgerald of December 1914 he wrote:

> With regard to Palestine, I suppose that while we naturally do not want to burden ourselves with fresh responsibilities such as would be imposed upon us by annexation, we are, I take it, averse to the prospect of a Russian advance Southwards into Syria, or of a too great extension of the inevitable French Protectorate over the Lebanon, etc...A buffer State is most desirable, but can we set one up? There are no visible indigenous elements out of which a Moslem Kingdom of Palestine can be constructed. The Jewish State is in theory an attractive idea; but the Jews, though they constitute a majority in Jerusalem itself, are very much in a minority in Palestine generally, and form indeed a bare sixth of the whole population...Would not the inclusion of a part of Palestine in the Egyptian Protectorate with the establishment at Jerusalem of a mixed Municipality chosen from a large number of elements and granted wide powers be a possible solution?[1]

Storrs's views are very important to attend to. As has been seen, he it was who held the most important and confidential talks with Abdullah in Cairo; it was he, again, who moved Kitchener to approach the Sharif in September, and he who drafted the messages, chose the messenger and interviewed him on his return. While Kitchener had not yet been replaced at Cairo and Cheetham was in charge at the residency, the Arab question was very much Storrs's province. This remained the case when Sir Henry McMahon, who had been foreign secretary to the government of India, became high commissioner and took charge of the residency in January 1915. McMahon's seems to have been a temporary appointment which he was to hold while Kitchener (who chose him) was secretary of state for war and thus unable to return to his post at Cairo.[2]

It was not a judicious appointment. The British representative at Cairo had to be, at that juncture, a man of great ability,

---

[1] P.R.O. 30 57/45 Kitchener Papers, Storrs to Fitzgerald, 28 Dec. 1914, cited above. Pirie Gordon's memorandum, quoted above, argued that Jerusalem would fare best under the Egyptian Muslims.

[2] 'I have seen Sir H. McMahon', wrote Kitchener to Grey on 1 Dec. 1914 (F.O. 800/102, Grey Papers); 'he will be glad to go to Egypt.' When his appointment was terminated at the end of 1916, McMahon wrote plaintively to Hardinge that it was only now that he was learning for the first time and 'at so late a date' of the temporary nature of his appointment. McMahon to Hardinge, Cairo 10 Nov. 1916, Hardinge Papers, vol. 27, fo. 58. Storrs's eminent position at the residency and his great ambition are commented on in a despatch from the French minister at Cairo (no. 280 of 21 July 1916), Archives du Ministère des A[ffaires] E[trangères], Paris, Guerre 1914–18, vol. 1567 (hereafter cited as A.E.).

decisiveness and energy, and not someone whose career – not hitherto particularly brilliant – was, as the viceroy at the time observed, 'practically over'. Commenting on the appointment a few months later, Hardinge told Nicolson: 'I had nothing to say to it and would not have advised it, if my opinion had been asked. He is a nice man and I like him very much, but his ability is of a very ordinary type while his slowness of mind and ignorance of French must be serious drawbacks to him.'[1] To Sir Ronald Graham, the adviser to the Egyptian ministry of the interior, who was a close friend, Hardinge was more outspoken. McMahon, he told him, 'has little knowledge of real administration and is more suited to governing a frontier province than a civilised community with all sorts of complex questions in which foreign interests are involved. He is also, like so many Indian Officials, dreadfully slow of mind.'[2] Graham himself supplies a few additional touches to Hardinge's portrait of McMahon: 'I get on very well with our old little Chief (generally known here as "the Locust"),[3] he wrote to Hardinge, 'but what a curious man he is – his slowness and absolute determination never to give a decision if he can possibly help it are at times quite disconcerting – while, with the exception of our old friend Durand, he is quite the laziest man I have met.'[4] The journalist Sir Valentine Chirol, who visited Cairo shortly after McMahon's arrival there, confirms and adds to these judgments: 'Doubtless,' he informed Hardinge in a letter of 18 April 1915, 'McMahon is very much handicapped by his ignorance of French as well as of Arabic, and he is nervous of giving himself away: Also, I am told, he is frightfully slow at the uptake and therefore very difficult to coach. The result is that he is creating the impression that he is a sort of "veiled prophet".'[5] These judgments are confirmed by the diary of a secretary at the residency who rose to become head of chancery, Mervyn Herbert. More than once, Herbert remarks on McMahon's slowness of mind and lack of interest in his duties, and on his astonishing ignorance. Herbert declared that McMahon relied on Clayton, Brunyate and Lord Edward Cecil especially to do the work for him. He was interested only in the Hijaz question, but Herbert

[1] F.O. 800/377 and 378, Nicolson Papers, Hardinge to Nicolson, 6 Jan. and 25 May 1915.
[2] Hardinge Papers, vol. 93, p. 262, Hardinge to Graham, 27 Jan. 1915.
[3] Sir L. Grafftey-Smith writes in *Bright Levant* (1970), p. 21, that McMahon's 'only visible enthusiasm was locusts. He had had some success with locust control in India, and would discuss his methods with all and sundry. Hence a nickname "Loki", which also became the combination of the Chancery safe [at the Cairo residency]'.
[4] Hardinge Papers, vol. 94, p. 344d, Graham to Hardinge, Cairo 16 Nov. 1915.
[5] Hardinge Papers, vol. 71.

added that even in the Hijaz question there was a lack of control, and no feeling that there was a man who really understood it at all.[1]

The way in which McMahon envisaged his duties in Egypt is significant. No one was more surprised by his appointment, he told his former superior the viceroy. He understood that he owed it to the fact that Egypt was drifting towards 'the creation of a Khediviate or Sultanate endowed with sovereignty, independence and powers out of all proportion to real needs and amounting to an insuperable obstacle to annexation which is likely to come at the end of the war. It appears to fall to my lot as an expert in native states, chiefs and Eastern Monarchs to correct this...'[2] This simple (and erroneous) view of the Egyptian political situation and of his duties in Cairo no doubt McMahon derived (mistakenly or not) from Kitchener. Taken together with his laziness, his slow intelligence, his unfamiliarity with the sophisticated and complicated politics of Egypt, it goes far to explain the manner in which McMahon mishandled the Sultan Husayn Kamil, alienated Egyptian ministers, and surrounded himself by what Husayn Kamil called a *camorra* of British officials to whom he abandoned (with what nefarious consequences were to appear shortly afterwards) his great powers and responsibilities.[3]

The hints and suggestions about McMahon's personality and methods thrown out by those who worked with him, and evoked by the evidence of his actions, are put into sharp focus by a remarkable despatch in which Defrance, the French minister at Cairo, having observed him for some six months discharging the duties of his office, summed up the new high commissioner. The despatch is worth citing at some length:

> The truth is that Sir Henry McMahon, well-intentioned as he is, had acquired no authority in Egypt: people here are still wondering what he is worth, what he is thinking and what he wants: he does not seem to have informed himself about any important question and gives the impression of being uninterested in Egypt, as though it is only physically and provisionally that he is occupying his office. Informally, intercourse with him is simple and agreeable. He fills with dignity his representational duties, but he seems inexistent if one addresses oneself to him in his capacity as British high commissioner and foreign minister of Egypt. He declares that everything is going perfectly well in Egypt and elsewhere, and seems to have no reason

[1] Mervyn Herbert's Diary, Middle East Centre, St Antony's College, Oxford. The diary is in two volumes, and all the relevant entries occur in volume one. See pp. 248–9, 292, 294–5, 314 and 350, where the passage summarized above (entry for 11 Nov. 1916) occurs.
[2] Hardinge Papers, vol. 71, McMahon to Hardinge, London 4 Dec. 1914.
[3] Kedourie, *The Chatham House Version*, particularly pp. 92 and 108–12.

for anxiety in his high and difficult station. When discussing business with him one has the feeling of talking to someone who has no cognisance of, who does not interest himself in the things which are being discussed with him and who, in any case, does not act of his own motion, gives no directive, to whom it does not occur to take any initiative.

...Sir Henry McMahon is, no doubt, a good official, able to carry out precise instructions, and accomplish a definite mission. But he does not seem to have the qualities necessary to direct, to lead, or to govern as the representative of the protecting Power.[1]

We may suspect that it was precisely these failings which recommended him to Kitchener, who had therefore no need to fear that a powerful personality might supplant him in his proconsular seat when he might want to resume it. And in extenuation of McMahon's behaviour, it must be said that he was well aware that Kitchener was his master and patron: he was, thus, careful to report to him frequently and in detail. Kitchener, in any case, would not have allowed him to forget the true position. If Chirol is to be believed, Kitchener was 'constantly sending messages and even writ[ing] himself to the effect that he will be soon back in Cairo.'[2] Shortly after McMahon's appointment Hardinge wrote to Crewe and expressed the opinion which, as has been seen, he entertained of McMahon. 'His fault', he told Crewe, 'is that his brain works so slowly, and it will probably grow worse with nobody to jog it.' Crewe, however, thought 'that his appreciation of the Arabian position is likely to be sounder than Kitchener's. The latter has not succeeded in grasping the fact which shines out steadily from the Moslem assurances of loyalty and support which you have sent home – that the Indian Mohammedans regard Turkey with sorrow but not with anger; that the Sultan as Khalif is not seriously shaken by the acts of his Young Turk Ministers; and that therefore it is quite uncertain whether Moslem India would approve the institution of an Arabian Khaliphate, even if brought about by agency within Islam.'[3] Contrary to what Crewe hoped, McMahon was sure to follow Kitchener's views in this as in other matters. And just as he left the conduct of Egyptian affairs to a junta headed by Lord Edward Cecil (whom Kitchener had, in August 1914, wanted to take charge of Egypt)[4] so he was content to leave Arab affairs in the hands of Storrs, who had the confidence of, and saw eye to eye with, the

[1] A.E., Guerre 1914–18, vol. 869, Defrance's despatch no. 217, Cairo 18 July 1915.
[2] Hardinge Papers, vol. 71, Chirol to Hardinge, Cairo 18 Apr. 1915, cited above.
[3] Crewe Papers, Cambridge University Library, C/22, Hardinge to Crewe, 14 Jan. 1915; C/24, Crewe to Hardinge, 18 Dec. 1914.
[4] Kedourie, *The Chatham House Version*, p. 411n84.

master whose agent McMahon for the time being was allowed to be. A short note of McMahon's to Crewe's private secretary,[1] shortly before he left London for Cairo indicates that he was indeed aware of Storrs's position and standing: 'I have', he wrote, 'made careful note of your remarks about Mr. Ronald Storrs. I have heard him highly spoken of by Lord Kitchener'.[2]

Kitchener was able to control affairs in Egypt not only indirectly through McMahon, but also directly through General Sir John Maxwell, the G.O.C. in Egypt. Maxwell was responsible to the war office and thus reported directly to Kitchener. It is also most probable that he owed his position to Kitchener's favour. Maxwell had commanded the British troops in Egypt from 1906 to 1912, and had then retired on half-pay. On the outbreak of war he was recalled from retirement and in September 1914 appointed once more to his old post in Egypt. Whether it was in order to defer to Kitchener's views, or simply because he himself shared them, Maxwell adopted exactly the same attitude as his secretary of state regarding Arab affairs and negotiations with the Sharif. His telegrams to the war office echoed and reinforced those of the residency to the foreign office. To take one example, on 9 November 1914 Cheetham telegraphs to the foreign office that a 'well-known and venerated' shaykh has just arrived from Syria; he is one of the leaders of the Arab movement, and reports that the majority of the Muslims are 'anxious for an understanding' with Great Britain but are deterred from taking action by their fear of France. If they are given a guarantee against a French occupation of Syria, suggests Cheetham, 'they would side whole-heartedly with Great Britain'.[3] The foreign office turns down the suggestion. A little while later, Maxwell telegraphs Kitchener: 'Could you let me know privately', he enquires, 'what the ultimate policy of England regarding Palestine and Syria in connection with the Arab movement will be? Among the Moslems there is considerable pro-English feeling, but all except the Maronites are anti-French. It is necessary to know what line will be taken, as there is a good deal of nibbling even among officers of the Turkish army...'[4] As will be recalled, Kitchener was plying Grey with exactly the same suggestions precisely at that time. Yet another example of conjugated effort on the part of McMahon, Maxwell and Kitchener is even more striking. It occurred a year

[1] Crewe acted for Gray when the latter was absent from the foreign office.
[2] Crewe Papers, 1/17, file 11, McMahon to F. M. Lucas, London 25 Dec. 1914.
[3] F.O. 371/2141, 69074/46756, Cheetham's telegram no. 251, Cairo 9 Nov. 1914.
[4] F.O. 371/2139, 77224/44923. Copy of Maxwell's telegram to Kitchener no. 332E, Cairo 27 Nov. 1914.

later, when it was thought that Baghdad would shortly fall to British arms and the terms of a suitable proclamation to the inhabitants of the conquered city were being discussed. McMahon had just issued his so-called 'pledge' to the Sharif, and Maxwell telegraphed to the commander-in-chief, India (repeating his telegram to the war office in London, who themselves sent a copy to the foreign office) as follows:

> In my opinion we should seize this excellent opportunity of issuing a proclamation giving verbatim text of our proposals to the Sharif of Mecca and Arab party, so far as Iraq and Mesopotamia are affected thereby...
> This is an opportunity of honestly and properly letting our intentions be known, and it would convince the Sharif that we are sincere, and would also do an infinite amount of good. Suspicion would be aroused if we did anything short of this, and Arabs are peculiarly suspicious.[1]

Simultaneously McMahon telegraphed:

> My advisors on Arabian questions are unanimously of opinion that opportunity of Baghdad Proclamation should be taken to publish the full text of our proposals as far as Mesopotamia is concerned to the Arab Party, and that this will have a good effect, whereas any divergence between statements at Baghdad and Cairo will rouse suspicions of the very suspicious Arab people, and do much harm.

Presumably for greater effect McMahon sent this telegram privately to Grey, who, as he recorded in a minute, was also approached by Kitchener in support of such a proclamation. But as Clerk rightly pointed out, since McMahon's letter to the Sharif was by no means clear, it was impossible to publish proposals about Mesopotamia 'until we ourselves know what those proposals are to be.' And in any case, as the India office also pointed out, McMahon's offers to the Sharif were 'conditional on Arabs performing their part of bargain, which is additional reason against proclaiming them as McMahon proposed.'[2] Since Baghdad did not fall then, the pressure jointly exerted by Kitchener, McMahon and Maxwell in the event led to nothing.

Shortly after his arrival in Cairo, Maxwell took a step which was to have significant consequences. As he wrote to Kitchener on 31 October 1914: 'I have closed down all intermediary intelligences and concentrated everything in Clayton's hands.'[3] G. F. Clayton, who had retired from the Egyptian army with the rank of captain in 1910

---

[1] L/P & S/53, pt 3, p. 4616/15, Maxwell's telegram no. 2094E, Cairo 31 Oct. 1915. Copy of Maxwell's identical telegram to Kitchener is in F.O. 371/2486, 163391/34982.

[2] F.O. 371/2492, 162361/15977, McMahon's telegram Private, Cairo 1 Nov. 1915, with minutes by Grey and Clerk. *Ibid.* 171785/159577, copy telegram to viceroy, London 8 Nov. 1915.

[3] Sir George Arthur, *General Sir John Maxwell*, 1932, p. 137.

and transferred to the Sudan government service, was then Sudan agent in Cairo and director of intelligence of the Egyptian war office (the governor-general of the Sudan being *sirdar* or head of the Egyptian army). When Maxwell put Clayton in charge of British military intelligence in October 1914, he promoted him to colonel, and by 1916 Clayton was brigadier-general. This rapid promotion is an index of the crucial position Clayton had come to hold in the direction of the war in the Middle East. A significant passage by T. E. Lawrence may serve to give an idea of the manner in which he quickly rose to such eminence: '...he worked', writes Lawrence, 'by influence rather than by loud direction. It was not easy to descry his influence. He was like water, or permeating oil, creeping silently and insistently through everything.'[1] These words are all the more revealing for being written by one who was, ostensibly at any rate, a friend and admirer. Maxwell had concentrated all military intelligence in his hands, and when the Arab Bureau was established early in 1916 it was he who chose its staff and was ultimately responsible for it. The fact that it was solely through him that the commander-in-chief received political intelligence meant that his views were likely to preponderate, and these, as will be seen, tended to reinforce Storrs's appreciations and Kitchener's predilections. But Clayton and his subordinates were not content merely to supply intelligence; they also advocated particular policies, and pushed them not only through the residency but also through military and naval channels to which they had access. By June 1916 the government of India was complaining about the Arab Bureau: 'We have come to the conclusion, after the experience of the last few months', the foreign department of the government of India telegraphed to the India office, 'that it is not suitable to make the Arab Bureau the mouth-piece of H.M.G.'s policy and principle as regards the Arab Question'. Shortly afterwards Hirtzel told the war office that the Arab Bureau should 'come out into the open', complaining that Hogarth, the director of the Bureau (who had the rank of commander in the Royal Naval Volunteer Reserve) was sending telegrams to the director of the intelligence division at the admiralty which were not being passed on to the foreign office or the India office.[2] It is

---

[1] *Seven Pillars of Wisdom* [1935], Penguin Books ed., 1962, p. 56.

[2] F.O. 882/2, Arab Bureau Papers, copy telegram from foreign department, government of India no. 3045, Delhi 20 June 1916; and letter from Clayton to Lt-col. C. N. French of the war office, Cairo 27 July 1916 in which Hirtzel's complaint is referred to. Clayton here agrees that the main channel of communication should be the foreign office, but still maintains that supplementary telegrams sent by himself to the director of military intelligence at the war office or by Hogarth to the director of the intelligence division at

generally agreed that for the good conduct of political and military affairs it is absolutely vital to keep intelligence appreciations and policy recommendations strictly apart. The Indian authorities, military and civil, were very much aware of this. When the Arab Bureau was instituted in the spring of 1916, India was informed that the Bureau was the 'central organ through which His Majesty's Government will lay down policy and principles'. They immediately queried this formulation, the significance of which does not seem to have been grasped in London, and after lengthy exchanges finally elicited a declaration from the secretary of state for India that the 'Bureau is merely an informing agency', and that policy was determined by the government.[1] But notwithstanding such affirmations, in Cairo during the war the rule that intelligence and policy must be kept apart was continuously and systematically flouted.

Many examples can be given of the head of military intelligence himself advancing and promoting particular policies. As has been seen, at the very outset Clayton acted in concert with Storrs to try and move Kitchener to approach the Sharif. He was also prominent among those who promoted the Sharif as the future Arab Caliph. A note by him of July 1915 argues that the Sharif is 'undoubtedly' the most suitable candidate for the caliphate from the British point of view, and that the terms of peace with Turkey should include a provision for the Sultan to renounce the caliphate which Husayn could then assume.[2] Again, a despatch of McMahon's of 15 February argued that the French were highly unpopular in Syria, that 'it is to England and England alone that both Syrian Christians and pan-Arabs are turning', that both parties will eagerly grasp 'at any deed or word on the part of England which may seem to hold out to them the support they seek', that French or Russian intervention in Syria would be viewed with 'the utmost disfavour or even hostility from the majority of the inhabitants, both Christian and Mohammedan', that British assurances to the Syrians might even precipitate a revolt in Syria 'by the various societies who are working against the Turks in that country', and that it would be worth considering the scheme of extending the dominion of the Sultan of Egypt into Syria as a

the admiralty should be considered 'of a more or less private nature'. 'I think,' he adds, 'it is as well to have some unofficial channel of communication as it is frequently desirable to send information for the private information of the D.I.D. or the D.M.I.' which the latter should be at liberty to disclose or not.

[1] F.O. 371/2771, file 18845 and particularly paper 94961, telegram to viceroy of 26 Apr., and paper 116183, telegram to viceroy of 14 June 1916.

[2] F.O. 882/12, fos. 116–17, note by Clayton, Cairo 24 July 1915. A report canvassing the claims of the Sharif by Lt H. Pirie-Gordon, RNVR and Lt H. C. Lukach was forwarded by Clayton to Cheetham with a covering letter dated 29 Mar. 1915, F.O. 141/587, file 545/1.

means of rendering unnecessary the acquisition of any portion of Syria by either France or Britain and thus obviating direct British involvement in Syria, and the ensuing friction with France. This despatch, as we discover, is very closely based on a note by Clayton of 8 February, large portions of which it incorporates verbatim.[1]

McMahon and Maxwell, Storrs and Clayton spoke thus with one voice and conveyed to the foreign office and to the war office the same information and the same recommendations, which their patron Kitchener underlined and seconded with his prestige and influence. When Kitchener died, Sir Mark Sykes drafted a message to be sent to the Sharif. Though couched in the solemn and grandiloquent language which he thought necessary to adopt in addressing Eastern potentates, the message does accurately describe – albeit in a mystificatory fashion – Kitchener's role in the Arab policy of the British government.

> In our councils [Sykes wrote] ever did he advise us of the Arab nation foretelling that in days to come they should rise once again to eminence and dominion among the peoples of the world, even as in the days of those great ones of the Arab race, saints, rulers, statesmen and warriors, who are dead even as he.[2]

But the Cairo officials also benefited from the support of Clayton's superior at Khartoum, Sir Reginald Wingate, governor-general of the Sudan and *sirdar* of the Egyptian army. Wingate had served in the East much longer than any of these officials, and enjoyed wide connexions in high political and official circles at home. He conducted a frequent and extensive correspondence with such personalities as Hardinge, Cromer, Curzon, Stamfordham and Sir Clive Wigram (the last two being private and assistant private secretary respectively to George V).[3]

From the first, Wingate was very eager to draw the Sharif to the British side, and conducted a correspondence with him through an intermediary, the Sudanese religious leader Sir Sayyid Ali al-Mirghani who, at one point, wrote – presumably with Wingate's authority – urging Husayn 'to rise and take over the reins of the holy Arabian Koreishite Khaliphate, which you represent, being a direct descendant of our Holy Prophet'; by so doing, Husayn would help the Mohammedans and the Arabs 'to recover their stolen Khalifate

[1] F.O. 371/2480, 23865/2506, McMahon's despatch no. 23, Cairo 15 Feb. 1915; F.O. 141/654, file 356/1 where Clayton's note of 8 Feb. is attached to the copy in the residency file. It will be recalled that about that time Lt Pirie-Gordon, an intelligence officer, produced a paper arguing that Egypt and Syria belonged naturally and historically together.
[2] F.O. 371/2773, 111398/42233.
[3] As may be seen from the Wingate Papers at Durham University.

and lost independence and civilization which the Turks have trodden down with their injustice.'[1]

A few months before, in May, Wingate sent to Grey a memorandum by Mirghani advocating that the Sharif should become Caliph and that Mecca should become the capital of the caliphate. In the private letter which accompanied Mirghani's note, Wingate wrote:

> I am well aware that it may be considered futile to talk of the formation of a new state without territory, without capital and without a ruler but however Utopian it may be there can be no doubt that when the psychological moment comes all Moslem eyes will be turned to Great Britain to whom they look for support in this – perhaps the supreme crisis – in their religious and national existence, and if I may venture to say so, I think it is for us to take the lead and to consolidate on our side – as far as we possibly can – the divergent views of various Moslem nationalities and Communities.[2]

In Wingate's mind two notions were conjoined from the start, much more clearly than they were in Kitchener's or Storrs's mind. These were the notions of an Arab caliphate and of a federation of Arab states which would lend support and give reality to such a caliphate. The scheme he favoured is exhibited together with his justification of it in a letter to Hardinge of 26 August 1915. He confessed that he was 'increasingly drawn to an attempted solution on Pan-Arabian lines' which 'might wean Sunnite Islam from the aggressive Pan-Islamism of the Ottoman school and create something like a true balance of power, spiritual and temporal in the central states of the Islamic world'. He continued:

> The geographical position of the Arabs and their control of the pilgrim routes, their sentimental claims to be the aristocrats of Islam and the natural guardians of the holy shrines and their strong racial characteristics combine to constitute them in my opinion, the natural and only effective counterpoise to Ottoman influences in the Near East and throughout Islam...

This meant the creation of an Arab caliphate. But an 'Arab "Pope" buried away in the sands of the Arabian Peninsula – even

[1] Wingate Papers, file 135/6, copy of letter from Mirghani to Husayn, 17 Nov. 1915.

[2] F.O. 371/2486, 77713/34982, private letter from Wingate to Grey, Khartoum 15 May 1915. Wingate had already convassed the same views in a letter to Hardinge (Hardinge Papers, vol. 93, pp. 484–91) of Mar. 1915, with which he had enclosed a long letter from 'one prominent member of the Arab party to another' which, Wingate declared, 'disloses...the arguments and aspirations of a political body who carry some weight and whose views represent, I believe, those of the majority of the better educated and non-fanatical Moslem Arabs of the Near East.' The letter, which was unsigned and very long, argues that Britain should promote an Arab caliphate. Wingate also attempted to promote the Arab caliphate through Cromer. Curzon, whom Cromer approached with this idea, was very sceptical of the whole scheme, and wrote to Cromer in a letter of 9 June 1915 (Wingate Papers, file 134/7): 'I am amused at the tacit assumption of all the Arab and Moslem writers that whoever the new Khalif is he will have to be bolstered up by us.' See also Kedourie, *The Chatham House Version*, p. 15, where another passage from the same letter is quoted.

though the integrity of these sands is fully secured to him – will appeal to Moslems nowhere'. On the contrary, he will become 'a living emblem of the decay of Islamic ideals'. Wingate therefore 'inclined to the view that, in the theory of the Arabian union, and by concessions to the Pan-Arabian ideal, may lie not merely a partial solution of many of our present difficulties, but possibly the formation of a really constructive scheme for the future'.

> I am under no delusion regarding the practical difficulties in the way, or the illusive character of Arabian political conceptions, but I conceive it to be not impossible that in the dim future a federation of semi-independent Arab States might exist under European guidance and support, linked together by racial and linguistic bonds, owing spiritual allegiance to a single Arab Primate, and looking to Great Britain as its patron and protector.[1]

More light is thrown on the views agitated in Wingate's entourage by a long paper written by his private secretary, Captain G. S. Symes, in February 1915 which Wingate sent to Grey. Symes discussed the issues raised by war with the Ottomans much more comprehensively than anyone had hitherto done. He tentatively proposed that the British should lay stress 'on the traditional claims of the Arabs (Koreish) to the Sceptre of Islam' and undertake to protect from outside interference an embryonic Arab caliphate. If this were done, he argued, 'the destruction of the temporal dominion of Turkey might assume, in Arab and Anglo-phil Moslem eyes, the character of a blow struck on behalf of the rightful protectors of Islam (the Arabs) against the Turkish Usurper of the Khalifate'. But Symes was concerned with much more than the caliphate, which he seemed to regard – in the prevalent European fashion – as a primarily religious office. Like his master he linked the Arab caliphate with the establishment of an extensive Arab state. Symes may, in fact, be considered the first British official to have advocated British support of pan-Arabism:

> The scope of Pan-Arab aspirations exceeds the limits of Arabia Proper and comprises an area bounded on the north by Kurdistan, on the west by the Mediterranean, on the south by the Red and Arabian seas, and on the east by the Persian Gulf. It is more than probable that by our actions in the near future in these regions the sincerity of our declarations and future policy in regard to Islam will be gauged and assessed by the Mohammedan world.

Symes urged that 'our intentions, *and those of our allies*, should be stated as clearly and definitely as possible at the first favourable opportunity.' What these intentions ought to be, Symes indicated

[1] Hardinge Papers, vol. 94.

in his paper. He was again probably the first British official to introduce into the discussion of British Middle-Eastern policy those accents of self-doubt, that eagerness to anticipate accusations of bad faith as yet unformulated, and to bow to demands as yet not made, which shortly afterwards were to become so familiar and influential:

> In this connection it will be remembered that by our alliance with France and Russia, and with the Egyptian precedent still fresh in Moslem minds, we are increasingly suspect as compared with Germany whose acquisitions of Moslem territory have hitherto been negligible. Unjustifiable though it may appear to us the character of grabbers of Moslem lands is attached to us by our opponents, and a sinister meaning will be given to our use of the terms 'protectorate', 'temporary or conditional occupation of territory', 'Spheres of influence', and even 'Economic Concessions'.

Symes therefore argued that it might be 'politic' to forgo any claim to economic control over the Euphrates valley, and to be simply confirmed in the occupation of Basra: 'Any advance we may find it necessary to make for strategic reasons, and any subsequent military operations in this region, would, conditional on local Arab support', he suggested somewhat obscurely, 'be undertaken on this understanding.' Syria was a more delicate matter. A declaration here was perhaps unwise, but it might 'tend considerably to allay Moslem suspicion, if not to satisfy Pan-Arab aspirations' if a guarantee were given that 'a right of access from the western terminus of the Hidjaz Railway to the Mediterranean would be recognized and facilities afforded for an "all Moslem" railway route from Mecca to a sea-port under Moslem Arab control'. This suggestion was, perhaps deliberately, just as cloudy as the earlier one regarding Mesopotamia, but what was clear was that Symes wanted a 'formal proclamation, expressed in a suitable Arabic' embodying these promises and guarantees to be issued 'at the first favourable opportunity.' Two paragraphs of the suggested proclamation are worth noticing. In the first, Symes proposed to tell the Arabs

> That Military operations against the Turco-German forces on the coasts of Arabia and in Mesopotamia, undertaken in support of the Arabs' cause, imply no intention of entering into possssion of, or alienating from their lawful owners, the Arab lands which are the rightful heritage of Islam.

This paragraph, it will be observed, is an echo of the Cairo proclamation of 4 December, cited above, which affirmed that Britain did not 'intend to possess any part of your countries neither in the form of conquest and possession nor in the form of protection or occupation'. But the second paragraph was original to Symes. It would have promised

That Great Britain and Her allies will recognize the principle that the main lines of access to the Hedjaz – and in particular the railway communications between the Holy Places and the Mediterranean Sea – should remain under independent Moslem control.[1]

When McMahon and Maxwell suggested, at the beginning of November 1915, that the proclamation to be issued when Baghdad was conquered should offer promises regarding an Arab national state, it was natural that Wingate should join his voice to theirs and urge that it should give 'the Arab nationalists an assurance that their interests both religious and material, will be carefully safeguarded.'[2]

Wingate's advocacy of the Arab caliphate and of Arab nationalism was so whole-hearted precisely because, like Storrs, he did not take it seriously and did not believe that mere words – however extravagant – spoken in support of these causes could possibly have any real consequences. As he told Clayton in November 1915, following the negotiations with the Sharif: 'After all what harm can our acceptance of his proposals do? If the embryonic Arab State comes to nothing, all our promises vanish and we are absolved from them – if the Arab State becomes a reality, we have quite sufficient safeguards to control it.'[3] His language in a letter to Hardinge some three years later is even more explicit. In this letter Wingate reminded Hardinge how in 1915 'when you were Viceroy and we were endeavouring to engineer the Sherif's revolt from the Sudan' he had informed him of Mirghani's views on the Arab caliphate:

> Sir Sayed Ali [he went on] no doubt thought that a great Arab success might place the Sherif in this proud position and the remote possibility of this proved an excellent war-cry – inasmuch as it rallied to the Sherif's standards many important tribes who had been long oppressed by Turkish misrule

[1] F.O. 800/48, Grey Papers, note by Symes, Khartoum 15 Feb. 1915 forwarded with a letter from Wingate to Grey of 27 Feb. A passage from Symes's autobiography (*Tour of Duty*, 1946, p. 34) seems to describe somewhat opaquely and obliquely his views at about that time: 'What might be the ultimate future of those semi-derelict Turkish provinces situated in Mesopotamia and along the Mediterranean and Red Sea littorals, which contained the vast Arabian deserts? Local populations differed greatly in physical type and conditions of life; but to most of them Arabic was the mother tongue, and a large majority professed the unifying creed of Islam. In the aggregate they seemed to possess almost all the attributes for political integration except up-to-date experience in the art of self-government. Such experience could be cultivated under the enlightened tutelage of a modern Power, or Powers. But European statesmen who repudiated imperialist ambitions of the bad old ("Colonial") days recognized the Arabs' fierce distrust of alien controls, or even queried the presumption that either the French, with their policy of assimilation, or the British with their *laissez-faire* technique, were ideally fitted to put Near-Easterns on a path of moral, as well as material development.' It is not clear to whom, unless to Symes himself, the expression 'European statesmen' is intended to refer.
[2] Hardinge Papers, vol. 94, Wingate to Hardinge, Khartoum 1 Nov. 1915.
[3] Wingate to Clayton, Khartoum 15 Nov. 1915, quoted in Kedourie, *The Chatham House Version*, p. 19.

whilst it afforded us an opportunity of dealing our Turco-German enemies a heavy blow by taking from them the Holy Places of Islam.

I admit to having been sufficiently opportunist to take the fullest advantage of the situation to treat the Sherif's revolt rather as a really useful war measure than as a means to an end for the renaissance of a great united Arab Empire.

There are others who may still retain such beliefs and I admire their enthusiasm but, personally, I am sceptical about their eventual success and as long as the movement served its purpose in knocking out one or two of the stones of the arch of the Central Powers I am satisfied that its object (as far as my intervention is concerned) has been achieved.[1]

The views of Storrs, Clayton and Wingate as they have been set out above should indicate amply enough the atmosphere reigning in British official circles in Cairo. The despatches of the French representative who, of course, was particularly sensitive to Syrian issues, supplement what is found in the British records, and help to convey a fuller idea of this atmosphere. When war with the Ottoman empire was not yet two months old, Defrance was already reporting that the British agency was exhorting the Syrians – so some of them informed him – to have confidence in Britain which would, at the proper time, ensure the 'independence' of Syria. Defrance believed these reports to have some foundation, and that over-zealous British officials were trying to persuade the Syrians in Cairo that the fate of their country depended solely on Britain.[2] In February 1915, the head of the French military mission in Egypt, Colonel Maucorps, wrote that Sir Ronald Graham had asked the French minister: 'What would you do if we were to land in Syria or Palestine?' The question was to him significant in two respects. In the first place, it was connected with the presence in the British agency of certain officials, including Storrs, 'who carry out among the Syrians an active campaign in favour of Britain, so that the latter might ask for British intervention.' In the second place,

> I think I ought to point out that a clear distinction is made here between Palestine and Syria, and that the British might undertake military action in Palestine, while respecting French rights in Syria. I have heard many Syrians here express the opinion that Palestine will belong to Britain and Syria to France.[3]

A week later, Maucorps reported on the views of George Lloyd, who was then serving in military intelligence under Clayton. In his earlier note, Maucorps had drawn attention to his very active role in the propaganda carried on in Cairo in favour of British inter-

---

[1] Hardinge Papers, vol. 39, Wingate to Hardinge, Cairo 28 Dec. 1918, cited above.
[2] A.E., Guerre 1914–18, vol. 867, Defrance's despatch no. 460, Cairo 23 Dec. 1914.
[3] A.E., Guerre 1914–18, vol. 868, note no. 4 by Maucorps, Cairo 21 Feb. 1915.

vention in Syria. Lloyd favoured British annexation of Haifa as the Mediterranean terminus of a railway from Mesopotamia: 'He represents...the idea of those who would like to make Great Britain the protector of Islam and to ensure for it – I quote his own words – at least the control of the Arab world.'[1] Defrance's despatches and telegrams of this period give examples of the way in which the censorship deleted references in the local press favourable to the French connexion with Syria, while allowing articles advocating British control of Syria. When Defrance complained of this to a high British official, he was told that it was difficult for the British authorities to prescribe to pro-British Syrians what line to take in the Syrian question since the British and French governments 'had not come to an agreement on this issue.'[2]

There is great contrast between the atmosphere in Cairo, and the views and activities of the Cairo officials, and that which reigned in New Delhi, and at Basra, which had been occupied by the Mesopotamia expeditionary force (supplied and controlled by the Indian army) on 23 November 1914. Shortly after its occupation, the viceroy urged an announcement that its occupation was permanent. Lord Crewe replied that the cabinet, having carefully examined Hardinge's proposal, decided that it would be a breach of the understanding among the Allies that a final settlement had to await the end of the war. To announce the annexation of Basra would entitle Russia to make similar announcements elsewhere.[3] But there is no doubt that Hardinge's views were widely shared in India and at the India office. In March 1915, Hirtzel wrote a long memorandum advocating that Basra and Baghdad be attached to India and governed by a governor-general 'enjoying the same measure of independence as the Governor-General of the Sudan'. The military secretary at the India office, Sir Edmund Barrow, dissented somewhat from this view, proposing instead the annexation of 'so much of the Basra wilayat as is essential for military reasons,' while the rest of Mesopotamia would remain under the suzerainty of the Caliph, with a British high commissioner or governor-general residing in Baghdad. The difference between these two views was clearly not fundamental.[4] As Crewe stated at the war

[1] *Ibid.*, note no. 8, Cairo 28 Feb., on conversation with George Lloyd.
[2] *Ibid.*, Defrance's telegram no. 40, Cairo 11 Feb. 1915, and his despatches nos. 47 and 49, Cairo 11 and 13 Feb. respectively.
[3] Crewe Papers I/19, file 3, Hardinge's private telegram, 7 Dec. 1914, and Crewe's private telegram, 9 Dec.
[4] Cab. 42/2/8, note by Hirtzel regarding the future settlement of Eastern Turkey in Asia and Arabia, 14 Mar. 1915, followed by Barrow's note, 16 Mar.

council meeting on 19 March, 'all shades of opinion at the India Office agreed that the Basra Vilayet must form part of the British Empire.' But neither the war council nor the cabinet took a decision in this sense, and as V. H. Rothwell has pointed out, 'the British administrators in [Mesopotamia] were scrupulous in not giving pledges that the British would remain precisely because they had no authority to do so from London or the Government of India.'[1] This was in marked contrast to the proceedings of Grey and Kitchener who gave out pledges regarding Arabia without the authority or knowledge of the cabinet or the war council, as well as to those of the Cairo officials who improved upon and embellished these pledges.

India's immediate concern was naturally Mesopotamia, but this is not to say that they had no views about policy in Western Arabia or the Levant. Thus, Kitchener was not the only one to think of contacting the Sharif. The resident at Aden (who was subordinate to the governor of Bombay) proposed to do so in December 1914 – that is after Kitchener's second message had, unbeknown to anyone at the India office, been sent to Mecca. Hardinge approved, and wished him to call upon Husayn to co-operate with the British 'by persuading the Arabs of the Hedjaz to dissociate themselves from the Turks', and if he were to do so 'we will not only now respect holy places, but will hereafter protect them, and support him and his family in retention of their hereditary rights and privileges'. Hardinge's proposal was thus very similar to what Kitchener had proposed in his first message. But Hardinge's message would have ended on a note which was absent from Kitchener's language, but which was very appropriate for an imperial Power addressing someone like the Sharif. Hardinge proposed to tell Husayn that 'our support, just as our displeasure, may mean much at end of war.'[2] But the viceroy's proposal came too late, and his message was never sent.

Again, both the India office and the government of India had views about the disposal of Ottoman territories in the Levant. As has been seen, Kitchener proposed, in November 1914, that British policy should aim at the recognition of an Arab Caliph at Mecca who would be guaranteed against both 'external aggression and internal interference', and that Syria should become the fief of this Caliph, revenue from which would maintain him in proper state. Kitchener also proposed that the Arabs should be told immediately that this

---

[1] Cab. 42/2/14, minutes of meeting of war council, 19 Mar. 1915; V. H. Rothwell, 'Mesopotamia in British War Aims 1914–18', *Historical Journal* XIII (1970), 274–5.

[2] Crewe Papers, I/19/4, Hardinge's telegram, 11 Dec. 1914.

was what the British desired, but that the French should, for the
time being, be kept in the dark. Grey consulted Crewe who
expressed grave doubts whether it would be possible to negotiate
with the Arabs behind the back of the French. Hardinge, whom
Crewe consulted in turn, pointed out that to guarantee the Muslim
holy places from all internal interference would be both undesirable
and impossible to fulfil. The proposed organization of Syria as a
caliphal domain, further, would make for serious difficulties with
the French whose interests were economic and political as much as
they were sentimental. 'In an Arabic Syrian State', he declared, 'the
reactionary Turk would be simply replaced by the unenterprising
Arab. Syria', he concluded, his language here indicating how Arab
and beduin were widely taken to be synonymous, 'is too advanced
in civilisation to tolerate a new Arab State.'[1] Kitchener's plan
aroused Hirtzel's objections as well: 'Would Christian opinion not
only in this country, but also in Russia and France', he wrote in
comment on the viceroy's telegram of 29 November, 'tolerate for
a moment the idea of actually setting up a new Moslem Power in
the Holy Land? I cannot believe it. It is bad enough to tolerate what
is already there: but to create a new Power, and to make the seat
of the Kaliphate, in a part of the world which, to the *least*
sentimental of men, must have an appreciably non-Moslem atmosphere, would seem to most plain Christians almost sacrilege.'[2] A
few months later Crewe himself made the same point when Constantinople was promised to Russia. It seemed to him, as he told
Grey, that Russia and France assumed that Britain had no interests
in the Levant:

> as regards Palestine ought we not to point out that its fate cannot be the
> exclusive interest of Russia as representing the orthodox faith and France
> (very facetiously) appearing on behalf of Rome? The Christians of the U.K.
> and its Dominions, and of the U.S. and of the Protestant countries of
> Europe...have a definite concern with the cradle of their religion.[3]

On the proposed Arab caliphate itself the India office also struck
a cautious note. When a copy of Mirghani's memorandum was sent
to them, they pointed out that it was by no means clear how
Mirghani intended the British government to act, and what effect
their action could have on the Sharif's position in the Muslim world.
Husayn should certainly be encouraged (by all means short of

[1] F.O. 800/98, Grey Papers, Crewe to Grey, 13 Nov. 1914, and copy of telegram from
Hardinge to Crewe Private and Personal, Delhi 29 Nov. 1914.
[2] Crewe Papers I/19, file 2, Hirtzel to Crewe, 1 Dec. 1914.
[3] Crewe Papers I/20, file 5, Crewe to Grey Private, 22 Mar. 1915.

military intervention) to throw off the yoke of Constantinople and
to declare the independence of the Hijaz: 'If, when he has asserted
his independence, he claims the Khalifate,' the foreign office was
told, 'it will be for Saiyid Ali el Morghani and others to acclaim
him as such. Whether the other Arab rulers will do so will doubtless
depend upon what the claim imports for them, and how far, if it
implies political sovereignty over territory which they at present
rule, they are willing to subordinate themselves and their subjects
to him.'[1] As the sequel was to show, these words of caution were
fully justified. Kitchener's hint, amplified by Storrs and echoed by
Mirghani, made a prodigious impression on the Sharif and his sons,
and encouraged them to entertain overweening ambitions. These
in turn disquietened and displeased Husayn's neighbours in the
Arabian peninsula, who remembered how the Sharif, on the pretext
of asserting the authority of the Ottomans, had, before the war,
waged war on Ibn Sa'ud in Najd and the Idrisi in 'Asir. This note
of caution generally marked the appreciations of the India office and
of the government of India and its agents. It is all the more striking
when contrasted with the unqualified enthusiasm expressed by Cairo
and Khartoum for the Sharif and his prospects. For example,
reporting on interviews with Ibn Sa'ud and the shaykh of Kuwait
at the end of December 1915, Cox reported that in the former's view
'no one [among the Arabian chiefs] cared in the least who called
himself Caliph, and [he] reminded me that the Wahabis did not
recognise any Caliph after the first four';[2] if the Sharif claimed the
caliphate 'his calling himself Caliph would not make any difference
to his status among other Chiefs and there would be no question
of their accepting any control any more than they do now'; Ibn Sa'ud
added that 'there was no doubt a certain amount of talk about the
Caliphate in Cairo, presumably because of the presence of a Sultan,
but as far as the Jezirat-al-Arab was concerned, he did not consider
that the question had any significance or interest for them'. The
shaykh of Kuwait, again, 'evinces general ignorance of the subject',
and neither he nor his dependents 'had any interest whatever in the
question.' These opinions confirmed Cox in 'the general impressions gained on this side of Arabia since the beginning of the war,
viz., that the question of the Caliphate has no serious interest for
the tribes or their Chiefs.' On this report Wingate commented as
follows:

[1] F.O. 371/2486, 84355/34982, India office to foreign office Secret, 24 June 1915.
[2] Though Ibn Sa'ud may have believed this, it does not seem to have been in fact the
correct Wahabi view; see article 'Imama', *Encyclopaedia of Islam*, new ed., by
W. Madelung.

The Quicksand

It is clear that widely differing opinions respecting the Khalifate are being expressed in India and Eastern Arabia to those held in Western Arabia and parts of Syria where the prestige of the Sherif of Mecca appears to be almost paramount. This prestige coupled with his known diplomatic skill and the advantage of his central position (at Mecca) render him in my opinion the sole candidate for the Khalifate who could count on a sufficient body of Arab (and anti-Ottoman) supporters, to declare himself as such, and subsequently to rally to his standard the remaining Arab factions who are opposed to Turkish domination of the Arabian Peninsula.[1]

Events were decisively to demonstrate how ill-founded Wingate's judgments were; but even when they were set down, there was little or no evidence to back them up. It was fanciful to speak of Husayn's 'paramount' prestige, and to believe that he could rally behind him a large body of supporters. It was moreover to fly in the face of the evidence to believe that the 'Arab factions' of the peninsula would accept his leadership.

This particular point was present to the mind of G. R. Clerk, head of the war department at the foreign office, who remarked in a minute written in August 1915 that there was need of 'great care' in British relations with the Sharif because, *inter alia*, his 'two Arab enemies are our two Arab friends – Idrisi and Bin Saud.'[2] In his caution, Clerk was at one with his colleagues, who time and again applied a brake to the forward policy recommended by Cairo. When, as has been seen, a few days after the outbreak of war with the Ottoman empire, Cheetham reported that the majority of the Syrian Muslims would whole-heartedly side with Britain if they were given a guarantee that France would not occupy Syria, Nicolson, the permanent under-secretary, minuted: 'We cannot ask for any guarantees from France as to Syria...Leave matter alone.'[3] When Cheetham, some two months later, pressed for independent British military action in Syria, declaring that according to intelligence sources a large proportion of the population of Syria and Palestine would welcome the advent of British forces, Lancelot Oliphant minuted that to act 'independently of our allies' was out of the question. Nicolson endorsed his view.[4]

Some two months later, when Symes's note of 15 February (mentioned above) reached the foreign office, it inspired Clerk to write a long minute examining the possibility of setting up a Muslim

[1] F.O. 882/8, note by P. Z. Cox on interviews with Ibn Sa'ud on 26 Dec., and with the shaykh of Kuwait on 31 Dec. 1915; Wingate to Clayton, Khartoum 15 Feb. 1916.
[2] F.O. 371/2486, 112369/34982, minute 13 Aug. 1915 on a memorandum by Symes about the Sharif, Khartoum 19 July 1915.
[3] F.O. 371/2141, 69074/46756, cited above, minute of 10 Nov. 1914.
[4] F.O. 371/2480, 2506, Cheetham's telegram no. 10, Cairo 7 Jan. 1915.

state which might secure for Britain the advantages, and avoid the drawbacks, of outright annexation. He confessed that the issue was complicated and difficult:

> The creation of a definite Arab State is, especially for foreign Christian Powers, practically an impossibility. We cannot do more than spread and encourage the idea. But what we can perhaps work for is a system of autonomous Arab states, recognizing and paying tribute to a spiritual Khalif at Mecca, but politically independent of him. Mesopotamia could be one such state, and Bin Saud could form another, and a federation might eventually come into being which would weld itself into a real Moslem Power.

These fanciful reflections about a spiritual caliphate at Mecca, to which a number of states – including Ibn Sa'ud! – would pay tribute show that the usually sensible Clerk was here quite out of his depth, and solely guided by the views of Symes and his Cairo and Khartoum colleagues. And to do him justice, he was not proposing a policy to be adopted; he was rather thinking aloud, and he kept on stressing how difficult the problem was. Even so, the response of the permanent under-secretary was sceptical: 'The project [of a spiritual caliphate buttressed by tributary states]', Nicolson minuted, 'is ingenious; but it will take time to work out and fructify and something will have to subsist. I am afraid too that Arab autonomous states would be rather quarrelsome.'[1]

Nicolson, in fact, believed that there were distinct advantages in maintaining intact the Ottoman empire in Asia, not least because its division among the Allies was bound to lead to friction; one difficulty in particular impressed him: 'I am quite sure of one thing', he wrote to Buchanan at Petrograd on 15 March 1915, 'that if [the Ottoman] Empire were to be partitioned and distributed there will be very great difficulty in settling as to who was to have control of Jerusalem and the Holy Places there.'[2]

Grey, as has been seen, was quite ready to let Kitchener entice the Sharif with large and vague promises, but he was immediately on his guard when Kitchener proposed in November 1914 that Syria be promised to the Arabs. He firmly minuted on Kitchener's letter: 'We cannot act as regards Syria'.[3]

The reason obviously was that two years before Grey himself had allowed without any reservation that Syria was within the zone of French influence.[4] Some two months after his minute on Kitchener's letter, British recognition of France's paramount position in Syria

---

[1] F.O. 800/48, Grey Papers, as cited above. [2] F.O. 800/377, Nicolson Papers.
[3] F.O. 800/102, Grey Papers, as cited above.
[4] Kedourie, *England and the Middle East*, p. 23.

had once more to be affirmed. In January 1915, Churchill conceived the plan of forcing the Straits at the Dardanelles. Included in his plan was a simultaneous attack on Alexandretta. Its purpose was that in case the attack on the Dardanelles failed, it could be represented as a mere demonstration to cover the seizure of Alexandretta: 'I believe', he told Kitchener, 'this aspect is important from an Oriental point of view.' But in August 1914 the British had agreed that the Mediterranean should be predominantly an area of French naval activity, and their consent had therefore to be obtained both for the attack on the Straits and the landing at Alexandretta. Of the latter scheme the French were very suspicious, and they objected strenuously to it. In order to obtain their consent to the Dardenelles operation, Churchill had to abandon the landing at Alexandretta, and to agree that the French vice-admiral in the Eastern Mediterranean should command in the Levant 'not only as I had proposed from Latakia to Jaffa, but including Alexandretta.' He had also to accept the French conditions stipulated by Augagneur, the French minister of the navy in a letter of 31 January, whereby no landing at Alexandretta or anywhere else on the Asiatic coast of the Mediterranean could be effected without prior consultation between the two governments, such consultation to include political as well as military issues.[1] Before agreeing to these conditions, Churchill had consulted both Kitchener and Grey. The latter wrote to Churchill on 26 January:

> I think it important to let the French have what they want in this Memo even about Alexandretta. It will be fatal to cordial co-operation in the Mediterranean and perhaps everywhere if we arouse their suspicions as to anything in the region of Syria. I hope you will close with this proposal. If it is not agreed to I foresee very untoward consequences.[2]

Shortly afterwards, what was implicit in Augagneur's letter to Churchill was made quite explicit. Delcassé, the foreign minister, visited London on 9 February and, in a discussion with Grey and Nicolson, declared that France claimed Syria and Alexandretta. This claim, so Delcassé understood, would not be opposed by Britain.[3] What the claim exactly meant would no doubt depend on the fate of the Ottoman empire, and whether it was to continue as

[1] Exchange of letters between Churchill and Augagneur on 27 and 31 Jan. reproduced in full in George H. Cassar, *The French and the Dardanelles*, 1971, pp. 251–6; see also *ibid.*, ch. 3 *passim*; the quotation from Churchill's letter to Kitchener, dated 20 Jan., is at p. 51.

[2] Martin Gilbert, *Winston Churchill*, vol. III, 1971, p. 267. Grey's letter is quoted from the Churchill Papers.

[3] A.E., Guerre 1914–18, vol. 868, Delcassé's telegram to Cambon, Paris 13 Feb. 1915.

a recognizable entity or be partitioned among the victors. What the term 'Syria' covered was again as yet undefined. Cambon, the French ambassador in London, writing to Delcassé in March, seemed to think that Palestine was separate from it, and he argued that one good reason for keeping the Ottoman empire in existence was that it was impossible otherwise to establish in Palestine a regime which would not be a source of friction among the Christian Powers.[1]

But whatever Syria was to include, or however the French were to assert their primacy there, by February Grey was more or less committed to acquiescing in French predominance in a large area of the Levant. It therefore comes as no surprise that he should have categorically rejected the suggestion which McMahon made in his despatch of 15 February. In this despatch, it will be recalled, McMahon, acting under Clayton's influence, argued that Syria should be attached to the Egyptian sultanate. In a private telegram which he himself drafted he told McMahon:

> It is perhaps well to say at once that it would mean a break with France if we put forward any claims in Syria and to claim it for Egypt would be equivalent to claiming it for ourselves.[2]

Like Hirtzel, Crewe, Nicolson and Cambon, Grey seems to have been concerned about the fate of the territory which all referred to as Palestine. In fact his attention was drawn to it as soon as the Ottomans had entered the war. His cabinet colleague Herbert Samuel spoke to him about it on 9 November 1914. He pointed out that 'the question of the future control of Palestine' was likely to arise, and that the Powers would not allow it to be given to any one of them. The opportunity might thus arise 'for the fulfilment of the ancient aspiration of the Jewish people and the restoration there of a Jewish state.' According to Samuel's note of their conversation, written on the same day,

> Grey said that the idea had always had a strong sentimental attraction for him. The historical appeal was very strong. He was quite favourable to the proposal and would be prepared to work for it if the opportunity arose. If any proposals were put forward by France or any other Power with regard to Syria, it would be important not to acquiesce in any plan which would be inconsistent with the creation of a Jewish state in Palestine. He asked whether I thought that Syria must necessarily go with Palestine. I said no...

Some three months later, on 5 February 1915, Samuel and Grey had another conversation about Palestine. Grey, as Samuel recorded at the time, was

[1] A.E., Guerre 1914–18, vol. 850, Cambon's despatch no. 129, London 4 Mar. 1915.
[2] F.O. 800/48, Grey Papers, telegram to McMahon, 8 Mar. 1915.

still anxious to promote a settlement of the question in a way favourable to Zionist ideas, but he is very doubtful of the possibility or desirability of the establishment of a British Protectorate.

...When I asked him what his solution was he said it might be possible to neutralize the country under international guarantee; to place the control of the Holy Places in the hands of a Commission in which the European Powers, and the Pope, and perhaps the United States, would be represented; and to vest the government of the country in some kind of Council to be established by the Jews. I expressed a doubt whether the Arab population, who number five-sixths of the inhabitants, would accept such a government. Grey said that a possible alternative would be, if it were found necessary to continue the suzerainty of Turkey, to establish a regime somewhat like that of Lebanon, but with the governor appointed by the Powers.[1]

When shortly afterwards Constantinople was conceded to Russia, the French informed the Russians that in compensation they demanded Syria, including Palestine. The Russians, so the British ambassador in Petrograd telegraphed, did not look with favour on this demand and rather hoped that Palestine would be internationalized. Grey's minute on Buchanan's telegram showed that he was still following the line of thought indicated in his second conversation with Samuel: 'Palestine', he wrote, 'might be given to Belgium, Christian, Liberal and now noble Belgium.'[2]

By March 1915, Grey had come to have one other idea about the future disposal of the Ottoman empire in Asia. This related to the Muslim holy places and the Arabian peninsula. As has been seen, he informed McMahon in a telegram of 14 April that the British government 'will make it an essential condition of any terms of peace that the Arabian Peninsula and its Moslem Holy Places should remain in the hands of an independent Moslem State.' Grey went on to add that it was not possible at that stage to determine how much territory should be included in this state.[3] Grey seems to have committed the British government to this 'essential condition' of any future peace settlement on the basis of a war council decision taken on 19 March. This decision was the outcome of a discussion ocasioned by a telegram from Buchanan at Petrograd. In this telegram (of 18 March 1915) the latter reported that the French ambassador had told the Russians that Syria, which France was claiming in compensation for the cession of Constantinople to Russia, included Palestine and the holy places. The war council

[1] Viscount Samuel, *Memoirs*, 1945, pp. 141 and 143–4.
[2] F.O. 800/88, Grey Papers, minute of 19 Mar. on Buchanan's telegram no. 320, Petrograd 18 Mar. 1915. Grey's minute is quoted in V. H. Rothwell, *British War Aims and Peace Diplomacy 1914–1918*, 1971, p. 26.
[3] F.O. 371/2486, 44598/34982, Grey's telegram no. 173, 14 Apr. 1915, cited above.

decided the following day that it was premature to discuss the partition of Turkey, but that the first desideratum of a peace settlement was the establishment of a 'Moslem entity'. This entity was to include 'Arabia'; but what else it was to include remained to be decided. Following this decision, Grey drafted this telegram to Buchanan:

> You can inform Minister of Foreign Affairs that when the Turks disappear as contemplated from Constantinople, we regard it as essential that some independent Moslem authority should exist as a political centre for Islam elsewhere. This authority need not be Turkish, but it must exist and be thoroughly Moslem and its centre will naturally be the Moslem Holy Places. Arabia will presumably be included in this Moslem State, and it will be necessary to decide whether it should include other, and if so, what territory in Asia Minor.
>
> Till this point has been decided it seems to us premature to discuss the possible division of Syria, Mesopotamia, or neighbouring regions amongst other Powers.[1]

As may be seen, the terms of this telegram are much less categorical than what Grey was to tell McMahon on 14 April. But the idea that the British had entered into a solemn commitment to create an independent state in Arabia seems to have become firmly anchored in Grey's mind. In his memoirs, he speaks of a 'promise to King Hussein that Arabia should be an entirely independent Moslem State', and he calls it a secret treaty.[2] Such a treaty, of course, never did exist. As for the government, its collective decisions regarding the future of the Ottoman empire up to the spring of 1915 were two in number. When war with the Ottomans seemed inevitable, the cabinet decided, on 2 November 1914, that 'Henceforward Great Britain must finally abandon the formula of "Ottoman integrity" whether in Europe or in Asia'. What this specifically meant or entailed was never considered, then or subsequently. Again, meeting on 9 March 1915, the cabinet agreed to the Russian demand for the annexation of Constantinople, provided it was made into a free port and the freedom of the Straits assured. At this meeting Kitchener and Churchill argued that 'we should intimate to Russia that it was our desire that we should occupy and hold Alexandretta, the French receiving on their part Syria.' But the proposal was not discussed and the cabinet took no decision on it.[3]

---

[1] F.O. 371/2449, 31923/25014, Buchanan's telegram no. 320, Petrograd 18 Mar., and Grey's telegram no. 380, 19 Mar. 1915; Cab. 42/2/14, for decision of war council.

[2] Viscount Grey of Fallodon, *Twenty-Five Years 1892–1916*, 1925, vol. II, p. 229.

[3] Asquith Manuscripts, Bodleian Library, Oxford, vols. 7 and 8. Asquith's cabinet letters of 3 Nov. 1914 and 9 Mar. 1915 respectively.

The Quicksand

A fortnight after this meeting, the French ambassador informed Grey of his government's opinion that 'as the question of Constantinople and the Straits had now been disposed of' unofficial discussions should be held between the French and the British on their various desiderata in Asia Minor.[1] It was no doubt in order to prepare for these discussions, which belief in the imminent fall of Constantinople made it seem urgent to conduct, that the prime minister appointed, on 8 April, a committee 'to consider the nature of British desiderata in Turkey in Asia'. Its chairman was Sir Maurice de Bunsen; G. R. Clerk represented the foreign office, Sir T. W. Holderness the India office, Admiral H. B. Jackson the admiralty, Major-General C. E. Callwell the war office, and Sir H. Llewellyn Smith the board of trade. The committee had one other member, namely Sir Mark Sykes, M.P., who was Kitchener's representative on the committee. Sykes had been advising Kitchener on Eastern questions since the outbreak of war, and it was at Kitchener's request, it seems, that Sykes was appointed to the committee.[2] As the most cursory examination will show, Sykes's influence on the *Report of the Committee on Asiatic Turkey* (Bunsen Report), which was completed at the end of June 1915, was profound.[3] This may be attributed as much to his prestige as a traveller and a writer who was believed to know the Ottoman empire intimately, as to the immense personal authority of his patron, an authority the like of which no other member of the Bunsen committee could invoke. As Sykes himself has written, he used to report nightly to Kitchener's personal military secretary and to receive 'instructions as to the points Lord Kitchener desired should be considered.'[4]

The Bunsen Report considered four alternative schemes for dealing with the Ottoman empire in Asia. The first was partition among the Allies; the second was the establishment of zones of interests in a nominally independent empire which would be under effective European control; the third was the maintenance of the Ottoman regime in Asia as independent in name and in fact, but subject to certain small but significant territorial excisions; and fourth, the maintenance of an independent empire decentralized on

[1] F.O. 371/2486, 34982, Grey's despatch to Bertie, 23 Mar. 1915. The despatch is reproduced in Grey, *Twenty-five Years*, vol. II, p. 230.
[2] Sykes's letter to Sir G. Arthur, Kitchener's biographer, 12 Sept. 1916, quoted in Kedourie, 'Sir Mark Sykes and Palestine 1915–16', *Arabic Political Memoirs*, (pp. 236–42), p. 237.
[3] The report and its appendices may be found in Cab. 27/1.
[4] Kedourie, 'Sir Mark Sykes and Palestine' *op. cit.*

federal lines, but again subject to territorial excisions. But whatever project was adopted would have to provide for the satisfaction of certain British desiderata. These were: (1) the recognition and consolidation of the British position in the Persian Gulf, (2) the prevention of discrimination against foreign trade, (3) fulfilment of pledges given or to be given to rulers in the Arabian peninsula 'and, generally, maintenance of the assurances given to the Sherif of Mecca and the Arabs', (4) security for undertakings such as oil production, in which Britain was interested, (5) development of corn supply in Mesopotamia, and a possible field there for Indian colonization, (6) maintenance of the British strategic position in the Eastern Mediterranean and in the Persian Gulf, (7) 'To ensure that Arabia and the Moslem Holy Places remain under independent Moslem rule. Dependent upon this, we should seek for a settlement which will appeal to, or at least not antagonise, Indian Moslem feeling, and will provide a satisfactory solution of the question of the Khalifate', (8) a satisfactory solution of the Armenian problem, and (9) 'A settlement of the question of Palestine and the Holy Places of Christendom'. Of the last three desiderata, the committee observed that they were questions which for the moment had to be set aside for discussion and settlement in concert with other Powers.

The committee's own preference was for the last scheme, namely to maintain an independent, but federal, Ottoman empire in Asia. But if this, the best solution, was not attainable, then the committee preferred the division of the empire into zones of interests. A policy of partition was, for them, a *pis aller*, to be acquiesced in only if the other two alternatives failed.

The committee's deliberations throw a great deal of light on the way its members viewed the Ottoman empire in Asia and its ethnic and geographic divisions, the caliphate and its future, and the religious interests which had to be taken into account in any future settlement. Thus, in considering the possibility of an independent empire run on federal lines – the scheme which they favoured – they argued that, excluding Arabia, 'Turkey in Asia falls ethnographically and historically into five great provinces – Anatolia, Armenia, Syria, Palestine and Irak–Jazirah'. Each one of these provinces had 'its own characteristics', which gave it 'an individuality of its own', thus naturally lending itself to the establishment within its borders of a form of local government.

This division of the Ottoman territory in Asia, and particularly the distinction in the Arabic-speaking parts of the empire between the three provinces of Syria, Palestine and Irak–Jazirah was of great significance in the committee's arguments, and it may also be said to have subsequently formed the basis of the Sykes–Picot arrangements. For in considering the alternatives of partitioning the empire, or dividing it into zones of interest, the committee proposed that the British sphere, in either case, should comprise the two provinces of Palestine and Irak–Jazirah in one continuous band of territory running from the foothills of southern Kurdistan in the north-east, to Rafah and Akaba in the south-west, taking in Haifa, Acre, Tadmor and Dayr az-Zor. The residue, constituted by the province of Syria, was to accrue to the French. The novelty of such a scheme lay in the proposed attribution of 'Palestine' to Britain. This represented a triumph for the ideas of Sir Mark Sykes.

As has been seen, the French were somewhat nervous of British designs on Alexandretta. Whether they knew it or not, the nervousness was justified. Kitchener wanted the annexation of the port in order to secure a wholly British line of communications between the Persian Gulf and the Eastern Mediterranean. He argued for this both in a war council meeting on 10 March and in a memorandum dated 16 March 1915 which he sent to the Bunsen committee. But his adviser Sykes succeeded in convincing him that Haifa would serve better as a British base on the coast of the Levant.[1] At the fourth meeting of the Bunsen committee he also succeeded in convincing his fellow members to adopt his scheme.

The committee were, of course, aware that France was claiming 'Palestine' and the Christian holy places. Sykes's scheme was designed precisely to prevent the French from establishing themselves in this area, where they would be contiguous to Egypt, and to 'Arabia' – 'a situation', affirmed the committee, 'which we could scarcely tolerate.' They were also aware that Russia objected to French control over the holy places, and they assumed that British control would likewise be resisted. They proposed therefore to meet the difficulty by separating the issue of 'Palestine' from that of the holy places 'to be decided as a separate question, in discussion with those who stand for the national and religious interests involved.'[2]

---

[1] Kedourie, 'Sir Mark Sykes and Palestine', *op. cit.*; Kitchener's memorandum of 16 Mar. 1915 is attached to the Bunsen committee report in Cab. 27/1. Admiral Fisher also strongly supported the annexation of Alexandretta; in a fervent letter of 11 Mar. 1915 he told Kitchener: 'We must put up a stiff fight for Alexandretta...the Politicians *both* sides (Balfour the worse!) want to pander to the French...We want the waterway of the Euphrates Valley up to Alexandretta and locks and dams will enable us to bring Barges carrying the 170 ton guns of the future with oil engines by a short Canal to Alexandretta from the Persian Gulf to the Mediterranean...' P.R.O. 30 57/80, Kitchener Papers.

[2] Para. 37. The same point is made in para. 96, where it is declared that the committee 'see no reason why the sacred places of Palestine should not be dealt with as a separate

The committee, as has been seen, considered the possibility of keeping the Ottoman empire in Asia nominally independent and dividing it into zones of interest to be apportioned among the Allies. But since Constantinople had already been promised to Russia, an alternative capital had to be found. At its eighth meeting, Sykes proposed to the committee that Damascus should be the new seat of the empire and and of the caliphate. His idea was adopted, and the committee suggested in its report (para. 60) the constitution of a distinct province centred on Damascus and lying between the French and the British zones. It is interesting to see the committee ready to consider an Arab city as the seat of an Ottoman caliphate, and particularly interesting to see Sykes proposing such a scheme. Sykes, we remember, was acting as Kitchener's representative, and his proposals were made with the latter's knowledge and consent. This episode therefore sheds a new light on the messages and hints Kitchener had so recently conveyed to the Sharif.[1]

Another suggestion, which emanated directly from Kitchener, sheds even greater light on the manner in which Kitchener understood these messages and hints. In his memorandum of 16 March arguing for the British annexation of Alexandretta, which has been mentioned above, Kitchener declared that 'should the partition of Turkey take place, it is to our interests to see an Arab kingdom installed in Arabia under the auspices of England, bounded on the north by the valley of the Tigris and Euphrates, and containing within it the chief Mahommedan Holy Places, Mecca, Medina, and Kerbela'. The committee substantially adopted Kitchener's suggestion. It began by recalling (para. 3) Grey's recent stipulation (when agreeing that Constantinople should go to Russia) that 'in all circumstances Arabia and the Moslem holy places should remain

question', but muddled and confused drafting has led to the inclusion in this paragraph of two seemingly contradictory statements: that Palestine 'has been included within the geographical limits assigned to the British sphere', and that 'it will be idle for His Majesty's Government to claim the retention of Palestine in their sphere'. The contradiction is resolved if 'Palestine' in the latter sentence is understood to mean the holy places.

[1] Towards the end of July 1915, Sykes discussed British desiderata in the Levant with the French military attaché at Cairo and told him of the plan to annex Haifa and a belt of territory eastwards to ensure British control of a proposed railway from Haifa to Mesopotamia. The British, he told Lt de St Quentin, had no ambitions over Damascus but he thought that it would be better to internationalize this city which was an Islamic religious centre. If the French, nonetheless, wanted to have Damascus, then he suggested that the Hijaz railway station should be 'vaticanized' to the benefit of the Sharif. Sykes also suggested that the area between Bethlehem and Jericho, including Jerusalem, with Jaffa as an outlet to the sea, should be placed under international administration. Note by St Quentin, no. 63, 'Visées anglaises sur la Syrie', Cairo 28 July 1915, A.E., Guerre, 1914–18, vol. 869.

under independent Moslem rule.' The committee also held (paras. 91–2) that following the outbreak of war

> we have entered into, and in some cases completed, negotiations with...the Sheikh of Koweit, the Amir of Nejd (Bin Saud), the Sheikh of Mavia, Said Idriss, and the Grand Sherif of Mecca. These negotiations vary in detail, but they have this much in common that in every case they offer a guarantee of independence in some form or another as a return for effective or successful support in the war against Turkey, It still remains to be seen in some cases whether the Chiefs will fulfil their part of the bargain.
>
> It must be confessed that, in the absence of any central or predominant Government or Chief in Arabia, and of the hesitation of the Arabs to meet the advances of His Majesty's Government and proclaim their own independence, it is not easy to give any more practical proofs of our friendliness than we have already done.

Given these undertakings (which, as has been seen, the committee regarded as by no means unilateral), and given the desire to ensure that no potentially hostile Power should be present in the Persian Gulf, the Arabian peninsula or the Red Sea coast, the committee considered (para. 94) that

> our desiderata will best be realised by stipulating that Turkey should recognise the independence of the territories comprising the kaza of Koweit and the sanjak of Nejd, withdraw all its troops from Arabia, and undertake, in accordance with a scheme which the Allied Powers will propose for acceptance, to grant complete administrative autonomy to the chiefs and States in such other parts of Arabia as may be recognised to be under Turkish sovereignty, and to abstain from all interference in their external and internal affairs. We should also require Turkey to guarantee administrative autonomy to the district containing the Shi-ite shrines of Kerbela and Najef.

This proposal the committee regarded as compatible with all the possible schemes for the Ottoman empire in Asia which the report had reviewed. They had also a somewhat more precise idea of the boundaries of 'Arabia' than Kitchener. They declared (para. 36) that

> a line starting from Akaba, at the head of the Gulf of Akaba, running thence to Maan, on the Hedjaz Railway, thence eastwards in a northerly curve to the limits of Koweit, would correspond roughly to a fair division between Arabia proper and those Arabs who belong to the districts of Damascus and Mesopotamia.

The report of the Bunsen committee was submitted on 30 June 1915. Shortly before, Sykes had set out for Athens, Cairo and Delhi taking with him a draft copy to show to British officials in the East and elicit their views. From Cairo, he sent two despatches dated 12 and 14 July, to the war office, in which he set out the reactions of McMahon and Maxwell respectively. In view of the correspondence which Cairo was shortly afterwards to conduct with the Sharif, these reactions are worth examining in some detail. McMahon dismissed out of hand the alternative of preserving the Ottoman empire in Asia, minus Constantinople and Basra, with its existing political and administrative structure. He did not much like, either, the idea of dividing the empire into zones of interests allotted to various Powers; such an ill-defined arrangement 'would be a source of constant anxiety and difficulty to the Egyptian Government.' The scheme which he favoured was that of outright partition, with Haifa rather than Alexandretta going to the British; for if Haifa went to the French, this would mean a French frontier, contiguous both to 'independent Arabia' and to Egypt, and this was 'doubly undesirable'. McMahon suggested also that Damascus should be included in British territory. Among the reasons he advanced were the 'intimate connection between Damascus and Mecca, Medina and Cairo, owing to the Haj pilgrimage', and the strong preference of the Damascene Muslims for Britain rather than France. Again, if a scheme of partition were adopted, McMahon proposed that 'the Palestine portion of British territory should be included in the dominions of the Sultan of Egypt. Jerusalem would thus nominally remain under a Moslem ruler, while the nature of its local self-administration could be adapted to meet international interests under British protection.' Finally, the high commissioner 'considered it of great importance that the seat of the Caliphate should not remain in Ottoman territory, and he believed that the fall of Constantinople would entail its loss for the Ottoman dynasty.'[1]

General Maxwell's views differed in some ways from those of his civilian colleague. The general concurred with the Bunsen committee in preferring a federal Ottoman empire to a partition. This would cause less friction with the Muslim world, and hold in abeyance the threat of a French naval base at Alexandretta. Maxwell went so far as to argue that even if the other Powers preferred partition, the British should still pursue a 'devolutionary' course in Mesopotamia and Palestine, these areas becoming

> provinces under the nominal suzerainty of the Sherif of Mecca but under our protection, the Sherif receiving a fixed annual tribute from both regions.
>
> Under this arrangement the Sherif might be induced to appoint the Sultan of Egypt as his representative in [Palestine] and appoint an hereditary governor for [Mesopotamia].

[1] F.O. 371/2476, 106764, Sykes's despatch no. 11 to Callwell, war office, Cairo 12 July, enclosed with McMahon's despatch no. 72, Cairo 21 July 1915.

Like McMahon, Maxwell wanted to see Damascus included in territory under British control or influence. Even more emphatically than McMahon he wanted to see the caliphate removed from the Ottomans; he indeed went so far as to say that he preferred a federal empire to partition only on such a hypothesis, and considered that 'this was not difficult of achievement if the powers of the Entente made the declaration of independence of the Sherif of Mecca a preliminary of the adoption of the devolutionary scheme by the Ottoman Government.'[1]

Simultaneously with the despatches describing Maxwell's and McMahon's views, Sykes sent another despath to the war office which may perhaps better describe the atmosphere in Cairo, and the ambitions entertained by some, at any rate, of the British officials there:

> I feel I should mention the fact that it would meet with the aspirations of many, and solve future difficulties, if France were willing to forego her rights in Syria and would allow us to control Ayalet no. 3 [i.e. that part of the Levant which the Bunsen committee had allotted to France], in return for compensation elsewhere, and the cession to her of certain branches of industrial enterprise and railways in Syria.
>
> The three Ayalets [i.e. Mesopotamia, Syria and Palestine] could then be under the government of the Sultan of Egypt and the spiritual dominion of the Sherif of Mecca. Worked as one unit these three regions are united by language and financially self-supporting.[2]

This despatch spells out the details of the settlement which McMahon's and Maxwell's criticisms of the Bunsen report had merely hinted at and sketched. It reminds us very much of the ideas mooted in their different ways by Storrs, Clayton, Wingate and Symes. But Sykes's despatches also make perfectly clear that on the eve of the McMahon–Husayn correspondence the Cairo officials were fully cognizant of the way the authorities in London were inclined to think of the post-war settlement, and of the commitments and obligations by which they felt themselves bound. The despatches also show that both McMahon and Maxwell were in favour of bestowing a 'spiritual' caliphate on the Sharif; also that neither was thinking of this Caliph actually governing extensive territories in the Levant or Mesopotamia. His province was, as McMahon put it, 'independent Arabia': as the context indicates, this territory began south of 'Palestine'. 'Palestine' itself both McMahon and Maxwell wanted to see attached, somehow or another, to Egypt.

[1] F.O. 371/2490, 108253, copy of Sykes's despatch to Callwell no. 12, Cairo 14 July 1915.
[2] F.O. 371/2490, 108253, Sykes's despatch to Callwell no. 14, Cairo 14 July 1915.

3. Mysteries of the McMahon–Husayn Correspondence

On the same day that Sykes sent his despatch of 14 July, Abdullah wrote a letter to his friend Storrs. With it he enclosed a memorandum which has come to be regarded as the first letter in the McMahon–Husayn correspondence.[1] That Abdullah should have written to Storrs was natural since it was he who was the recipient of Abdullah's confidences in Cairo in February and April 1914, and since he had sent on Kitchener's messages the following September and November. But it seems that Abdullah's role in the negotiation was more than that of an intermediary or a representative of his father's. Some eighteen months later, his younger brother Faysal told Captain T. E. Lawrence that the Arab rising was first imagined by Abdullah 'who reckoned that the Hejaz was capable of with-standing Turkey, with the aid of the [Ottoman] Syrian and Meso-potamian armies, and our diplomatic help. He approached Lord Kitchener to this end and obtained satisfactory assurances,' Law-rence reported, 'but the scheme was put off on Feisal's representing that Turkey was too strong for them.' As has been seen, Kitchener did not in fact give any assurances and this, rather than Faysal's sage advice, explains why matters were not taken further. But Abdullah seems to have remained the moving spirit in a plan to secure independent Sharifian rule in the Hijaz and to obtain the caliphate for his family. This, at any rate, was the information which reached the authorities at Khartoum shortly before Abdullah despatched his letter. Their informant – a 'well educated and intelligent member of a famous (Sherifian) family who had left Mecca seven months ago' and who was an associate of Abdullah's – told them that he was 'in a very great measure "the power behind the throne"', but that his father, though willing to consider the use of British arms to achieve the independence of the Hijaz, was rather more cautious about 'taking any active or open steps in the further, and far more important, matter of the assumption of the Khalifate.'[2]

[1] Abdullah's letter is not included in the official white paper, Cmd. 5957; a translation may be found in George Antonius, *The Arab Awakening*, 1938, p. 413.
[2] Lawrence's diary while with Faysal at Yenbo 2–5 Dec. 1916, F.O. 882/6, Arab Bureau Papers, p. 15; secret memorandum by Symes, Erkowit 19 July 1915, F.O. 882/12, pp. 108–9.

The Quicksand

This caution led to a first tentative enquiry concerning the possibility of obtaining help from the British when he sent a messenger who reached the Sudan on 12 July 1915 and whose mission was to enquire whether the British were willing to assist the Sharif 'and his Arab supporters' with arms and ammunition.[1] About the same time, or shortly thereafter, the Sharif sent Faysal to Damascus (where he arrived in September) and to Constantinople in order to discover whether Arab officers and troops in Syria would join a rising, and whether concessions could be obtained from the Ottoman government. It would seem that Faysal gave a memorandum to Sa'id Halim the *sadri-i azam* (Grand Vezir) in which he asked for autonomy for the Hijaz under Husayn and his descendants. The request, if it was really made, was not satisfied, and Faysal returned to Mecca, again via Damascus, towards the end of 1915.[2]

But these two exploratory moves were quite eclipsed by the memorandum which Abdullah sent to Cairo on 14 July. This audacious document could not have been the work of the Sharif or Faysal whom the evidence shows to have favoured cautious policies; it bears the hall-mark of Abdullah's inspiration who, then and later, liked to play for high stakes and nursed grandiose, not to say overweening, ambitions.

The audacity of this memorandum is best appreciated by examining the demands which it contained, to ensure the acceptance of which Abdullah asked Storrs to do his best. The note purported to speak on behalf of 'the Arab nation' and demanded that 'England acknowledge the independence of the Arab countries' over an area bounded on the east by Persia, on the south by the Indian Ocean, on the west by the Red Sea and the Mediterranean up to Mersina, and on the north by a line running from Mersina in the west, through Urfa, Mardin and Amadia, to the Persian border in the east. The memorandum allowed one concession, namely that 'the position of Aden' was to remain 'as it is'. To this large territorial claim was joined another far-reaching demand: 'England to approve of the proclamation of an Arab Khalifate of Islam'. The protection of this extensive and populous domain was to be ensured by a treaty whereby 'both high contracting parties' were 'to offer mutual assistance to the best ability of their military and naval forces, to face any foreign Power which may attack either party. Peace not to be decided without agreement of both parties'. Britain was also 'to

[1] F.O. 882/12, p. 106, Wingate's telegram to Clayton, Khartoum 12 July 1915.
[2] Amin Sa'id, The Great Arab Revolt, vol. I, pp. 106 and 109.

acknowledge the abolition of foreign privileges in Arab countries, and to assist the Government of the Sherif in an International Convention for confirming such abolition.' In return for all this Britain was offered 'preference in all economic enterprises in the Arab countries whenever conditions of enterprise are otherwise equal'. The note ended with an ultimatum: 'the Arab nation' required an answer within thirty days; otherwise 'they reserve to themselves complete freedom of action', and the Sharifian family would consider itself 'free in word and deed' from the bonds of their declaration previously sent in answer to Kitchener's message.

This message reached Cairo on 18 August. Storrs was clearly amused by it, as by an exorbitant and absurd demand which initiates a long and leisurely process of bargaining in an oriental bazaar. 'As I struggled through his difficult writing and even more difficult Arabic', he tells us in his autobiography, 'I found myself murmuring

> In matters of commerce the fault of the Dutch
> Is offering too little and asking too much.'

He also discloses the modest limits within which, in spite of his own flamboyant missives, he thought the Sharif's ambitions should be confined: 'It seemed to me that having been little more than a sort of Erastian Administrator for the Turks, the Sharif and his people would be well treated and amply rewarded if they were gratuitously enabled to defeat and evict their traditional enemy and were guaranteed immunity from external aggression in their permanent possession of the two Holy Cities, together with the independent sovereignty of their country of origin, the Hejaz. If to this a sufficient majority of Moslems chose to add the Khālifat [sic], that was their business, and not ours; though, as uniting the strongest religious with the weakest material power, it would be greatly to our interest.'[1] These remarks are borne out by the note he wrote at the time in which he remarked of the Sharif that 'it may be regarded as certain that he has received no sort of mandate from other potentates', and that he 'knows he is demanding, possibly as a basis for negotiation, far more than he has the right, the hope, or the power to expect'. He suggested therefore that boundaries could be reserved for subsequent discussion, that the caliphate 'has already been left to the decision of Islam; the British Government having been especially precise upon the point', and that the Sharif should be told

---

[1] Storrs, *Orientations*, pp. 152–3.

The Quicksand

that 'the chief point for immediate decision [was] the expulsion of the Turks and the Germans and the maintenance of tranquillity and solidarity in Arabia.'[1]

This appreciation clearly governed the advice which McMahon tendered to London. The Sharif's pretensions, he wrote, were 'in every way exaggerated', but to discuss them now in detail might seriously discourage him. He proposed to tell the Sharif that the discussion of boundaries was premature, and to confirm the British government's 'friendly sentiments and promises as expressed in Lord Kitchener's communication of last November.' Grey drafted a telegram approving this language, but it was held up pending the expression of opinion by the India office who had indicated that they did not entirely share McMahon's view. In a letter of 24 August, Hirtzel agreed that the Sharif's proposals were 'obviously unacceptable' as they stood and probably incompatible with the rights and interests of other Arab chiefs with whom the British government had engagements. But to answer his definite proposals with the generalities proposed by McMahon 'will not only not engage him for our cause, but may lead him to think that we were not serious in our overtures'. The India office suggested therefore that McMahon should invite the Sharif to send a representative to Egypt in order to 'negotiate a preliminary agreement for securing the independence, rights and privileges of the Sheriffate'. If the Sharif agreed, it might then be possible 'to come to close quarters with his proposals, and to reduce them to reasonable dimensions.' This suggestion was adopted by the foreign office who made a small but significant change before incorporating it in their telegram of instructions sent to McMahon on 25 August. The change was suggested by Clerk who seems to have been very cautious in his attitude to the Sharif's overtures. When Symes's memorandum of 19 July on the Sharif, mentioned above, reached him on 23 August he wrote that it showed the need of exercising great care in the relations with the Sharif, and this for two reasons: first that the Sharif was sitting on the fence waiting to be sure of Turkey's downfall before taking action, and second that his 'two Arab enemies are our two Arab friends – Idrissi and Bin Saud.'[2] He now suggested that the Sharif should be told that the British government were prepared to *discuss* rather than *negotiate* a preliminary agreement.

[1] F.O. 371/2486, 125293/34982, note by Storrs, Cairo 19 Aug., enclosed with McMahon's despatch no. 94 Secret, Cairo 26 Aug. 1915.
[2] F.O. 371/2486, 112369/34982.

Mysteries of the McMahon–Husayn Correspondence

The India office had another suggestion to make. Since it was necessary to answer the Sharif's question about the caliphate, the answer 'might take the form of a reference to the penultimate sentence of Lord Kitchener's message of November last, with the addition that he must consult his co-religionists as to whether he should proclaim himself Khalif.' The penultimate sentence of Kitchener's message, as will be recalled, read: 'It may be that an Arab of true race will assume the Khalifate at Mecca or Medina'. The foreign office adopted this suggestion as well and the telegram drafted by Clerk dealt with the caliphate as follows:

> if the Sherif after consulting his co-religionists proclaimed himself Khalif he may rest assured that HMG will acknowledge the resumption of the Khalifate by an Arab of true race, as already indicated in Lord Kitchener's communication of last November.

Nicolson, rather sceptical of negotiations with the Sharif, and even more cautious than Clerk, tried to make these assurances more precise and less far-reaching, and the passage as finally sent to McMahon read as follows:

> if the Sherif *with the consent* of his co-religionists *is* proclaimed Khalif he may rest assured that HMG will *welcome* the resumption of the Khalifate by an Arab of true race, etc.

Nicolson's intent is made clear by a marginal note in which he justified the change of 'acknowledge' into 'welcome': 'Our "acknowledgement"', he wrote, 'might be interpreted as indication that we considered we had a view in the matter.'[1]

Whether these two points, however, were to be included in his reply to the Sharif was left to McMahon's discretion. He chose not to include them. Regarding the invitation to send a representative to Egypt, he did not consider that the moment had arrived 'when we can usefully discuss even a preliminary agreement, and it might at this stage injure the Sherif's chances of the Khalifate to advertise his dealings with us by sending a son or other notable to treat with us'. As for the caliphate, McMahon did not use the formula suggested by the foreign office 'as the terms of my message will be sufficiently clear to him on this point.'[2] What McMahon in fact wrote to the Sharif in his letter of 30 August was as follows:

> to this intent we confirm to you the terms of Lord Kitchener's message...in which was stated clearly...our approval of the Arab Khalifate when it should

[1] F.O. 371/2486, 117236 and 118580/34982, McMahon's telegram no. 450, Cairo 22 Aug., Hirtzel's letter, 24 Aug., and telegram to McMahon no. 598, 25 Aug. 1915 and minutes.
[2] F.O. 371/2486, 125293/34982, McMahon's despatch no. 94 Secret, 26 Aug., cited above.

be proclaimed. We declare once more that His Majesty's Government would welcome the resumption of the Khalifate by an Arab of true race.

This text, which was most probably composed by Storrs, constitutes a double departure from the instructions of the foreign office. In referring to Kitchener's message of November 1914, it did not use the cautious conjectural mode in which this had been couched: 'It may be that an Arab of true race', but adopted Abdullah's more emphatic reformulation whereby the British government was committed to the 'approval' of the caliphate, 'when it should be proclaimed'. In the second place the conditional approbation of the Arab caliphate expressed in the foreign office telegram – 'if the Sherif with the consent of his co-religionists is proclaimed Khalif' – was transformed into an absolute and unqualified welcome. These changes of emphasis were entirely in line with the embellishments which earlier messages to the Sharif had undergone at the Cairo residency. The Arabic version was made even more emphatic and pointed. The 'Arab of true race' who was to resume the caliphate was here further described as from the 'blessed stock' of the Prophet. The allusion could not but be unmistakle to the Sharif who was amir of Mecca precisely because he was the direct descendant of the Prophet.[1] In the correspondence which followed, every letter from McMahon was prefaced by respectful allusions to Husayn's descent from Muhammad. These rhetorical flourishes were no doubt thought to be harmless, indeed useful, lubricants of Anglo-Sharifian relations, and quite devoid of any real consequences. This emerges clearly from a comparison of Storrs's real view of the Sharif's demands, with the magniloquence which he affected in the hope no doubt that the Sharif would be taken in. The hope probably rested on Storrs's belief that Abdullah, whom he considered 'the mainspring of the Sherif's family', wanted the caliphate more than anything else. This appears from a letter to Fitzgerald, Kitchener's secretary, written shortly after McMahon's letter to the Sharif of 30 August. In it Storrs declared:

If, as now begins to seem possible, he is able to conciliate his powerful neighbours of Nejd, Yemen and Asir, and impress upon them that he has no idea of pretending to any temporal rights within their territories, his chances of a general – though hardly yet of universal – recognition as Caliph will be very great.[2]

[1] The English version of this letter in Antonius, *The Arab Awakening*, pp. 415–16, correctly includes this phrase as it appears in the Arabic text. It is inexplicably omitted from the official version in Cmd. 5957 which is declared to be based on a comparison of the English drafts with the Arabic text.
[2] P.R.O. 30/57, 47 Kitchener Papers, Storrs to Fitzgerald, Alexandria 6 Sept. 1915.

In order fully to appreciate the effect of Storrs's rhetoric on its recipient, we have to remember that Wingate, who carried on a parallel correspondence with the Sharif through the intermediary of the Sudanese notable, Ali al-Mirghani, also adopted the same stratagem and encouraged Mirghani to use extravagant language about the 'holy Arabian Koreishite Khalifate', and the Sharif's right and duty to restore it to the Arabs.[1] Wingate, indeed, would have liked to go even to go even further than Storrs. As has been seen, he was very sceptical about the prospects of an Arab empire or Arab unity; yet he wanted to add some rhetoric about Arab unity to the rhetoric about the Arab caliphate which was being purveyed to Husayn. In a telegram of 30 August 1915, he wrote to Clayton:

> If the Foreign Office concurred I should personally recommend the insertion of a pious aspiration on the subject of the Sherif's ideal of an Arab union, in other words something might be added to ensure his remaining definitely on our side at any rate until our success in the Dardanelles enables us to give more authoritative expression to our views.[2]

Cairo's change of wording and of emphasis passed unremarked at the foreign office, but Hirtzel at the India office noticed it immediately, pointing out that the new formula went 'dangerously far'. In a later minute he recalled that the expression 'approval of the caliphate' had been first used by the Sharif and then repeated in McMahon's letter. 'But', Hirtzel pointed out, 'Lord Kitchener's message had said nothing so precise and Sir H. McMahon went beyond the instruction of H.M.G.'[3]

To McMahon's letter of 30 August, the Sharif promptly returned a long, carefully ambiguous, even obscure answer. The one demand of his which McMahon had fully conceded was that Britain should 'approve' the proclamation of an Arab caliphate. The Sharif now brushed the matter off as of no particular importance. 'God', he piously exclaimed in his letter of 9 September, 'have mercy on [the caliphate's] soul and comfort the Moslems for their loss'. The important demand was that concerning the boundaries; it was not on his own behalf that he was making this demand, but on behalf of the 'people'. The boundaries which he had proposed in his letter of 14 July were 'necessary to our existence' and 'the essential essence of our life, material and moral'. But the letter also contains two passages which invited further bargaining, and left the door open for an abandonment of the original demands: 'they ['our

---

[1] Kedourie, *The Chatham House Version*, p. 18.   [2] Wingate Papers, file 135/2.
[3] L/P & S/10/523, p. 3935/1915, minute by Hirtzel, 27 Oct. 1915 and L/P & S/11/119, p. 1951/1917, minute by Hirtzel, 31 May 1917.

people'] have decided to discuss this point in the first resort with the Power in which they now have their confidence and trust and whom they regard as their ultimate appeal, namely the Illustrious British Empire.

'Their reason for this aim and confidence is the reciprocity of interests, the necessity of regulating territorial divisions and the wishes of the populations concerned, so that they may know how to base their future life and avoid finding Great Britain or any of her allies in opposition to or in conflict with their wishes, which God forbid!'[1] The second passage appeared even more clearly to leave the decision on boundaries in British hands: 'Whatever the illustrious Government of Great Britain finds conformable to its policy on this subject, communicate it to us and specify to us the course we should follow.

'In all cases it is only God's will which shall be executed, and it is God who is the real factor in everything.'

A few weeks later, the Sharif attempted to hustle the British into admitting his claims by sending a letter to Mirghani in which he explained that if modifications were made to 'our demands' concerning boundaries, this would not only be 'annoying' to the Arabs, but would very highly 'affect all the Mohammedans'. The Arabs 'will then become positive that the cause for making such difficulties is the intention to exterminate the Arabs and destroy their faith and unity. I do not think in this case that there is any man who does not know that a General Call (to the Jehad) in the ears of the Mohammedan world will differ from the call of the Ottomans'. This threat, that he would proclaim a *jihad* against the British and their Allies, the Sharif coupled with a reference to an anti-Ottoman rising in the Shi'ite holy city of Karbala as an earnest of the profits the British might reap from satisfying his demands. The inducement was as ill-founded as the threat was blatant, since the Sharif had absolutely no connexion with Karbala, and disorders there being the consequence of endemic bad relations between the Shi'ites and their Sunni Ottoman rulers, not a blow struck in favour of Arab nationalism.[2] The Sharif's letter to Mirghani was clearly a crude gambit designed to stampede the British into a panic decision, and it ought not to have taken in an experienced negotiator. Yet McMahon was,

[1] In this, as in the previous quotation from the Sharif's letter of 9 September, I have preferred the version suggested at the sub-committee which considered the corespondence in 1939, to the wooden translations produced in 1915 at the residency, which manage to make Sharifian prose even more ungainly than it already is.

[2] F.O. 882/12, letter from the Sharif to Mirghani, undated and unsigned, received in October 1915.

or at any rate affected to be, impressed by it. When shortly afterwards, the government of India objected to the injudicious haste with which promises had been made to the Sharif, he was ready to cite this letter in proof that if the British did not hurry, the Germans and the Turks would get the support of the Arabs. Clayton likewise professed to take this letter at face value.[1]

Just as the Sharif's letter of 9 September was coming to the knowledge of the authorities at Cairo, an event occurred which proved to have a far-reaching influence on their subsequent actions. This was the arrival at Cairo of Lieutenant Muhammad Sharif al-Faruqi. This young infantry officer – he was born at Mosul in 1891 – had been ADC to the commander of the 12th army corps stationed at Mosul which was transferred to Syria at the outbreak of war. From what he told Clayton, it was at this juncture that he entered a secret society composed of Arab army officers, the 'chief member' of which was the chief staff officer of the 12th army corps, 'a certain Yasin Bey' as Clayton put it. According to Faruqi, the members of this society engaged in subversive activities in Syria, and tried to encourage mutinies and desertions in the Ottoman 4th army, which had been assembled to launch an attack on the Suez Canal. These activities came to the ear of its commander, Jemal Pasha, who set investigations on foot. Some of the officers, including Faruqi, were imprisoned, but no satisfactory evidence could be obtained against them, and they were released. But the authorities, now clearly on their guard, posted them away from Syria, and Faruqi found himself at Gallipoli, in command of an infantry company. He remained in the firing line for ten days, and then, on the pretext of arranging a truce for the burial of the dead, managed to desert to the enemy, and was promptly sent to Cairo. The intelligence department, and no doubt Clayton in person also, had several conversations with him, the gist of which the latter conveyed in a memorandum of 11 October 1915, to which a statement by Faruqi (whether written or dictated by him, or reconstructed from his conversation is not clear) was attached.[2]

Clayton was obviously impressed by Faruqi. The latter's statement began: 'I am a descendant of Omar Ibn El Khattab, the 2nd Khalifa of El Islam who had the title of El Farug, which means separator. He was so called for having separated the right from the wrong.' Clayton, for his part, asserted that Faruqi was 'according

---

[1] F.O. 371/2486, 165761/34982, McMahon's telegram to Grey no. 674, Cairo 5 Nov. 1915; Wingate Papers, 135/5, Clayton's telegram to Wingate, Cairo 13 Nov. 1915.

[2] F.O. 371/2486, 157740/34982, enclosed with McMahon's despatch no. 121, Cairo 12 Oct. 1915.

to his own statement, a prominent member of the Young Arab party (Military) and his contention is borne out by the fact that his family is one of some eminence among the Arabs, and also by Aziz Bey Ali El Masri, himself a sworn member of the same party.'

Faruqi presented an impressive and grandiose, if somewhat hazy, picture of the officers' secret society, and its activities in Syria. It had a Central Office at Damascus 'in continual communication with the Headquarter Office', branches 'In every important town or station', a cypher, and a treasury amounting to £100,000, accumulated from members' subscriptions. The society was indeed so powerful that 'neither Turks [n]or Germans have dared to attempt to suppress it, though fully aware of the fact that its attitude has been, at least passively hostile, and in the cases of many of its members actively sympathetic towards the Allies, more especially Great Britain.'

The members of the society had sent an officer to Mecca who, on their behalf, had paid allegiance to the Sharif. They had also taken 'a solemn oath on the Koran that they will enforce their object and establish an Arab Caliphate in Arabia, Syria and Mesopotamia at all costs and under any circumstances, sacrificing for this object all their efforts and property and, if needs be, their lives.'

Faruqi declared that the officers' emissary to the Sharif had found out that the latter was in communication with the British who had 'given their consent to the Sherif establishing an Arab Empire, but the limits of his Empire were not defined. It was mentioned that the dominions of the Sherif shall include "the Sherif and those who follow him".' This statement of Faruqi's, it is interesting to note, seems a garbled version of the last paragraph of Kitchener's second message to the Sharif, a paragraph which, as will be recalled, Storrs had added on his own authority. What Faruqi now went on to say shows how this paragraph was understood, and what far-reaching conclusions its recipients derived from it: 'When this phrase reached Damascus', Faruqi declared, 'it was suggested that the northern line of limit of the Sharif's Empire should be "Mersina–Diarbekr" line.

'About three months ago representatives were sent to Jedda [Faruqi went on] with instructions that if England agreed to these limits they were to discuss them with other articles of the agreement, otherwise they were to come back without discussing the other points, and I do not know what happened to this mission.' Faruqi's declaration thus shows that Abdullah was encouraged to send his letter of 14 July 1915 to Storrs by the hope of a military rising in Syria, to be carried out by the officers' society, and that the boundaries of the future Arab state which he was encouraged to put forward by Storrs's incautious rhetoric were suggested by, and perhaps even agreed with, these officers.

That Faruqi should have known the main lines of the Sharifian proposals must have impressed his British interlocutors with his bona fides and importance. In his report Clayton certainly showed no misgivings about Faruqi's standing; the latter, he wrote, 'maintains that he is accredited by the Committee and that through him the reply of England may be given.' But when we turn to Faruqi's own statement, we may conclude that Clayton was perhaps somewhat too eager to look upon this young lieutenant as the authorized representative of a powerful and far-flung secret society. For what Faruqi said was this:

> I am not authorised to discuss with you officially our political programme, but if no agreement between your and our representatives who came to Jedda has yet been made I can, for the sake of shortening negotiations, keeping in mind the complications of social problems of the Arabs amongst themselves and the political complications between us and one of the Powers of Europe (France), for the above reasons and for the confidence in myself and my party and all Arabs, and the good wishes of the English towards the Arabs, and my conviction that England does not wish to alienate the Arab from her, give answers to any questions you wish to make re the agreement and if necessary make modifications in its articles including the Mersina–Diarbekr line; modifications which I promise to try my utmost to convince most of them to go by my agreement.

This involved, obscure and labyrinthine language was hardly that of an 'accredited' agent who could negotiate and make binding agreements on behalf of his principals. It is the language, rather, of one who is unsure of his own position; who, while wishing to impress with large claims and beguiling promises, is yet careful to leave open an avenue of retreat from what he might persuade his interlocutors to accept as binding commitments and clear straightforward engagements.

Faruqi claimed that 'We, the Arab party, are a power which cannot be disregarded. 90% of the Arab officers in the Turkish army and a part of the Kurd officers are members of our Society'. Some of them in Mesopotamia had already joined the British, but the greater part were still hesitating. If he and the British could come to an 'arrangement, I guarantee to go to Mesopotamia and bring over a great number of officers and men especially from the 35th Division of El Mosul, who all know me.' But unless an 'arrangement' was arrived at, and that 'within a few weeks', Faruqi's fellow conspirators 'have decided to throw in their lot with Turkey and

Germany and secure the best terms they can'. The Germans and the Turks were 'fully alive to the situation and have already approached the leaders of the Young Arab Committee and, indeed, have gone so far as to promise them the granting of their demands in full.' Clayton was prodigiously impressed by this language. Faruqi's disclosures, he wrote in his report, 'together with the experience of the past year, during which there have been considerable opportunities of studying the Pan-Arab movement, lead to the conviction that the proposals now put forward are of very grave and urgent importance.' Clayton was utterly convinced that the Sharif's proposals – which were the same as Faruqi's – should receive a speedy and favourable answer. For him there could be little doubt that 'the attitude of the Sherif is that of the majority of the Arab people' who had been waiting 'patiently' for a whole year for Britain to deliver them from the Turkish yoke. But, Clayton sententiously remarked, 'even the patience of the Oriental is not inexhaustible'. If a favourable reply were returned, the 'Committee would at once begin to work actively and their operations, begun in the Hedjaz where the Sherif is a great power, would soon extend to Syria and Palestine where the Turkish forces are much reduced, and to Baghdad and Mosul where the Committee's influence is perhaps greatest.' If the proposals were rejected, or even if the issue were evaded, the Young Arab party would 'definitely' be thrown into the hands of the enemy: 'Their machinery will at once be employed against us throughout the Arab countries, and the various Arab Chiefs, who are almost to a man members of or connected with the Young Arab party, will be undoubtedly won over. Moreover,' Clayton concluded his report, 'the religious element will come into play and the "Jehad", so far a failure, may become a very grim reality, the effects of which would certainly be far-reaching and at the present crisis might well be disastrous'.

It is a remarkable report to have been written by a director of military intelligence. The one thing the report does not, in fact, do is to assess the value of the information it presented, or to indicate on what grounds the assertions of an unknown young deserter should be so unquestioningly accepted. Clayton refers to his study of the Pan-Arab movement during the previous year. But the evidence, such as it was, was rather insubstantial and inconclusive. Of the Sharif the British really knew very little, and of the secret society in Syria even less. Clayton had no way of independently verifying Faruqi's story, but his report shows no diffidence, no hesitation, no attempt to indicate to his superiors that perhaps Faruqi should be taken with a grain of salt. When his report was received at the India office at the beginning of November, Hirtzel's immediate reaction was that the 'whole thing is not very impressive', and Holderness also pointed out that the evidence which Clayton actually marshalled did not amount to very much,

> as the Arab deserter, Faroki, has to be taken at his face value, and the only chief who is mentioned by him as privy to the negotiations is the Shariff of Mecca. But this is the best we have. For the rest we have to accept the word of Colonel Clayton, General Maxwell and Sir H. McMahon, who profess themselves satisfied after long enquiries that there is a large and solid Arab party, that can be detached from the Turks, which is worth detaching. By this they mean that if we won over the party by the promise of an independent Arabia, free from the Turk and under British guarantee of protection, there would be defections of Arab units from the Turkish Army, and a rally to our side in Egypt and Mesopotamia of important chiefs.[1]

As is well known, apart from the Sharif's rebellion, none of the developments listed in Holderness's minute eventuated. Was Clayton, then, completely incompetent as director of intelligence, and were his superiors in Cairo misled equally with him? Or was it less a case of simple incompetence, and more that of a desire to form and influence policy getting in the way of a dispassionate evaluation of intelligence? There is some evidence in support of the latter supposition. Thus Clayton seems to have had no doubts whatever about the consequences for policy of Faruqi's disclosures and proposals. In a letter dated 9 October 1915 – that is, two days before the date of the report which has been reviewed above – Clayton wrote to Wingate: 'I shall take the opportunity [when reporting to London the interviews with Faruqi] of rubbing in the fact that if we definitely refuse to consider the aspirations of the Arabs, we are running a grave risk of throwing them into the arms of our enemies.'[2] The following day, 10 October, Storrs wrote to Fitzgerald, Kitchener's secretary: 'The Arab question is reaching an acute stage.

'I gather from the Sherif, as does Clayton from Faróki that they feel, rightly or wrongly, that their time has come to choose between us and Germany. The latter promises all things but is mistrusted: the Arabs have more confidence in, and would accept much less from, us.

'I have thrashed the thing out at great length with Clayton, and beg you to give all possible prominence to the note being sent home by the G.O.C. in this week's bag.'[3]

[1] L/P & S/10/523, p. 4024/1915, minute by Hirtzel, 2 Nov. and by Holderness, 6 Nov. 1915.
[2] Wingate Papers, 135/4.   [3] P.R.O. 30/57, 47.

The Quicksand

As Storrs announced, Maxwell forwarded Clayton's report on Faruqi to the war office on 12 October – as did McMahon on the same day to the foreign office – sending at the same time a telegram to Kitchener to draw his attention to this important document:

> I am forwarding today by mail a memorandum on the Arab question which is now very pressing.
>
> A powerful organisation with considerable influence in the Army and among Arab Chiefs, viz: the Young Arab Committee appears to have made up its mind that the moment for action has arrived. The Turks and Germans are already in communication with them and spending money to win their support. The Arab party however is strongly inclined towards England but what they ask is a definite statement of sympathy and support even if their complete programme cannot be accepted.
>
> Sherif [of] Mecca, who is in communication with the Arab party, also seems uneasy and is pressing for a declaration of policy on the part of England.
>
> If their overtures are rejected or a reply is delayed any longer the Arab party will go over to the enemy and work with them, which would mean stirring up religious feeling at once and might well result in a genuine Jehad. On the other hand the active assistance which the Arabs would render in return for our support would be of the greatest value in Arabia Mesopotamia Syria and Palestine.
>
> The question is important and requires an early decision.

The urgent, indeed alarmist, tone of this telegram derives directly from Clayton's memorandum. Maxwell, then, proved as uncritical as his director of intelligence in building such an imposing structure of speculation on the flimsy foundation of Faruqi's assertions, which proved in the event to be totally erroneous. But it is not necessary to invoke hindsight; even at the time it was patent that no tangible evidence existed to confirm, or disprove, the allegation that there was a 'powerful organisation with considerable influence' in the Ottoman army, that the Germans were negotiating with it, or that its support 'would be of the greatest value in Arabia Mesopotamia Syria and Palestine'. In fact, as we know now, the Ottomans were then very popular in Syria.[1] Indeed if Faruqi's statement is read carefully, it is possible to deduce from it that if a secret society was once active among the Ottoman officers in Syria, the vigilance of the authorities had long ago neutralized it, by measures such as that whereby Faruqi found himself commanding an infantry company at Gallipoli.

Kitchener took Maxwell's telegram very seriously. He, of course,

[1] Isaiah Friedman, 'The McMahon–Hussein Correspondence and the Question of Palestine', *Journal of Contemporary History* v, 2 (1970), 90, citing contemporary German official reports.

had not yet seen Clayton's memorandum and Faruqi's statement, and there is no knowing whether, had he done so, he would have endorsed Clayton's and Maxwell's extravagant conclusions. In the event, he sent Maxwell a telegram the following day, 13 October, declaring that the government were 'most desirous of dealing with the Arab question in a manner satisfactory to the Arabs' and asking him to 'telegraph to me the headings of what they want'. Kitchener also moved Grey to ask McMahon by telegram on 14 October to send his view on the 'definite statement of sympathy and support from us' which he understood the Arabs to desire.[1]

In answer to Kitchener's request for details of the Arab demands, Maxwell replied with another telegram on 16 October. The telegram is crucial in understanding the mind of the British officials at Cairo and deserves careful scrutiny. Maxwell began by referring Kitchener to McMahon's telegram no. 450 of 22 August – cited above – in which the latter had set out the demands contained in Abdullah's original memorandum of 14 July. From Maxwell's language it now appeared that this memorandum represented much more than Sharifian pretensions; this document had now become 'the proposal of the Arab Party through the Shereef of Mecca.' In speaking thus, Maxwell was accepting and confirming Faruqi's story that the Sharif's demands were really those of the officers' secret society. Maxwell could not possibly know what had gone on between the Sharif and the officers, and was thus in no position to endorse Faruqi's assertions. Maxwell, however, had no hesitation in asserting that 'behind all the Arab potentates there is a large and influential party actually in the Turkish army' who would 'actively' work against the Ottoman regime if 'a reasonable basis for negotiation' could be arrived at quickly. Maxwell stressed the necessity and urgency of wasting no time in reaching an agreement,

> otherwise they and the potentates will throw in their lot with the Turks, a contingency which will increase very materially our difficulties in Mesopotamia and Arabia, also with Senoussi, and make very much easier the invasion of Egypt.

These dire warnings were repeated and emphasized in the concluding sentence of his telegram:

> We are up against the big question of the future of Islam...I feel certain that time is of the greatest importance, and that unless we make definite and agreeable proposals to the Shereef at once, we may have united Islam against us.

What 'reasonable basis for negotiation' did Maxwell have in mind?

[1] F.O. 371/2486, 150309/34982.

we have reason to believe that they [i.e. the Arab Party] would accept considerable modification [of the Sharif's proposals] in negotiation with Great Britain. The time is past in my opinion for vague generalities, and our best course seems to me to eliminate what we cannot and will not allow, and to treat the rest as a basis for negotiation. But we must bear in mind in so doing that even if we insist on retaining the Villayet of [Basra] as British, the rest of Mesopotamia must be included in the negotiation, likewise on the West, the Arab party will, I think, insist on Homs, Aleppo, Hama and Damascus being in their sphere.[1]

This telegram constitutes the first intimation to the government of the alleged demand of the Arab party that the four cities, Homs, Aleppo, Hama and Damascus, should belong to 'their sphere'. In stating this, and that Mesopotamia north of the Basra *vilayet* should be 'included in the negotiation', Maxwell was relying on Clayton's report of Faruqi's views. In his memorandum of 11 October, cited above, Clayton reported at length on Arab territorial demands as set out by Faruqi who, Clayton wrote, stated that

a guarantee of the independence of the Arabian Peninsula would not satisfy them, but this together with the institution of an increasing measure of autonomous Government, under British guidance and control, in Palestine and Mesopotamia would secure their friendship. Syria is of course included in their programme but they must realise that France has aspirations in this region, though El Faruqi declares that a French occupation of Syria would be strenuously resisted by the Mohammedan population. They would however no doubt seek England's good offices towards obtaining a settlement of the Syrian question in a manner as favourable as possible to their views and would almost certainly press for the inclusion of Damascus, Aleppo, Hama, and Homs in the Arab Confederation.

As may be seen, Faruqi's views, as reported by Clayton, are neither clear nor definite. The impression carried away from this passage is of someone hedging and sparring for position, testing his interlocutor's ground and at the same time unsure of his own. The tentativeness and haziness apparent in this passage is increased by Faruqi's other observations and Clayton's comments on them. The passage cited above continued as follows:

In El Faruqi's own words 'our scheme embraces all the Arab countries including Syria and Mesopotamia, but if we cannot have all, we want as much as we can get'.

It was preceded by a paragraph in which Clayton seemed to be giving his estimate of what Faruqi and his friends wanted and could be induced to accept:

[1] F.O. 371/2486, 152729/34982, Maxwell to Kitchener no. 2030E Secret, Cairo 16 Oct. 1915, copy forwarded by war office to foreign office on 18 Oct.

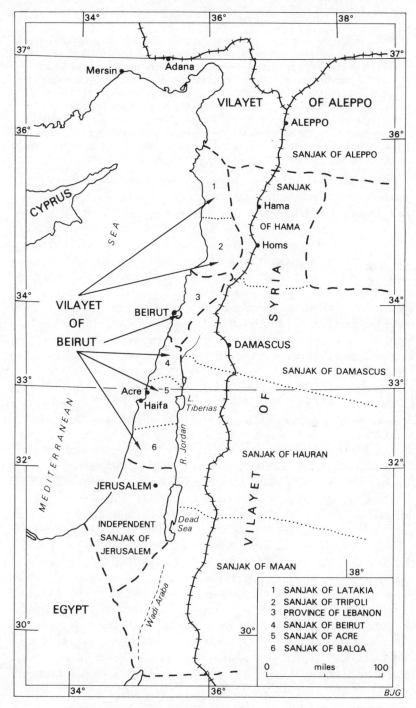

Map 1. Ottoman administrative divisions in the Levant

The Quicksand

They realise that to carry out the idea of an Arab Empire in its entirety is probably outside the region of practical politics at present, and he [i.e. Faruqi] at any rate appreciates the fact that England is bound by obligations to her Allies in this war. The more experienced probably are aware that England could hardly be expected to regard with equanimity the establishment of a powerful and united Arab Empire, marching with Egypt and on the flank of the highway to India. But they do ask that England should promise to assist them to obtain a reasonable measure of independence and autonomous Government in those Arab countries where England can fairly claim that her interests are greater than those of her Allies.

This passage reinforces the impression which the other two passages just cited unmistakably convey, namely that the issue was wide open, that large demands were being made for the sake of bargaining, exactly as Abdullah had done in his memorandum of 14 July. This was seen by Hirtzel when Clayton's memorandum reached him at the beginning of November; in his minute cited above he wrote that 'one point is abundantly clear viz. that a great deal of room was left for bargaining' and quoted in support of his argument another statement of Faruqi's also quoted by Clayton: 'We would sooner have a promise of half from England than of the whole from Turkey and Germany. We will accept reasonable terms from England, but nothing short of our entire programme from any other Power.'[1]

A comparison between Clayton's memorandum and Maxwell's telegram of 16 October leads us to suspect that most probably a process of bargaining did go on, and that Faruqi was persuaded to scale down his demands to what his interlocutors thought reasonable. Clayton describes at length Faruqi's demands and expectations and concludes that the Arab party 'would almost certainly press for the inclusion of Damascus, Aleppo, Hama and Homs in the Arab Confederation'. Maxwell's telegram is more clear-cut and categorical: '...our best course seems to me to eliminate what we cannot and will not allow and to treat the rest as a basis for negotiation ...even if we insist on retaining the Villayet of [Basra] as British, the rest of Mesopotamia must be included in the negotiation; likewise, on the west, the Arab party will, I think, insist on Homs, Aleppo, Hama and Damascus being in their sphere.' What Maxwell is saying is clear enough: as a basis of negotiation we can discuss the possibility of including in a future Arab state in the east, Mesopotamia north of Basra, and in the west Homs, Aleppo, Hama and Damascus. In writing as they did, Maxwell and Clayton must clearly have believed that they had come to some understanding with

[1] L/P & S/10/523, p. 4024/1915, cited above.

Faruqi, and that this understanding had some value because, as Clayton put it, Faruqi was 'accredited by the Committee' and 'through him the reply of England may be given'. In this they were mistaken for, as has been seen, Faruqi had been most equivocal about his standing and powers, declaring that he was 'not authorised to discuss with you officially our political programme', but that he could, 'for the sake of shortening negotiations...give answers to any questions you wish to make re the agreement and if necessary make modifications in its articles...modifications which I promise to try my utmost to convince most of them to go by my agreement.' But even if Faruqi were really 'accredited', he was, as events were shortly to show, an unreliable agent. As McMahon wrote some ten months later, Faruqi was 'a man of considerable intelligence, and has had military experience as an officer in the Turkish army, but he is a Syrian Arab of the visionary, impractical type, common among Syrians. I have means of supervising his correspondence with the Sherif,' McMahon went on, 'and am by no means satisfied with the manner in which he interprets the Sherif's messages to me, nor mine to the Sherif.'[1]

In the present instance, though Maxwell and Clayton thought that they had come to an agreement with Faruqi, very soon afterwards he was holding quite another language. A month or so after Clayton's memorandum and Maxwell's telegrams, Sir Mark Sykes (who had arrived in Cairo on his way back from a visit to India and Mesopotamia) saw Faruqi and reported his demands to the war office:

> Following [he telegraphed on 20 November 1915] is the best I could get, but it seems to me satisfactory both as regards ourselves and France.
>
> Arabs would agree to accept Alexandretta, Aintab–Berijik–Urfa–Midiyat–Zakho–Rowanduz as approximate northern frontier. They would agree to a convention with France to allow her a monopoly of all concessionary enterprise in Palestine and Syria: the latter being defined as bounded as far south as Deir Zor by the Euphrates, thence to Deraa and to Ma'an along the Hejaz railway.[2]

To this new interlocutor, Faruqi was speaking quite a different language. He no longer confines the western territory of the prospective Arab state to the four cities of Aleppo, Homs, Hama and Damascus. It is the whole of Palestine and Syria which he claims.

---

[1] Hardinge Papers, vol. 23, fo. 165, McMahon to Hardinge, Ramleh 22 July 1916. The episode is described in detail in McMahon's despatch no. 334, Cairo 21 Nov. 1916, F.O. 371/2782, 242008/217652. Saint Quentin, the French military attché at Cairo, was to write later that Faruqi's mode of life was indecorous (*manque de tenue*) and that he was known to be an intriguer. Service historique de l'armée, papers of the Mission militaire au Hedjaz, 17N489, note no. 72 by St Quentin, Cairo 26 Aug. 1917.

[2] F.O. 882/13, Sykes's telegram no. 19, Cairo 20 Nov. 1915.

This again is what he tells the Sharif in the first letter which he wrote to him from Cairo. In this letter, dated 6 December 1915, Faruqi writes:

> I discussed with them [the British] the negotiations which had gone on between you and them regarding the formation of an Arab state under the leadership of Your Highness, and your request that they should recognize this independence within the boundaries Mersina–Midyat. I had learnt about these and other matters from my brother [i.e. fellow member of the secret society] Yasin Bey, and we had agreed that I should mention them to the British so that they might feel confidence in, and rely upon, me. As a result of my statements, they had confidence in me, and they subsequently explained their answer to Your Highness whereby they exclude what is west of the line, Damascus–Homs–Hama–Aleppo–Mersin–Alexandretta, on the ground that their ally France had interests [there] and that they could not alienate her for our sake...When they informed me of these details and asked me for my personal opinion, I replied to them in a personal capacity in conformity with what I knew, and with the discussions with Yasin Bey and some other brothers. I said that it was not possible in any way to give up a single span of territory in Syria, and that I did not know of any non-Arab land west of the line Damascus–Aleppo as they pretended...This discussion took place with those in authority here, and I also talked on this subject with one of their deputies who specializes on behalf of their state in the Arab question, and who is called Sir Mark Sykes. This personal discussion took place repeatedly, and I think they are convinced [of my point of view] and that they have understood that we are more useful to them than they to us, and their interest [in the matter] greater than ours.[1]

Here Faruqi gives his version of the discussions which Clayton and his colleagues had conducted with him in early October, and Sykes in mid-November. He informs the Sharif that he had rejected the suggestion made to him about the limits of the prospective Arab state in the west, and that he had refused to give up 'a single span' of Syria. This is likely to have been his initial position; it is as likely that subjected to the persuasions of the British officials in Cairo, he gave in to them and acquiesced in their proposals; but that, as was his wont, in writing to the Sharif he represented matters to be quite otherwise; and that, in his discussions with Sykes, he should confront the new negotiator with the old demands and attempt to strike a better bargain. No other explanation will account for the confidence with which Clayton, Maxwell and, as will be seen, McMahon in turn asserted that a state comprising the four Syrian cities and Mesopotamia north of Basra would be a satisfactory basis of negotiation with the Arabs. The alternative, namely that they

---

[1] Muhammad Tahir al-'Umari, *Muqaddarat al-'Iraq al-siyasiyya* [Political Destinies of Iraq], 3 vols., Baghdad, 1925, vol. I, pp. 222–3; Faruqi's letter to the Sharif, Cairo 27 Muharram 1334/6 Dec. 1915.

should have all three conspired to mislead their government in so important a matter, is absurd and untenable.

What agreement they thought they had reached with Faruqi is further elucidated by a report written towards the end of October by Aubrey Herbert, M.P., which was received at the foreign office on 5 November 1915. After being wounded in fighting on the western front, Herbert was sent to Egypt in December 1914, where for a few months he served as intelligence officer under Clayton. He then joined the Gallipoli expedition and was again wounded in the fighting. He was evacuated to Egypt on 9 October 1915, and shortly afterwards invalided home. He wrote the report just mentioned during the voyage from Egypt to Britain.[1] As a member of parliament and a younger son of the Earl of Pembroke who, moreover, had a brother who was then a secretary in the Cairo residency, and as someone who had himself served in the intelligence department, Herbert was the recipient of confidential information which the Cairo officials may well have wished to convey to London through his intermediary. His report is indeed concerned with the secret negotiations being then conducted with Faruqi; and though his report is entitled 'Personal Views on the Arab Situation', the details which he records, as well as the arguments rehearsing the urgency of an understanding with the Arabs, were clearly obtained from Clayton and other high officials:

> When I arrived in Cairo about ten days ago, the Arab question had reached a crisis. I saw the General, Clayton, Cheetham, and the High Commissioner. They all agreed that it was almost of supreme importance to get the Arabs in with us, that the opportunity would be lost if this was not done soon, and that whilst the Arabs would accept modifications in the frontiers [for] which they are asking, Homs, Hama, Damascus and Aleppo were essential to them. If this estimate of the situation is correct, it is vital to reconcile the French to making the large concessions involved by A) the promise of generous compensation elsewhere, (Nigeria?) or B) by convincing them of the acute danger of this situation, which left to itself may drift beyond our control, doing only a little less damage to the French cause than to ourselves, or lastly, C) by persuading the French to accept a wider sphere of influence with a larger measure of autonomy for the inhabitants of that sphere. This would mean a policy of British disinterestedness in Palestine, in favour of France. Almost any other method of achieving co-operation with the Arabs would be preferable. For though Palestine may not be indispensable to us either as a war frontier or bridge in peace time to Mesopotamia its value in both aspects is considerable.[2]

What Herbert is here saying is that Homs, Hama, Damascus and Aleppo constitute the minimum demands of the Arabs which have

[1] See the extracts from his diary published as *Mons, Anzac and Kut*, 1919.
[2] F.O. 371/2486, 16459/34982.

4-2

to be conceded if they are to join the Allies. This is certainly what Grey understood him to be saying. In a letter to Kitchener dated 4 November, he wrote:

> Aubrey Herbert who has just come back from Egypt says that all that is necessary to get the Arabs is to promise definitely the four towns of Damscus, Aleppo, Homs and Hama.[1]

But, it may be asked, where did this talk of Homs, Hama, Damascus and Aleppo originate? The conjunction is peculiar, and would not have readily occurred to Faruqi who, in Clayton's and Maxwell's reports, was said to be insisting on them as an irreducible minimum. Aleppo and Damascus were two relatively important and populous cities, Homs and Hama small, sleepy, provincial towns. In terms of Ottoman administrative divisions, again, the joining together of these four places made no sense, since Aleppo and Damascus were the capitals of two *vilayets*, while Homs and Hama were included in the *vilayet* of which Damascus was the capital. Also if Damascus, Homs and Hama were undoubtedly Arab, the same was not so true of Aleppo which was a mixed city, quite different in character from the other three, having its connexions and its trade overwhelmingly to the northwards in Kurdish- and Turkish-speaking territories. But if these four places were considered Arab, this was nothing peculiar to them, as the Sharif rightly pointed out in his letter to McMahon of 5 November 1915. This was also what Faruqi said he had pointed out to his Britsh interlocutors. In his lettter to the Sharif of 6 December 1915, cited above, he declares that he told them 'that I did not know of any non-Arab land west of the line Damascus–Aleppo as they pretended.'

In this letter, Faruqi also states that the suggestion to confine Arab claims to these four places came from the British side. In this, he may be taken to be telling the truth, for it is inherently improbable that so far-fetched and so peculiar a suggestion should have come from him. What, then, did the British have in mind when they broached the idea to him? In 'A Note on "Damascus, Homs, Hama and Aleppo"' published in 1961,[2] Emile Marmorstein has pointed out that in chapter 58 of *The Decline and Fall of the Roman Empire* Gibbon, relating the victories of the crusaders over the Muslims, declared, on the authority of the Muslim historian Ibn al-Athir (1160–1234) as cited by the French orientalist de Guignes, that at the end of the first crusade,

> the four cities of Hems, Hamah, Damascus and Aleppo were the only relics of the Mohammedan conquests in Syria.

[1] F.O. 800/102, Grey Papers.   [2] In *St Antony's Papers*, no. 11.

That these four places were joined together in the discussions with Faruqi, and that it was proposed that they should constitute the territory of the Arab state in Syria is thus seen to be the outcome of a literary reminiscence. This is the most convincing explanation of this odd and extraordinary proposal. It is interesting (and, as will be seen from part II below, somewhat ironical) that the only other independent use of this argument drawn from medieval history to be found in British official documents is most probably due to the erudite Arnold J. Toynbee. In February 1919 he was a member of the Turkish section of the British delegation at Paris, a section headed by Sir Louis Mallet. The prime minister, Lloyd George, happened to require then an answer to French claims to Syria, which were being buttressed by historical arguments. At his request, Mallet and Toynbee produced a memorandum in which the following passage occurs:

> In this connection His Majesty's Government point out that during the period of the crusades not only Deir-el-Zor [in eastern Syria] but Aleppo, Hama, Homs, and Damascus were never included in the boundaries of the Latin principalities...[1]

It is not known whether Lloyd George made use of this memorandum but a copy is to be found among his papers.[2] It does not seem, however, that either Toynbee or anyone else hit on this episode in the history of the crusades in order to explain and clarify the language of McMahon's letter.

Marmorstein (who wrote before the archives were opened) argues that it was Sykes, with his romantic historical imagination, who hit upon the notion of confining the Arabs of Syria to Homs, Hama, Damascus and Aleppo because the Muslims had been similarly confined eight hundred years before. But Sykes was not in Cairo when Faruqi first arrived there and, as had been seen, when he did interview the latter Homs, Hama, Damascus and Aleppo were not mentioned at all. It is also unlikely that the pedestrian McMahon, the stolid Maxwell, or the unimaginative Clayton would have hit upon such a fanciful notion. Of those whom we know to have been intimately involved in the Arab negotiations, only Storrs can have been its author. Readers of his memoirs know how much Storrs prided himself on being more than a mere dull official, and what a parade he made of his profound cultivation and his rare erudition.

---

[1] F.O. 608/107, file 384/1/6, paper 1562. A minute by Mallet dated 6 February 1919 on the jacket states that the memorandum consists of 'notes made by Mr Toynbee and me...on the P.M.'s instructions'.

[2] Lloyd George Papers, Beaverbrook Library, F.13/3/23.

The Quicksand

May it not then have seemed to him an exquisite private joke deftly to reduce to their due proportions the Sharif's territorial ambitions – which, as we know, he found absurdly inflated – by means of an esoteric and obscure historical allusion?

In his memorandum cited above, Aubrey Herbert has something else to say. He discusses, as has been seen, various ways by which the French could be induced to give up Homs, Hama, Damascus and Aleppo. The least desirable of these ways in his eyes was that which involved 'a policy of British disinterestedness' in favour of France in Palestine. We may infer from this that when he and his highly placed informants in Cairo spoke of Homs, Hama, Damascus and Aleppo forming the territory of an Arab state, they meant this and no more. It will be recalled that as recently as the previous July both McMahon and Maxwell had expressed views on the Bunsen committee proposals, and both of them insisted that Palestine should, somehow or another, be under direct British control. McMahon wanted Haifa to be annexed by the British, and 'the Palestine portion of British territory' to be included in the dominions of the Sultan of Egypt. Maxwell, for his part, preferring a 'devolutionary' scheme for the Ottoman empire, wanted to see Mesopotamia and Palestine becoming 'provinces under the nominal sovereignty of the Sherif of Mecca' who would appoint the Sultan of Egypt as his representative in Palestine and merely receive in exchange a fixed annual tribute. In their minds, we may then say with confidence, 'Palestine' and 'Homs, Hama, Damascus and Aleppo' were two quite different things. As Aubrey Herbert's report shows, what they were afraid of in October was that conceding the latter to the Arabs might mean abandoning the former to France.

Shortly after the despatch of McMahon's despatch of 12 October with which Clayton's report was enclosed, the Sharif's letter of 9 September, the contents of which have been described above, reached Cairo. In a telegram of 18 October McMahon summarized its contents.[1] The summary, so far as it went, was, literally speaking, an accurate one. But by the very fact of its being a summary, it managed to impart to the Sharif's letter a coherence and a definiteness which it did not possess. When sending the full text in translation (which went by surface mail and therefore arrived in London too late to be taken into account in the discussion on policy) McMahon remarked in his covering despatch that the letter was 'probably purposely and as is the custom of the Sherif – couched in vague terms.' Of this vagueness he certainly gave no hint

[1] F.O. 371/2486, 152901/34982, McMahon's telegram no. 623, Cairo 18 Oct. 1915.

in his telegram of 18 October. Nor did he draw attention to the fact that the Sharif, while seeming to insist on the original demands of 14 July, yet still left the door open, as has been seen, to more bargaining. It is doubtful whether McMahon or his advisers saw that this was the case, for, as he wrote in his despatch, he considered the letter to be 'a plain intimation that the Sherif of Mecca and the Arab communities whose policies and ideas he represents, are ready to side with us in the present war on condition that we can accept their main demands and especially the territorial boundaries defined in the Sherif's previous communication'.[1] There is, of course, no telling whether the foreign office would have concurred in this reading of the Sharif's language, if they had known it in good time, just as there is no telling whether they would have accepted Clayton's estimate of Faruqi – and thus acquiesced in Cairo's proposals – if they had seen the full text of his report (which reached them only on 25 October),[2] instead of having to rely, in reaching a crucial decision, only on Maxwell's and McMahon's urgent and alarmist telegrams. The minutes, as will be seen, at any rate indicate that the officials in London were more cautious and less impetuous than their Cairo colleagues.

What is clear is that McMahon read the Sharif's letter in the light of the discussions with Faruqi. This appears from the personal telegram which he sent to Grey on 18 October – the same day on which he reported on the Sharif's letter. This telegram was in answer to the telegram of 14 October in which Grey, as has been seen, asked McMahon to give his view on the 'definite statement of sympathy and support from us' which the Arabs were said by Maxwell to desire. In this telegram, McMahon referred both to the Sharif's letter and to Faruqi's statements, stating in so many words that the former had to be considered in the light of Faruqi's views. This was an *idée fixe* which McMahon had come to have. Even before receiving the text of the Sharif's letter, he was writing to Grey (in his despatch of 12 October) that this letter 'should throw light' on Faruqi's representations. He was thus quite oblivious of the fact that the Sharif not only did not know Faruqi, but at that time was not even aware of his existence. McMahon's telegram went on to explain Faruqi's views:

From further conversation with Faroki it appears evident that Arab party are at parting of the ways, and unless we can give them immediate assurance of nature to satisfy them they will throw themselves into the hands of

[1] F.O. 371/2486, 163827/34982, McMahon's despatch no. 126, Cairo 19 Oct. 1915.
[2] Enclosed with McMahon's despatch no. 121 of 12 Oct., F.O. 371/2486, 157740/34982.

Germany who he says has furnished them fulfilment of all their demands. In the one case they seem ready to work actively with us which will greatly influence the course of Mesopotamia and Syria campaigns while in the other Arabs will throw in their lot against us and we may have all Islam in the East united against the Allies.

Arab party say they cannot longer hesitate because they must act before Turkey receives further assistance from Germany. Matter therefore is urgent.[1]

Two days later, on 20 October, McMahon followed up his two telegrams of 18 October with another telegram in which he transmitted news of the Hijaz and Arabia as given by the Sharif's messenger. The messenger, whom McMahon declared (on what evidence is obscure) to be 'of some consequence', had stated that

> the Arabs are anxiously awaiting the results of the negotiations with England. Sheikh Rabegh in particular was most friendly and with many other Chiefs is only waiting for some such guarantees [as asked for by the Sharif] to fall on the Turks. The Shereef is in correspondence with the Imam ı chia whom he wishes to dissuade from aiding the Turks. He himself when asked by the messenger why he would not show his hand, replied that so long as he had no definite treaty with England he had to reckon with the possibility of the Allies making peace with the Turks at whose mercy he would then find himself.[2]

As it happens, the shaykh of Rabigh (a small port north of Jeddah) was to give a great deal of trouble to the British and to the Sharif when the latter rose against the Ottomans, while the Imam Yahya remained steadfastly loyal to the Ottomans all through the war. McMahon, of course, did not know any of this. It is true that information about Rabigh would have been difficult to obtain, but the situation in the Yemen could have been ascertained by enquiry from Aden. No such enquiry was made, and McMahon's telegram is quite innocent of any suspicion that the Sharif's emissary might not be the best of informants, and that these matters were at best very hazy and uncertain. Indeed his telegram contained another item, the significance of which he failed to see, or at any rate underline. He wrote that his own agent who had gone with the *mahmal* (the ceremonial empty litter which it was customary to send to Mecca yearly from Egypt) and had accompanied the Sharif's emissary from Jeddah to Cairo, reported that 'the merchants of Jeddah instigated by the Turks have sent to the Porte a petition against the Shereef'. This piece of information might have alerted McMahon and his subordinates to the possibility that enthusiasm

[1] F.O. 371/2486, 153045/34982, McMahon's unnumbered personal telegram to Grey, Cairo 18 Oct. 1915.
[2] F.O. 371/2486, 154423/34982, McMahon's telegram no. 626, Cairo 20 Oct. 1915.

for the British connexion was not as universal as the Sharif claimed, and it certainly chimed with what Ali Asghar, Storrs's agent, as has been seen, had to report from Mecca in the first half of October 1914, concerning the prevalence there of pro-Ottoman and pro-German sentiments. But the information does not seem to have attracted comment either in Cairo or in London.

In his personal telegram to Grey of 18 October McMahon, relying on 'further conversations' with Faruqi, declared that 'Arab party would accept an assurance on the following lines':

> England accepts principle of independent Arabia under British guidance and control within limits propounded by Sherif of Mecca, in so far as England is free to act without detriment to the interest of her present Allies (this refers to French in regard to whom see remarks on modification of North West limit of Arabia)...
>
> In regard to North-Western boundaries proposed by Sherif of Mecca, Faroki thinks Arabs would accept modification leaving in Arabia purely Arab districts of Aleppo, Damascus, Hama and Homs, whose occupation by the French they would oppose by force of arms.
>
> He also accepts the fact that British interests necessitate special measures of British control in Basrah Vilayet.
>
> If we consider letter of Sherif of Mecca in light of Faroki's views I do not think either Sherif or Arab party are likely to regard any less wide assurances as acceptable.[1]

It is clear that in spite of McMahon's talk of 'further conversations' with Faruqi, his telegram constitutes a mere repetition of Maxwell's two earlier telegrams, and like them is based on Clayton's report of 11 October. But in describing what would be acceptable to the Arabs McMahon introduced a change in wording which, slight as it was, was later to occasion much dispute and controversy. In his report, Clayton had written that the Arabs 'would almost certainly press for the inclusion of Damascus, Aleppo, Hama and Homs in the Arab Confederation', while Maxwell, in his telegram of 16 October had declared that 'the Arab party will, I think, insist on Homs, Aleppo, Hama and Damascus being in their sphere.' McMahon, we observe, now speaks of the Arabs insisting on the 'districts of Aleppo, Damascus, Hama and Homs' being in their sphere. There is nothing in the papers to indicate that the word 'districts', which McMahon now introduced, was intended to make any substantive change in the Arab demands as they had been described by Clayton and Maxwell. If it was more than a gratuitous redundancy, its purpose may have been to clarify and emphasize the meaning of Maxwell's and Clayton's language. But who introduced

---

[1] F.O. 371/2486, 153045/34982, cited above.

this word into the draft of McMahon's telegram, and for what reason, must remain unknown since the relevant file at the Cairo residency seems to have disappeared.

McMahon's personal telegram of 18 October was given prompt consideration at the foreign office. Clerk wrote a long minute in which he expressed the view that 'the best solution is an independent Arabia'. Two 'important limitations' had however to be considered, namely French claims and ambitions and the British advance in Mesopotamia. Clerk held that it was 'difficult to challenge the position which France claims, and has to some extent secured by acquiring special interests in the North-Western portion of Arabia as now defined by the Arabs'. As for Mesopotamia, he did not think that a solution 'which would provide for Arab independence and yet safeguard our vital interests, is necessarily impossible. Moreover,' he added, 'we shall have to be ready to resign acquisitions of territory in Mesopotamia if we are to get the French to give up their Syrian dreams.' Clerk saw yet another difficulty in the proposals put forward by Cairo,

> namely who is, or are, to rule this Arab empire? Bin Saud can run Nejd, Sherif Hosein can govern the Hedjaz, the Idrisi or Imam Yahya may be master of the Yemen, but no-one is indicated as Emir of Damascus or Caliph of Baghdad.

This point Clerk considered clearly of some importance, for two days later he reverted to it in a somewhat different manner, and in a short minute on McMahon's telegram no. 626 of 20 October, cited above, he wrote: 'The real difficulty will be to make sure that the Sherif speaks for all the Arabs'.

But Clerk was on the whole inclined to authorize McMahon to take preliminary and provisional action. His cautious recommendation was that

> subject to any fresh considerations which may arise out of Sir H. McMahon's despatch no. 121 [forwarding Clayton's report on the discussions with Faruqi, which McMahon had mentioned in his personal telegram to Grey but which had not yet been received] when we get it I would submit that he should be told that H.M.G. agree in principle to the establishment of an independent Arabia, and that we are ready to discuss the boundaries of such a state, and the measures to be taken to call [it] into being with qualified Arabian representatives without delay.

Clerk was aware of the haste with which he had set down his views, and would have liked more time for consideration, but he was also clear that no amount of consideration would alter his belief that 'we should try to come to terms with the Arabs, for which purpose we should start negotiation forthwith.' On the same day, 19 October, Nicolson commented on Clerk's suggestion. He minuted:

> I doubt if it will be easy in view of the conflicting rivalries and jealousies of the Arab Chiefs to set up 'an independent Arab State.' But we might proceed on the lines suggested by Mr Clerk. Sir H. McMahon urges a quick decision – and I should therefore urge an interim reply.[1]

This minute is silent about the serious doubts which McMahon's recommendations aroused in Nicolson. The reason may be that the matter being represented as extremely urgent, Nicolson did not feel he could stand in the way of what seemed to be informed, expert advice. But shortly afterwards, in a private letter to Hardinge he gave free rein to his misgivings:

> I have no great confidence [Nicolson wrote on 11 November 1915] in the possibility of the erection of an independent Arab State. It is quite impossible, I am sure, to bring into unity rival and warring Arab Chieftains. I am not at all fascinated by the overtures which the *Sheriff of Mecca* has lately been making to us. It seemed to me that he felt himself in a precarious and dangerous position and was anxious to obtain some kind of protection from us...To imagine we could ever bring about the establishment of an Arab State under one ruler appears to me to be a fantastic dream and I am surprised the proposal has been seriously entertained.[2]

If these were Nicolson's real views, it does seem surprising that he should have done so little to prevent McMahon's suggestions being 'seriously entertained'.

Grey was as prompt in dealing with McMahon's request for instructions as Nicolson and Clerk. A telegram was drafted by him, approved by Kitchener, added to by the India office, and sent to McMahon on 20 October, two days, that is, after the receipt in London of his personal telegram to the foreign secretary. But McMahon seemed to labour under a gnawing sense of extreme urgency. Grey's telegram to him crossed one of his, also sent on 20 October, in which he referred to his telegram no. 626 where he had reported what the Sharif's emissary had to say about conditions in Arabia. This, McMahon insisted,

> shows that situation is developing rapidly and requires dealing with without delay, Arab organization having now reached point at which it might be directed against either, and especially in view of the fact that Sherif's position is obviously becoming one of difficulty and even danger.[3]

[1] F.O. 371/2486, 152901/34982.   [2] Hardinge Papers, vol. 94, p. 344a.
[3] F.O. 371/2486, 154122/34986, McMahon's telegram no. 627, Cairo 20 Oct. 1915.

The Quicksand

It is difficult to resist the impression that McMahon was either trying to hustle the government into a quick decision – in the belief, perhaps, that here was a bargain not to be missed – or that he himself sincerely believed that the situation brooked not even the few days' delay needed for counsel and consultation. Neither supposition is to the credit of his judgment.

In any case Grey, as has been said, did not keep him waiting. His telegram of 20 October informed the high commissioner:

> You can give cordial assurances on the lines, and with the reserve about our Allies, proposed by you. Stipulation that Arabs will recognize British interests as paramount and work under British guidance etc., should not be included unless it is necessary to secure Arab consent, as this might give impression in France that we were not only endeavouring to secure Arab interests, but to establish our own in Syria at expense of French.
>
> There is no difficulty in speaking without reserve about Arab Peninsula and Holy Places. The general reserve you propose is however necessary more especially for North Western Boundaries.
>
> As regards Mesopotamia proposed sphere of British control, namely Basra Vilayet, will need extension in view of British interests in Baghdad province and area actually in our occupation. Our treaties with Arab chiefs will of course stand.
>
> But the important thing is to give our assurances that will prevent Arabs from being alienated, and I must leave you discretion in the matter as it is urgent and there is not time to discuss an exact formula.
>
> The simplest plan would be to give an assurance of Arab independence saying that we will proceed at once to discuss boundaries if they will send representatives for that purpose, but if something more precise than this is required you can give it.
>
> You should keep Wingate informed.[1]

The third paragraph of this telegram did not figure in Grey's original draft, but was inserted after representations from the secretary of state for India. Chamberlain (who had succeeded Crewe at the India office), as he told the viceroy, 'only accidentally' became aware of Maxwell's and McMahon's telegrams, and this as late as 20 October. 'I was most anxious to consult you before Grey sent his answer', he wrote to Hardinge on 22 October, 'but he urged so strongly the need for an immediate decision that all I could do was to ask Grey to introduce some words to safeguard what I call Indian interests'. As we also learn from another letter of Chamberlain's, the pressure for a quick answer to McMahon came not only – and perhaps not even primarily – from Grey; Kitchener was as – or perhaps even more – vehement: 'It is evident,' Chamberlain wrote to Hardinge on 12 November 1915, 'that the authorities in Egypt,

---

[1] F.O. 371/2486, 155203/34982, Grey's telegram no. 796, 20 Oct. 1915.

and Kitchener himself, attach great importance to these Arab negotiations. They appear to think that the Arabs are on the brink of a general and combined rising against the Allies in co-operation with the Turks, and they further appear to believe that it is still possible to snatch the brand from the burning by such offers as McMahon has made. I am,' he added, 'very sceptical about all their assumptions'.[1] The paragraph which Chamberlain was able to insert in these panic conditions was, as the sequel showed, most inadequate and, in effect, left McMahon a free hand.

In the last paragraph of his instructions, Grey asked McMahon to keep Wingate informed of his negotiations. This was the reiteration of a request which Grey had made once at the end of August, and repeated in another personal telegram sent on 14 October, on the same day, that is, as he had asked the high commissioner to report what assurances would be acceptable to the Arabs. In reply to this telegram, McMahon informed Grey on 20 October that time did not permit him to ascertain Wingate's views on the proposals he had sent in his personal telegram of 18 October.[2]

As it happened, in the interval between Grey's approval of McMahon's proposals and the latter's sending his well-known letter of 24 October to the Sharif, Wingate, although unbidden, did propose a form of reply to the Sharif. In a telegram of 23 October to Clayton, he suggested that the Sharif should be written to as follows:

> H.B.M.'s Government will recognize and support, and further will exercise her good offices with her allies to this end, the principle of Arabian independence within the boundaries defined on behalf of the Arab peoples, by the Sherif of Mecca; without prejudice to the claims by Great Britain and her allies to exercise such local measures of protection and control over certain districts as may be necessary to secure these territories from foreign aggression, to promote the welfare of the local populations, and to safeguard their economic interests.[3]

There is no evidence that Wingate's formula was seriously considered by McMahon and his advisers. Yet in eschewing territorial precisions, Wingate without knowing it conformed better than the high commissioner to Grey's instructions. In his telegram no. 796 of 20 October Grey, it will be recalled, had written:

[1] Hardinge Papers, vol. 121, pp. 196 and 214. See also Chamberlain's telegram to viceroy of 22 Oct. (copy in F.O. 371/2486, 162458/34982) where it is said that Kitchener and Grey accept the view that unless a 'definite and agreeable proposal' was made to the Sharif, there was a risk of 'genuine jihad and united Islam against us.'

[2] F.O. 800/48, Grey Papers, Grey's personal telegrams to Wingate, 31 Aug. and 14 Oct., and Wingate's personal telegram, 20 Oct. 1915.

[3] F.O. 882/2, fos. 132–3, Wingate's telegram to Clayton, Khartoum 23 Oct. 1915.

The simplest plan would be to give an assurance of Arab independence saying that we will proceed at once to discuss boundaries if they will send representatives for that purpose...

Grey, that is, like Clerk and Nicolson, regarded the assurances to the Sharif as mere provisional preliminaries to be replaced at leisure by a properly negotiated and detailed arrangement. This was also what Wingate aimed at in his elastic and comprehensive formula, which was thus much preferable to McMahon's obscure and misleading letter which was later to lead to controversy and accusations of bad faith.

McMahon, then, took full advantage of the discretion which Grey allowed him to use in dealing with the Sharif. Furthermore, he and his advisers were well aware that this was what he had done. Sending a copy to Hardinge of his letter of 24 October to the Sharif, he wrote on 28 October: 'As you will have seen they left the formulation of the terms to the Arab party almost entirely to my discretion, and as it had to be done in the shortest possible time, it was a difficult and delicate task.'[1] Clayton, writing to Sir William Tyrrell two days later, to send him a copy of the letter to the Sharif, declared that this letter was the result of the government 'giving what amounted to a free hand to the High Commissioner in the matter'. What seemed particularly to recommend the terms of the letter to Clayton was that Faruqi 'has seen the conditions proposed and in the main, agrees with them', and that Aziz Ali al-Misri also agreed.[2]

In his letter of 28 October to Hardinge, McMahon, as has been seen, declared that the answer to the Sharif 'had to be done in the shortest possible time'. Thus, once again he expresses his sense of the extreme urgency of the matter, but again does not indicate the reasons for this hurry. One possible reason, namely that the Sharif's messenger had to go back quickly to the Hijaz, may be ruled out. In a report to the French minister of war dated 30 October 1915, Vice-Admiral Huguet, commanding the French man-of-war *Montcalm* which had escorted the ship carrying the *mahmal* to Jeddah, wrote that the Sharif's emissary who had been transported from the Hijaz to Suez aboard a British man-of-war, had left Cairo on 26 October suddenly, unexpectedly and in a hurry (*inopinément au plus vite*) aboard the British cruiser *Venus*.[3] If Huguet's report is accurate, it would seem that the departure of the Sharif's emissary

[1] Hardinge Papers, vol. 94, p. 319.
[2] F.O. 882/2, fos. 134–7, Clayton to Tyrrell, Cairo 30 Oct. 1915.
[3] A.E., Guerre 1914–18, vol. 870.

was speeded up by the British authorities so that he might put McMahon's letter in the Sharif's hands as quickly as possible.

In his letter of 24 October 1915, then, McMahon began by saying that the Sharif's letter of 9 September had made him realize that the boundaries issue was 'one of vital and urgent importance', and that he was now communicating a statement regarding it 'on behalf' of the British government. The statement (which is the best-known passage in the whole correspondence) had this to say about territorial boundaries:

> The districts of Mersina and Alexandretta and portions of Syria lying to the west of the districts of Damascus, Hama, Homs and Aleppo cannot be said to be purely Arab and should be excluded from the proposed limits and boundaries.
>
> With the above modification, and without prejudice to our existing treaties with Arab chiefs, we accept those limits and boundaries, and in regard to those portions of the territories wherein Great Britain is free to act without detriment to her Ally, France, I am empowered in the name of the Government of Great Britain to give you the following assurances and make the following reply to your letter:–
>
> Subject to the above modifications, Great Britain is prepared to recognize and support the independence of the Arabs within the territories included in the limits and boundaries proposed by the Sherif of Mecca.
>
> Great Britain will guarantee the Holy Places against all external aggression and will recognize their inviolability.
>
> When the situation admits, Great Britain will give to the Arabs her advice and will assist them to establish what may appear to be the most suitable forms of government in those various territories.
>
> On the other hand, it is understood that the Arabs have decided to seek the advice and assistance of Great Britain only, and that such European Advisers and officials as may be required in the formation of a sound form of administration will be British.
>
> With regard to the Vilayets of Baghdad and Basra, the Arabs will recognize that the established position and interests of Great Britain necessitates special measures of administrative control in order to secure these territories from foreign aggression, to promote the welfare of the local populations and to secure our mutual economic interests.[1]

In the covering despatch with which the copy of this letter was sent to London, McMahon again stressed the extreme urgency of the matter in order to justify his having acted without further reference to Grey. He went on:

[1] F.O. 371/2486, 163832/34982, text of letter to Sharif enclosed with McMahon's despatch no. 131 Secret, Cairo 26 Oct. 1915. The last three phrases of the last paragraph seem an echo of the latter half of Wingate's telegram of 23 Oct. cited above. If so, then Wingate's language was preferable, since his draft did not speak of 'mutual economic interests', a phrase needlessly giving rise to queries and contentions.

The Quicksand

> The composition of a reply which would be acceptable to the Arab party and which would at the same time leave as free a hand as possible to His Majesty's Government in the future has been a difficult task.

The task, difficult as it may have been, was not well discharged. McMahon's letter had a specious air of precision; but its language was in reality vague, involved, roundabout and obscure and, as the sequel proved, a fertile source of disputes and recriminations. It bears all the marks of Storrs's tongue-in-cheek, brittle cleverness. Wingate's simple formula, cited above, would have been infinitely preferable. And what made McMahon's proceedings even less businesslike was that, as he disclosed in the despatch, a verbal gloss on the terms of his letter was given to the Sharif's emissary so as 'to facilitate its comprehension' by his master. What was said to him in Cairo, and what he reported in Mecca alike remain unknown. Wingate in Khartoum also gave a verbal interpretation of McMahon's offer. This was for Mirghani's benefit to enable him to explain matters to the Sharif. From the few details of the interview which he recorded (in a letter to Clayton of 1 November 1915), it would again seem that on territorial issues he was more straightforward and that his language was less compromising than that of the high commissioner and his advisers. Wingate wrote that he had pointed out to Mirghani 'the necessity for the reservations which we have made in Syria, Palestine and Mesopotamia.' And Mirghani did in fact transmit Wingate's language to the Sherif. 'In what they told you before', he wrote in a letter of 17 November 1915, 'that the discussion of the frontier question was premature, they meant that the Arabian Government had not yet come into existence and that the most important problem was first to have it brought to life and that any other question was secondary'.[1]

McMahon's despatch provides some clues about his intentions in writing as he did to the Sharif:

> I have been definite in stating that Great Britain will recognise the principle of Arab independence in purely Arab territory...but have been equally definite in excluding Mersina, Alexandretta and those districts on the northern coasts of Syria, which cannot be said to be purely Arab, and where I understand that French interests have been recognized. I am not aware of the extent of French claims in Syria, nor of how far His Majesty's Government have agreed to recognize them. Hence, while recognizing the towns of Damascus, Hama Homs and Aleppo as being within the circle of Arab countries, I have endeavoured to provide for possible French pretensions to those places by a general modification to the effect [that] His Majesty's

[1] Wingate Papers, 135/5 and 6.

Government can only give assurances in regard to those territories 'in which she can act without detriment to the interests of her ally France'.

. . . .

I venture to emphasize [he went on] the fact that the eventual arrangement would be very greatly facilitated if France would consent to forego any territorial claims she may have in purely Arab territories, such as Damascus, Hama, Homs and Aleppo. The inclusion of such districts in Arabia will be insisted on by the Arabs...

And again:

I would also once more lay stress on the religious importance attached to Damascus by Arabs, not only as one of the three points of departure of the Sacred Carpet [i.e., with Cairo and Hebron], but as, in their eyes one of the principal Holy Places.

As appears then from this despatch, McMahon's circumlocutions were designed to seem to offer the Sharif a substantial territory, while in fact offering him nothing at all. Even the four Syrian towns which, as the Cairo officials unanimously declared, would be insisted upon as an irreducible minimum by the Arabs, were conceded with one hand, only to be taken away with the other. As for the territory outside these four towns, it was entirely outside the ambit of this qualified and restricted concession.

In the despatch, as has been seen, McMahon speaks of 'the towns of Damascus, Hama, Homs and Aleppo', of 'purely Arab territories, such as Damascus, Hama, Homs and Aleppo', 'districts' upon the inclusion of which in Arabia the Arabs will insist. In his personal telegram to Grey of 18 October, McMahon, it will be recalled, spoke of the 'purely Arab districts of Aleppo, Damascus, Hama and Homs'. It was in this telegram that the word 'districts' was used for the first time to describe the four Syrian towns. The evidence of this despatch shows that McMahon attached no special significance to the word 'districts', and that for him it was synonymous with 'towns' and 'territories'. But the word, vague and redundant as it is, did figure in his letter to the Sharif which speaks of 'the districts of Damascus, Hama, Homs and Aleppo', and its exact meaning and significance subsequently gave rise to much puzzlement and ingenious interpretations.

The difficulty of fathoming the high commissioner's meaning was much aggravated by the way in which his words were translated into Arabic. This, as appears from his memoirs, was Storrs's responsibility. Storrs was oriental secretary at the residency, and liked to give the impression that he was at home in Arabic and other oriental languages. Witness his memoirs, which are studded with diacritical marks, quotations from the Arabic and allusions to his

99

The Quicksand

enjoyment of the beauties of Arabic literature. But as a colleague of his in Palestine has written, though Storrs was a good linguist, he 'pretended that he knew far more than he actually did – dropping a few words of Hebrew to visiting Italian ecclesiastics and a few words of modern Greek to bemused Palestinian Jews.'[1] Storrs's very anxiety to parade his expert knowledge of Arabic provides evidence in support of this judgment. For his memoirs contain inaccuracies which are not misprints, and which are incompatible with even an elementary knowledge of this language. Thus he must transliterate the Arabic word for caliphate (which is hardly necessary since the word has acquired a familiar English form), and writes *Khālifat* which is quite impossible, the correct transliteration being of course *khilāfa*. Again, he insists on writing in Arabic characters the word *himāya* and produces حمايه instead of حمايه, thus providing an Arabic transcription of the way in which the word would be pronounced by, say, an Englishman unable to produce the sound ḥ.[2] The mistake is characteristic of someone who does not know, but wishes to convey the impression that he knows, the language. As regards McMahon's letters to the Sharif, Storrs admitted somewhat defensively that

> Our Arabic correspondence with Mecca was prepared by Ruhi, a fair though not profound Arabist (and a better agent than scholar); and checked, often under high pressure, by myself.[3]

As may be seen from Ruhi's translations of the letters to the Sharif,[4] his Arabic style was not of the best. It was ungainly and inelegant; and he sometimes made grammatical mistakes which, if not glaring, yet do reveal that he did not possess a command over the language such as would enable him to cope easily with this kind of correspondence. If Ruhi's Arabic was, in Storrs's not very expert estimation, only 'fair', his English seems to have been no better. Thus, C. E. Wilson, the governor of the Red Sea province who organized communications with the Hijaz before the Sharif's rebellion, reported on one occasion, when a letter from Husayn was received and

---

[1] Edwin Samuel, *A Lifetime in Jerusalem*, 1970, p. 52.
[2] Storrs, *Orientations*, pp. 153 and 142.
[3] *Ibid.* p. 154.
[4] A facsimile of the Arabic text of the letter of 24 October 1918, as supplied to the Arab delegations to the Palestine conferences, London 1939, is reproduced in Z. N. Zeine, *The Struggle for Arab Independence*, Beirut, 1960, plate 1. The same author has photographically reproduced in an Arabic work, *al-Sira' al-duwali fi'l-sharq al-awsat wa wiladat dawlatayy Suriya wa Lubnan* [International Conflict in the Middle East and the Birth of the Two States of Syria and Lebanon], Beirut, 1971, appendix 1, facsimiles of most of McMahon's other letters.

translated by Ruhi at Port Sudan, that 'Some parts of the letter Ruhi found somewhat difficult to put into proper English'.[1]

Thus it was by the conjugated efforts of a Persian secret agent, and an indifferent and shaky Arabist, who many years before had 'savour[ed] rather than studi[ed]'[2] the language for three terms at Cambridge, that the involved and obscure communications which the high commissioner sent on behalf of 'the Government of Great Britain' were turned into Arabic.

It was, then, through the agency of Ruhi and Storrs that the word 'districts', which figured in the original of McMahon's letter, was rendered into Arabic as *wilāyāt* (sing. *wilāya*). This is patently a mistranslation. A possible translation of the word 'district' would have been *iqlīm* or *muqāta'a* or *nāhiya*. The most natural meaning of *wilāya* in the context of McMahon's letter, on the other hand, is 'province', i.e. one of the main administrative areas, *vilayet* in Turkish, into which the territory of the Ottoman empire was divided. But the conjunction of the four place-names, Damascus, Homs, Hama and Aleppo, makes this interpretation impossible, since Homs and Hama were not – and never had been – *vilayets*. How, then, to account for the presence of this word in the Arabic version of McMahon's letter? May it not be that the word *wilāyāt* is not at all meant to be a translation of the word 'districts'? As has been seen, in McMahon's despatch of 26 October 1915, 'towns' and 'districts' were used interchangeably. It may then be that Ruhi was here not so much translating a word, the exact significance of which he may have found difficult to fathom, as conveying its meaning – which he would have ascertained from Storrs. It so happens that in colloquial spoken Arabic the word *wilāya* can mean 'town'. This, interestingly enough, is confirmed by the Sharif's answer to McMahon's letter. In this answer, dated 5 November 1915, Husayn spoke of the *wilāya* of Mersina, meaning without any doubt the town of Mersina. Ruhi, says Storrs, was a 'fair' Arabist: does not this account for the presence of this colloquial usage in the middle of a formal document, which attempts – however haltingly – to use the appropriate written, literary language? Storrs also tells us that Ruhi's translations were checked by himself 'often under high pressure': may not this, coupled with his sketchy knowledge of

[1] F.O. 882/19, Wilson to Clayton, Port Sudan 19 March 1916. The florid style of British communications to the Sharif may have also been due to Ruhi. Lt.-Col. Vickery, British representative at Jeddah in 1919, was 'credibly informed' that 'Ruhi used to adress the King [Husayn] with the most extravagant titles when he wanted anything out of him'. F.O. 882/20, fo. 210.

[2] Storrs, *Orientations*, p. 15.

Arabic, in turn account for his failure to spot the anomaly, and to substitute, say *mudun* (sing. *madīna*), an appropriate word in the literary language, for Ruhi's *wilāyāt*?

McMahon's letter introduced yet another complication fertile of much later controversy. When Clayton first mooted, in his report of 11 October, the idea of the four Syrian towns constituting the irreducible Arab demand in Syria, he put the matter in this way: the Arab party, he wrote,

> would almost certainly press for the inclusion of Damascus, Aleppo, Hama and Homs in the Arab Confederation.

In his telegram of 16 October, Maxwell took up Clayton's theme and reiterated that

> the Arab party will, I think, insist on Homs, Aleppo, Hama and Damascus being in their sphere.

McMahon's personal telegram to Grey of 18 October made an identical report:

> In regard to North-Western boundaries proposed by Sherif of Mecca, Faroki thinks Arabs would accept modification leaving in Arabia purely Arab districts of Aleppo, Damascus, Hama and Homs, whose occupation by the French they would oppose by force of arms.

It is this formulation which Grey approved in his telegram of 20 October, where he wrote:

> The general reserve you propose is…necessary more especially for North Western Boundaries.

But in his letter to the Sharif of 24 October, McMahon, without authority and for reasons which must remain unknown owing to the disappearance of the relevant residency file, significantly modified the formula. Instead of telling the Sharif that the four towns would form the territory of the Arab state in Syria – which is what he himself, Maxwell and Clayton unanimously declared to be the Arab demand – McMahon chose to tell the Sharif that

> portions of Syria lying to the west of the districts of Damascus, Homs, Hama and Aleppo cannot be said to be purely Arab, and should be excluded from the limits demanded.

That this formulation had no substantive significance appears clearly from an exchange between Grey and McMahon which took place shortly afterwards. On 6 November Grey telegraphed to McMahon that a French representative was shortly expected in London to discuss the boundaries of a Arab state, and went on:

Mysteries of the McMahon–Husayn Correspondence

I propose to concentrate on getting French consent to inclusion of Damascus, Hama, Homs and Aleppo in Arab boundaries.

McMahon answered:

Arabs attach very great importance to inclusion of Damascus, Hama, Homs and Aleppo in Arab boundaries and have, in fact, repeatedly expressed the determination to fight for those territories if necessary.[1]

McMahon's change of formulation thus made the bizarre notion of confining the Arab state in Syria to the four towns even more bizarre. It also made it well-nigh unintelligible, by turning these towns into a boundary, such that territory to the east of it was 'purely Arab', and to the west of it not 'purely Arab'. Even apart from the fact that Aleppo could not be said to be 'purely Arab', a boundary of this kind was a nonsense, the more so in that McMahon's letter in no way indicated how far north or south this boundary would extend. Thus the antiquarian fancy which sought to confine the Arabs to the territory left to the Muslims during the crusades was made even more fanciful by McMahon's maladroit formulation.

As has been seen, Grey's telegram of 20 October included a passage relating to Mesopotamia which was suggested by Austen Chamberlain. It ran as follows:

As regards Mesopotamia proposed sphere of British control, namely Basra Vilayet, will need extension in view of British interests in Baghdad province and area actually in our occupation.

McMahon himself had reported that Faruqi 'accepts the fact that British interests necessitate special measures of control in Basrah Vilayet', and Grey's words were clearly meant to instruct the high commissioner to emphasize the British position – stemming from military occupation – in Basra and to the north. But McMahon, no doubt anxious to clinch a deal with the Sharif, chose to muffle what he was desired to emphasize, and spoke of 'special measures of administrative control' – an expression which had not occurred either in his own telegrams or in Grey's instructions – in Basra and Baghdad needed 'to secure these territories from foreign aggression, to promote the welfare of the local populations and to secure our mutual economic interests'. McMahon may have thought, however, that he was genuinely effecting a reconciliation between his superior's instructions and what had been agreed with Faruqi. What

[1] F.O. 371/2486, 166421 and 166819/34982, Grey's telegram no. 860, 6 Nov. and McMahon's telegram no. 677, Cairo 7 Nov. 1915.

McMahon and his advisers were themselves prepared to concede to the Sharif appears from a draft of McMahon's letter to the Sharif, which may have been prepared by Clayton – it is on intelligence department paper – in anticipation of approval by Grey. 'With regard to the Vilayet of Baghdad and Basra', the draft declared, 'the Arabs will recognize the vital economic interests of Great Britain and will guarantee to safeguard them'.[1]

When the details of McMahon's letter to the Sharif arrived at the India office, Hirtzel took great exception to them. 'These assurances', he minuted, 'are incompatible with any of the schemes discussed by the interdepartmental committee'. British annexation of Basra, he also rightly pointed out, was 'a common feature of all the schemes of the inter-departmental committee (though in para. 88(6) it is suggested, with reservations, that it might not be necessary under the scheme of a reformed and decentralized Ottoman Empire), and has always been put forward as a *sine qua non* by the G[overnment] of I[ndia]'.[2] The passage of the Bunsen committee report to which Hirtzel alludes here goes on:

> This question [the administration of Basra by a local government] is, however, one which primarily affects the Government of India, with whom it would rest to say whether they would be prepared to risk what might amount to little more than substituting, as far as Basra is concerned, the intrigues of a local Mesopotamian administration for those of the Turkish Imperial Government.

But as Hirtzel pointed out, the Bunsen Report was never seriously examined by the government.[3] He might have added that neither McMahon, in making his proposals, nor Grey in responding to them seems to have taken any notice of it. And McMahon, at any rate, we remember, not only was familiar with it, but had actually suggested modifications which were incompatible with what he was now putting forward; and still more incompatible with the original draft of his letter to the Sharif.

The viceroy also expressed dismay at McMahon's action. The latter had used the discretion left to him

> without due regard to Indian interests, by the inclusion of provinces of Baghdad and Bussorah in the proposed independent Arab State, only 'special measures of advanced administrative control' in these two Vilayats being reserved to His Majesty's Government or the Government of India. We think we should not have been committed to such a policy, and that we should have been consulted before a pledge of such vital importance to future

---

[1] F.O. 882/19.
[2] L/P & S/10/523, p. 3935/1915, minute by Sir A. Hirtzel, 27 Oct. 1915, cited above.
[3] *Loc. cit.*, minute of 26 Oct. 1915.

of India was given...We have always contemplated as a minimum eventual annexation of Bussorah Vilayet and (? some form) of native administration in Baghdad Vilayat under our close political control. McMahon guarantees apparently putting annexation out of the question.[1]

McMahon defended himself by saying that his formula

was intended to give us everything short of definite and open annexation i.e. a free hand regarding military measures, internal administration as well as development and commercial and industrial enterprize.

and that

it practically amounts to our monopoly of all administration and control in those Vilayets and was interpreted in that sense by Arab representatives here.[2]

This telegram shows once again the impolicy of McMahon's proceedings. What he had said to the Sharif about Baghdad and Basra, as the viceroy complained, clearly ruled out British annexation. For the rest, it was quite vague since the 'special measures of administrative control' of which he spoke could, if left without further specification, be interpreted in a hundred different ways. Instead of telling the Sharif how exactly he should understand this phrase, it was to the viceroy that we see him supplying his own private gloss. For good measure, he adds that the phrase 'was interpreted in that sense by Arab representatives here.' How this interpretation was recorded, and how authoritative and acceptable to the Sharif it might be was left quite obscure.

When the commander of the British troops in Mesopotamia, General Nixon, came to hear of McMahon's promises to the Sharif, he put forward yet another, very weighty objection:

Apart from the fact that such a commitment appears to be premature and will prejudice existing British interests at Basra and Baghdad and future of this great country [he wrote in a telegram of 14 November 1915] it seems to me to involve complete misconception of attitude of inhabitants of vilayets. It moreover overlooks the important and fundamental fact that four-fifths of the population of Basra and two-thirds of Baghdad vilayets are Shiahs.[3]

Nixon was of course right in calling the fact to which he drew attention important and fundamental. McMahon and his advisers do not seem to have at any time appreciated its import, and that to the Shi'ite population of Mesopotamia the Sharif and the handful

[1] F.O. 371/2486, 165415/34982, copy of viceroy's telegram, 4 Nov. 1915.
[2] F.O. 371/2486, 165761/34982, McMahon's telegram no. 674, Cairo 5 Nov. 1915.
[3] F.O. 371/2486, 171826/34982.

of disaffected Ottoman officers who plotted with him were of less consequence than even to the Sunnis of the Levant and of Arabia.

The India office were concerned not only about McMahon's references to Mesopotamia. They had serious misgivings about the dangerous vagueness of his promises, and of the manner in which they might be implemented. Thus Hirtzel pointed out in a minute of 9 November that

> The problem of Palestine has not been expressly mentioned in these negotiations. Jerusalem ranks third among the Moslem holy places, and the Arabs will lay great stress on it. But are we going to hand over our own holy places to them without conditions? Whatever may be the attitude of western Christianity on this subject, the very strong feeling of Russia will have to be reckoned with.

Holderness agreed:

> The question of Jerusalem illustrates the absurd and visionary character of the scheme. There is also the question of the Lebanon.[1]

McMahon would no doubt have replied that both the Lebanon and Palestine were excluded from his promise to the Sharif, first because they were not within the territory of the four towns, and second because they were in an area where, as he told the Sharif, Britain could not make promises 'without detriment to the interests of her Ally, France'. As he put it in his despatch to Grey of 26 October cited above:

> I am not aware of the extent of French claims in Syria, nor of how far His Majesty's Government have agreed to recognize them. Hence, while recognizing the towns of Damascus, Hama, Homs and Aleppo as being within the circle of Arab countries, I have endeavoured to provide for possible French pretensions to those places by a general modification to the effect [that] His Majesty's Government can only give assurances in regard to those territories 'in which she can act without detriment to the interests of her ally France'.

Valid as McMahon's argument would have been here, yet Hirtzel and Holderness were justified in thinking that an exact specification was more businesslike, and less open to dispute.

Holderness had another point to make, quite as important. Cairo justified its haste by alleging that, if promised what they wanted, the Arabs would rise. For instance, in a telegram of 1 November, Maxwell was confidently asserting that Faruqi 'and others of his party here, including Aziz Bey El Masri, have accepted the proposals

[1] L/P & S/10/523, p. 4082/1915.

[made by McMahon to the Sharif] and are ready to act.'[1] Assuming this to be the case, what form would agreement with the Arabs take?

> Is there to be [asked Holderness in a minute of 6 November] a bi-lateral treaty with reciprocal promises, or is a unilateral proclamation by the British Government to the Arabs of Arabia to suffice?...The only person with whom a treaty could be made is the Grand Sheriff. He cannot pledge anyone but himself, and he would insist on secrecy. There could be no uprising from this of the Arabs at large.[2]

No one at the foreign office or in Cairo thought of these points, or asked himself by exactly what mechanism or agency a secret letter from McMahon in Cairo to the Sharif in Mecca would result in an uprising in Syria and in Mesopotamia. Nevertheless, such an uprising the Cairo authorities confidently promised and, to help bring it about, Grey was prepared to jettison long-standing and substantial British interests. In a telegram of 6 November which he himself drafted Grey told McMahon:

> Our primary and vital object is not to secure a new sphere of British influence, but to get Arabs on our side against Turks.[3]

A copy of this telegram went to the India office, and it drew this comment from Hirtzel:

> Granted that we do not want a new sphere of influence for its own sake, what is vital to the security of India and (I believe) the peace of the world, is that it should not pass into the control of any other power. If the war has not taught this, what has been the meaning of our whole policy in Turkish Arabia and the Persian Gulf for the last century? And unless the cause of the Allies is literally *in extremis* I can see no justification for this extraordinary *volte face*.

The passage from Grey's telegram which has been just cited roused Hirtzel's particular indignation: 'if published it would', he wrote, 'cover its author' – whose identity he did not know – 'with ignominy.'[4]

Grey might not have agreed with Hirtzel's formulation of traditional British interests in the Middle East. But if his first priority was, as he put it, 'to get Arabs on our side against Turks', he was also at the same time singularly and paradoxically sceptical of Arab

---

[1] F.O. 882/6, Maxwell's telegram to British minister, Athens, Cairo 1 Nov. 1915. The telegram concerned negotiations by a secret agent possibly with highly-placed Ottoman personalities.
[2] L/P & S/10/523, p. 4068/1915.
[3] F.O. 371/2486, 166421/34892, Grey's telegram no. 860, cited above.
[4] L/P & S/10/523, p. 4068/15, cited above.

ability to accomplish anything of value in the war. When Austen Chamberlain protested to him about the manner in which McMahon had disposed of Mesopotamia,

> the best comfort he could give me [wrote Chamberlain in a minute of 27 October 1915] was that the whole thing was a castle in the air which would never materialize.[1]

The conjunction of these two contradictory ideas, namely that the Arabs were supremely important, and that they did not matter at all, must in the end explain why Grey gave in to McMahon's eager urgings. But to entertain these two contradictory ideas was to be caught in a ruinous incoherence. Sir Arthur Hirtzel, whose comments show him to have been the most clear-sighted and sagacious of those involved in this episode, pointed it out at the time, and it is fitting that he should have the last word:

> Sir E. Grey [he declared in his minute of 2 November] does not think that [McMahon's] assurances matter much because the scheme will never materialize. But it would surely be attributing too much stupidity to the Young Arab party to assume that they will not manoeuvre us into a position in which – whether or not they get what *they* want – we shall not get what *we* want without eating some very indigestible words.[2]

The vast structure of recrimination, accusation and self-accusation which after the war was erected upon the McMahon–Husayn correspondence gives Hirtzel's words the character and status of a prophecy.

Grey's haziness and incoherence in these negotiations is matter for constant wonderment. His declared objective was, as he himself put it, 'to get Arabs on our side against Turks'. Or, as he put it shortly afterwards to McMahon: ...an effective Arab movement against Turks would be worth the future inconvenience as regards Baghdad', but the Arabs should act 'at once'.[3] Grey was moved to speak thus by a protest of Chamberlain's against McMahon's proceedings.[4] Yet at the very same time in a conversation with the French ambassador, he declared that what was of 'paramount importance' was to secure a separation between the Arabs and the Turks, instead of a combination between them.[5] Chamberlain once again had to point out that this was not at all what had been

---

[1] L/P & S/10/523, p. 3935/1915, cited above.
[2] L/P & S/10/523, p. 4024/1915, cited above.
[3] F.O. 371/2486, 166807/34982, Grey's telegram no. 874, 11 Nov. 1915.
[4] *Ibid.* Chamberlain's memorandum of 8 Nov. 1915.
[5] F.O. 371/2486, 169450/34982, Grey's telegram to Bertie, no. 878, Paris 10 Nov. 1915.

promised through and by the Cairo officials, and that for which Basra and Baghdad had been given up to the Sharif. McMahon's offer had been conditional not only on the separation between the Arabs and the Turks, but on the immediate active co-operation of the Arabs against the Turks. Only if this materialized, Chamberlain insisted, was McMahon's offer binding, and only in such circumstances should the French be asked to make similar concessions in Syria.[1]

It is well known that the prospect, held out by Faruqi, of a large-scale rebellion in or desertion from the Ottoman armies in Syria and Mesopotamia – and it was this which moved McMahon to propose, and Grey to approve the terms embodied in the former's letter of 24 October – in the end failed utterly to materialize. As has been seen, Clayton, Maxwell and McMahon all failed to subject Faruqi's allegations and promises to critical examination, and the only sceptical voice which was heard – but to no purpose – was that of the India office. As it happened, very shortly afterwards, it was Faruqi himself who disclosed that the hopes he had aroused were chimerical. For when Sykes interviewed him about 20 November he was no longer speaking of a mighty and secret Arab military organization which would on its own paralyze Ottoman power in the Levant. On this occasion, as will be recalled, he made large territorial claims which would have to be conceded as the price of Arab co-operation. But he also declared that there would be no Arab rising without substantial Allied military intervention in Alexandretta!

> This, Faroki insisted [so ran Sykes's telegram], was dependent on the Entente landing between Mersina and Alexandretta and making good the Cilician Gates or the Amanus Pass; stipulating further that, until this has been done, the Sherif should take no action...The necessity of immediate and adequate action in the Gulf of Alexandretta was also urged by Faroki, who added that the Germans would forestall them if the Entente did not seize this opportunity: the Arabs would in their own interests be obliged to reconsider the situation, once the Turks or Germans got into Syria.[2]

Sykes's telegram arrived in London through the foreign office, but there is no record in its papers of anyone commenting on this remarkable disclosure which totally and suddenly undermined the assumptions on which British policy towards the Sharif had been based.

In the meantime the Sharif himself had indicated that he was in

---

[1] *Ibid.* 174595/34982, Chamberlain's memorandum, 12 Nov. 1915.
[2] F.O. 882/13, Sykes's telegram to war office, no. 19, Cairo 20 Nov. 1915, cited above.

no hurry – was indeed rather reluctant to take action against the Ottomans. His answer to McMahon's letter of 24 October arrived in Cairo about 10 November. This letter, dated 5 November, contained a remarkable paragraph which nothing in the previous correspondence would have led its recipient to expect:

> In your desire to hasten the movement we see not only advantages, but grounds of apprehension. The first of these grounds is the fear of the blame of the Moslems of the opposite party (as has already happened in the past), who would declare that we have revolted against Islam and ruined its forces. The second is that, standing in the face of Turkey which is supported by all the forces of Germany, we do not know what Great Britain and her Allies would do if one of the *Entente* Powers were weakened and obliged to make peace. We fear that the Arab nation will then be left alone in the face of Turkey, together with her allies, but we would not at all mind if we were to face the Turks alone. Therefore it is necessary to take these points into consideration in order to avoid peace being concluded in which the parties concerned may decide the fate of our people as if we had taken part in the war without making good our claims to official consideration.

The first, and perhaps the most surprising, assertion here is the imputation to McMahon of a desire to hasten the movement. In this the Sharif professes to see 'grounds of apprehension'. But McMahon had written nothing to give rise to such remarks. The urging, on the contrary, had all come from the Sharif himself, or from Faruqi, and McMahon had done no more than obediently respond to it. Thus in his original memorandum of 14 July the Sharif had set a time limit of thirty days in which the British government had to accept or refuse his demands. Again, in his letter of 9 September he wrote that 'the whole country, together with those who you say are submitting themselves to Turco-German orders, are all awaiting the result of these negotiations'. It was no doubt in response to this statement that McMahon, in his letter of 24 October, wrote: 'I have realised, however, from your last letter that you regard this question [of the boundaries] as one of vital and urgent importance'. The Sharif now wrote as if McMahon was trying to involve him by some trickery and against his will in something doubtful and perilous. What if he were accused of dividing Islam; and what, further, if the Allies were defeated? Before making a move to help Great Britain, the Sharif wanted to be guaranteed against such an eventuality. It is as though it was McMahon and not he himself who had initiated the correspondence the previous July. He was no doubt led to adopt this stance by the eager and effusive manner which McMahon adopted, and even more by the parlous state of the Gallipoli expedition. Nicolson was right in thinking that the Sharif was sitting on the fence, and that if he thought events were moving against the British, he would come down on the other side.[1] Crewe, who was acting for Grey at the foreign office, regarded the Sharif's proposals as absurd, and considered the prospect of an agreement not at all hopeful.

McMahon, on the other hand, saw nothing absurd in the Sharif's language. On the contrary; the evacuation of Gallipoli made the situation facing the British in Syria and Mesopotamia quite serious, and rendered 'alienation of Arab assistance from Turks a matter of great importance, and we must make every effort to enlist the sympathy and assistance, even though passive, of Arab people'. Thus McMahon, a month or so after holding out dazzling prospects of Ottoman collapse in the Middle East following the defection of the Arabs, was now content with the mere sympathy and passive assistance of the Arabs. This he was prepared to purchase by conceding what the Sharif desired. He proposed, in particular, to assuage the Sharif's worries – as expressed in the paragraph quoted above – by assuring him that 'Great Britain has no intention to conclude peace in terms of which freedom of Arabs from Turkish domination does not form essential condition.'[2] He insisted that a successful understanding with the Arabs depended on some such assurance. The foreign office, also shaken no doubt by the aftermath of Gallipoli, approved his language in a telegram drafted by Clerk[3] and in his letter to the Sharif of 14 December, McMahon wrote:

> We fully appreciate your desire for caution, and have no wish to urge you to hasty action, which might jeopardise the eventual success of your projects, but, in the meantime, it is most essential that you should spare no effort to attach all the Arab peoples to our reunited cause and urge them to afford no assistance to our enemies.
>
> It is on the success of these efforts and on the more active measures which the Arabs may hereafter take in support of our cause, when the time for action comes, that the permanence and strength of our agreement must depend.
>
> Under these circumstances I am...directed by the Government of Great Britain to inform you that you may rest assured that Great Britain has no intention of concluding any peace in terms of which the freedom of the Arab peoples from German and Turkish dominance does not form an essential condition.

When he came to see this passage, Chamberlain was very disturbed and wrote a letter to Grey which is worth quoting in full:

[1] F.O. 371/2486, 172416/34982, minute by Sir A. Nicolson on telegram from McMahon, unnumbered, Mudros (where McMahon had gone to confer with Kitchener then on a visit to the Gallipoli front) 16 Nov. 1915.

[2] F.O. 371/2486, 181834/34982, McMahon's telegram no. 736, Cairo 30 Nov. 1915.

[3] *Ibid.* telegram to McMahon no. 961, 10 Dec. 1915.

Are we not getting into a great mess with these negotiations of MacMahon's?

He has now informed the Grand Sheriff that 'you may rest assured that Great Britain has no intention of concluding any peace in terms of which the freedom of the Arab peoples from German and *Turkish* domination does not form *an essential condition.*'

Had he any authority for this pledge and, if he had, must not you at once tell the Russians that you are precluded from entertaining Djemal Pasha's proposals?[1]

I have not overlooked the paragraph which precedes the one I have quoted from MacMahon's letter; but what does it mean? When will 'the time for action' by the Arabs come?

MacMahon seems to me to be 'all give and no take' in his negotiations and he is pledging us to things which we may be unable to perform.

Given the policy recommended by the General Staff and approved yesterday by the War Committee the Arabs will (at best) take no action and MacMahon's 'time for action' will not have arrived. Are we then to add the independence of 'Arabia' to all the other objects which we have pledged ourselves, to secure before we made peace?

Is it not necessary to review the whole situation carefully and then to issue full and very clear instructions to MacMahon? It seems to me that telegrams are not sufficient.[2]

In the last paragraph of his letter, Chamberlain put his finger on the fundamental vice from which British policy towards the Sharif suffered. It was that the ignorance, the enthusiasm and the *parti pris* of the Cairo officials were hardly ever questioned or resisted in the foreign office, which was content passively to acquiesce, by telegram, in decisions for which Cairo likewise had urgently requested approval by telegram. As Clerk complained somewhat later: 'We cannot work out a consistent Arab policy on three-weeks' old reports from subordinate officials, telegraphic requests for large sums of money, munitions and stores from the High Commissioner and gobbets of Hedjaz news buried in the voluminous pages of Arab Bureau reports, themselves already growing out of date, which is all we get at present.'[3] The foreign office papers certainly contain no systematic consideration of the aims to be pursued, or the methods to be adopted, or of the character and ambitions of their Arab interlocutors. This is in great contrast to the measured and shrewd appreciations by Hirtzel and Holderness which abound in

---

[1] This is an allusion to reports transmitted by the Russians to the effect that Jemal was willing to go over to th side of the Allies provided he was recognized as the ruler of Syria.

[2] F.O. 800/98, Grey Papers. The letter is dated 29 Nov. 1915, but this seems a slip; no doubt 29 December is meant, which is when Chamberlain would have seen a copy of McMahon's despatch no. 172 (F.O. 371/2486, 198266/34982) of 14 Dec. with which a copy of his letter to the Sharif of the same date was enclosed.

[3] F.O. 371/2774, 144045/42233, minute by G. R. Clerk, 25 July 1916.

the India office papers. But their views had almost no influence for, as Hardinge put it so well, 'Grey was bounced by Kitchener and Chamberlain by Grey'.[1] Nothing better illustrates Hardinge's point than Grey's minute on Chamberlain's letter. It said, simply: 'I have spoken to Mr Chamberlain about this'.

In his letter of 5 November 1915, the Sharif had something to say about the territorial offer contained in McMahon's telegram of 24 October:

> we renounce our insistence on the inclusion of the *wilāyas* of Mersina and Adana in the Arab Kingdom. But the two, *wilāyas* of Aleppo and Beirut and their sea coasts are purely Arab *wilāyas*.

The Sharif's language here made the confusion produced by McMahon's letter of 24 October worse confounded. For whereas McMahon used *wilāya*, understood to mean 'town', in a consistent, albeit inappropriate, manner, the Sharif is clearly using the term in two different and inconsistent ways. He means by it on the one hand 'province', or *vilayet* in the Ottoman administrative usage, as when he speaks of the *wilāyas* of Aleppo and Beirut (which were Ottoman *vilayets*). But he also clearly uses it to mean 'town' as when he speaks of Mersina being a *wilāya*, for Mersina was not a *vilayet*. It was, rather, included in the *vilayet* of Adana. But Adana and Mersina are joined together in the Sharif's letter, and it must therefore remain obscure whether in speaking of the *wilāyas* of Mersina and Adana, the Sharif meant the towns of Mersina and Adana, or the town of Mersina and the *vilayet* of Adana. It is most probable that he meant the former, but no one at Cairo or in the foreign office queried his language or thought it necessary to ask him what he meant.[2]

What is at any rate clear is that the Sharif ignored and disregarded McMahon's language about 'portions of Syria lying to the west of the districts of Damascus, Homs, Hama and Aleppo' which henceforth disappears from the correspondence. The Sharif, not having present to his mind Ibn al-Athir or Gibbon, must have been puzzled by this phrase. By saying that these 'portions' of Syria 'cannot be said to be purely Arab' McMahon, the Sharif may have thought, meant that there were large non-Muslim populations there. But the only areas where there were sizeable numbers of non-Muslims were the *vilayets* of Aleppo and Beirut, and to rebut a possible

[1] Hardinge Papers, vol. 94, p. 194, letter to Sir Ronald Graham, Delhi 8 Dec. 1915.
[2] The confusion is not lessened by the official translation published in 1939, which speaks of the *vilayets* of Mersina and Adana, and the *vilayets* of Aleppo and Beirut.

contention based on this fact the Sharif asserted that these two *vilayets* were undoubtedly Arab, because 'there is no difference between a Moslem and a Christian Arab: they are both descendants of one forefather'. This, of course, was special pleading since Muslims by no means considered Christians their equals, and since the *vilayet* of Aleppo did contain large numbers of Kurds, Turks and Armenians. The interesting point, however, is that this seemed to the Sharif the best way of meeting McMahon's so peculiarly phrased reservation. That he should have brought the *vilayets* of Aleppo and Beirut into the debate was also a direct consequence of McMahon's defining the Arab state by excluding from it 'portions of Syria lying west of Damascus, Homs, Hama and Aleppo', on the untenable pretext that they could not be said to be purely Arab, instead of simply laying it down, in conformity with Faruqi's presumed statement, that the Arab state would comprise the territory of the four towns.

McMahon was, in the event, quite ready to abandon his fanciful notion. He suggested that in his reply he should agree that 'with the exception of tract around Marash and Aintab, vilayets of Beirut and Aleppo are inhabited by Arabs, but in these vilayets as elsewhere in Syria our ally France has considerable interests, to safeguard which some special arrangements will be necessary.'[1] Grey had recently discussed the Sharif's approaches with Cambon and had declared that the boundaries of his state in Syria would have to be settled in agreement with France, and that a French delegate should be appointed to discuss the matter.[2] It was this conversation which initiated the process culminating in the so-called Sykes–Picot agreement, which may thus be seen as the direct consequence of the Sharif's demands and of the British attempt to reach agreement with him. Thus, when McMahon's proposed answer to the Sharif regarding Aleppo and Beirut reached the foreign office, negotiations with Picot, the French delegate, were afoot. McMahon was therefore cautiously instructed to say that 'as the interests of others are involved, the point required further consideration by H.M.G. and a further communication in regard to it will be sent later.'[3] Consequently, in his letter to the Sharif of 14 December McMahon wrote:

> With regard to the *vilayets* of Aleppo and Beirut, the Government of Great Britain have fully understood and taken careful note of your observations,

[1] F.O. 371/2486, 181834/34982, McMahon's telegram no. 736, Cairo 30 Nov., cited above.
[2] A.E., Guerre 1914–18, vol. 1681, Cambon's telegram no. 2448–9, London 21 Oct. 1915. Cambon suggested in this telegram Picot's appointment as delegate.
[3] F.O. 371/2486, 181834/34982, telegram to McMahon no. 961, 10 Dec. 1915.

but, as the interests of our ally, France, are involved in them both, the
question will require careful consideration and a further communication on
the subject will be addressed to you in due course.

The word *vilayet* in this passage appears in Arabic as *wilāya* which
is therefore used here not in the loose colloquial sense which had
obtained in the letter of 24 October but in the precise, official sense
appropriate to an official document. But the confusion still subsisted,
since earlier in his letter McMahon had spoken of 'the exclusion of
the districts of Mersina and Adana from boundaries of the Arab
territories', and the word used to translate 'district' was still the
word *wilāya*. But Ruhi and Storrs – who were presumably again
responsible for the translation – were here merely echoing the
Sharif's confused Arabic usage.

The 'further communication' of which the above passage speaks
was never sent to the Sharif, so that in Syria the boundaries of the
Arab state, as contemplated in this correspondence, remain quite
undetermined. But the Sharif had raised another issue in his letter:
that of Basra and Baghdad. He declared that these *vilayets* were
'parts of the pure Arab Kingdom' greatly valued by the Arabs and
not to be given up. But, in order to facilitate agreement, he was
willing

> to leave under the British administration for a short time those districts now
> occupied by the British troops without the rights of either party being
> prejudiced thereby…and against a suitable sum paid as compensation to the
> Arab Kingdom for the period of occupation, in order to meet the expenses
> which every new kingdom is bound to support…

The foreign office were puzzled as to the exact meaning of the
expression 'Arab Kingdom', and Oliphant commented: 'For sheer
insolence it would be difficult to find any passage to equal' this
paragraph.[1] But McMahon found the Sharif's proposals satisfactory,
'showing a desire for mutual understanding on reasonable lines'. It
was, he said, 'quite impossible to come to any general understanding
with Arabs without some acknowledgement that Irak is in theory
part of Arabia proper'; the Shi'ites, it is true, were numerous in Iraq,
but so were Christian Arabs in the west but, since the Arab
movement was 'based on national not religious grounds', 'neither
fact appears to me to preclude general agreement on lines suggested'.
Again, contrary to what India said, the Sharif was not a nonentity:
'Everything tends to prove that he is of sufficient commanding
importance by position of descent and personality, to be the only

[1] F.O. 371/2486, 170984 and 172416/34982, minutes on two telegrams from McMahon at
Mudros 14 and 16 Nov. giving summaries of the Sharif's letters.

possible central rallying point for Arab cause'. He therefore was in favour of accepting some such arrangement as the Sharif had suggested: 'What they obviously desire is some assurance of our considering the question of a quitrent or subsidy'. This was to ignore the Sharif's stipulation that Basra and Baghdad were to remain under British administration 'for a short time' only. Here too, the foreign office (who sought Hirtzel's advice on the subject) were much more cautious than the high commissioner. He was told to say that British interests required that Baghdad and Basra should be considered in detail and carefully – and this the present situation did not allow. 'This need not, however,' the foreign office telegram added, 'preclude eventual consideration of a perpetual lease or any other reasonable financial proposal'.[1] McMahon therefore wrote as follows to the Sharif:

> The Government of Great Britain…are ready to give all guarantees of assistance and support within their power to the Arab Kingdom, but their interests demand, as you yourself have recognized, a friendly and stable administration in the *vilayet* of Baghdad, and the adequate safeguard of these interests calls for a much fuller and more detailed consideration than the present situation and the urgency of these negotiations permit.

Why the *vilayet* of Basra is not mentioned in this passage McMahon did not explain. But it is at once evident that this new formula is much vaguer and much less binding than the one McMahon had employed on his own initiative, and that as in the case of Syria, the effect of his letter was to make it quite uncertain what exactly the Sharif was being offered.

In his letter of 5 November Husayn, dealing with McMahon's stipulation (in his letter of 24 October) that his offer was 'without prejudice to our existing treaties with Arab chiefs', sought to restrict the scope of this stipulation by making it apply to Baghdad and Basra where the 'Arab Kingdom', he wrote, would respect 'your agreements with the Sheikhs of those districts, and especially those which are essential'. This was clearly unacceptable, and in his reply of 14 December, McMahon sought to insist that his stipulation applied to all engagements. He clearly had in mind such treaties as Britain had with Ibn Sa'ud, the Idrisi, the ruler of Kuwait, and the shaykhs of the Trucial Coast. But the point was made in a most maladroit fashion. McMahon (or Storrs, who most probably drafted the letter) accepted Husayn's talk about 'the Arab Kingdom', and wrote that

[1] F.O. 371/2486, 181834/34982, McMahon's and foreign office telegrams, cited above.

it is, of course, understood that this [stipulation] will apply to all territories included in the Arab Kingdom, as the Government of Great Britain cannot repudiate engagements which already exist.

This awkward and misleading formulation was later to be exploited by Husayn.

In the despatch with which he forwarded a copy of his letter, McMahon explained that he had omitted a reference in the letter to a possible future settlement of the Mesopotamian question on a financial basis, 'but I have verbally hinted something to this effect to the Sherif's messenger.'[1] What McMahon exactly hinted, and what the messenger understood and conveyed to the Sharif remain unknown. This was not, as has been seen, the first occasion when McMahon preferred this method to the exact recording of proposals on paper. The method may have its advantages, but with two interlocutors like the Sharif and McMahon it was likely to increase, rather than diminish, the risk of false impressions and misunderstandings. The Sharif, too, on occasion preferred verbal to written communications. Thus his letter of 5 November was accompanied by an oral message from Abdullah to Storrs in which, as Storrs recorded in a note of 12 November 1915, the former strongly emphasized the point that the restrictions contained in his written reply should not be taken too seriously.[2] This message was not at any time reported to the foreign office, and considering how far McMahon was prepared to go in agreeing to the Sharif's written demands it does not seem that – assuming he knew of it – he in any way took it into account.[3]

Neither, it seems, did the Sharif. For his answer to McMahon's letter of 14 December (dated 1 January 1916) was, on the face of it, as insistent about the original territorial claims as he had ever been. By then, he had received Faruqi's first letter – mentioned above – and used it to argue that his demands were 'the result of the decisions and desires of our peoples'. By then, also, the withdrawal from Gallipoli was a well-known fact, and the Sharif may have thought that this would make the British more amenable to

[1] F.O. 371/2486, 198266/34982, McMahon's despatch no. 172 Secret, 14 Dec. 1915, cited above.
[2] Wingate Papers, 135/5.
[3] An echo of this oral message may possibly be heard in what Sykes, who had reached Cairo shortly after the Sharif's messenger, was to tell Chamberlain. Writing to Hardinge on 18 Jan. 1916, the secretary of state for India said that according to Sykes the Arabs 'fully recognized that any authority which they might assert over the Basrah vilayet would be purely nominal, and that they would be dependent on British administration for the preservation of order there'. Hardinge Papers, vol. 122, p. 13.

conceding his original demands. If they did not give in, on the other hand, this would allow him, if prudence so dictated, to abandon the negotiation and throw in his lot with the Ottomans. As regards Basra and Baghdad therefore, he pointedly ignored McMahon's retreat from his offer of 24 October, his answer not referring at all to what McMahon had actually written, but only to his oral message about a British subsidy or rent in respect of the two provinces:

> With regard to what had been stated in your honoured communication concerning El Iraq as to the matter of compensation for the period of occupation, we, in order to strengthen the confidence of Great Britain in our attitude and in our words and actions, really and veritably, and in order to give her evidence of our certainty and assurance in trusting her glorious Government [he wrote in a fine show of insouciant, open-handed magnanimity], leave the determination of the amount to the perception of her wisdom and justice.

About Syria he was utterly emphatic and more uncompromising than he had been so far. Echoing the language which Faruqi alleged he had held in Cairo, the Sharif declared:

> it is impossible to allow any derogation that gives France, or any other Power, a span of land in those regions.

What the regions exactly were was not clear, the Sharif speaking of 'the northern parts and their coasts'. If the French were to occupy those parts, they 'being neighbours to us will be the germ of difficulties and discussion with which there will be no peaceful conditions.' Indeed, such a situation 'may oblige us to undertake new measures which may exercise Great Britain, certainly not less than her present troubles'. This being the risk, the Sharif, exchanging the magnanimous for the minatory tone, '[did] not find it necessary to draw your attention to the fact that our plan is of greater security to the interests and protection of the rights of Great Britain than it is to us'.

Without asking for instructions, McMahon answered in a letter (dated 25 January 1916) which was vague and oblique in substance, and fulsome in manner. He '[took] note' of the Sharif's remarks about the *vilayet* of Baghdad which were to be given 'careful consideration' after the enemy's defeat. As for what he, in imitation of the Sharif, called 'the northern parts', his reply to the Sharif's assertions and threats was merely that

> nothing shall be permitted to interfere in the slightest degree with our united [i.e. British and French] prosecution of this war to a victorious conclusion. Moreover, when the victory has been won, the friendship of Great Britain

and France will become yet more firm and enduring, cemented by the blood of Englishmen and Frenchmen who have died side by side fighting for the cause of right and liberty.

The Sharif's letter of 1 January, addressed as it was to a great power, might have been considered truculent, or even insolent in manner. But McMahon did not think so. The Sharif's letter and messages, he reported to London by telegram, were 'of friendly and satisfactory nature'.[1] And it is with placation and flattery that he responded:

> We fully realise and entirely appreciate the motives which guide you in this important question, and we know well that you are acting entirely in the interests of the Arab peoples and with no thought beyond their welfare.

And again,

> In this great cause Arabia is now associated, and God grant that the result of our mutual efforts and co-operation will bind us in a lasting friendship to the mutual welfare and happiness of all.

When Chamberlain saw this exchange, he commented:

> Sir H. McMahon's 'gush' seems to me to lower British prestige and to be of a character to confirm the Grand Shareef in his impression that he is more important to us than we are to him.[2]

Against strictures of this kind, McMahon had a defence. It is best set out in a letter to Hardinge of 4 December 1915, in which he tries to refute the accusation that, in his dealings with the Sharif, he had neglected Indian interests:

> I found myself at the moment in the difficult position of having to give in great haste such assurances in respect to a nebulous state of affairs, both present and future, as would satisfy a somewhat nebulous community and prompt them into taking sides with us instead of the enemy.
> I had necessarily to be vague as on the one hand HMG disliked being committed to definite future action, and on the other any detailed definition of our demands would have frightened off the Arab.

In his letter of 24 October he had attempted to secure in Mesopotamia 'without mention of annexation...everything that annexation confers'; he had clearly been more cryptic than he had intended since Hardinge, Sir Percy Cox and the secretary of state for India had read various 'unintended' meanings into it. But whatever view was taken of his exchanges with the Sharif

[1] F.O. 371/2771, 16451, McMahon's telegram no. 70, Cairo 26 Jan. 1916.
[2] L/P & S/10/586, p. 540/1916, minute by Chamberlain, 17 Feb. 1916.

I do not for one moment go to the length of imagining that the present negotiations will go far to shape the future form of Arabia or to either establish our rights or to bind our hands in that country. The situation and its elements are much too nebulous for that. What we have to arrive at now is to tempt the Arab people into the right path, detach them from the enemy and bring them on to our side. This on our part is at present largely a matter of words and to succeed we must use persuasive terms and abstain from haggling over conditions – whether about Baghdad or elsewhere.[1]

McMahon's case, then, was that his engagements to the Sharif were mere words, and mere words can do no harm. This frivolous attitude did not sit well with the great responsibility of his office, and it was moreover utterly contemptuous of the Sharif and the Arabs. This attitude was shared by his principal advisers, Storrs and Clayton, and by Wingate at Khartoum. Clayton gave vent to it in a letter written at about the same time:

> India [he wrote to Wingate on 12 November 1915] seem obsessed with the fear of a powerful and united Arab state, which can never exist unless we are fools enough to create it.
> I don't for a moment deny the menace that would arise were such a state to be created as the Arabs dream of, but I shouldn't have thought that anyone could consider it within the bounds of practical politics and it will have to be our business to see that it does not ever become a possibility, owing to our backing one horse to the exclusion of the others.[2]

It is of course the case that McMahon's two letters of 24 October and 14 December which contain his promises, and which have to be taken together, offer almost nothing at all in the way of territory. But the vagueness and imprecision of their language, their cryptic and oblique manner, the rhetoric about the Arab caliphate and Arab freedom which they employed (for all of which he and his Cairo advisers were very largely responsible) combined to make McMahon's letters misleading and deceptive not only for their recipient, but for British officials and ministers as well, who were later to be quite at sea about their exact meaning and significance. Grey indeed was unwittingly prophetic when (in words quoted at the head of part 1) he minuted a despatch of McMahon's in February 1916:

> This Arab question is a regular quicksand.[3]

The fundamental objection to McMahon's methods was well put by Hardinge and by Hirtzel. The former, commenting on McMahon's letter to him of 4 December 1915, quoted above, wrote to Chamberlain:

---

[1] Hardinge Papers, vol. 94, pp. 356–7.   [2] Wingate Papers, 135/5.
[3] F.O. 371/2767, 20954/938, undated minute (c. 5 Feb. 1916) on McMahon's despatch no. 16, Cairo 24 January 1916.

Mysteries of the McMahon–Husayn Correspondence

When McMahon gave Irak away to the Arabs without reserve, I wrote very strongly to him in a private letter. He has replied in a very curious letter, recognizing the justice of our complaint, by implying that the negotiations are merely a matter of words and will neither establish our rights, nor bind our hands in that country. That may prove eventually to be the case, especially if the Arabs continue to help the enemy, but I do not like pledges given when there is no intention of keeping them.[1]

Hirtzel, for his part, when he saw the text of the Sharif's letter of 1 January and McMahon's answer of 25 January 1916 had this comment to make:

Altogether, these negotiations rest on a very insecure basis, and if we are not very careful we shall lay ourselves open to charges of bad faith from all parties.[2]

The Sharif's letter of 1 January 1916, as has been seen, McMahon found satisfactory. His telegram, however, said nothing about its intransigent tone regarding French claims in Syria. When, therefore, Nicolson read the full text of the letter at the beginning of February he was unpleasantly surprised and complained that McMahon had given no indication of its 'rather ominous language' on the subject. Hirtzel also was disturbed by the letter, holding that it was 'absolutely destructive' of the Anglo-French negotiations which were then afoot. He therefore suggested that the French should be told of the Sharif's attitude, so that the British might not be accused later of bad faith. Nicolson then told Cambon of the Sharif's views and recorded the French ambassador's reply in a note of 2 March 1916. Cambon, he wrote, did not take it very seriously and

remarked that the Shereef would not be an Arab if he did not say something of the kind. I told him that we had not yet communicated to the Shereef the proposals as to the northern limits as we intended to wait till we had received the consent of Russia.[3]

McMahon's letter to the Sharif of 25 January 1916 was the last in the correspondence to deal with territorial issues. The Sharif acknowledged it with a letter dated 18 February which began by stating that

its contents filled us with the utmost pleasure and satisfaction at the attainment of the required understanding and the intimacy desired.

[1] Hardinge Papers, vol. 121, p. 330, Hardinge to Chamberlain, 24 Dec. 1915.
[2] L/P & S/10/586, p. 540/1916, cited above.
[3] F.O. 371/2767, 39490/938; Nicolson's minutes of 5 Feb. on the Sharif's letter of 1 Jan. are in *ibid.* 20954/938, cited above; and Hirtzel's in L/P & S/10/586, p. 540/1916, cited above.

These words McMahon took to mean that the Sharif 'considers that negotiations are now complete and that time for action on his part has arrived'.[1] If the British side of the correspondence was, as Hirtzel said, distinguished by its 'disingenuousness', the Sharif, it must be admitted, was himself not exactly straightforward. Not only were McMahon's letters in no sense a treaty or a binding engagement, but, such as they were, they had settled nothing, rather had left everything hanging in the air. The Sharif's expression of pleasure at 'that attainment of the required understanding' is quite surprising, and in fact lays him open to a charge of equal disingenuousness. Holderness was thus justified in writing that

> As to disingenuousness, the Grand Sharif and his party cannot with decency cast this in our face. If we are disingenuous, much more are they. We are prepared, as I understand, to give them independence, in the sense of freedom from the Turk and other external powers and liberty to create an Arab Khalifate, if they will actively side with us. If they fail to carry out their side of the agreement, they cannot hereafter complain if we should say it was off.[2]

The temptation of the caliphate, together with McMahon's eager and deferential manner, may indeed be the explanation of the Sharif's behaviour. He may have felt that when the time came for serious negotiations, the vagueness of his correspondence with McMahon would have its uses, and that it would enable him to claim, and perhaps to obtain, much more than could be gained by detailed prior negotiation. This tactic explains, for instance, why in his letter of 1 January, he so generously leaves the amount of the rent which Britain was to pay him for Basra and Baghdad 'to the perception of her wisdom and justice.' It is at this juncture also that he suddenly recurs to the caliphate which had figured in his memorandum of 14 July 1915, but which he deprecatingly dismissed once McMahon had assured him (in his letter of 30 August) that the British government 'would welcome the resumption of the Khalifate by an Arab of true race'. In a letter to Mirghani dated 28 December 1915 he 'refers more definitely than in any previous communication', McMahon wrote, 'to the assumption by himself of the Khalifate'. What the Sharif actually said gives the reader vivid sense of his vaulting ambition, and his utter certainty that he was called upon to become the Caliph of all the Muslims:

> I had not claimed before to be the qualified chief of the Emirs (the Caliph) but I explained to them more than once that I was ready to extend my hand

[1] F.O. 371/2767, 40645/938, McMahon's telegram, Cairo 1 Mar. 1916.
[2] L/P & S/10/586, p. 705/1916, minutes by Hirtzel and Holderness, 23 and 25 Feb. 1916.

to any man who would come forward and take the rein of authority. I was, however, chosen in every quarter and even forced to take up the question of their future prospects.

He objects to the idea that his caliphate might be conditional on approval by the Muslims, including the Shi'ites of Mesopotamia:

> I can see no ground for making (further) conditions such as the universal agreement of the Emirs and tribes which were mentioned, especially the 'Shias', i.e. the Persians, who [he contemptuously declares] lack the necessary qualifications and every other right (to decide the question of the chosen Caliph of Islam).[1]

It is not surprising that with the letter of 18 February came an oral message from Abdullah asking for £3,000 'for myself for my scheme'; the scheme, the messenger explained, consisted in choosing a powerful committee of Muslims from the Arab countries which would offer his father the caliphate: 'The latter is aware but feigns ignorance of these measures'. If the British could be got to work for the Sharif in his quest for the caliphate, what a *coup* this would be! And Storrs indeed obliged, sending the money by return.[2]

Nicolson, it will be recalled, writing at the beginning of February 1916, said that the Sharif had not been told of the northern limits of the Arab state. In speaking thus, Nicolson was rightly assuming that these limits had been left undetermined in the correspondence with the Sharif, and implicitly referring to the statement in McMahon's letter of 14 December that a communication on the subject would be sent to him 'in due course'. It was to make such a communication possible that Anglo-French negotiations began at the end of 1915, and issued the following May in the Asia Minor agreement, commonly known as the Sykes–Picot agreement. On 8 March 1916 Nicolson wrote privately to McMahon in order to acquaint him with the progress of the negotiations:

> We have submitted the agreement to which we and France have come to in principle in respect of the northern limits of the future Arab State or Confederation of Arab States to Petrograd, and we are waiting for the views of the Russian Government on the subject. I may tell you privately that we have been obliged to do this, as the French claims extend considerably eastward beyond the limits of Syria proper...We then have to consider the question as to the manner in which to approach the Sheriff on the subject of boundaries and other matters.[3]

[1] F.O. 371/2767, 30674/938, McMahon's despatch no. 26, Cairo 7 Feb. 1916. The Arabic text of the Sharif's letter is not in the file; the translation sent by McMahon was done in Khartoum.

[2] F.O. 371/2767, 45855/938, McMahon's despatch no. 42, Cairo 29 Feb. 1916; F.O. 141/461, 1198/48, memorandum of Storrs, 11 Mar. 1916.

[3] F.O. 800/381, Nicolson Papers.

The Quicksand

It was Sykes who went to Petrograd in order to obtain Russian consent to the Anglo-French arrangements. On his return to London, he telegraphed to Clayton to ask him to send 'two Arab officers representative of intellectual Syrian Arab mind' with whom Picot might hold discussions about the boundaries of the Arab state in the framework of the agreement, and particularly about an outlet to the sea for the Arab state in Syria: 'Present French view', he told Clayton, 'is Syrian littoral (Palestine excluded) all blue under Tricolor'. Clayton, however, was not in favour of putting the Arabs in touch with Picot:

> Any agreement on main principles between Allies is all to the good, but to divulge it at present and to insist on any particular programme would, I am convinced, be to raise considerable feeling.

And again, more emphatically:

> I feel it would be most impolitic to raise now with Arabs Syrian question which is quiescent for the moment.[1]

The Sykes–Picot agreement was finally settled at the end of April 1916, and Cairo was immediately informed. The officials there insisted unanimously that the details should not be divulged to the Sharif. Thus Clayton telegraphed to the war office on 3 May:

> The present arrangement seems the best possible. It does not clash with any engagements which have been given to the Sherif and has the advantage of clearly defining our position vis a vis other parties.
> At the same time, I feel that divulgence of agreement at present time might be detrimental to our good relations with all parties and possibly create a change of attitude in some of them which would be undesirable just at present and would certainly handicap our intelligence work. It might also prejudice the hoped for action of the Sherif who views French penetration with suspicion. Although the agreement does not clash with our engagements to him, it is difficult to foresee the interpretation he might place on the two spheres of influence.
> Lapse of time, accompanied by favourable change in the situation, will probably render acceptable in the future what is unpalatable today.[2]

Again D. G. Hogarth, the director of the newly-established Arab Bureau writing to Captain Reginald Hall, the director of the intelligence division at the admiralty, on the same day, 3 May, thought that the agreement was 'remarkable' and, under the circumstances, the best that could be obtained: 'Sir Mark Sykes no doubt

[1] F.O. 371/2768, 70889 and 76013/938, telegram no. 287, Sykes to Clayton, 14 Apr., and Clayton reply, telegram no. 278, Cairo 20 Apr. 1916.
[2] F.O. 882/16.

achieved the utmost in persuading M. Picot to resign the eastern part of Syria with the chain of important inland Cities to independent Arab government, to leave Haifa to us, and to accept the internationalization of Palestine'. But he too was firmly inclined to let sleeping dogs lie:

> At the same time the conclusion of this Agreement is of no immediate service to our Arab policy as pursued here, and will only not be a grave disadvantage if, for some time to come, it is kept strictly secret. Early in the course of our negotiations with the Arab Independence Party it appeared as if we might be called upon at any moment to define precisely the policy of the Allies, as a condition of any anti-Turkish action by the Sherif of Mecca: but that necessity has not been realized and seems unlikely to arise. The Sherif, while receding neither from the claims which he put forward last autumn for the inclusion of the whole of Syria with Palestine up to lat. 37° N., [in] the area of Arab Independence, nor from his avowed hostility to French penetration, has dropped all discussion of geographical limits since the beginning of the current year, and has promised Arab action at an early date without making our agreement about his claims in any way a condition preliminary. Therefore, as regards him at any rate, it has become our policy to remain uncommitted in the matter of boundaries and to give him no cause to think that we are in any better position than we were to define these. For any definition was bound to clash with claims on which he has laid stress.[1]

As may be seen from the course of the negotiations as set out above, Hogarth describes with perfect accuracy how matters stood at the time when he was writing his letter. But his statements become rather hazardous when he asserts that 'it has become our policy to remain uncommitted in the matter of boundaries and to give him no cause to think that we are in any better position than we were to define these.' There is no evidence at all that such a policy was discussed, let alone agreed or authorized. If it was a policy, then the decision to adopt it must have been taken privately by the officials at Cairo. But in these Arab affairs, it was not the first time that this had happened.

As may have been expected, McMahon made himself the echo of his officials' view. On 4 May, he telegraphed:

> Although there is nothing in arrangement agreed between France and Russia and ourselves as defined in your telegram that conflicts with any agreements made by ourselves or assurances given to Shereef and other Arab parties, I am of opinion it would be better if possible not to divulge details of that arrangement to Arab parties at present.
>
> Moment has not yet arrived when we can safely do so without some risk of possible misinterpretation by Arabs.[2]

[1] F.O. 882/14.
[2] F.O. 371/2768, 84855/938, McMahon's telegram no. 329, Cairo 4 May 1916.

As these documents therefore show, the Cairo officials had no doubts about the compatibility of the Sykes–Picot agreement with what they had said to the Sharif. But then what they had said was so vague and ambiguous that it was compatible with almost anything. The documents also show that it was their deliberate decision to maintain this ambiguity, and to avoid for as long as possible telling the Sharif how things stood exactly. And in this decision Grey acquiesced.[1] There is no record of his having consulted anyone before doing so. This, then, is the explanation why 'the further communication' promised in McMahon's letter to the Sharif of 14 December 1915 was never sent.

If there was thus an element of mutual bluff between the Sharif and McMahon, there was also a great deal of ignorance and self-deception on the part of the latter and of his subordinates. To take one example, in his telegram of 26 January which described the Sharif's letter of 1 January as friendly and satisfactory, McMahon reported that at the Sharif's (verbal) request he was providing his messenger with a letter of introduction to the Idrisi ruler of Asir.[2] It will be recalled that Clayton's intelligence paper of 6 September 1914, so important in getting Kitchener to initiate the war-time contacts with the Sharif, unhesitatingly affirmed that Ibn Saʿud, the Sharif and the Idrisi were combining 'with a view to throwing off the Turkish domination and working towards an Arabia for the Arabs'. It did apparently not strike anyone as ironical that the Sharif should now require the good offices of the British in approaching the Idrisi. Again, another paper on 'The Politics of Mecca' produced by Lieutenant T. E. Lawrence of the intelligence department in January 1916, showed great credulity about the power and influence of the Sharif. Lawrence's paper declared that relations between the Sharif and the Idrisi had improved: for this there was no evidence, and if the Sharif's request for an introduction meant anything, it meant that there had been no friendly contact between these two parties who had, not so long ago, been involved in hostilities. The Sharif, the paper continued, had close relations with the Imam of the Yemen and looked upon him 'as the person to carry out his ideas' in that country: here again there is no evidence to support these assertions, and the Imam's subsequent record, when he stood by the Ottomans till the end of the war, in fact belies them. The Sharif was also, the paper affirmed, in touch with the so-called Mad Mullah of Somaliland 'and has pressed on him the same counsel of

[1] *Ibid.* Grey's telegram no. 371, 6 May 1916.
[2] F.O. 371/2771, 16451, McMahon's telegram no. 70, Cairo 26 Jan. 1916, cited above.

inactivity, pending directions how he may best act in conformity with the general lines of Arab politics'. Needless to say, the Mad Mullah never paid any heed to the Sharif or to 'the general line of Arab politics.' On all these issues, the Aden authorities were well informed, but Lawrence clearly ignored, or was ignorant of, this authoritative source. His paper included a section on 'The Sherif's Methods' which added a mysterious and romantic touch to the story: 'He send his orders and suggestions – and in the flux of Arab politics the latter are always the more potent – by letter, unsigned and unsealed. They are en clair, and if the country is quiet are carried by messengers of importance. In secret missions to the Arabs of Syria, or to CONSTANTINOPLE he uses women to carry his letters'. This worthless concoction based mostly on the assertions of the Sharif's messenger the high commissioner solemnly sent under cover of a despatch to the foreign secretary.[1] To say that all this information was hopelessly unsound is not to rely on hindsight. For, as has been seen, both the India office and the government of India questioned at the time the reliability of the information emanating from Cairo. And in this particular instance, Oliphant, who was at the foreign office, and dependent like everyone else on the appreciations provided by Cairo, shrewdly minuted McMahon's despatch: 'I am inclined to think that this account is somewhat partial and highly coloured'.

In trying to persuade Hardinge that his way of dealing with the Sharif's demands was harmless, indeed beneficial, McMahon appealed to the viceroy's concern for the Mesopotamian expeditionary force: 'The safety of our Baghdad force', he wrote in his letter of 4 December 1915, cited above, 'requires both Arab and camel to be friendly. It seems to me worth a few persuasive words and a little money to get this result if one can'.[2] Exerting his best efforts, McMahon came up with a scheme which he thought would much weaken Ottoman forces in Mesopotamia. In a telegram of 21 March 1916, he suggested sending Faruqi and Aziz Ali al-Misri to Mesopotamia where they would 'win over' the Arabs in the Ottoman army. But, wrote McMahon, they 'demand for themselves and Arab military element...some definite assurance of British policy towards Arabia.' They would be, explained McMahon, 'tolerably content' with the assurances given to the Sharif. In a telegram of the following day, drafted by Grey and amended by Kitchener,

---

[1] F.O. 371/2771, 30673/16451, McMahon's despatch no. 25, Cairo 7 Feb. 1916: Lawrence is recorded as the author of the report on a copy in F.O. 141/461, 1198/39.

[2] Hardinge Papers, vol. 94.

McMahon was allowed to give such assurances if necessary, but he was to be careful not to go beyond the assurances already given to the Sharif.[1]

When Hirtzel saw this exchange of telegrams, he was disturbed. 'I was', he minuted, 'under the impression that we had negotiated an agreement with the Grand Shereef as the person generally recognized in western Arabia and Egypt as the Arab leader, and that he and we and nobody else were reciprocally responsible for the fulfilment of its terms. Sir H. McMahon's remark [that Faruqi and Misri would be 'tolerably content' with the assurances given to the Sharif] suggest that there are others to be separately satisfied and who may not accept what he has accepted'. A letter was sent to the foreign office drawing attention to this point. In consequence, another telegram, drafted by Oliphant, and approved by Nicolson, by the India office and the war office was despatched to McMahon. The telegram, reproducing almost verbatim the language of the India office letter, was despatched on 5 April to Cairo. The telegram pointed out that the Sharif had repeatedly purported to speak on behalf of all the Arabs; while there was no clear evidence whether this claim accorded with the facts, it had not been questioned by the British government: 'If the claim be well founded it is a matter for consideration', the telegram went on, 'whether individual assurances should be given to other and ex hypothesi less responsible Arabs'. If McMahon, the telegram concluded, had not already given these assurances to Faruqi and Misri, he should bear this point in mind.[2] The point which Hirtzel made was elementary. If, as the Cairo officials maintained, the Sharif was the spokesman of all the Arabs, then they should not have been so eager to give 'assurances' to others. Since they were ready to do so, we may suspect that they would have involved themselves in yet more ambiguous declarations and equivocal promises.

In the meantime, the commander of the Mesopotamian expeditionary force, Sir Percy Lake, had indicated his scepticism as to the usefulness of Faruqi and Misri and his refusal to allow them into Mesopotamia. This evoked a curious response on McMahon's part. When making his original suggestion McMahon had in mind, it will be recalled, the possibility of large-scale desertions from the Ottoman army to be brought about by these two agents. But he now completely changed his position and claimed that Lake's refusal

[1] F.O. 371/2767, 54229, McMahon's telegram no. 204, Cairo 21 Mar., and Grey's no. 215, 22 Mar. 1916.
[2] L/P & S/10/586, p. 1076 b/1916, Hirtzel's minutes and letter to foreign office, 28 Mar.; F.O. 371/2767, 54229, telegram no. 262 to McMahon, 5 Apr. 1916.

would disturb the Arabs and diminish their confidence in British assurances. In any case, it had not been intended for Faruqi and Misri to pass over the Turkish lines; rather their simple presence in Mesopotamia was thought 'to afford Arab element in Turkish army much required guarantee of unity of interest and good faith and materially assist in establishing good local relations'. How this was to be done was not specified: 'our agents would have to be given free scope in their choice of means'.

This telegram evoked a scathing memorandum to Grey which Chamberlain wrote out himself on 3 April:

> I do not find this telegram very easy to understand.
>
> The decision to which it refers is that El Faruki and El Masri should not proceed to Mesopotamia. As it now appears that Sir H. McMahon never contemplated that they should pass over to the Turkish lines (as was supposed here) it is not clear of what use he thought they could be. It is not believed that either of them have any influence in Irak. How was 'practical use' to be made of them there?
>
> 'An impression is gained', Sir Henry telegraphs 'that there is visible limit to the patience of those in whom we have raised feelings of expectation'. This is the severest criticism I have seen of Sir H. McMahon's policy. *He* raised the expectations. We have given assurances by his mouth much wider than we at home intended; we have given money and arms and promised more. The Shereef has done nothing, and we are now to be told by Sir Henry that it is we who fail to fulfil the expectations we have raised! Will Sir Henry ever realise that there are two sides to a bargain and that the Shereef has his part to play and that it is now 'up to' him [the Shereef] to make the next move?
>
> What does he mean by 'continuing to give all guarantees short of definite action'?
>
> He has given guarantees as already stated in excess of our intentions. He safeguarded French freedom of action in Syria but not ours in Mesopotamia. But by his declarations we hold ourselves bound and there has been no suggestion that we should secede from them. If he only desires to repeat himself, he has authority to do so, but does he mean that he is to give further assurances, and if so what?
>
> 'The Turks and Germans are exploiting our inaction'. What action did Sir Henry lead the Arabs to expect beyond the grant of money and arms? What was his authority for promising other action than this? We have done our part. It is surely time that the authorities in Egypt realised that we are as necessary to the plans of the Grand Shereef as he is to ours. I have a very uncomfortable feeling (supported by a passage in, I think, the last letter but one from the Grand Shereef) that Egypt has given him the impression that we need him more than he needs us.[1]
>
> This is not the fact if his schemes are to materialise, and in any case it is a very unfortunate impression to leave on his mind.
>
> I am very uneasy about the whole handling of the question by Egypt.

[1] Chamberlain may have been referring to the Sharif's letter of 1 Jan. 1916, in which he writes: 'I do not find it necessary to draw your attention to the fact that our plan is of greater security to the interests and protection of the rights of Great Britain than it is to us'.

As usual, Grey passively responded to pressure. He ordered that McMahon should be told that his difficulty about assurances was not understood and reminded that 'the sole question is whether and when the Arabs will do their part'. A telegram in this sense was sent to him, also on 5 April.[1]

It may have seemed, at first sight, rather impatient of Chamberlain to tax McMahon with not insisting that the Sharif keep his side of the bargain. For did not the Sharif say in his letter of 18 February that he had sent his son Faysal to raise a rebellion in Syria, while his son Ali, operating from Medina, would occupy the Hijaz railway? And was he not therefore justified in stating that this 'beginning of the principal movement' was to be taken as 'a foundation and a standard to our actions'? These confident assertions were based on the Sharif's hope and expectation of a rising in Syria which he would lead. There is evidence to show that he was encouraged in this hope by the promises of some Arab officers and notables in Damascus which were probably conveyed to him through his son Faysal who passed through Damascus on his way back from Constantinople in the autumn of 1915. One Arab chronicler has stated that on this occasion Faysal met secretly a small, ostensibly representative committee composed of Yasin al-Hashimi, chief of staff of the 12th division then stationed in Syria (it was his name which Faruqi invoked when he first arrived in Cairo), who spoke on behalf of the *'Ahd* party – a small secret group of Arab officers – General Ali Rida al-Rikabi, who represented another small secret group, known as the *Fatat* party; shaykh Badr al-Hasani, who was said to speak on behalf of the *ulama*, and who told Faysal that these 'supported his father in his rising against the Turks, to save the nation from their tyranny and oppression'; Nasib al-Atrash, a Druze chieftain who declared that the Druzes would be the first to support the rising; and Shaykh Nawwaf al-Sha'lan, son of Nuri al-Sha'lan, paramount chief of the Ruwala tribes who spoke not only on his own behalf, but as representing the Arab tribes in Syria. All these are said to have assured Faysal of their readiness to take action against the Ottomans.[2] Yasin al-Hashimi, in particular, is said to have declared: 'We ask for nothing, we need nothing, for we have

---

[1] F.O. 371/2768, 62377/938, McMahon's telegram no. 232, Cairo 1 Apr., and telegram to him no. 263, 5 Apr. 1916 (drafted by Nicolson on Grey's instructions). Chamberlain's memorandum is with these papers.

[2] Amin Sa'id, *Asrar al-thawra al-'arabiyya al-kubra wa ma'sat al-sharif Husayn* [Secrets of the Great Arab Revolt and the Tragedy of Sharif Husayn], Beirut [c. 1960], pp. 55-7. This work is a new edition, containing additional material, of vol. 1 of the same author's The Great Arab Revolt, published in Cairo in 1934, to which reference was made above.

everything. You only have to lead us and to march in the vanguard.'[1]
On the strength of these assurances, the Sharif and his sons meeting
at Ta'if in December 1915 decided to rise against the Ottomans. They
also decided that Faysal would go back to Damascus to settle
details, and that Ali would go to Medina to organize a rising of the
tribes there.[2] As has been seen, the Sharif told the British of these
decisions in his letter of 18 February 1916. He also felt confident
enough to send in March a minatory telegram to Enver Pasha
demanding a general pardon for the political prisoners whom Jemal
Pasha had arrested and tried for treason in Syria, together with
autonomy for Syria, and that the sharifate of Mecca should be made
hereditary in his house.[3] The Sharif and his son Abdullah (who
seems to have been the chief instigator of these events) no doubt
reasoned that they could not possibly lose. Either the Ottomans
would give in, and the Sharif would become at a stroke the leader
of the Arab world; or they would refuse, and he would lead a
rebellion in Syria and the Hijaz which would enjoy the mighty
support of the British empire. It is thus not surprising that, with
such beguiling prospects before him, the Sharif should have thought
the exact settlement of boundaries a secondary issue to be attended
to in due course, when the whole of Arabia and the Levant were
at his feet.

If this was the calculation, then the Sharif had a great disappointment in store. When the time for action came, none of the Damascus
conspirators proved ready to act, and their grandiose talk of a rising
in which the army, the Druzes, and the beduins would join, turned
out to be mere talk and bombast. There has survived a letter
addressed by one of the conspirators, Nasib al-Bakri, to the Sharif
which indicates both the extent of the plan and its flimsy foundations. The letter, dated 9 March 1916, was written from Medina,
where Bakri had stayed behind, having come in the entourage of
Enver and Jemal Pashas when, accompanied by Faysal, they visited
Medina in late February. Bakri reports that he had discussed with
Ali, the Sharif's eldest son who (as will be recalled) had been sent
to Medina by his father, 'the programme of the caliphate and the
establishment of its foundations', and that the latter had asked him
to give the Sharif an account of their deliberations. If the Ottoman
government acquiesce in the Sharif's demands, Bakri argues, their
money and arms should be taken and a force should be fitted out

[1] Amin Sa'id, *The Great Arab Revolt*, vol. I, p. 109.
[2] Amin Sa'id, *Secrets*, p. 57.
[3] Amin Sa'id, *The Great Arab Revolt*, vol. I, p. 110.

and sent to Damascus where Faysal would remain. The force, which would be double what the government had requested, would wait in Damascus for the proper opportunity when it might be used in a movement against the Ottomans on the pretext that their conduct of the war was leading to th loss of Muslim areas. Bakri is here no doubt referring to the Russian offensive in Eastern Anatolia which led to the capture of Erzerum. If, on the other hand (Bakri went on), the government procrastinated in replying to the Sharif's demands, then the Sharif should not insist, but should await a suitable opportunity for a rising, justified by the government's disregard of the rights of the Hijaz, and its disrupting of Islamic unity. If, finally, the government refused the Sharif's demands outright, which Bakri thought remote, then Faysal would have to come back from Damascus, leaving the movement without a head.

Bakri admits that the military leaders who had taken part in the conspiracy had been moved away from Syria. But the movement, he assures the Sharif, still exists: 'However,' he goes on, 'owing to present circumstances which are known to Your Highness, we have not been able to effect anything or to meet any of the leaders or the principal men. We therefore thought it necessary, myself and His Highness Faysal, to renew any old connexion we may have had with any leader or person whatever'. Bakri had therefore secretly assembled Druze chiefs in his home, where they met Faysal and swore mighty oaths that they were ready and waiting for a sign from the Sharif. But, declares Bakri, they made it a condition that Faysal should make peace between them and the beduin tribes (with whom they had a traditional enmity) and that all the latter should also join the movement. Bakri goes on to relate that Nuri al-Sha'lan, the powerful beduin chief – from whose son Nawwaf Faysal had received promises of support the previous autumn – now came to Damascus, summoned by Enver Pasha. He sent Faysal a message to the effect that he was still of the same mind and determined to keep his word, but that since the government was now strong, it was advisable not to meet, but to wait for thirty or forty days in order to see what the government would do and what its situation would be.

It was fairly clear from all this that the conspiracy organized the previous autumn was now falling apart, but Bakri put on a bold front and told the Sharif that he hoped that 'in a short while our affairs will develop as had been anticipated, and that all the forces [in Syria], whether beduin or Druze, civilian or military, would act in unison to raise high the standard of the Arab caliphate. It should also be apparent to Your Highness', Bakri insisted, 'that the failure of our society to act and the dispersal of some of its members has in no way affected our programme; on the contrary, all this has only served to increase our energy and our eagerness to proceed with the contemplated action.'[1]

As became clear very soon, Nasib al-Bakri was only whistling in the dark. The Druzes, the beduins, the civilians, the military all remained absolutely quiescent. Even Yasin al-Hashimi, whose potent name Faruqi had invoked, and who had been ready to make such large promises to Faysal, continued to serve the Ottomans faithfully until the end of the war. As late as 1918 he was approached by an emissary of Faysal's – now established at Akaba – with a request that he should join the Sharifian cause. But he refused saying that he was engaged on military duties which he could not abandon – he was then the commander of an Ottoman division stationed at Tulkarm in Palestine.[2] The Sharif's discomfiture soon became known to Cairo. An oral message accompanying a letter of 29 March 1916 from the Sharif to McMahon seemed to say – its language as usual was somewhat obscure – that if there was to be a rising in Syria, this had to be effected by means of a force sent from the Hijaz, 'because he [Faysal] had no hope in the Syrians starting any movement, not because of his mistrusting them, but because the notables and leaders of the party and those who steer the movement have all departed. We have therefore to depend on the natives of the Hijaz for starting the local movement or seizing the railway lines or any other movement'. With his letter, the Sharif sent a copy of what purported to be a letter to him from Faysal in Damascus which expatiated on the defeats which the Ottomans were sustaining at the hands of the Russians, but which contained very little about affairs in Syria. The letter, however, ended: 'Nuri [Sha'lan] is here and we have made a sworn agreement and action is being taken; may God be our helper. Nothing can be done without money.'[3]

Very shortly afterwards, McMahon received another letter from the Sharif, dated 18 April. This letter constitutes the Sharif's final admission that all his grandiose plans were now in shambles:

[1] The letter is reproduced as document no. 17 in Sulayman Musa (ed.), *al-Thawra al-'arabiyya al-kubra: watha'iq wa asanid* [The Great Arab Revolt: Documents and Records], Amman, 1966, pp. 48–51.
[2] Amin Sa'id, *Secrets*, pp. 258–9.
[3] F.O. 371/2768, 88001/938, McMahon's despatch no. 88, Cairo 25 Apr. 1916, enclosing letter of 29 Mar. from the Sharif.

Were it not for the eight Firkas (divisions) of Turkish troops in those districts[1] [Syria] they would have risen and done their duties long ago. They are then unable to be the first to rise, and the rising must start from here first, and as soon as we rise up we will lay hold on the railway line from Medina, and then advance gradually upon Syria. Then they (Syria) will be able to rise up.

The letter contained one quite misleading statement. The Sharif said that

we have done all that is in our power to destroy the railway line which connects Syria with the Hijaz...

This was presumably a reference to the activities of his son Ali round about Medina. But Ali was certainly unable then or later to cut the railway or to dislodge the Ottomans from Medina where they remained undefeated until after the armistice of Mudros, and where the Ottoman commander in fact refused to surrender to such a craven and contemptible foe.

The Sharif's letter also contained a surprising, not to say outrageous, suggestion. Having asserted that his troops had cut the Hijaz railway at Medina, the Sharif went on:

It will be absolutely necessary therefore that a sufficient number of British troops should land at a convenient point which it may be possible to reach, start from that point and occupy the railway line connecting Syria with Anatolia...

This, he eloquently pointed out, would

make it easy for our friends in Syria to rise up with their followers who expect relief to come to them from the eyes of needles on account of their sufferings owing to the transgressions which are known to you.

The Sharif expatiated further on the utility and importance of a British landing in Syria:

Moreover we find it necessary that the British troops should take up a point from which it should be easy for them to begin operations as we have already, in order to seize the railway line, and this will facilitate the advance of the British troops on Irak and the advance of the Russian troops from Erzerum to Erzinjan.[2]

It is not clear whether McMahon appreciated the absurdity of these suggestions which required that a British expeditionary force should

---

[1] It would be interesting to know what Arabic word the Sharif used here for 'districts', but the original of his letter was not sent to London, and the file has only the translation done in Cairo.

[2] F.O. 371/2768, 95498/938, McMahon's despatch no. 104, Cairo 10 May 1916, enclosing the Sharif's letter of 18 Apr. 1916.

effect the very rising in Syria which Faruqi had promised would not only make such a force unnecessary but would actually bring the Ottoman empire to its knees. In any case, there is no record of anyone, whether in Cairo or at the foreign office, pointing out that if British troops were to fight the Ottomans in Syria, then it was quite supererogatory to have engaged in this long-drawn-out correspondence and have held out the splendid prospect of the caliphate etc. to the Sharif of Mecca.

But the Sharif had more pressing matters to attend to than to advise his British ally on grand strategy. The minatory telegram which he sent to Enver when he thought that he could rely on a rising in Syria, together with the activities of his son Ali in the Medina region, had aroused the suspicions of the Ottoman government. Jemal Pasha sent his deputy commander Fakhri Pasha together with reinforcements for the garrison at Medina, and the Sharif must have feared that the government was getting ready to suppress him.[1] Faysal later told T. E. Lawrence that he advised his father to delay taking action, but 'Abdullah (whom Faisal calls Mifsud [sic. It may be that *mufsid* (mischief-maker) is meant]!) told his father that Faisal was afraid, and the revolt was ordered for June.'[2] Faysal, as is notorious, disliked and was jealous of his elder brother, and these feelings may have dictated his language on this occasion. For it may well be that the Sharif now felt so compromised that he had no option but to declare a rebellion against the government – however inauspicious the circumstances – and hope that the British would come to his rescue.

This, of course, was far removed from the great expectations with which he and the British had begun. But the Sharifian cause had been advocated so strongly by the Cairo officials, they had put so much of themselves in it, that it veritably became their cause. Thus, within days of the beginning of the Sharif's revolt, Kinahan Cornwallis of the Arab Bureau, who became and remained one of the staunchest partisans of the Sharifians, was explaining how it was imperative, now that the rebellion had started, for the British to support Husayn by launching a great attack in Sinai.

> We have helped him [he wrote to Hogarth on 21 June 1916] to start his rebellion and it is just as necessary to us as it is to him that we should see him through. His local outbreak is nothing but the effects of its failure on our operations in the east will be very great. We seem to have a great chance

[1] Amin Sa'id, The Great Arab Revolt, vol. 1, p. 115.
[2] F.O. 882/6, Lawrence's diary, 2–5 Dec. 1916 when he was with Faysal behind Yenbo, cited above.

now of strengthening our position both in Mesopotamia and the Canal by making such a show of force in Sinai as to prevent the Turks from sending an expedition south. It is true that we haven't the troops in Egypt now, but we ought to get them.

...The War Council should be made to realize the importance of its connection with our armies in Egypt and Mesopotamia and that speedy action now will save a great deal in men and money later on. Action from Sinai would be a quite sufficient menace to the Turks.[1]

Clayton, again, in an undated memorandum which must have been written at the end of 1916 or the beginning of 1917 gave quite a new version of the reasons for which the Sharif's movement had seemed so important:

The main factor that recommended the Sherif's revolt was that whether it succeeded or failed our military commitment would be small and we should be able to counteract by diplomacy alone the evil effect in Eastern eyes upon British prestige caused by the evacuation of Sinai the retreat from Ctesiphon the retirement from Lahej and the evacuation of Gallipoli.

This was indeed a far cry from his memorandum of 11 October 1915 where nothing less than the collapse of Ottoman power in the Hijaz, the Levant and Mesopotamia was anticipated. But in this later memorandum too, Clayton was extravagantly enthusiastic about the results of the Sharif's rebellion:

The Sherif's revolt has shattered the solidarity of Islam, in that Moslem is fighting against Moslem. It has emphasised the failure of the Jehad, and endangered the Khalifate of the Sultan. The gravity of this blow to Turkey can be estimated by the furious protest of pro-Turk Moslem elements. The intrigues of the Committee of Union and Progress and of German Orientalists have been to a large extent counteracted.

The agreement carries on and completes our policy in Arabia, as exemplified in the agreements with the Hadramaut, Oman, Muscat, Koweit and with Bin Saud. With the last named, it gives Great Britain a band of influence running across Arabia from Red Sea to Persian Gulf as a bar to the progress of hostile activity and penetration, it has rendered pro-British a large body of anti-Turk sentiments in Turkish Arabia, Syria and Mesopotamia and it has impaired the loyalty of the Arab divisions of the Turkish army. Its effect is continuing and even should the Sherif only succeed in holding out until peace is declared it will be found to have had a cumulative effect which may influence greatly the final situation.[2]

Almost every appreciation in this report can be shown to be either exaggerated or fanciful or mistaken. But Clayton's most egregious error perhaps was to compare what he called the 'agreement' with the Sharif – by which he can only have meant McMahon's letters

[1] F.O. 882/4.   [2] F.O. 882/4.

to Husayn – with the precise and businesslike instruments which had hitherto regulated British relations with the rulers of the Arabian peninsula. These agreements or treaties never gave rise, during their currency, to the misunderstandings, disputes, accusations or self-accusations which McMahon's confused and maladroit productions have engendered and still, even now, continue to engender.

PART II
THE FLY IN THE
FLY-BOTTLE

To show the fly the way out of the
fly-bottle.
> WITTGENSTEIN,
> *Philosophical Investigations*

4. Husayn Interprets McMahon's Promises, 1916–17

Having come to the end of his long, involved and inconclusive negotiations with the Sharif of Mecca, Sir Henry McMahon, in a private letter to Sir Edward Grey, uttered a veritable *cri de cœur*:

> In dealing with the Arab question, I feel at times somewhat bewildered at the numerous agencies who have a hand in it.[1]

Anyone who has followed the complications, ambiguities and equivocations which the previous chapter has attempted to unravel will sympathize with the high commissioner's bewilderment. His sentiments were echoed over a year later by a junior member of the foreign office, Harold Nicolson who, at the request of the secretary of state, was asked to write a memorandum 'showing exactly under what obligations we are to the Arabs and to our Allies with regard to Turkey'. Nicolson, as will be seen, found it by no means easy to comply, since exactitude was precisely what did not distinguish British obligations towards the Sharif.

> The above observations as to our commitments to the Sherif [Nicolson wrote towards the end of his paper] are tendered with some diffidence, as the matter has been dealt with through many and varied sources, and it is a little difficult to be sure that the papers in the Department represent the whole of what actually passed.[2]

Yet at the time when these 'commitments' – to use Nicolson's words – were being entered into, the authorities in London seem to have had little doubt as to what they entailed. For them, they meant no more than that in the Levant, Aleppo, Hama, Homs and Damascus would be the nucleus of an Arab state, the exact boundaries of which were to be determined by negotiation with France. This assumption appears quite clearly from the course of their discussions with Picot. These discussions are summarized in letters which Lieutenant-Colonel A. C. Parker of the war office[3] (who was a member of the committee set up to negotiate with Picot) addressed

---

[1] F.O. 800/48, Grey-Papers, McMahon to Grey, Cairo 19 Apr. 1916.
[2] F.O. 371/3044, 153075/1173, memorandum by H. Nicolson, 13 July 1917.
[3] On whom see Kedourie, *The Chatham House Version*, p. 20.

to Clayton. From these letters it is clear that what Picot was pressed to concede in Syria (all of which he claimed for France) was precisely the territory of the four towns. Thus, at the third meeting of the negotiators on 21 December 1915,

> M. Picot said that after great difficulties he had obtained permission from his Government to agree to the towns of Aleppo, Hama, Homs and Damascus being included in the Arab dominions to be administered by the Arabs under French influence.

Another point which the negotiators assumed was that Palestine – however delimited – had not been committed in the negotiations with the Sharif. In his letter of 23 November 1915 reporting the discussions which took place at the first meeting with Picot, Parker reported that with regard to the French claim for 'the whole of Palestine'

> it was pointed out that the question of Jerusalem, Nazareth and other places was a question apart, and affected various other nations including Russia: and that this question could not now be gone into.[1]

Again, the results of the discussions with Picot as at the end of January 1916 were summarized in a memorandum which Sir A. Nicolson sent to Grey with a minute which said:

> The four towns of Homs, Hama, Aleppo, and Damascus will be included in the Arab state or Confederation, though in the area where the French will have priority of enterprise...[2]

Finally, in the formal note from Grey to Cambon setting out the details of the so-called Sykes–Picot agreement, Grey declared that

> since His Majesty's Government recognise the advantage to the general cause of the Allies entailed in producing a more favourable internal political situation in Turkey, they are ready to accept the arrangement now arrived at, provided that the co-operation of the Arabs is secured, and that the Arabs fulfil the conditions and obtain the towns of Homs, Hama, Damascus and Aleppo.[3]

These successive passages, with their cumulative reiteration of the names of the four towns, are significant. They show that the

---

[1] Parker's letters are conveniently reproduced in the 'Summary of Historical Documents from the Outbreak of War between Great Britain and Turkey, 1914, to the Outbreak of the Revolt of the Sherif of Mecca in June 1916', dated 29 Nov. 1916, which was prepared by the Arab Bureau and sent to London enclosed with Cairo despatch no. 360 of 20 Dec. 1916. A print of the 'Summary' is in F.O. 371/6237, E155/4/91; Parker's letters are at pp. 22–4 of this print.

[2] Cab. 37/142/6, print of Nicolson's minute, 2 Feb. 1916.

[3] Grey to Cambon, 16 May 1916, reproduced in *Documents on British Foreign Policy 1919–39*, series I, vol. IV, 1952, p. 245.

authorities in London firmly believed that any scheme for dealing with the fate of the Ottoman empire had to include the provision that these towns should be part of an Arab state. They believed that this had been promised to the Sharif – but not absolutely: as Grey put it, the Arabs on their part had 'to fulfil the conditions'. It was however matter for self-congratulation that the French had been induced to endorse McMahon's promise of October 1915.

But would the Sharif fulfil the conditions? When Grey wrote his letter, Husayn had not yet declared himself against the Ottomans, and it was impossible to say whether in fact he would do so at all. When, at last, in June 1916, Husayn rose against his own government, this was because he felt himself compromised beyond recall, and was afraid that the Ottomans might succeed in getting rid of him. For all the elaborate plotting that had gone on for the previous eighteen months, his rebellion was a hasty ill-organized affair. The report of Colonel C. E. Wilson, governor of the Red Sea province in the Sudan who was sent to act as British representative in Jeddah, is clear and explicit on this point. In a despatch dated 7 July 1916, i.e. less than a month after the Sharif's rising, he wrote:

> The Grand Sherif appears to have started his revolt without sufficient preparation and somewhat prematurely; he has entered into a struggle which is taxing his powers to a high degree and intrigue among his own people, which appears to be rampant, does not tend to make matters easier for him.[1]

Clayton was very surprised by the rising. The French minister in Cairo reported him as saying that no precise agreement had been made with the Sharif, either about the aid to be given to him or about the benefits to be vouchsafed to him or about his territorial demands. According to the minister, as Clayton understood the matter, the Sharif

> had simply been promised by England that his own independence from Turkey, and that of the other great chiefs of Arabia would be recognized. It would seem also to have been agreed that so far as Mesopotamia was concerned, where British economic interests require the establishment and proper functioning of a stable and well-organized government and administration, special treaties would be made between England and the chiefs of the region. As regards the territories which would eventually belong to France, it would seem to have been agreed that the Arabs would have to reach an agreement in due course directly with us.[2]

[1] F.O. 371/2774, 144050/42233, enclosure with McMahon's despatch no. 168, Cairo 24 July 1916.
[2] A.E., Guerre 1914–18, vol. 1681, Defrance's despatch no. 232, Cairo 24 June 1916; and vol. 1682, despatch no. 248 Very Confidential, Cairo 5 July 1916.

The Fly in the Fly-bottle

If allowance is made for Clayton's natural desire to persuade the French minister that French interests had been fully taken into consideration in the negotiations with the Sharif, his cursory report of the state and import of these negotiations was essentially sound and accurate. But as was to be seen shortly, a great gap existed between a view such as Clayton's and the pretensions of the Sharif. In fact, no sooner had the Sharif burned his boats with the Ottomans, than he started to claim the caliphate and to allege (through Abdullah) that in correspondence with him the British had promised to back him up in making good his claim. He was, in other words, producing his own gloss on the exchanges with Cairo. While on a visit to Jeddah on 29 June 1916, Cornwallis was told by Faruqi that the Sharif designed to assume eventually the titles of 'King of the Arabs' and 'Calipha of the Moslems', and that he also intended to invade Syria.[1] Wingate in Khartoum, for his part, curiously enough, would not believe that Husayn had such ambitions:

> It is quite a mistake [he wrote to a correspondent at the end of August 1916] to say that the Sherif is striving to seize the Khalifat for himself – he knows full well that the Khalifat must fall to the authority who is most acceptable to the Sunni Moslems throughout the world, and until he can lay claim by his success to the acclaim of united Islam, he is not likely to advance any such personal theory.[2]

What Wingate does not seem to have envisaged is that the Sharif should require the British so to act as to obtain for him 'the acclaim of united Islam'. This is what Storrs discovered the following October. While on a visit to Jeddah, he was approached by Abdullah with a request that the British government should refer to his father privately and preferably also publicly as *amir al-mu'minin* (commander of the faithful), since this would produce a good effect on the Arabs: 'they had even ventured to hope for some such communication from His Majesty the King', Abdullah declared. Since this title was one which pertained exclusively to a Caliph, Storrs quickly pointed out that if by this Abdullah envisaged the title of Caliph, then he must know that the British government had repeatedly declared that the caliphate was exclusively an affair for Muslims; how could they accept the Sharif as Caliph when not even in the Hijaz was he recognized as such? Storrs was no doubt literally correct, but was it not also the case that the British government had also declared their approval of the Arab caliphate, and hinted

[1] F.O. 882/4, Cornwallis's report, Cairo 8 July 1917.
[2] P.R.O. 30 57/91, Kitchener Papers, Wingate to Lord Middleton (a former secretary of state for India), Khartoum 26 Aug. 1916.

broadly that they hoped to see the Sharif assume the dignity? And did they not back their statements to the tune of three thousand pounds which Storrs himself had sent to Addullah for this very purpose? It is most likely therefore that Abdullah sensed in Storrs's seemingly forthright protestations a hint of bad faith. In any case, he did not persist in his request, but asked instead that his father should be addressed as 'Majesty' and 'king'. This request also Storrs turned down.[1]

Two weeks after Storrs's visit, without prior consultation or indeed warning, Husayn was suddenly proclaimed king of the Arab Nation. From Ruhi's account, it appears that Abdullah was the directing brain behind the operation. He ordered his 'tools' in Jeddah to spread rumours that a large number of Powers, including Britain, France and Russia, had acknowledged Husayn's new title; he dictated the terms of a congratulatory telegram which the merchants and notables of Jeddah had to send to his father, and he instructed the telegraph office to refuse telegrams couched in different terms. On the evening of 30 October, a meeting was held at the municipality in Jeddah in which was read the text of a petition sent to Husayn by the 'Ministers, notables, natives and Ulema' of Mecca. The terms of this document, which was no doubt inspired if not composed by the Sharif, are significant in showing the extent of Husayn's religio-political ambitions. In this intentionally ambiguous document Husayn is grandiloquently celebrated as king of the Arabs and the saviour of Islam because he is the descendant of the Prophet who is reported to have declared that 'the ruler should remain amongst [his own tribe, Quraysh]':

> You are Qoraysh and indeed you are the chosen of Hashim [Muhammad's great-grandfather] and we confess, in the day of judgment, between the hands of God, the Exalted, that we know not of any Muslim amir who is more pious than you...and that no one but you can manage our affairs according to God's wishes.
>
> .   .   .   .
>
> Oh, our Lord and the Saviour of Islam from the hands of its hypocritical enemies, we praise God who honoured us by you and caused the hosts of God to be victorious by your blessedness, and the spirituality of your forefather, may prayer and peace be upon him. We will be drawn nearer unto God if we fight against whomsoever fight against you and we are the friends of those who are your friends...
>
> .   .   .   .
>
> Verily we recognize His Majesty our lord and master El Hussein Ibn Ali, as our King, we the Arabs, and he will act amongst us according to the book of God the Almighty and the laws of His Prophet, may prayer and peace

[1] F.O. 882/5, Storrs's Jeddah diary, 17 Oct. 1916.

be upon Him. We, therefore, take the oath of obedience, loyalty and sincerity to him in secret and in open and we consider him also to be our religious leader until all the Moslem world be of one opinion concerning the Islamic Caliphate...[1]

When Abdullah was asked the reason for such a sudden action, his reply was that there was no suddenness in the matter 'as we were negotiating secretly about the matter with His Majesty's Government', while Husayn himself declared that the British had addressed him 'as the Caliph which is a higher dignity than Kingship', and that therefore it was natural for him to think that he did not have to seek approval before assuming the lesser dignity.[2]

Sharifian protestations may been partly the outcome of a genuine misunderstanding. As has been said in the previous chapter the British had discovered that Faruqi was in the habit of reporting to the Sharif interviews with British officials which had in fact not taken place. McMahon now explained, in a despatch following Husayn's assumption of the kingship, that a telegram from Faruqi to the Sharif in the previous July had stated that 'I have discussed with the High Commissioner regarding the title of King of the Arabs and I saw him willing to admit this idea with the greatest facility.'[3] This, according to McMahon, was a fabrication. What was not a fabrication, and what gave the Sharif some ground for assuming British acquiescence, and even approval, was that money had been sent to Abdullah specifically to further the cause of his father's caliphate. Again, the language in which the Sharif was addressed was perhaps ambiguous, but also suggestive in the extreme. A note in the Arab Bureau papers admits that the 'secret negotiations' to which, as has been seen, Abdullah referred, related to this despatch of funds, 'and he would have us believe', the note went on, 'that he was justified in inferring, and that in fact he did infer, from them that H.M.G's repeated public announcements regarding the Caliphate were not to be taken too seriously'.[4] It is not clear why the writer of this note should be so incredulous, since actions, it is commonly accepted, are louder than words. Again, the ambiguity of Cairo's language could legitimately have made the Sharif read more into the letters he received than their writers intended. McMahon, at any rate, seems to have sensed, too late, that such could be the case, and in

[1] F.O. 371/2782, 233117/217652, 'Note by Hussein Effendi Ruhi', 30 Oct. enclosed with C. E. Wilson's despatch no. 12, Jeddah 31 Oct. 1916.
[2] F.O. 371/2782, 242002 and 242008/21765, Wilson's despatches nos. 14 and 15, Jeddah 5 and 11 Nov. 1916 respectively, enclosing transcripts of telephone conversations with Abdullah and his father, and a letter from the Sharif dated 4 Nov.
[3] F.O. 371/2782, 242008/217652, McMahon's despatch no. 334, Cairo 21 Nov. 1916.
[4] F.O. 882/5, fo. 104.

a letter to Hardinge (now once more permanent under-secretary at the foreign office) was anxious to deny that his messages could have been misunderstood. He was, he told Hardinge, shocked at Husayn's assumption of the kingship, and he went on:

> Whatever references the Sherif may make to terms and expressions used in previous, and what would appear to be imaginary, communications, the records of our correspondence will, I am sure, prove not only that we have abstained from saying anything that implies the future existence of any supreme ruler in Arabia, but also that geographical terms that in English may have been loosely expressed by such words as Country, Kingdom, Empire etc., have in the Arabic version been expressed by the interchange of such words as 'mamlakah', 'doulah' and 'hukumah' none of which necessarily imply the existence of a king. Also in certain important passages the term Arab Government has been expressed in the plural.[1]

If, as McMahon thought, the Arabic words he cited did not 'necessarily imply', neither on the other hand did they necessarily rule out, the existence of a king. But one of the words he cited does 'necessarily imply the existence of a king', since 'mamlakah' signifies 'realm' or 'kingdom'. McMahon was here most probably relying on Storrs's imperfect Arabic. Storrs, it will be remembered, had translated 'mamlakah' as 'possessions' in a note of May 1915 addressed to the high commissioner.[2] The inaccuracy is here characteristic: the Arabic words for 'kingdom' and 'possessions' have a common root, but while 'kingdom' is *mamlaka*, 'possessions' is *amlāk* (sing. *mulk*). But it is of course not true that Cairo had 'abstained from saying anything that implies the future existence of any supreme ruler in Arabia', for (to mention only one of the many declarations) on Kitchener's instructions the hope had been expressed – to be subsequently made even more emphatic – that 'an Arab of true race will assume the Khalifate at Mecca or Medina', and a Caliph is the supreme ruler not only in Arabia, but over all Muslim lands. Again, in the same message, Storrs on his own responsibility had added: 'It would be well if Your Highness could convey to your followers and devotees, who are found throughout the world, in every country, the good tidings of the freedom of the Arabs'. This particular statement, we may recall, was read by the emissary of the Damascus officers – and therefore no doubt by the Sharif as well – to mean that the British had 'given their consent to the Sherif's establishing an Arab Empire', and led to the formulation of the demands set out in Abdullah's note of 14 July 1915.[3]

[1] Hardinge Papers, vol. 27, McMahon to Hardinge, Cairo 10 Nov. 1916.
[2] F.O. 141/461, file 1198 cited in part 1 above.
[3] Faruqi's statements as recorded in Clayton's report, in part 1 above.

The Fly in the Fly-bottle

But the Sharifian claims had an even more solid justification. As Holderness of the India office now pointed out in a letter to the foreign office, all through the correspondence with McMahon the Sharif purported to speak for the Arabs as a whole, and insisted that he was only the transmitter and executant of their demands. This claim, which had no basis in fact, was never once questioned: indeed the British authorities had discussed with him in great detail the limits of the Arab state, and negotiated with him what he regarded as an alliance.[1] If this was so – and unquestionably it was so – then the Sharif could reasonably consider himself entitled to British acquiescence in – if not approval of – his proclamation as king of the Arabs and prospective Caliph.

Husayn did not easily give up his ambitions. Great Britain and France objected to the title king of the Arabs and agreed – after lengthy debate – to recognize Husayn as king of the Hijaz. To have so easily and so soon after his revolt achieved a regal rank was no doubt a great achievement, but Husayn did not mean to confine his rule to this province. Syria and Mesopotamia were what he coveted. Early in 1917, the Damascene notable Rafiq al-Azm wrote to Husayn suggesting that emissaries should be sent to other Arabian rulers to gain their support for the movement. Husayn turned the suggestion down as derogatory, sternly reminding his correspondent of his pre-eminent position: 'You have doubtless heard', he told Rafiq al-Azm, 'of those Syrians who were present on the day when I was proclaimed King, and who proclaimed me as such on behalf of their countrymen, the people of Aleppo and Irak.'[2]

But it is clear that in Husayn's mind the kingship of the Arabs was only a preparation for the caliphate in which he hoped to succeed the Ottomans. The lengths to which he went in order to wrest a public acknowledgement of his claim from the British were remarkable in their pertinacity and ingenuity. Thus Husayn began a memorandum of 10 April 1917 to Wingate, the new high commissioner in Egypt, as follows:

> When Great Britain repeatedly and plainly declared, by writing, her desire to restore the Arab Caliphate, and when I found that the affairs of the Ottoman Government were being handled by the Turanians, in such a manner as to deprive all the Moslems of the world of that happiness and welfare of which only a small part was being enjoyed by the Moslems of Turkey, I thought that to leave things as they were and abstain from negotiations, instead of remedying the situation that would be

[1] F.O. 371/2782, 221869/217652, India office to foreign office, 4 Nov. 1916.
[2] F.O. 141/736, Husayn to Rafiq al-Azm, 16 Mar. 1917.

pleasing to God and to the Moslems, was a crime upon which I need not dwell.[1]

The import of these words is clear. The Arab caliphate of which the British were said to have 'repeatedly and plainly' desired the restoration was, in Husayn's view, no mere 'spiritual' caliphate, but a political power which would replace that exercised by the Ottomans. And for the first time in these Sharifian negotiations, someone in Cairo realized that Husayn meant one thing by the caliphate, while the British who had so insouciantly dangled it before his eyes meant quite another. The writer of an unsigned Arab Bureau paper dealing with Husayn's memorandum cited Kitchener's hint in the message of October 1914, and its emphatic amplification by McMahon the following August, and added:

> it should be noted that to the Sharif, both temporal and spiritual power are included in the word 'Caliphate' and a much wider meaning has therefore been given by him to the extracts quoted above than was intended by H.M.G.[2]

It is probable that the Arab Bureau paper came to Wingate's attention, but the covering despatch with which he forwarded Husayn's memorandum to London is utterly silent on this point, Wingate merely saying that Husayn was 'evidently' referring to Kitchener's message and McMahon's letter.[3]

Neither did Wingate try to explain to Husayn the divergence between his view of the caliphate and that of the British, and a little while later Husayn obstinately returned to the subject. On 28 July 1917, Husayn explained to Wilson and Lawrence what the latter, in a long and curious report, called 'his dogmatic position'. The report is a jumble of glib assertions about Islam and the caliphate, some inaccurate and others fanciful; it shows that Lawrence was hopelessly out of his depth in these matters, and that he was easily gulled by Husayn. It will be recalled that when Storrs visited Jeddah in October 1916, Abdullah asked that the British government should address Husayn as *amir al-mu'minin*, and that Storrs, rightly apprehending that this was tantamount to his recognition as Caliph, refused. Husayn now disclaimed to Wilson and Lawrence any interest whatever in the caliphate, but he obliquely hinted that he would like the title of *amir al-mu'minin*:

[1] F.O. 371/3048, 92524/22841.

[2] F.O. 882/12, fos. 237–40, 'Notes on the statement forwarded under cover of a letter from the King of the Hejaz to H. E. The High Commissioner, dated 10.4.17'; the 'Notes' bear the date 23 Apr. 1917.

[3] F.O. 371/3048, 92524/22841, McMahon's despatch no. 89, Cairo 21 Apr. 1917.

The title Emir el-Muminin was one that a sincere Moslem might adopt. It made no pretence to any succession to the prophet, but was objectionable politically, on account of the word 'Emir'. It was no use being Emir, without the power or pretence of giving orders, not to a sect, or a country or two, but to the Moslem world. The main divisions of Shia and Sunni would unite under this title, but the smaller sects, and especially the alien congregations in India and Africa, would resent the implications of authority, as, no doubt, would the Great Powers.

Lawrence, obviously una ware that the office of Caliph and that of *amir al-mu'minin* were one and the same, went on the declare his 'personal opinion'

> that the title of Emir el-Muminin would not be repugnant to him, if it came not as his assumption but as the homage of his followers. It is generally used by the tribes today from Kaf to Kunfida, and will apparently be acceptable to the Sheikhs of urban Syria. His present objection, that it involves the power of command in Islam, does not hold good; since it is as fair to interpret it only in a doctrinal sense.

Husayn, though he misled Lawrence and Wilson by alleging that Caliph and *amir al-mu'minin* were distinct and different, yet insisted that the office meant exercise of power over the whole Muslim world. But in his own comment Lawrence seems to give credence to the erroneous but widespread view that the power in question was not political power pure and simple, but power, as he puts it, 'in a doctrinal sense'. In the despatch with which he sent Lawrence's report, Wilson has a passage remarkable for its utter confusion, and its naive acceptance of Husayn's arguments and pretentions:

> I agree with Captain Lawrence's concluding remarks and as he [i.e. Husayn] appears opposed to a Caliphate on principle I am of opinion that his ultimate aim is to be recognized as Emir el Muminin by the Moslem world generally and not as Caliph as I have previously thought, but his object all along has I think been the same viz. to be the recognized Head of Islam.[1]

In saying that Husayn's aim was to be 'the recognized Head of Islam', Wilson clearly assumed that Husayn wanted to be some kind of Muslim Pope. For this reason, he had been prepared to defend Husayn's assumption of kingship over all the Arabs. He had recommended, to start with, a 'qualified approval' of Husayn's action on the ground that 'the title sounds more than in fact it really is or is intended by the Sherif to be', its main purpose being, in

---

[1] F.O. 882/12, fos. 265–9; Lawrence's report was published in *The Arab Bulletin* and reprinted in T. E. Lawrence, *Secret Despatches from Arabia*, 1939, ch. XXIV. For the relation between the titles 'caliph' and *amir al-mu'minin* see T. W. Arnold, *The Caliphate* [1924], 2nd ed. 1965, *passim*.

his view, to cut away the ground from under the feet of those who were saying that Husayn was delivering the Muslim holy places to the British.[1] A few days later, he reinforced his argument about the harmlessness of the Sharif's action:

> As stated in my Despatch No. 14 of the 5th November, I think that the title sounds more than in fact it really is or is intended by the Sherif to be. He cares far more in my opinion about eventually becoming Caliph than for any temporal title...[2]

Wilson, thus, had in common with the Cairo officials a dangerous tendency to believe that large claims made by the Sharifians did not matter, since they were, at most, mere grandiloquence. As the passage just quoted also shows, he suffered under the misapprehension that the caliphate was not itself a temporal office. This misapprehension could occasion a great deal of mischief since Wilson was from 1916 to 1919 the chief British military and political representative in the Hijaz, and since he also believed that Husayn's claim to the caliphate was 'the greatest asset which we would obtain from his revolt'.[3] He was therefore singularly incapable of appreciating the extent of Sharifian ambitions, and of dealing with them in a firm, unambiguous manner. His presence in Jeddah, far from helping Husayn to appreciate the political realities, was likely to increase his illusions, to promote false expectations on his part, and thus in the end to make for misunderstanding and recriminations.

Wilson's attitude to the Sharif's claims and pretensions is exemplified by a report of his written in September 1916 in which he asserted that the Sharif 'is no Petty Chief and his revolt, if made successful, will be of the greatest possible advantage to the BRITISH EMPIRE now and in the future'. His view was that the British government

> has certainly encouraged the revolt and therefore must bear the responsibility for it, and whatever promises of assistance, definite or indefinite, were or were not made, it is obvious that the Sherif and the Arab Chiefs do not consider that the support they expected and relied on, and which the Sherif understood was promised him, has been given.

Wilson's tone in this report makes clear that in this he agreed with the Sharif.[4]

The Sharif indeed was not slow to complain that promises of help

---

[1] F.O. 371/2782, 242002/217652, Wilson's despatch no. 14 of 5 Nov. 1916, cited above.
[2] F.O. 371/2782, 242008/217652, Wilson's despatch no. 15 of 11 Nov. 1916, cited above.
[3] F.O. 141/736, Wilson to Arab Bureau, 7 June 1917.
[4] F.O. 882/4, fos. 326–31, Wilson's 'Notes on the Military Situation in the Hedjaz', 11 Sept. 1916.

which the British had made were not kept. When he rose, he was able to overpower the small Ottoman garrisons in Mecca and Ta'if, and, with the help of the British navy, to take control of Jeddah; he could do little else against the Ottoman government. He attributed his inability to cope with the Ottoman troops or to occupy Medina to the failure of the British to cut the Hijaz railway which he declared had been promised to him. He first made this allegation in a letter to McMahon of 25 August 1916, repeated it shortly afterwards to Wilson, and returned to it in the memorandum of April 1917 to Wingate mentioned above. His refrain was that if the railway had been cut as 'decided in the contents of the Agreement', he would have been able to take Medina and to reach the vicinity of Damascus. There had of course been no such promise, but neither McMahon, nor Wilson, nor Wingate, said anything to refute this baseless allegation.[1]

The Sharif was also prompt in asserting territorial claims which he claimed had been agreed in the correspondence with McMahon. Very soon after his rebellion, the British government sanctioned a subsidy to Husayn of £125,000 a month. When he was informed of this, he replied in his letter of 25 August:

> Your Excellency knows that the above-mentioned monthly pay of £125,000...will be deducted from the amount which we left to the justice of Great Britain to decide for our deficient Government which is under Great Britain's guardianship and protection during her occupation of Basra and Iraq.

The Sharif was here referring to his letter of 5 November 1915 in which he had agreed to a British occupation of Basra and Baghdad 'for a short time' in exchange for 'a suitable sum paid as compensation to the Arab Kingdom for the period of occupation'. On foreign office instructions, it will be recalled, McMahon answered that the Basra and Baghdad called for 'much fuller and more detailed consideration than the present situation and the urgency of these negotiations permit'. The foreign office had also instructed McMahon to tell the Sharif that the postponement of the negotiation over the two *vilayets* did not preclude 'eventual consideration of a perpetual lease or any other reasonable financial proposal'. McMahon, it will also be recalled, chose not to include this point in his reply but, as he told the foreign office, 'verbally hinted something to this effect to the Sharif's messenger'. We do not know either what exactly he said to the messenger, or what the messenger

[1] F.O. 371/2775, 195007 and 213985/42233, and F.O. 371/3048, 92524/22841 respectively for the Sharif's letters of 25 Aug. and 9 Sept. 1916, and his memorandum of 10 Apr. 1917.

reported to the Sharif. When the Sharif now recurred to his views of the previous November, McMahon refrained from answering his allegations, and contented himself with saying to the foreign office somewhat cryptically that the 'reference to future monetary compensation for our occupation of Basrah and Iraq needs no further comment at the present moment.'[1] Was this because his earlier 'verbal hint' had been more compromising than he cared to reveal? The episode at any rate underlines the perils of diplomacy by messenger. The Sharif recurred in a veiled manner to this point in his memorandum of 10 April 1917 in which he asked for increased subsidies. He threw out vague hints about British obligation to protect his boundaries, based on what he called 'the agreement', and affirmed that 'To this end a subsidy was assigned to us, the causes, object and duration of which were well known'.[2] Since the claim made in his letter of 25 August 1916 was never answered, let alone rebutted, Husayn was naturally assuming that the British government had accepted his view of their mutual obligations. This was not in fact the case, and silence on the earlier occasion thus proved damaging and dangerous. Continued silence, when the Sharif now reiterated his claim, was even more impolitic. For, in the meantime, Husayn had tried to assume the kingship of all the Arabs, and had come up against the strong objections of the Allies. They had compelled him to accept the lesser title of king of the Hijaz. This was done in order to limit Husayn's pretentions and confine them to a limited territory. To allow unchallenged the claim that money paid by the British now was only an advance on what was due to him as rent for Basra and Baghdad was implicitly to acquiesce in what had so shortly before been explicitly rejected, namely that Husayn was king of more than the Hijaz. Yet neither Wingate nor the foreign office suggested that Husayn's interpretation of past British actions and statements should be challenged.

In his memorandum, Husayn declared that he was only alluding to the question of the boundaries promised to him because he had already addressed Wilson on the subject, and because his secretary, Fu'ad al-Khatib, had discussed the matter while on a recent visit to Cairo. The latter had indeed expounded his master's views at some length in a conversation with Hogarth on 12 February 1917. Fu'ad al-Khatib put forward no claim on the basis of alleged British promises. Rather he argued that Husayn could not be expected to confine himself to the Hijaz which was too small and too poor. His

[1] F.O. 371/2775, 195007/42233, McMahon's despatch no. 219 Secret, 11 Sept. 1916.
[2] F.O. 371/3048, 92524/22841, cited above.

future kingdom, as he envisaged it, had to comprise 'Syria and Damascus'. Responding to Hogarth's questioning, Fu'ad al-Khatib added that 'it was, of course, understood that Basra and all the lower river region must remain under Great Britain. As for Baghdad and Mosul, he hoped they would have Home Rule under the King in Damascus'. Hogarth questioned Fu'ad al-Khatib on two other subjects. The first concerned the Jews in Palestine:

> Fuad declared Arabs and Jews understood one another now, and that there would be no friction. The alliance between Jews and the C.U.P. did not hold in Syria. Fuad had evidently no idea that any special arrangement might be proposed for Palestine and contemplated it as an integral part of the Arab Kingdom. He stated that he was in relation with prominent Zionist and other Palestinian Jews and had full assurance of support from there.

The second, and more important, topic which Hogarth broached was that of the French. His interlocutor, he writes, betrayed no knowledge of any Franco-British agreement relating to Syria.

> I then recalled to him the old French interest in and ambition about Syria. Suppose the French still desired the Syrian coast? Fuad said at once that the Syrian interior, without the coast, would be of practically no value to the Arab Independent State. The King at Damascus, without command of Beyrout, was not a possible condition. Lebanon, too, was the 'heart of Syria'. I asked why he attached so much importance to Beyrout which is not the natural port of Damascus. He replied it was the port of all Lebanon, and also the place of origin and development of higher Syrian education and of Arab ideals. If the French must have something, let them take the coast northward from Junieh. Then the Arab State would have as ports Beyrout, Saida, Haifa and Jaffa.

The ambitions which Fu'ad al-Khatib was here describing had come to be expressed fairly soon after the Sharif's rebellion. From Jeddah in a despatch of 28 September 1916 Wilson reported Aziz Ali al-Misri as declaring that he and Abdullah would go to Cairo after the fall of Medina, and try to meet McMahon secretly 'on the subject of Syria and French [aims] there, with the idea of making a secret treaty between the British Government and the Sherif'.[1] Soon afterwards, the French military attaché in Cairo reported Captain Lawrence as saying to him: 'Abdullah will be talking to us about his future Arab kingdom which is to include Palestine and Syria. We will advise him to begin by taking Medina in the first place'.[2] It was not only the British who were apprised of these ambitions; the Sharifians took

[1] F.O. 371/2775, 205736/42233, Wilson's despatch no. 5, Jeddah 28 Sept., enclosed in McMahon's despatch no. 253, Cairo 6 Oct. 1916.
[2] Service historique de l'Armée, Papers of the French military mission to the Hijaz, 17N499, St Quentin to Brémond, no. 42 (107), Cairo 14 Oct. 1916.

no care to hide them from the French, whose interest in Syria they well knew. In conversation with Si Kaddour Ben-Ghabrit, a Moroccan dignitary whom the French government sent as a member of Brémond's mission to the Hijaz, Husayn and Abdullah referred to the establishment of an Arab government in Syria, and Abdullah in particular revealed '*la fougue de sa jeune ambition*' – as the French foreign minister put it – by speaking of the conquest of Syria and even of Iraq.[1]

We may suspect that in betraying no knowledge of the Sykes–Picot agreement in his conversation with Hogarth, Fu'ad al-Khatib was showing no more than a prudent discretion. For as early as October 1916, the main provisions of the agreement were well known in Syrian circles in Cairo: a Lebanese notable, Emile Edde, came back then from a visit to France with the details which had been given to him by the French politician Flandin.[2] It is highly unlikely that knowledge which was widespread in the Syrian community in Cairo would have remained hidden from Fu'ad al-Khatib, who was himself Lebanese. The reason why Husayn and Abdullah were so forthcoming about their ambitions, and why Fu'ad al-Khatib was so confidently explicit about Sharifian territorial demands we may gather from the penultimate paragraph of Hogarth's report where he said that he

> could detect a fixed belief, underlying Fuad's talk, that Great Britain would eventually use force, if necessary, to establish the Arab State against all comers: and he once said that, in the interior, the Arabs would even welcome a British Protectorate, if it was a necessary condition of freedom from other interference.

Of the existence of such a 'fixed belief' there is no doubt whatever, nor is it difficult to account for. It arose from the incautious and sometimes unauthorized language which was held to the Sharifians over a period extending from Abdullah's visit to Cairo in February 1914 until the receipt of his letter of July 1915; from the generally known fact that the Cairo officials were antagonistic to French claims in the Levant; and lastly perhaps from Faruqi's misleading reports to Husayn of which, as has been seen, the British were aware, but which they took no steps to expose or deny. The final paragraph of Hogarth's report indicates another reason for Sharifian confidence:

[1] A.E., Guerre 1914–18, vol. 1688, telegram from Fleuriau no. 1484, London 7 Nov. and telegram from minister of foreign affairs no. 3786, Paris 10 Nov. 1916.

[2] A.E., Guerre 1914–18, vol. 874, Defrance's despatch no. 423, Cairo 22 Oct. 1916. The French minister states in this despatch that he himself had not been informed of the provisions of the agreement.

The Fly in the Fly-bottle

The entry of the French Military Attaché into the room put an end to our conversation and I have not thought it well to resume it, for fear of giving Fuad an inkling that things are even now, not expected to turn out quite as the King of Hijaz and he himself forecast them.[1]

Hogarth's reticence here is characteristic of the attitude assumed by the Cairo officials towards Sharifian claims. As has been seen, they had urged that the details of the Sykes–Picot agreement should be withheld from the Sharif, and presumably Hogarth was now only following the same line of conduct. But Fu'ad al-Khatib's claim and expectations were incompatible not only with this agreement, but also with McMahon's letters to the Sharif of 24 October and 14 December 1915 which by definition could be assumed to be known to the Sharifians. For Hogarth timidly to refrain from recalling to a Sharifian official what they promised and – more pertinently – what they did not promise for fear of arousing disappointment, was to store up for the future dangerous misunderstandings and even more grievous disappointment.

In discussing boundaries with Hogarth, Fu'ad al-Khatib did not claim that Sharifian desiderata were justified by past British promises. But the case was otherwise with his master. Just as Husayn claimed that the British had undertaken to cut the Hijaz railway in order to facilitate his rebellion, and just as he professed to regard the British subsidy as part payment for his consent to their occupation of the Mesopotamian provinces which British troops were then engaged in conquering, so he also pretended that by his agreement with the British, the whole of Syria belonged to him. He made this claim in conversation with Wilson at the beginning of April 1917, accusing the British of going back on their promise and of being 'not perfectly open with him'.[2] But Husayn produced no document to prove his contention. Clayton was very puzzled by this claim:

I cannot make out [he wrote to Wilson] what the Sherif means by his interpretations of McMahon's letter. I have not yet succeeded in unearthing from the Residency files a copy of the original Arabic which was sent, but it is there somewhere and must be produced. I cannot imagine that any ambiguity can have produced the meaning which the Sherif has read into it and I can only think that, being very nervous, he is trying to do a bit of a bluff. His refusal to send extracts of the letters he quotes rather gives colour to this.[3]

The search in the residency files proved unavailing, and Storrs who had been sent on a mission to Basra was telegraphed to about them.

---

[1] F.O. 882/6, fos. 182–5, 'Future of Arab Movement' by D. G. Hogarth, 12 Feb. 1917.
[2] F.O. 882/12, fo. 212, Wilson's telegram, Jeddah 9 Apr. 1917.
[3] F.O. 882/12, fo. 215, Clayton's letter, Cairo 18 Apr. 1917.

He declared that the letters were in his file,[1] but they were not found. They remained in fact missing for many years, and since Husayn consistently refused to show British representatives the letters on which he was basing his allegations, the Cairo officials remained in doubt as to whether Storrs in his translations did not inadvertently say or imply something which had not been intended, and which enabled Husayn to make these large claims.

Such claims were repeated, albeit more circumspectly, by Abdullah and Faysal when Wilson saw them shortly after the interview with Husayn at the beginning of April 1917. Abdullah, Wilson reported, was 'obviously under the impression that Baghdad is to be incorporated in the Arab Kingdom'. Abdullah also gave his own – highly misleading – version of the British promises regarding Syria. He stated that the Sharif's claims had included Syria and that

> the High Commissioner had replied to the effect that the British Government had no objection to granting the Sherif's demands, but that the question of Syria could not be discussed as Great Britain could not interfere with her Ally France who had some interests in that country and that therefore nothing could be settled about [it] at that time.
>
> Abdullah stated that the Sherif considered that he had been promised the whole of Syria but on being asked admitted that this was not the case.

In falsely alleging that McMahon had said that 'the British Government had no objection to granting the Sherif's demands' over Syria, Abdullah was clearly probing the position in the hope that Wilson would, out of politeness perhaps, not object to such a claim, and that his acquiescence would later prove a useful argument. Faysal also had recourse to the same tactic:

> He frequently stated [Wilson also reported] that the majority of Syrians disliked the French and asked me whether I did not think that Great Britain would assist the Sherif to obtain the country. I replied that I had never seen the letters which had passed between his father and the High Commissioner but that I felt sure that if the Syrians did not want to be under the Sherif's rule we certainly would not force them to be; also that we entered into negotiations with the Sherif because he was the principal Arab leader with whom we could get into communication but we did not thereby acknowledge the Sherif as Ruler of all the Arabs.
>
> Faisal agreed with the above but stated that he felt sure that the vast majority of the Syrians would welcome the Sherif...[2]

---

[1] F.O. 141/825, file 1198, Wingate's telegram no. 32417, Cairo 19 Apr., and Storrs's telegram, Basra (which he had just reached) 2 May 1917.

[2] F.O. 882/16, fos. 233–6, 'Note on conversations with the Emirs Abdullah and Faisal', Wedj 1 May 1917.

Wilson's response on this occasion was firm and unambiguous. This was uncharacteristic both of his own attitude to Husayn and to Sharifian claims, and of the way in which Cairo usually conducted business with Mecca. It would have been much to the advantage of both sides if such clarity had been usually the rule in their written and oral exchanges. As it was, Wilson's language on this occasion remained exceptional. Naturally, the Sharifians did not care to recall it thereafter but neither did Wilson or other officials recur to it again. On the contrary, the next bout of Anglo-Sharifian negotiations was to be the occasion of new equivocation and misunderstanding.

5. Sykes, Picot and Husayn

These negotiations came about in consequence of new military developments. The first months of 1917 saw a British offensive in Mesopotamia which led to the capture of Baghdad early in March, and the beginnings of an attack on Palestine which was to lead to the capture of Jerusalem in December. The invasion of Palestine raised the issue of French rights there as they had been recognized in the Sykes–Picot agreement. The French were not tardy in claiming a voice in the administration of the territories about to be conquered. But the new prime minister, Lloyd George, was unwilling to share with the French the fruits of victory. As he told Lord Bertie, the British ambassador in Paris, in April 1917, the French would have to accept a British protectorate in Palestine: 'we shall be there by conquest and shall remain'.[1] But there could be no question then of openly disowning the Sykes–Picot agreement, and at an Anglo-French conference held on 28 December 1916 the British had agreed that when the British troops entered Palestine, a French Muslim detachment would be associated in the operations, and a French political officer would be attached to the British commander-in-chief. In the event, it was Picot who was appointed French political officer. This agreement made necessary the appointment of a British counterpart to Picot, who would see to it that British objectives were safeguarded and French designs nullified. Sir Mark Sykes was chosen for this post. He was to be designated chief political officer, and the real significance of his appointment may be gathered from clause three of the document setting out the 'Status and Functions of Chief Political Officer and French Commissioner' which the foreign office issued to Sykes. This clause declared that 'The General Officer Commanding will communicate with the French Commissioner through the Chief Political Officer and the French Commissioner will communicate with the General Officer Commanding through the Chief Political Officer'. Sykes was thus to interpose himself between Picot and the British commander-in-chief who, under military law, was naturally the ultimate authority in occupied enemy territory. What Sykes had to do was

[1] Lady Algernon Gordon Lennox (ed.), *The Diary of Lord Bertie of Thame*, 1924, vol. II, p. 123.

spelled out at a conference held on 3 April 1917 at 10 Downing Street at which were present Lloyd George, Lord Curzon (lord president of the council and member of the war cabinet), Hankey (secretary of the war cabinet) and Sykes himself. The two ministers, the cursory and reticent minutes tell us,

> impressed on Sir Mark Sykes the difficulty of our relations with the French in this region, and the importance of not prejudicing the Zionist Movement and the possibility of its development under British auspices. The attachment of a French Commissioner and of two French Battalions to General Sir A. Murray's force was a clear indication that the French wished to have a considerable voice in the disposal of the conquered territories...

Lloyd George, in particular,

> laid stress on the importance, if possible, of securing the addition of Palestine to the British area.[1]

It was then as a result of this decision that Sykes arrived in Cairo during April 1917, and was joined there by Picot. Earlier in the month, Jean Gout, of the *sous-direction d'Asie* at the Quai d'Orsay had written a memorandum arguing that French interests required that the Sykes–Picot agreement should no longer be kept a secret from the Syrians and from the king of the Hijaz. If the terms of the agreement were not divulged to them the Syrians, seeing the British advance in Mesopotamia, would begin to doubt the ability of the French to protect them, 'and like all weak men', would turn towards what seemed to be the preponderating power. Again, the Arabs who surrounded Husayn were lulling themselves with false hopes, and being unaware of their legitimate share in the Ottoman booty, dreamt of establishing anew the empire of the caliphs: 'When the reality will be suddenly unveiled to them, they will hold us responsible for the bankruptcy of their chimeras, and instead of working peaceably with them, we will have to act against them, perhaps even by military means'. It was bad for French influence, Gout declared, systematically to hide from those concerned the plans which had been made: 'The moment seems therefore to have come,' he concluded, 'when we should put the question to our English allies and, by agreement with them, to make known to the Syrian leaders and to the Melik of the Hedjaz what our aims are, what help we are offering, and what guarantees we are disposed to give them'.[2]

---

[1] Cab. 24/9, G.T. 372. Sykes's instructions are included in an appendix to the minutes, which also incorporate the text of the decision taken at the Anglo-French conference of 28 Dec. 1916.

[2] A.E., Guerre 1914–18, vol. 1694, memorandum by J. Gout, 5 Apr. 1917.

As events were to show, Gout proved remarkably prescient. Though there was shortly afterwards an attempt to dispel the illusions to which his memorandum referred, other illusions were subsequently fostered among the Sharifians, to dispel which the French had in the end to expel Faysal from Syria by force of arms.

The Sykes–Picot agreement, it will be recalled, was kept secret at the urging of the Cairo officials. It was they who now advocated that Husayn should be informed of its details. In a telegram of 27 April 1917, Wingate reported that Picot's arrival in Cairo was making Husayn anxious, that he had expressed a 'strong desire' to meet Sykes, and that the latter was going to Jeddah. Wingate considered it 'very necessary' that Husayn should 'be now informed of general lines of our agreement with France'. The foreign office acquiesced.[1] A few days before, Sykes and Picot had met three 'delegates representative of Moslem Syrian feeling' and explained to them the Anglo-French arrangements regarding the Levant and Mesopotamia. In reporting the outcome of these meetings Sykes claimed that these 'delegates' agreed on the following points:

(1) That they desired that Great Britain and France should be prepared to contemplate the establishment of an Arab State or confederation in an area approximating to Areas A and B [as described in the Sykes–Picot agreement].

(2) That for defence and protection such a state or confederation would be obliged to rely upon France and Great Britain.

(3) In return France and Great Britain should have a monopoly of exploitation, finance and political advisers in that state or confederation.

Further [Sykes went on], delegates agreed that for a new and weak state such as the Arab must be, Palestine presented too many international problems to assume responsibility for, but that in the event of the Jews being recognized as a millet or 'nation' in Palestine, they insisted that equal recognition must be accorded the actual population.

Sykes also declared that he had told these 'delegates' 'quite clearly and definitely' that

as regards Bagdad there could be no doubt that H. M. G. would reserve for itself the right to maintain a permanent military occupation, and insist that the local government would have to be of a kind sufficient to maintain law and order so that British commerce should not suffer; at the same time I did not know what form of Government H. M. G. would establish there.

Picot, for his part, informed his government that he had announced to the Syrians that France was the only Power to whom they should

[1] F.O. 371/3054, 86526, Wingate's telegram no. 464 Urgent, Cairo 27 Apr., and foreign office telegram no. 442, 28 Apr. 1917.

look for their liberation, and that 'no one here doubts any more that England has renounced any ambitions in Syria. Her partisans have abandoned the struggle'. But neither Sykes nor Picot disclosed to his respective government the identity of these so-called 'delegates', who chose them or in what manner they were chosen, or how binding their acquiescence was in the schemes which had been put before them. Yet another possibility of confusion and equivocation may be seen in Sykes's statement that a main difficulty in these talks

> was to manoeuvre the delegates, without showing them a map or letting them know that there was an actual geographical or detailed agreement, into asking for what we are ready to give them.[1]

Whether or not Sykes did obtain the acquiescence of the 'delegates' to the schemes he unveiled before them, what he and Picot had to say to them would undoubtedly have become generally known very soon in Cairo and in the Hijaz. So that what he would have to say to Husayn on his forthcoming visit would not be entirely unexpected. At any rate, Wingate obtained the approval of the foreign office for the language which he instructed Sykes to hold in Jeddah. Sykes was to 'reassure' Husayn about French aims in the 'interior of Syria'; but he was also to tell the king that his rule 'cannot be imposed upon peoples who do not desire it'; and, further, he was to 'make it clear that in Baghdad and district whilst desirous of promoting Arab culture and prosperity, we will retain the position of military and political predominance which our strategical and commercial interests require'. A letter which Clayton sent on the same day to Wilson at Jeddah repeats and amplifies Wingate's instructions. Sykes was to 'indicate gently' that special measures had to be taken as regards Baghdad where British military and political preponderence had to be ensured 'at any rate for a considerable time'. Sykes also was to point out 'what is an undoubted fact, viz: that the Arab movement as represented by himself, cuts no ice whatever in Mesopotamia, and that therefore it is quite out of the question to force it upon them.'[2] Though Wingate's instructions contained no new departure in British policy, yet they were unwontedly forthright and unequivocal. The question was whether Sykes would speak as clearly and as unambiguously as these instructions required him to do. The doubt arises because he was partial to grandiloquent phrases in addressing oriental personages, because he could not bring himself to treat someone like Husayn

---

[1] F.O. 882/16, Sykes's telegram to director of military operations, war office London, no. 18, Cairo 30 Apr. A.E., Guerre 1914–18, vol. 877, Picot's telegram no. 5, Cairo 2 May 1917.

[2] F.O. 882/12, fos. 241–4, Clayton to C. E. Wilson, Cairo 28 Apr. 1917.

seriously enough to warrant speaking to him plainly and precisely, and finally because, as will be seen, it is doubtful whether Sykes now believed that it was desirable or possible for a Power like Britain to aim at a 'position of military and political predominance' in Baghdad.

Wingate concluded his telegram by saying that if Sykes's visit to Jeddah proved successful, a second meeting with Husayn when Picot would be present might be arranged.[1] As is well known, Picot did subsequently join Sykes at Jeddah and did hold important conversations with Husayn. What his government wished Husayn to be told may be gathered from the instructions given to Si Mustapha Cherchali, an Algerian notable who was sent to take charge of French Muslim pilgrims in Mecca. Before Picot's forthcoming visit to Jeddah became known to them, the ministry of foreign affairs had suggested that Cherchali should make known to Husayn the French views on the future of Ottoman territories in Asia. He was to tell Husayn that on the Syrian coast it was necessary to have a 'special regime' under the 'direct supervision [*égide directe*]' of the French government, and that in the areas where the Arab element was dominant France would encourage the creation of emirates in Aleppo, Damascus, and Mosul, the rulers of which would have links with the king of the Hijaz, and who would engage to call exclusively on French advisers '*pour mener à bonne fin leur œuvre de civilisation*', and on French capital for the economic development of the country. 'As for Jerusalem and Palestine', the instructions went on, 'a *modus vivendi* which would ensure respect for all religions would be examined, and the Sharif will not be left out of the deliberations.'[2]

Sykes met Faysal at Wejh on 2 May and, as he reported in a telegram of 6 May 1917, 'explained to him the principle of the Anglo-French [agreement] in regard to Arab Confederation'. Sykes gave no details of his conversation but informed Wingate that 'Faysal accepted the principle after much argument and seemed satisfied'. Sykes then went to Jeddah where he had a meeting with Husayn on 5 May which lasted for three and a half hours. Again Sykes gave no details of their conversation, merely recording that he had 'explained the principle of the agreement as regards an Arab Confederation or State, in accordance with my instructions.' These instructions, it will be recalled, required Sykes to stress that the

[1] F.O. 371/3054, 87289/89526, Wingate's telegram no. 472, Cairo 28 Apr., and foreign office telegram no. 446, 30 Apr. 1917.
[2] A.E., Guerre 1914–18, vol. 1695, instructions to Cherchali, 1 May 1917.

British would retain in Baghdad 'the position of military and political predominance which our strategical and commercial interests require'. In his telegraphic report Sykes does not say whether he had drawn Husayn's attention to this important point. But there is reason to believe that Sykes, on this occasion at any rate, eschewed precision and plain-speaking. He told Brémond, the head of the French military mission at Jeddah, that it would be well if, while discussing Franco-Arab questions with Husayn, he could make generous concessions to the king (*il serait bon que le Colonel Brémond aborde ce sujet en étant très large au point de vue des concessions*) and not insist too much on precision, so as to allow these ideas to ripen in the head of the Sharif.[1] Sykes's estimate of the favourable outcome of his negotiations appears from the message which he asked to be conveyed to Picot, namely that 'I am satisfied with my interviews with Sherif Feisal and King of the Hijaz, both of whom now stand at the same point as was reached at our last joint meeting in Cairo with t.ie three Syrian delegates, and that as the King of the Hejaz stated he earnestly desired to see M. Picot, I took the liberty of fixing an interview for 19th May'.[2]

On 17 May, Sykes and Picot met Faysal at Wejh and they travelled together to Jeddah where the two envoys met Husayn on 19 May for a meeting which lasted for three hours. 'The interview', wrote Sykes, 'closed most inconclusively M. Picot being unfavourably impressed by the King.' A second meeting took place on the following day. At both meetings Faysal and Fu'ad al-Khatib were present, and Wilson came to the second meeting. At this meeting Husayn asked Fu'ad to read a declaration the gist of which, according to Sykes, was that

> His Majesty the King of the Hedjaz learned with satisfaction that French Government approved Arab national aspirations [,] that as he had confidence in Great Britain he would be content if the French Government pursued the same policy towards Arab aspirations on Moslem Syrian Littoral as British did in Baghdad.

On the same occasion Faysal gave the following message from his father to Sykes:

> We are ready to co-operate with France in Syria to the fullest extent and England in Mesopotamia but we ask for help from England with Idrisi and Ibn Saud without in any way infringing on their independence. We beg that

[1] Service historique de l'armée, Paris, section d'outremer, papers of the military mission to the Hijaz, 17 N 498, Brémond's telegram to Defrance no. 1440, Jeddah 7 May 1917.
[2] F.O. 371/3054, 93335/86256, Wingate's telegram no. 496, Cairo 7 May repeating Sykes's telegram from Jeddah of 6 May 1917.

Sykes, Picot and Husayn

Great Britain will endeavour to induce them to recognize the King's position
as leader of Arab Movement.[1]

As on his previous visit, Sykes gave no details whatever of what went
on between himself, Picot, Faysal and Husayn, the sole record of
the interviews which he furnished being a telegram which recorded
the statements quoted above.

The brevity of Sykes's report was to lead later to questions being
raised as to what exactly had been said during these meetings. But
unlike the meetings with Faysal and Husayn earlier in May, the later
meetings were reported at the time in some detail by some of those
present: by Picot himself, by Colonel Wilson, and by Fu'ad
al-Khatib. These reports make it possible to form an idea of the
course of the discussion, and of the meaning and significance of
Husayn's declaration quoted above. One issue which has aroused
much debate is whether Husayn was informed on this occasion of
the existence and tenor of the Sykes–Picot agreement, which, as has
been seen, both Wingate and Gout desired should be done. The
information which these reports provide will serve to settle this
particular issue. When Sykes went on his first visit to the Hijaz at
the beginning of May, Clayton wrote to Wilson in order to give him
some idea of Sykes's mission and of the line he was proposing to
take with Husayn. Clayton said:

> Sykes will explain to you exactly how matters stand in regard to the
> agreement with the French as represented here by Picot. It is too lengthy
> to explain in a letter, nor is it possible to do so without the aid of the map
> which Sykes will show you. I think when you see exactly how matters stand,
> you will think that they are a good deal better than we thought at one time,
> and it is not impossible that the Sherif may be rather relieved at finding the
> arrangement much more favourable than he had feared.[2]

From Clayton's language it is clear that Sykes took with him to the
Hijaz the details of the Asia Minor agreement. Picot, reporting to
his government on his discussions with Husayn, ended his account
by saying:

> In sum, the King now knows our agreements which has not upset him as
> much as had been feared.[3]

That the terms of the Asia Minor agreement were revealed to Husayn
at the first interview with Sykes and Picot is, finally, confirmed by

[1] F.O. 371/3054, 104269/86256, Sykes's telegram, Aden 24 May 1917.
[2] F.O. 882/12, fo. 241, Clayton to Wilson, 28 Apr. 1917, cited above.
[3] A.E., Guerre 1914–18, vol. 877, Picot's telegrams nos. 13–18, via Aden 24 May 1917.

the contemporary testimony of Fu'ad al-Khatib. He complained to Colonel S. F. Newcombe, head of the British military mission to the Hijaz, that

> no fresh information has been given the King as to the country's future except a hasty perusal and explanation (with little opportunity given him to think it over or criticise) of the Sykes–Picot agreement.[1]

Some three years later, Fu'ad al-Khatib emphatically asserted in conversation with Rashid Rida that Husayn had on that occasion been quite content with the terms of the agreement.[2] Finally, a memorandum by Sykes written in June 1918 gives further support to the contention that Husayn was well aware of the Sykes–Picot agreement. Sykes's memorandum was occasioned by a telegram from Wingate reporting that Husayn was asking through his agent in Cairo for the details of this agreement of which he professed to have just learnt from an article in an Arabic newspaper published in Paris in the French interest. In his memorandum Sykes firmly declared that Husayn 'has frequently been given the outline and detail of the agreement in question both by myself, M. Picot, Colonel Brémond and Commander Hogarth who was specially sent down for the purpose'. As he informed the Eastern Committee 'he was quite sure that the King of the Hedjaz had some months back, been fully informed of the Sykes–Picot agreement, and that he had now read it again in good Arabic and feigned indignation.'[3]

Husayn's declaration to Picot that 'he would be content if the French Government pursued the same policy towards Arab aspirations on Moslem Syrian Littoral as British did in Baghdad' was, then, clearly linked to the arrangements mooted in the Sykes–Picot agreement. In the agreement Baghdad (as well as Basra) formed part of the so-called red zone where Britain was allowed to establish such direct or indirect administration or control as it desired, or thought fit to arrange with the Arab state or confederation of Arab states. The same right was accorded to France in the so-called blue zone. These two zones, therefore, were meant to have a different regime from that of the areas designated 'A' or 'B' where an Arab state or confederation of states was to be set up. The reason for this difference in treatment clearly stemmed from the desire of the

---

[1] F.O. 882/16, fo. 134, 'Note by Sheikh Fuad El Khatib taken down by Lt Col. Newcombe' enclosed with Wilson's letter to Clayton, 24 May 1917.

[2] Kedourie, *The Chatham House Version*, p. 27, quoting Rashid Rida writing in *al-Manar*, vol. 33, 1933, p. 797.

[3] F.O. 371/3381, 107379/146 for Sykes's memorandum, and Cab. 27/24, Eastern Committee meeting 18 June 1918, where Wingate's telegram was discussed.

British and the French eventually to annex, or closely to control, the red and the blue zones respectively. The distinction between these two zones, on the one hand, and areas 'A' and 'B' on the other, in respect of administrative and political arrangements, was affirmed in a memorandum by Sykes and Picot as late as 17 May 1917, two days, that is, before their meeting with Husayn.[1]

The question then arises whether Husayn, in his declaration to Picot, was agreeing to the French annexing or closely controlling the 'Moslem Syrian Littoral' (whatever this meant), since this is what the British were entitled to do in Baghdad. The answer to this question, as will be seen, is bound up with Sykes's attitude to the agreement he had negotiated a year earlier, and to his views on what British policy should be in the red zone, and particularly in Baghdad. In spite of the joint memorandum with Picot which has just been mentioned, there is reason to believe that he inclined rather to treat the red zone – or at any rate Baghdad – very much like the areas reserved for the Arab state. The future of Baghdad came to the fore at the beginning of March 1917, when it became clear that the city would shortly fall to British arms. On 6 March, the secretary of state for India asked Sir Percy Cox to submit a draft proclamation, suitable for publication when British troops entered the city. The proclamation, the secretary of state stipulated, had to contain 'friendly references to Arab State and King Husain.' Cox complied promptly and sent a draft two days later. The draft recalled that the war had not been sought or started by the British, that Basra had been peaceful and prosperous during the two years of British occupation, and it promised good treatment, and the protection of life, honour, religion and property. The draft also referred to Turkish misgovernment which had prompted 'King Hussein of Mecca' to rise 'for defence of the Arab cause', to expel the Turks from the Hijaz and to make himself independent. The draft went on:

> It is the same causes which led three great Arab leaders of Eastern Arabia, viz. Bin Saud, ruler of Nejd; Bin Subah, ruler of Koweit; and Bin Mardas, ruler of Mohammerah, to meet together and make common cause and to announce to Islamic world at a public assemblage in Koweit last November their complete unity and accord in working for interests of the race. At this meeting they testified their firm intention to support Shereef Hussein and to co-operate to the utmost with British Government for the expulsion of the Turks for ever from the soil of Arabia so that under more benign auspices the Arab cause may achieve advancement and a glorious future. It is for those who have the cause of Islam and of the Arab race and Arab

[1] F.O. 371/3044, 12049/1173.

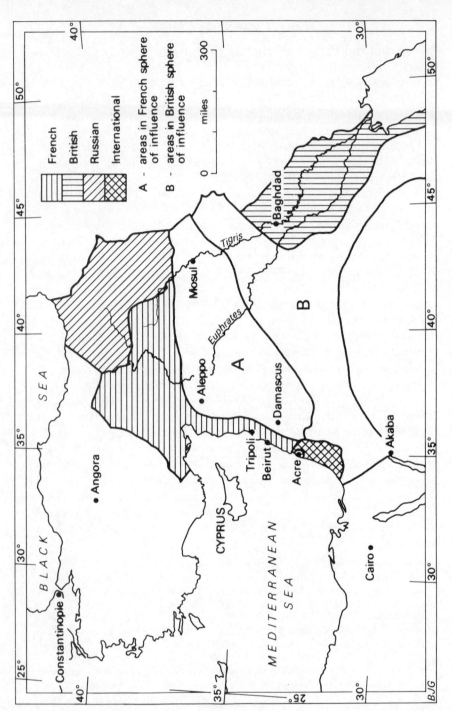

Map. 2. The Asia Minor, 'Sykes–Picot', agreement

progress at heart to co-operate with forces and Government of Great Britain in accomplishing the complete expulsion of the Turks, and thereby assisting to bring war to a speedy conclusion, and to ensure their own emancipation. For the present they can best promote that end by going quietly about their daily vocations and assisting the British authorities to carry on normal administration.[1]

This draft proclamation displeased Hirtzel a good deal. He held that it showed that Cox was contemplating 'a close administration, amounting practically to annexation', and that this was not the policy of the government, 'so far as they have yet defined their policy'. But Hirtzel considered that the correspondence between McMahon and Husayn had committed the British government to recognize and support the independence of the Arabs within certain limits which – he argued – included the *vilayets* of Baghdad and Basra,

> only they have claimed that in these vilayets 'the Arabs will recognize that the established position and interests of Gt. Britain necessitate special measures of administrative control' (Sir H. McMahon to Grand Shereef 26th Oct/15). This claim has not been admitted, but the Shereef merely said that he 'might agree to leave under the British administration for a short time those districts now occupied by the British troops, [i.e. the *vilayet* of Basra only] without the right of either party being prejudiced thereby (especially those of the Arab nation which are to it economic, and vital) against a suitable sum paid as compensation to the Arab Kingdom for the period of occupation' (5th Nov. 1915). In reply to this Sir H. McMahon wrote that 'our interests demand...a friendly and stable administration in the vilayet of Baghdad, and the adequate safeguarding of these interests calls for a much fuller and more detailed consideration than the present situation and the urgency of these negotiations' (17th Dec. 15).

Hirtzel interpreted these exchanges to mean that the British had 'never even claimed the right of a British administration for Baghdad', but that Basra's was a different case, on Husayn's own admission, and because it had already been occupied when negotiations with him began. Hirtzel therefore held it necessary on the grounds alike of 'expediency and honour' not to pre-empt Baghdad for annexation by India, which he suspected Cox's proclamation of trying to do. As he put it in another minute a month later, he was concerned not so much to settle the political future of Mesopotamia there and then, as to prevent anything being done which would, whether intentionally or not, 'queer the pitch for an Arab administration afterwards, in whatever sense the term may then [i.e. at a peace settlement] be interpreted.'[2]

[1] F.O. 371/3042, 51001 and 52609/212.
[2] L/P & S/10/666, p. 1019/17, Hirtzel's minute of 9 Mar., and pp. 1419 and 1434/17, his minute of 9 Apr. 1917.

For these reasons, Hirtzel preferred a draft proclamation 'to the People of Baghdad and Irak' which had been produced by Sykes. The 'rhetorical part' of this document seemed to Hirtzel 'admirable', but he had serious reservations about one of its passages. As originally drafted this paragraph read:

> But you people of Baghdad are not to understand from this that it is the purpose of the British Government to impose upon you a foreign yoke or alien institutions. It is the desire of the British Government that the Arabs of Irak and Baghdad shall in future be a free people enjoying their own wealth and substance under their own institutions and laws.

Hirtzel considered it 'important now to avoid uttering words which we may hereafter have to eat if the Arab State proves a failure. In that event we shall almost certainly have to annex Baghdad, and we ought not to tie our hands now'. The passage in Sykes's proclamation just quoted was 'a direct and unconditional promise of independence to the vilayets of Basra and Baghdad'. This ought not to be given, and for Sykes's

> It is the desire of the British Government that the Arabs of Irak and Baghdad shall in future be a free people...

Hirtzel proposed to substitute

> It is the desire of the British Govt that the *Arab State* shall be free...

This was consonant both with McMahon's promises and with the Sykes–Picot agreement, and left the British government a free hand in Baghdad should the prospective Arab state collapse. Similarly, Hirtzel suggested that the proclamation should be addressed only to the Arabs of Baghdad and not, as Sykes proposed, to the Arabs of Baghdad and Iraq, since the latter area included Basra.[1]

Sykes's draft, presumably with Hirtzel's amendment, was examined further at a meeting between Sykes and representatives of the India office and the foreign office. No record of the discussions at this meeting has survived, but the passage which attracted Hirtzel's criticism was there further modified as follows:

> But you people of Baghdad are not to understand from this that it is the wish of the British Government to impose upon you alien institutions. But remember it rests with those who are well advised among you to prepare the way so that the British people may when the time comes give freedom to those who have proved themselves worthy to enjoy their own wealth and substance under their own institutions and laws.

[1] L/P & S/10/666, p. 1019/17, cited above.

The draft, amended in this way, came before a meeting of the war cabinet held on 12 March 1917. But considerably amended as it had been, it still aroused misgivings in Austen Chamberlain who circulated to his colleagues a memorandum, dated 10 March. Chamberlain declared himself 'uneasy' about 'the wide terms of the promise' conveyed in the draft, a promise which might lead to charges of breach of faith in the future. He went on:

> I am not aware that the Cabinet has ever definitely decided what the exact political position of the Baghdad vilayet should be, and I doubt whether it is possible to decide that question at this moment.

Chamberlain proposed yet another amendment to the passage which had already been twice amended. He proposed that this key passage should read as follows:

> But you people of Baghdad are not to understand from this that it is the wish of the British Government to impose upon you alien institutions. It is the desire of the British Government that the Arabs of Irak and Baghdad shall in future be free from oppression, and enjoy their wealth and substance under institutions and laws congenial to them.

Chamberlain's memorandum was countered by a memorandum which Sykes – who, together with Hirtzel, was invited to be present for the discussion of this item – read to the cabinet, the terms of which deserve some examination. In view of the conflicting views before them, the war cabinet decided to remit the two drafts they had before them together with Chamberlain's amendments to a committee made up of Curzon, Milner, Chamberlain and Hardinge, who 'should make such alterations as were necessary in the draft and report their decision to the War Cabinet'. This committee produced yet another draft of the controverted passage which read as follows:

> But you people of Baghdad, whose commercial prosperity and whose safety from oppression and invasion must ever be a matter of the closest concern to the British Government, are not to understand that it is the wish of the British Government to impose upon you alien institutions. It is the hope of the British Government that the aspirations of your philosophers and writers shall be realized and that once again the people of Baghdad shall flourish enjoying their wealth and substance under institutions which are in consonance with their sacred laws and their racial ideals.

The new draft proclamation, addressed 'To the People of Baghdad', was approved by the war cabinet on 14 March and Cox was instructed to publish it.[1]

The authorized version of the proclamation, its inflated rhetoric notwithstanding, in effect, took almost all political significance out of Sykes's original draft. That ministers and officials disagreed with the policy he was advocating is amply clear from a comparison of the successive drafts of the key passage in the proclamation, from Hirtzel's minutes, Chamberlain's memorandum and the cabinet minutes. Sykes's policy did not prevail on this occasion, but it is important to examine the assumptions on which he based it since these governed his approach to the negotiations with the French and the Sharif. Sykes disagreed with Chamberlain's amendment which, he contended, would tell the Arabs that 'Whether you behave well or ill, we shall give you good treatment, but we shall settle your affairs for you.' This the Arabs would not accept: 'The Arab is above all proud; he does not want favours granted him. If we desire to get on with the Arabs', he affirmed, 'we must not patronise but we must be firm'. Therefore, 'If we set up autonomy as an ideal, we get the sympathy of every Arab nationalist, we make it almost impossible for the French to go in for forcible dominion [in Syria], and we pave the way for a better state of things in Egypt.' Otherwise, 'we pave the way for discontent, and a coalition between the Arabic speaking Egyptian nationalists and the Arab intellectuals'. To support his case, Sykes also made a distinction between southern and northern Mesopotamia:

> The political conditions and possibilities in the area between Kut and Kerkuk are entirely different to the conditions between Kut and Basra. The southern area is a country which has relapsed into complete barbarism and anarchy, and it is inhabited practically by savages with no intellectual class, and I am pretty sure the Arab nationalist party would be glad to see us rule it. The northern area has been the centre for organised government from time immemorial, and has sent an annual quota to the military and civil service schools, and consequently has in peace time a large intellectual class. The members of this class are, it is true, scattered and terrified, but it is of the greatest importance to demonstrate to them that their ideals are not contrary to ours and to leave the door open for them to come in on our side without loss of dignity.

This particular justification for a British annexation of Basra was fanciful since there was really no demonstrable difference between this *vilayet* and Baghdad in respect of social, political, or intellectual

[1] Cab. 23/2, minutes of war cabinet 94, 12 Mar. with Chamberlain's and Sykes's memoranda annexed, and minutes of war cabinet 96, 14 Mar. 1917. Text of proclamation as telegraphed to Cox in F.O. 371/3042, 56627/212.

characteristics. Quite as fanciful was Sykes's apprehension of an alliance between Egyptian nationalists, who were pro-Ottoman and anti-Sharifian, and those whom he called Arab intellectuals. His strongest argument, in fact, is that if Baghdad were given over to the Arab nationalists, this would make it very difficult for the French to annex or closely control territory in the Levant. The argument was likely to appeal to Lloyd George and other members of his administration who were bent on preventing the French from establishing a foothold in an area so close to Egypt. Sykes's thinking is revealed in a proposal which he makes in this memorandum, which if it were accepted, would radically alter the Asia Minor agreement which he himself had negotiated a year before:

> if we are courageous, we have every prospect of being supreme in region (B), and beloved in region (A). If we do not play up to Arab racial pride in Baghdad, then we shall make Baghdad a restless appanage instead of a centre of influence.
>
> Baghdad is a natural capital of practically all the inhabited areas of region (B). If we make it an Arab capital we shall control the Arabs, because we shall control Baghdad commercially, and by clause 6 we can maintain troops there.

Sykes was thus arguing for the disappearance of the distinction established in the Asia Minor agreement between the so-called red area (in which Baghdad was included), and the regions called 'A' and 'B'. In the red area, it will be recalled, Great Britain was 'allowed to establish such direct or indirect administration or control as [it] desire[s] and as [it] may think fit to arrange with the Arab State or Confederation of Arab States'. Areas 'A' and 'B', on the other hand, constituted the territory of 'an independent Arab State or a Confederation of Arab States', the sole difference between them being that in area 'A' France, and in area 'B' Great Britain, was alone to supply 'advisers or foreign functionaries'. In support of his argument that Baghdad should be made the capital of area 'B', Sykes declared that 'by clause 6 we can maintain troops there'. It is not clear what he meant since clause 6 of the Asia Minor agreement gave no such right, and indeed nowhere in the agreement was the presence of British or French troops expressly provided for. Later on in his memorandum Sykes insisted that it was important to offer the Arabs 'local autonomy' in Baghdad because 'there is much in a name'. If this were granted, 'the Arabs will not object to the presence of British troops and a British General, British advisers, and British merchants'. These were mere affirmations, unsupported by any evidence. Sykes had no ground for asserting that the Sharifians would not object to the presence of British troops in Baghdad. This assumption could only have stemmed from Sykes's refusing to take the Sharifians seriously. We see here therefore a dangerous ambiguity similar to that which had earlier led Grey and the Cairo officials to make wide and vague promises on the mutually contradictory grounds that the Sharif would not rise unless such promises were made, and that the promises anyway did not matter because the Sharifian movement would come to nothing. In the present case, Sykes does not ask himself how the Arabs could possibly allow British troops to be stationed in Baghdad, if they were as intent on 'local autonomy' as he represents them to be. His arguments, as has been seen, did not impress the war cabinet.

Two days after approving the text of the Baghdad proclamation, the war cabinet established a committee to oversee the administration of Mesopotamia. Curzon was to be chairman, with Milner, the secretary of state for India and the under-secretary of state for foreign affairs as members. When the committee began its life, the secretary of state for India was Chamberlain and the under-secretary at the foreign office was Lord Robert Cecil. In addition Hirtzel, Holderness, Graham and Clerk were appointed associate members. Sykes was appointed secretary.[1] This appointment notwithstanding, Sykes's policy over Baghdad was rejected almost totally by the committee. At its first meeting on 19 March 1917 the Mesopotamia administration committee decided that the occupied territories in Mesopotamia should be administered by the British government, and not by the government of India, and that the Basra *vilayet* should remain 'permanently' under British administration. The committee also resolved

> That it would be premature to determine at present what should be the precise form of Arab government to be ultimately set up in the Baghdad Vilayet and contiguous Arab sphere, but that the provisional British Administration to be established in the occupied territories outside of the Basra Vilayet should be framed with a view to such a development in the future.[2]

The terms of this resolution indicate clearly enough that the dispute over the terms of the Baghdad proclamation related to matters of substance, and that the consensus among ministers and high officials was that, contrary to what Sykes had advocated, Baghdad should not at that stage be considered as forming part of the prospective Arab state.

[1] Cab. 23/2 minutes of war cabinet 98, 16 Mar. 1917.
[2] Cab. 27/22, first meeting of the Mesopotamia administration committee, 19 Mar. 1917.

The committee's decision that Basra and Baghdad should be separately administered aroused the misgivings of Cox and of the government of India, and Chamberlain raised the issue at the second meeting of the committee, on 8 May 1917. He doubted whether it was in fact practicable to treat Baghdad and Basra differently. The discussion which followed provides yet further evidence how far removed the committee's thinking was from Sykes's ideas. In answer to Chamberlain's observations, Curzon remarked that the possibility of a separate peace with Turkey must not be forgotten, and the terms of such a peace might require the restoration of Baghdad to Turkey: hence Baghdad must have a separate administration. Again, if the British were to retain Palestine, they might have to surrender Baghdad. These remarks elicited an interesting exchange between Hirtzel and McMahon, who had been invited to this meeting of the Mesopotamia administration committee. Hirtzel, with his punctilious regard for what had been promised to Husayn, declared that the British were pledged not to make a peace with Turkey which involved handing back Arabs to Turkish rule. He was, of course, referring to McMahon's letter of 15 December 1915 in which the high commissioner had informed Husayn that he was 'directed by the Government of Great Britain to inform you that you may rest assured that Great Britain has no intention of concluding any peace in terms of which the freedom of the Arab peoples from German and Turkish domination does not form an essential condition'. But the author of this categorical pledge now denied that it was as 'rigid' as Hirtzel stated. Curzon supported his contention. The upshot of the committee's deliberations was a decision to inform the viceroy that though the intention was that separate administrative systems should be established in Basra and Baghdad, he was to rest assured that 'HMG had not in view the immediate establishment of an Arab Administration' in Baghdad.[1]

Following the first meeting of the committee Hardinge had informed Wingate that

> It would be too early as yet to determine the precise form of government to be ultimately set up in the Baghdad vilayet, though they propose, if it be possible, to erect an Arab facade, while keeping a firm hold on the external relations and general administration of the vilayet.[2]

It was presumably on the strength of this telegram that Wingate, as has been seen, instructed Sykes when he was setting out on his

[1] Cab. 27/22.
[2] F.O. 371/3051, 68626, Hardinge to Wingate Private and Secret, 31 Mar. 1917.

first visit to Jeddah, to inform Husayn that in Baghdad 'we will retain the position of military and political predominance which our strategical and commercial interests require'. As has also been seen, Sykes, in reporting on his first meeting with Husayn, did not disclose whether he spoke on Baghdad as Wingate had instructed him. It is true that shortly afterwards he informed George Lloyd that he had made it 'fully plain' to Husayn that 'there must be no doubts in his mind as to the permanency of our military occupation of Baghdad.'[1] Again, the joint memorandum of 17 May 1917 by Sykes and Picot, cited above, distinguished between the red and blue zones on the one hand, and areas 'A' and 'B' on the other. But, as will appear, the language which Sykes held to the Sharifians during his second Jeddah visit makes it unlikely that he was as forthright on his first visit as he claimed, or that he really believed in the distinction between the red zone and area 'B' which the joint memorandum had just reaffirmed.

If Picot's report is to be believed, at his first meeting with Husayn on 19 May, he left the king under no misapprehension about French aims. He declared that when the circumstances of the war would allow it, the French government was determined to provide in Syria the same 'efficacious help' to the king as the British were providing in Iraq and Baghdad, and thus 'to facilitate, through the occupation of the coast where the population desired the French presence, the eventual liberation of the Arab race, which is the goal of our efforts'. This declaration, Picot reported, embarrassed the king, for Husayn was going to lay claim to the whole of Syria, both Christian and Muslim. The discussion which lasted no less than three hours was, according to Picot, somewhat confused and the impression which he derived from it was distinctly unsatisfactory (*nettement fâcheuse*).[2] In his account of the interview, Fu'ad al-Khatib, who was present, adds a significant detail. He states that Picot twice proposed to Husayn 'an agreement in Syria with France as you have with Great Britain in Baghdad,' which the king refused.[3] It is not clear what Husayn understood by such a proposal, but Picot, if he made it, must clearly have been relying on the distinction which he and Sykes had so recently reaffirmed between the red and blue zones on the one hand, and areas 'A' and 'B' on the other. In proposing the same arrangement in Syria as in Baghdad Picot would be

[1] F.O. 371/6259, E1031/1031/91 'Notes by George Lloyd on Various Arabian Questions', 4 June 1917. An incomplete copy of the report is in F.O. 882/16, fos. 141–2.
[2] A.E., Guerre 1914–18, vol. 877, Picot's telegram nos. 13–18, via Aden 24 May 1917.
[3] F.O. 882/16, fos. 131–6, 'Note by Sheikh Fuad El Khatib taken down by Lt Col. Newcombe'.

assuming that Baghdad would not form part of the proposed Arab state.

The same evening Sykes acted in order to break the deadlock. He summoned Fu'ad al-Khatib and asked him to get the king to agree to Picot's request. Later in the evening he sent a message to Fu'ad al-Khatib through Wilson, reiterating his request, and repeating his message the following morning. Fu'ad al-Khatib declared to Newcombe, of the British military mission at Jeddah, that it took him three hours

> to convince the King to accept Sir Mark Sykes's wish. He agreed at last because he said that he trusted what the British Commissioner says: He knows that Sir Mark Sykes can fight for the Arabs better than he can himself in political matters and knows that Sir Mark Sykes speaks with the authority of the British Government and will therefore be able to carry out his promises.[1]

It was thus as a result of Sykes's intervention and in exchange for his promises that Husayn made on 20 May the declaration cited above to the effect that 'he would be content if the French Government pursued the same policy towards Arab aspirations on Moslem Syrian Littoral as British did in Baghdad'. What then did Sykes promise? Though Fu'ad al-Khatib gives no details of the inducements which he was asked to convey to Husayn, there can be little doubt as to what these were. Sykes, it is fairly clear, must have promised or broadly hinted that at the peace settlement Baghdad would form part not of the red zone (which could be annexed or closely controlled by the British) but of area 'B' (which was to form part of the proposed Arab state). Nothing but this private understanding can possibly explain Husayn's sudden readiness to concede Picot's demand which only the previous day he was bent on resisting. And as transpired at the meeting, Sykes's private assurances made Husayn utterly confident in the soundness of his own contention that McMahon had promised him Baghdad. Wilson's account of this meeting shows plainly what happened, and in its fashion eloquently expresses the uneasiness and bewilderment at what took place of a man who was essentially straightforward, if not very intelligent. In his letter to Clayton of 24 May cited above, Wilson began by citing Husayn's declaration and by observing that it was by no means clear to which territory in Syria it referred: 'I am not clear', he wrote, 'and probably Picot and the Sherif are not clear, whether Syria i.e. including Damascus etc. is meant; or

[1] F.O. 882/16, 'Note by Sheik Fuad El Khatib', *loc. cit.*; Wilson's letter to Clayton, 24 May 1917, fos. 102–14.

merely the Syrian coast claimed by France: one may have meant Syria the other only the Syrian coast'. But it was the linking of Syria with Baghdad which particularly aroused his anxiety:

> Although Sykes and Picot were very pleased at this happy result and the Sherif had made the proposition himself I did not feel happy in my own mind and it struck me as possible that the Sherif, one of the most courteous of men, absolutely loyal to us and with complete faith in Great Britain, was verbally agreeing to a thing which he never would agree to if he knew our interpretation of what the Iraq situation is to be.
>
> I therefore asked Sykes 'Does the Sherif etc. know what the situation at Baghdad really is' and he replied 'they have the Proclamation'. I said nothing more for a few minutes as I was an onlooker but later remarked that the Proclamation said nothing much more than asking Arabs to co-operate in the Government.
>
> Sykes then asked Fuad if he had read the Proclamation of General Maude and Fuad said he had and the matter then dropped...

What Wilson understood by the 'Iraq situation' is clear, for he knew that Sykes, as has been seen, was instructed to tell Husayn that in Baghdad 'we will retain the position of military and political predominance which our strategical and commercial interests require,' and he was disturbed to see that Sykes did not emphasize this point as his instructions required him to do. In his letter Wilson recurs again and again to the dangerously equivocal outcome of the meeting of 20 May:

> As you know I have all along been a strong advocate of being as open as possible with the Sherif. My considered opinion is that we have not been as open and frank as we should have been at this last meeting.
>
> Special representatives of Great Britain and France came expressly to fix things up with the Sherif and when the latter agreed to France having the same status in Syria as we are to have in Iraq surely the main points of our agreement re Iraq should have been stated to prevent all chance of a misunderstanding which might have far reaching consequences.
>
> What made me feel that the Sherif and Picot had different ideas as to what the position of France in Syria was to be was:
>
> 1. That the Sherif agreed to France in Syria being in the same position as we in Iraq.
> 2. That Picot was so obviously delighted at getting the Sherif to verbally agree to this.
>
> Later in the evening (20th) Newcombe came and told me he had had a long talk with Faisal and Fuad and amongst other things told me that it was Sykes who urged Fuad to get Sherif to agree to the two points stated at the meeting and that Sykes had told Fuad or Sherif to leave everything to him, this was the first time I heard that Sykes was responsible for the Sherif's action...
>
> By urging the Sherif to agree to the formula re France and Syria Sykes has undoubtedly taken a very heavy responsibility on his shoulders and if I had known (at the meeting), that the Sherif had only agreed to the formula

on Sykes' urgent persuasion, I should certainly have tried hard to get some principal facts re our position in Iraq stated at the meeting.

Everything may be alright as Baghdad and Iraq except Basra may be going to be entirely Arab and independent with British advisers, financial control etc., if so well and good but if the Sherif puts one construction on MacMahon's letter and we another, there is likely to be serious trouble.

I feel very strongly that the Sherif should be told exactly what our interpretation is of our future position in Iraq which position has every right to be much more prominent than that of the French in Syria.

From George Lloyd I gather that Baghdad will almost certainly be practically British, if this is so then I consider that we have not played a straightforward game with a courteous old man who is as Sykes agrees, one of Great Britain's most sincere and loyal admirers, for it means that the Sherif [agreed] verbally to Syria being practically French which I feel sure he never meant to do.[1]

The line pursued by Sykes becomes somewhat clearer when we consider Picot's account of these negotiations. His version of Husayn's declaration of 20 May was somewhat different from that which Sykes reported. According to Sykes Husayn had declared that he would be satisfied if French policy in the 'Moslem Syrian Littoral' would be the same as that pursued by the British in Baghdad. This is not what Picot understood Husayn to have said, for he informed Paris that Husayn would like to see not the 'Moslem Syrian Littoral' but rather 'Moslem Syria' (*la Syrie musulmane*) treated on an equality with Baghdad. This report puzzled the ministry of foreign affairs in Paris. They wondered whether an error in transmission had occurred, and whether Husayn had referred to 'non-Moslem Syria' rather than to 'Moslem Syria'. For as they correctly pointed out, it was in '*non-Moslem Syria*, that is to say in the blue zone, that our situation is equivalent to that of Britain in the red zone, which does in fact include Baghdad'. Picot hastened to dispel the misapprehension. There had been, he telegraphed, no error in transmission:

The doubt which had crept into the mind of the Department results from the fact that though Baghdad is included in the red zone, the British mean to treat it in the [same] way as the Arab areas of the B zone (*lui appliquer le [même] régime qu'aux régions arabes de la zone B*), and only Irak [i.e. Basra and southern Mesopotamia] would have a special regime.

Naturally enough, Paris found this news very surprising since they had had no inkling of such a change in British policy.[2] It should

[1] F.O. 882/16, *loc. cit.*, Wilson's letter to Clayton, 24 May 1917.
[2] A.E., Guerre 1914–18, vol. 877, Picot's telegrams nos. 13–18, via Aden 24 May; telegram to Picot no. 127–8, Paris 29 May; Picot's telegram no. 24–7, Cairo 8 June; and telegram to Picot no. 138, Paris 11 June 1917.

have been just as surprising to Picot who, as has been seen, a short while before, on 17 May 1917, had signed a declaration jointly with Sykes affirming the difference in status between the red and blue zones on the one hand, and areas 'A' and 'B' on the other. In this declaration nothing had been said about altering the status of Baghdad. The information which Picot now disclosed to the ministry of foreign affairs in answer to their query he could only have obtained from Sykes. But what he had been led to believe was a change in British policy was nothing of the kind. It was rather that Sykes was pursuing his own views – views which had been rejected shortly before when the Baghdad proclamation was discussed by the cabinet in London. For this Sykes had, and knew that he had, no authority whatever. But by passing off these views as British policy to Picot, and surely also to Fu'ad al-Khatib, he thought he would settle the difficulty between Husayn and the French. He took care however not to reveal to anyone in Cairo or London the details of his negotiations. On the contrary. Thus Clayton answering Wilson, who had asked for 'some statement of the result of the interview between Sir Mark Sykes and the King of the Hejaz', wrote:

> I understood verbally from Sir Mark Sykes that he made it clear to the Sherif that a further large measure of control and also British Military occupation would be necessary in Iraq for some considerable time to come, and this is most undoubtedly true.[1]

Again, after his return to London, it was only obliquely that Sykes indicated his preference for doing away with the distinction between the red zone and area 'B'. Thus, commenting on the paper, cited earlier, in which Harold Nicolson summarized British obligations in regard to Ottoman territory, Sykes correctly pointed out that annexation was not mentioned in the Asia Minor agreement, though it was open to the signatories to annex certain areas, and he added:

> However, I submit that formal annexation is quite contrary to the spirit of the time, and would only lay up a store of future trouble.[2]

But these words by no means disclose that Sykes had in fact already put into practice the policy he was here advocating. It was not until the middle of August 1917 that Sykes explicitly advocated that the blue and red zones should be assimilated to areas 'A' and 'B' respectively, and proposed that if the French objected, they should be told that this was the policy the British intended to follow in Mesopotamia.[3]

[1] F.O. 882/16, fos. 129–30, Clayton to Wilson, Cairo 26 June 1917.
[2] F.O. 371/3044, 153075/1173, minute by Sykes, 18 July 1917.
[3] F.O. 371/3059, 159558, Sykes's memorandum, 14 Aug. 1917.

But did Sykes's policy, or rather his stratagem, serve to settle the issue between Husayn and the French? By no means. For one thing nobody knew the exact extent of 'Moslem Syria' of which, according to Picot, Husayn spoke, or whether it was identical with the 'Moslem Syrian Littoral' to which Sykes reported him as referring. Husayn, at any rate, understood from the Jeddah negotiations something diametrically opposed to what Picot had understood. Wilson need not have feared that the 'courteous old man' was being tricked; on the contrary, it was Husayn who was priding himself on having tricked Picot. At the end of July 1917, in a private conversation with Lawrence, Husayn declared that he had refused to permit the French annexation of Beirut and the Lebanon, and had refused a detailed discussion of boundaries.

> He is extremely pleased [Lawrence went on] to have trapped M. Picot into the admission that France will be satisfied in Syria with the position Great Britain desires in Iraq. That he says means a temporary occupation of the country for strategic and political reasons (with probably an annual grant to the Sherif in compensation and recognition)...

Husayn's language establishes that what he understood by the expression 'Moslem Syrian Littoral' was poles apart from what Picot understood by 'Moslem Syria'. Picot understood Husayn to agree that non-Moslem Syria would be fully under French control, while Husayn meant that the whole of Syria – including its littoral, i.e. the Lebanon – would be part of the Arab state as Sykes had indicated that Baghdad would be.

In transmitting Lawrence's report to London, Wingate remarked that 'we must eventually take steps to correct any erroneous opinion he [Husayn] may have, or profess to have formed, in regard to the Syrian Littoral and Palestine and of the provinces of Baghdad and Basra'. It was in order to dispel Husayn's misapprehensions, we remember, that Sykes and Picot visited Jeddah. Far from dispelling them, the visit produced new misunderstandings, the consequence of Sykes's diplomacy. But when he read Wingate's despatch, Sykes professed to see in it no cause 'for real apprehension or action'. He presumed – on what grounds he did not state – that 'if all goes well we in Irak intend to set up some kind of Arab Government under our auspices and if the government we set up wishes to accept a nominal suzerainty of the King of the Hejaz we should have no objection. Similarly', affirmed Sykes, on what grounds again is obscure, 'the French are quite ready (though naturally they won't say so), to do the same on the Syrian littoral'. Sykes was sure that the French did not desire to annex the

Lebanon, because this would mean Maronite deputies in the French Chamber![1] Sykes's policy, we may thus conclude, depended not on actual negotiations and agreements, but on his own hazardous estimates of future contingencies and hypothetical *arrière-pensées*. It is instructive to set side by side with his own speculations those of his colleague Picot whom he involved in the elaborate game of mutual deception and self-deception which was played at Jeddah in May 1917. When Ribot, the French minister of foreign affairs asked Picot what Husayn meant exactly by the expression 'Moslem Syria', Picot replied that he saw grave disadvantages in seeking to define it too precisely:

> If we mean to take advantage of our agreements relating to Asia Minor, we shall be led sooner or later to occcupy Beirut and the coast. Everything will then be easy for us as also for the British, because the Arabs always acquiesce in the *fait accompli*, and they have again ingenuously confessed this to me repeatedly during my recent journey.[2]

After the departure of Sykes and Picot from Cairo, Clayton realized that Husayn believed, or professed to believe, that the two envoys had promised him Syria and Mesopotamia unconditionally. In a letter to Sykes he pointed out that Husayn had been given nothing in writing, and wondered whether it was not advisable to give him an *aide-mémoire* 'of what you actually told him'.[3] What has been set out above makes it highly doubtful whether an *aide-mémoire* could have been composed in a way such as to receive the assent of all three interlocutors. In any case, there is no evidence that it was ever written.

One more feature of the game of mutual bluff which Sykes, Picot and Husayn played at Jeddah in May 1917 falls to be noticed. As has been seen, in return for his declaration to Picot, Husayn asked Sykes through Faysal that the British should use their influence to induce the Sultan of Najd and the Idrisi of 'Asir to recognize Husayn as 'leader of the Arab Movement'. This was clearly yet another attempt to secure somehow an acknowledgement of Husayn's primacy. Sykes actually took up this request and asked Sir Percy Cox at Basra and the resident at Aden to take up the matter with Ibn Sa'ud and the Idrisi respectively. He presumably believed that in

---

[1] F.O. 371/3054, 174974/86526, Wingate's despatch no. 179, Ramleh 16 Aug., enclosing note by Lawrence, 30 July 1917. The minute, initialled by Sykes, though it is not in his handwriting, is of 15 Sept. 1917.

[2] A.E., Guerre 1914–18, vol. 877, Picot's telegram no. 24–7, Cairo 8 June 1917, cited above.

[3] F.O. 882/16, fos. 143–7, Clayton to Sykes, Cairo 22 July 1917.

Arab affairs words were mere words and of no consequence. As he told Cox: 'If Ibn Saud could by some means convey to Sherif that he regards him as titular leader of Arab cause without in any way committing his local position I believe much good would result'. Ibn Sa'ud and the Idrisi had good reason to fear Husayn's ambition and were in no way inclined to acknowledge his primacy. To make such an approach would only serve needlessly to irritate them and excite their suspicions; and both Cox and the resident at Aden refused to act on Sykes's suggestion.[1]

Though nothing came of this attempt, Husayn became confident, as a result of Sykes's promises to Fu'ad al-Khatib, that his own interpretation of McMahon's promises was correct. At the meeting of 20 May in Jeddah, Wilson reported, Husayn

> has gone trumps on a letter he has from Sir Henry MacMahon the contents of which are unknown to Fuad or Faisal or anyone of the Sherif's advisers.
>
> My fear [Wilson told Clayton] is that the Sherif has possibly put one construction on the contents of this letter and we another, if this turns out to be the case a very serious and awkward situation will certainly arise (particularly if we are unable to produce our copy which I understand has not yet been found)...[2]

Since the translations of McMahon's letters were mislaid, Cairo was unable to refute or even to challenge Husayn's allegations. He persisted in them. Towards the end of November 1917, at a meeting with Wilson he again referred to McMahon's letters and expressed 'complete faith' in the word of the British government. Syria was his: Arab notables who were executed by the Turks had informed him that they were dying for him and his cause; his honour was involved as he had promised the Syrians he would give them help and never desert them. Wilson was again alarmed by this, and stressed once again that the Arabic translations which were said to have been 'locked up by Storrs somewhere' had to be found.[3]

It was not only Syria (and Mesopotamia) that Husayn believed to be his. The old dream of securing the caliphate with British help was also still alive. In conversation with Cornwallis towards the end of 1917, Abdullah harked back to it. He now took the line that Arab independence would be complete only when the caliphate reverted to the Arabs and Husayn

> was on all counts the man most fitted, and his assumption of the office would bind the Arab nation to a degree which was otherwise impossible. In

---

[1] F.O. 371/3054, file 86256, which contains the relevant correspondence.
[2] F.O. 882/16, Wilson to Clayton, Jeddah 24 May 1917, cited above.
[3] F.O. 141/654, file 356/144, Wilson's telegram, Jeddah 26 Nov. 1917.

The Fly in the Fly-bottle

particular [he solemnly assured Cornwallis] the difference which at present existed between his Father and the important Emirs of the Arabian Peninsula could be solved without difficulty.

I pointed out [Cornwallis went on] that the King had already told Colonel Wilson that he had no wish to become Caliph but the Emir replied that he would have no choice in the matter. Custom decreed that the decision should be made for him by others and he would have no knowledge of the project until the day on which he was publicly proclaimed.[1]

---

[1] F.O. 371/3396, 19575, Wingate's despatch no. 2, Cairo 6 Jan., enclosing note by Cornwallis, 3 Jan. 1918, on conversation with Abdullah.

6. Wingate, Hogarth and Husayn

The Jeddah conversations of May 1917, then, did nothing to recall to Husayn the exact terms of his correspondence with McMahon, and the very limited and hypothetical character of British undertakings as they were set down in McMahon's letters of 24 October and 15 December 1915. Far from dispelling illusions, these conversations, equivocal and tortuous as they were, left Anglo-Sharifian relations more obscure than ever, and confirmed Husayn in his ambitions and pretensions. It soon became necessary to make another attempt to clarify matters to Husayn. The Balfour declaration of 2 November 1917 in favour of a Jewish national home in Palestine, Allenby's advance into Ottoman territory and his capture of Jerusalem in December, approaches by the Ottomans to Husayn in favour of a settlement,[1] all were believed to require a restatement of British policy to Husayn. During November Sykes and Clayton exchanged telegrams in which they expressed anxiety about the Arab movement and the attitude of the Sharif and the Syrians of Cairo. Both, wrote Clayton on 28 November, were suspicious of French designs in Syria, and the latter viewed 'with little short of dismay' the prospect 'of seeing Palestine and even eventually Syria in hands of Jews whose superior intelligence and commercial abilities are feared by [all] alike'. This made the Arabs receptive to 'German-inspired Turanian propaganda' and paved the way for 'attractive proposal for independence under nominal Turkish suzerainty'. Among the measures which Clayton recommended to counteract such dangers was that the French should 'make a definite pronouncement disclaiming any idea of annexation in Syria (including blue area) and emphasising their intention of assuring liberty of *all* Syrians and helping them along the path towards independence and Government by people. This', Clayton affirmed, 'is particularly urgent'.[2] Wingate hastened to support these views in another

---

[1] F.O. 371/3380, 146, Wingate's telegram no. 1394, Cairo 24 Dec. 1917 reporting that Jemal Pasha had sent two letters to Faysal and to Ja'far al-'Askari (an Ottoman officer who had deserted to the Sharif and who was now Faysal's chief of staff) arguing that Allied aims in Syria and Mesopotamia would be an effective bar to the creation of an Arab empire – the only justification of the Arab revolt – and suggesting negotiations.

[2] F.O. 371/3054, 227658/86256, Wingate's telegram (Clayton for Sykes) no. 1281, 28 Nov. 1917.

telegram the following day. Husayn, he declared, 'has in no degree abated his original pretensions concerning Syria and apparently still nourishes illusion that through the good offices of His Majesty's Government he may be installed as, at any rate nominally, overlord of greater part of the country'. If this illusion were dispelled, he would either be driven to abdicate or to make the best possible terms with the Turks. Like Clayton, Wingate believed that a French disclaimer of annexation was necessary; he also declared, somewhat obscurely, that 'we must... continue to envisage the possibility of the King establishing such political relations with the future Government or Governments of Syria as will encourage the belief that an Arab State or Confederacy has been created of which he is Moslem overlord. By this means Sheriff's revolt against the Ottoman Empire could be justified in Moslem eyes, and his future financial independence to some extent provided for'.[1] In all this, it will be noticed, no mention is made of McMahon's promises and stipulations. Rather, unconditional disclaimers of annexation and grandiose proclamations in favour of 'independence and Government by people' are advocated, to what end is not very clear. Was it to do away with an unwelcome French foothold in the Levant? Was it to avert Husayn's possible defection to the Ottomans? In either case, the calculation was faulty. The French would certainly not give up their claims so easily; and as for Husayn, the Cairo officials should have been well placed to know that he was utterly dependent on them for money and arms, that any threat by him to defect was an empty one, and that the Ottoman army would have in the end to be confronted and defeated not by a Sharifian, but by a British army. It is at any rate worth noting how utterly different now were the reasons alleged by the Cairo officials for supporting Husayn from what they had been two years before.

An opportunity soon arose to make yet another declaration to Husayn. Relations between him and Ibn Sa'ud had always been tense and were now worsening. To prevent a damaging conflict between the two rulers who were both British clients, and to encourage Ibn Sa'ud to take action against the Ottomans and their supporter Ibn al-Rashid, the amir of Ha'il, the chief political officer at Baghdad sent one of his political officers, H. St J. Philby, on a mission to Ibn Sa'ud. After seeing Ibn Sa'ud, Philby was to travel overland to Jeddah where he would meet an official sent by the Cairo authorities. They would see Husayn and try to diminish his suspi-

[1] F.O. 371/3054, 228069/86256, Wingate's telegram no. 1286, Cairo 29 Nov. 1917.

cion of Ibn Sa'ud, and would then both go to Najd for the same purpose. The official chosen by Cairo for this mission was Storrs, but at the last minute Allenby required his services in Jerusalem which he had just occupied and Wingate appointed Hogarth to go to Jeddah in his stead.[1]

Wingate suggested taking advantage of Hogarth's visit to inform Husayn about the lines of British policy. On 31 December, he sent an 'urgent' telegram stating that Husayn was sure to ask Hogarth 'what our ultimate line will be about (1) Syria and (2) Bagdad', and that it was 'very necessary at present juncture that we should make a communication to Shereef on these subjects'. Wingate suggested these 'formulas':

> 1. Jews must be accepted by Arabs in reservations (or colonies) in parts of Palestine to be settled at Peace Conference. Rest of Syria to be Arab but precise status to be left to peace conference. If Syrians demand it we should welcome (a) King Hussein's overlordship if local autonomy secured and (b) Faisal at Damascus but French must be consulted as chiefly interested.
> 2. That Bagdad is to be Arab under British protection but its precise Government must await wishes of inhabitants and result of Peace Conference.

And as usual in these Arab negotiations, an urgent answer was requested:

> Hogarth leaves here January 2nd. May approval or otherwise be communicated to me if possible by then.

We may note with interest the entire absence in Wingate's 'formulas' of any reference to McMahon's letter which, after all, embodied what the British had been willing to concede, and on the basis of which, they were entitled to believe, Husayn had thrown in his lot with them. The 'formulas', furthermore, gratuitously made new and dangerously vague promises about Faysal's position, Syrian 'local autonomy' and the like. They also volunteered a declaration about Palestine on the assumption that Husayn was entitled to have a say in its future. This was no doubt a response to the unfavourable reaction which, as has been seen, the Balfour declaration had elicited in Syrian circles in Cairo. But Wingate had no ground for assuming (as he seems to have done) that on this their views and Husayn's were identical. Husayn's reaction to the capture of Jerusalem was the subject of an anxious exchange between London and Cairo. A telegram of 18 December, drafted by Sykes,

---

[1] F.O. 371/3061, 244397/191347, Wingate's telegram no. 1403, 27 Dec. 1917. The whole of file no. 191347 relates to Philby's mission and the relations between Hijaz and Najd.

enquired whether it was significant that Husayn had not offered congratulations on the capture of Jerusalem. Wingate answered the following day that Husayn had sent personal congratulations through his representative, but before committing himself officially Wingate thought that he wanted to have the opportunity of digesting newspaper reports of Zionist meetings in London. A few days later Clayton offered an alternative explanation of Husayn's silence over Jerusalem. It was due, he thought, to Husayn's fear of hostile propaganda if he displayed public sympathy with Christians in their capture of a Muslim holy city.[1] As Hogarth's interview with Husayn's was shortly to show, Clayton's explanation was nearer to the truth than Wingate's.

The instructions which Wingate had requested in his telegram of 31 December were sent on 4 January 1918. They had been drafted by Sykes and approved by Hardinge who suggested, however, the omission of one paragraph. Sykes's draft began:

> The following formulas would be best:
> That the Entente Powers are determined that the Arab race shall be given full opportunity of once again forming a nation in the world. That this can only be achieved by the Arabs themselves uniting, and that Great Britain and her Allies will pursue a policy with this ultimate unity in view.
> That the Entente Powers will only approve of measures and forms of Government in Mesopotamia and Syria which put no obstacle in the way of ultimate unity.

It is this last paragraph which Hardinge thought it best to omit.

> We must be particularly careful [he minuted] to give no handle to any scheme by which our hold on Basra would be affected

and the general affirmations in the preceding paragraph rendered the specific assurances about Mesopotamia and Syria 'unnecessary'. But Hardinge did not query the wisdom of these general affirmations, or enquire how they tallied with McMahon's promises, or with the assurances given at Jeddah the previous May by Sykes and Picot.

Sykes's draft instructions went on:

> That so far as Palestine is concerned we are determined that no people shall be subjected to another, but that in view of the fact
> a) That there are in Palestine shrines, Wakfs and holy places, sacred in some cases to Moslems alone, to Jews alone, to Christians alone, and in others to two or all three, and inasmuch as these places are of interest to vast masses of people outside Palestine and Arabia, there must be a special régime to deal with these places approved of by the world.

[1] F.O. 371/3061, 240633 and 245447/214354, telegram to Wingate no. 1216, 18 Dec., Wingate's telegram no. 1367, 19 Dec., and Clayton's telegram no. 1416, 30 Dec. 1917.

b) That as regards the Mosque of Omar it shall be considered as a Moslem concern alone and shall not be subjected directly or indirectly to any non-Moslem authority.

The statements made in the above passage are no doubt unexceptionable, but one may again ask why, unless Husayn had a special claim over Palestine and its holy places, they should have been addressed to him. And as has been seen, a special claim of this kind had never been admitted by the British government. But Sykes, it appears, did think that the British government should, unbidden and of its own motion, acknowledge such a claim. At Sykes's suggestion, a telegram was sent to Wingate on 16 November 1917, proposing that the mosque of Omar and the area around it should be handed over to a representative of Husayn's and that no non-Muslim should be allowed to enter it without a pass issued by the British political officer, and counter-signed by Husayn's representative. Wingate discussed the proposal with Allenby and answered on 19 November, expressing 'great doubts' over its advisability; to hand this area over to Husayn 'might induce the belief that we had fixed on him as the Khalifa of Islam'; furthermore, Wingate continued,

the admission of King of Hedjaz's representative in an official position in Jerusalem might give rise to aspirations which are very clearly excluded in Sykes–Picot agreement.

The foreign office accepted Wingate' advice, but some three weeks later, on 11 December, Sykes in a telegram to Clayton suggested that it would have 'useful political effects' if Faysal were invited to Jerusalem as his father's representative. Clayton replied three days later that Faysal's presence in Palestine at that juncture 'would complicate situation seriously and inevitably militate against any Arab–Jew entente'.[1]

The last 'formula' drafted by Sykes relates to Zionism, and the same point arises here too, namely whether Husayn was entitled to be officially informed of, and to have his approval implicitly sought for, the Balfour declaration. Husayn, then, was to be told

That since the Jewish opinion of the world is in favour of a return of Jews to Palestine and inasmuch as this opinion must remain a constant factor, and further as His Majesty's Government view with favour the realisation of this aspiration, His Majesty's Government are determined that in as far as is

[1] F.O. 371/3061, 214354, 221385, 235199 and 237239/214354, telegram to Wingate no. 1078, 16 Nov.; from Wingate no. 1233, Cairo 19 Nov.; to Wingate no. 1103, 21 Nov.; from Sykes to Clayton no. 1175, 11 Dec.; from Clayton to Sykes no. 1340, 14 Dec. 1917.

compatible with the freedom of the existing population both economic and political, no obstacle should be put in the way of the realisation of this ideal.[1]

Armed with these 'formulas', Hogarth went to Jeddah, where Philby, coming from Najd where he had seen Ibn Sa'ud, had already arrived. Between 8 and 14 January Hogarth had ten interviews with Husayn. From his report it is clear that Husayn's anxieties were not those which Wingate's or Sykes's 'formulas' were designed to assuage. In the first place, the king 'hardly touched on Mesopotamia and neither said nor asked anything of importance about the future of either Baghdad or Basra. I was careful', Hogarth wrote, 'to let these questions as far as possible alone and he never seemed desirous of raising them.' The reference to Mesopotamia in Sykes's draft – which Hardinge wisely omitted – was therefore a literally gratuitous commitment. Equally gratuitous were the references to the holy places and Jewish settlement in Palestine. While Husayn, wrote Hogarth in his report to Wingate,

> accepted without demur H.M.G's declaration on this matter, as conveyed in Foreign Office telegram no. 6 of November 6, 1916 to yourself,[2] he left me in little doubt that he secretly regards this as a point to be reconsidered after the Peace, in spite of my assurance that it was to be a definitive arrangement. He compared ourselves and himself (in his habitual homely way) to two persons about to inhabit one house but not agreed which should take which floor or rooms! Often in the course of our conversations he spoke with a smile of accounts which he would settle after the war, pending which settlement he would press nothing. I doubt if he has any fixed plan or foresees his way; but I have no doubt that in his own mind he abates none of his original demands on behalf of the Arabs, or in the fulness of time, of himself.

As for Jewish settlement in Palestine, the position, Hogarth declared in his report, 'is, I think, very much the same as in the preceding case.' In the 'Notes' on his conversations with which he supplemented his report, Hogarth added that Husayn 'agreed enthusiastically' to the 'formula' of the foreign office telegram. Hogarth rightly remarked in his report that Husayn 'probably knows little or nothing of the actual or possible economy of Palestine and his

---

[1] F.O. 371/3054, 245810/86256, Wingate's telegram no. 1418, Cairo 31 Dec. 1917, and telegram to Wingate no. 24, 4 Jan. 1918. The 'formulas', now known as 'The Hogarth Message' have been published in Cmd. 5964, *Statements made on behalf of His Majesty's Government during the year 1918 in regard to the Future Status of certain parts of the Ottoman Empire*, 1939, *Accounts and Papers*, vol. XXVII, 1938–9.

[2] F.O. 371/2782, 221869/217652. In this telegram it was suggested that Husayn be informed that H.M.G. and their Allies could not recognize him as king of the Arabs, as such a title might provoke disunion among Arabs. But he was to be assured that he would continue to be regarded as 'The titular head of the Arab peoples in their revolt against Turkish misrule'.

ready assent to Jewish settlement there is not worth very much.' But the fact remains that Husayn 'readily' and even 'enthusiastically' assented to the 'formula' which Hogarth conveyed to him. The fact that he did so is surely as significant as his motives for doing so, on which Hogarth speculates. As Hogarth points out, Husayn had no fixed plan, but felt sure that his ambitions would be fully satisfied after the war. The reason for this belief comes out clearly from another passage in Hogarth's report:

> As regards our Agreement with himself, the King volunteered (apropos of nothing in particular) the declaration that he recognized the possible necessity of modification owing to the course of the war and changes in the mutual relations of the Allies. He has real trust in the honour of Great Britain, but very little in that of France: and undoubtedly he expects differences of opinion to arise among the Allies before and at the Peace Conference. I think he has some hope of forcing France's hand when it comes to the point, and expects us to back him. He lived too long in Constantinople not to have imbibed the policy of playing one Power against another. He listened to my protestation of our perfect accord with France, and of the latter's good intentions towards the Arabs, with politeness, but lack of conviction.
>
> In conclusion I may say that the King is more assured than ever both of our power to help him and the Arabs, and of our intention to do so, and that he leaves himself confidently in our hands. But he is not easy in his mind either about Central Arabia or about the loyalty of his own Hedjaz people.

Husayn's neglect of specific territorial arrangements stemmed, then, from his belief that existing agreements relating to them did not matter, that come the peace settlement, Britain and France would fall out, Britain would be his champion, and he would obtain all that he desired. The lack of interest which Husayn showed in Palestine as such, and his lack of concern over the Balfour declaration and Zionist aims appears from the message which he sent through Hogarth to the inhabitants of the newly occupied Jerusalem. In its English translation the message reads as follows:

> I...inform you that I am in such circumstances as you are already aware of. I advise you to continue and to double your thanks to God for what he has given you namely tranquility and safety for yourselves, your property and all that you care for receiving your full rights and privileges etc. etc. [sic.]
>
> But notwithstanding all this, in case anything might happen which you consider harmful or the like communicate it to the Governor General at your end who will no doubt immediately give orders that such harm be made away with this being an obligation under 'agreement with and unity in action' with Great Britain who is known of being honest.[1]

[1] F.O. 141/654, fo. 365. The Arabic original is not in the file.

The Fly in the Fly-bottle

It is particularly interesting that the difficulties which Husayn made about sending such a message did not arise from his claiming Palestine as part of the territories which had been promised to him, but from his desire to advertise himself in the message as king of the Arabs or the Arab nation. Hogarth had to exert himself in order to dissuade him from it. Husayn, he reported, objected that

> unless he might sign as 'King of the Arabs' or the 'Arab Nation', the addressee would ask what business it was of his. Even when warned he must not so sign, he drafted the message at first patently on the assumption that he held that position; and I had to get him to redraft it in a different tone.

Once he realized he could not get his way on this particular point, Husayn made no difficulties about sending a message which, as has been seen, advised the Arabs of Jerusalem to obey the British and look up to them as their legitimate rulers. That the assertion of his claim to kingship over the Arabs was Husayn's overriding concern appears again from an episode of a few months later, which also relates to Palestine. Wilson reported in July 1918 that Husayn had received letters from notables in Jerusalem telling of 'certain difficulties they were in' and asking him to act as an intermediary with the military governor:

> His Highness said he was not in favour of such letters being written to him from Palestine. He could only deal with them as 'Hussein ibn Ali' [i.e. not in an official capacity] and he thought it undesirable that such appeals should be addressed to him.[1]

Husayn's ambition to be recognized as the ruler of the whole Arab world in fact loomed largest in his conversations with Hogarth, whose 'formulas' could do nothing to assuage Husayn's chagrin and annoyance that Ibn Sa'ud should so obstinately refuse to recognize his claim.

> He both fears Ibn Saoud as a centre of a religious movement, dangerous to the Hedjaz [wrote Hogarth], and hates him as irreconcilable to his own pretension to be 'King of the Arabs'. This latter title is the King's dearest ambition...He opposes to our argument that he cannot be 'King of the Arabs' till the Arabs in general desire him to be so the counterargument that they will never so desire till he is so called; and he brought forward more than once the plea, that, if we destroy the one great Moslem power, Turkey, we are bound in our interest, to set up another.
>
> .   .   .   .
>
> It is obvious that the King regards Arab Unity as synonymous with his own Kingship, and (for reasons given above) as a vain phrase unless so regarded. He treats our proclamations and exhortations about it as good intentions but no more and has no faith in their effect until we support the

[1] F.O. 686/39, note of interview with Husayn by C. E. Wilson, Jeddah 21 July 1918.

embodiment of the idea in one single personality – himself. 'Arab Unity' means very little to King Hussein except as a means to his personal aggrandisement. He made this very clear in the matter of the message to Jerusalem Arabs which I was asked to suggest to him.[1]

There remains to notice one significant feature of Hogarth's negotiations. In broaching the subject of Palestine and its international control, Hogarth reminded Husayn of 'proviso in original Agreements safeguarding special interests of our Allies and especially France.' Hogarth seems to have used such an argument on his own initiative for, as has been seen, it had occurred neither to Sykes nor to Wingate to refer to McMahon's letters. In specifically invoking the stipulations laid down in these letters, Hogarth is quite exceptional among those British officials who negotiated with Husayn.

In spite of this reminder of what McMahon had actually said, Hogarth's conversations could by no means produce an agreement as to what was and what not due to Husayn. The 'formulas' with which he had been supplied were too elastic and ambiguous to achieve this. No sooner had Hogarth returned to Cairo than Wingate asked for further assurances to be given to Husayn. The Bolsheviks had recently published the war-time secret treaties, among them the Sykes–Picot agreement, and in a speech made at Beirut on 6 December 1917, the Ottoman leader Jemal Pasha gave publicity to these revelations and taunted Husayn with complicity in the dismemberment and subjugation of Muslim lands.[2] In a telegram of 22 January 1918, Wingate reported an 'urgent appeal' by Abdullah for a definitive refutation of Jemal's assertions. Wingate himself declared that general or vague assurances would be not only useless but also harmful. An explicit and total denial was necessary, and he asked for authority to notify Husayn officially

1. That H.M.G. is still determined to secure Arabs' independence and to fulfil promises made through him at beginning of Hedjaz revolt.

2. That H.M.G. will countenance no permanent foreign or European occupation of Palestine Irak (except province of Basrah) or Syria after the war.

3. That these districts will be in possession of their natives and that foreign interference with Arab countries will be restricted to assistance and protection.[3]

[1] F.O. 371/3383, 25577/675, Hogarth's 'Report' and 'Notes' on his mission to Husayn, dated 15 Jan., enclosed with Wingate's despatch no. 15, Cairo 27 Jan. 1918. Fragments from the 'Report' and the 'Extracts from Notes on Conversations with King Hussein' attached to the 'Report' were published in the White Paper Cmd. 5964 (1939) cited above. The relation of these fragments to Hogarth's report as a whole is discussed below.

[2] Kedourie, *England and the Middle East*, p. 107.

[3] F.O. 371/3380, 14373/146, Wingate's telegram no. 154, Cairo 22 Jan. 1918.

The second and third paragraphs of Wingate's suggested declaration went far beyond a mere recapitulation of the promises which he wished to recall in the first paragraph. So did Sykes's 'formula' drafted in response to Wingate's telegram, which he asked to be discussed at a meeting of the Middle East committee. In a minute of 25 January, he proposed that the committee should authorize Wingate to tell Husayn that the British were 'determined' that 'the peoples of Syria, Mesopotamia and Arabia' should be given the opportunity for self-determination.[1]

Before the committee could meet to consider Wingate's proposal, another telegram, dated 29 January, was received from him, in which he transmitted yet another request from Husayn for recognition as king of the Arabs:

> He represents that such recognition now would benefit his cause and help to refute enemy propaganda about annexationist aims of Entente in Arab countries.[2]

The committee met on 2 February to consider Wingate's two telegrams. They had also before them a telegram from Sir Percy Cox at Baghdad who reported that the anxieties described in Wingate's telegram of 22 January were unknown in the area for which he was responsible, and protested against Mesopotamia being made a pawn in negotiations with Husayn. Cox had always disliked the mention of Mesopotamia in McMahon's letters to the Sharif, and now suggested that if a new declaration of intentions was necessary, the terms of the proclamation published on the fall of Baghdad were sufficient. A telegram from the government of India supported Cox,[3] and at the committee meeting, Lord Islington, the under-secretary of state for India, strongly argued that no new assurances regarding Mesopotamia should be given to Husayn. If Mesopotamia could not be mentioned, then Syria had likewise to be omitted: the committee thus rejected Wingate's and Sykes's suggestions in this respect. But Wingate, as has been seen, was also suggesting that an undertaking should be given that Palestine also should not be permanently occupied by a European power, and that it would be included among the districts to be 'in possession of their natives'. Given the language that Hogarth had been so recently instructed to hold, and

---

[1] F.O. 371/3380, *loc. cit.*

[2] Cab. 27/23, minutes of Middle East committee meeting no. 54 in which may be found Wingate's telegram no. 199, Cairo 28 Jan. 1918. The foreign office copy had disappeared when the relevant volume came to be bound; see F.O. 371/3396, 18007.

[3] F.O. 371/3380, 18462 and 19106/146, copies of telegrams from Cox, Baghdad 25 Jan., and viceroy, Delhi 28 Jan. 1918.

did hold, to Husayn on Palestine, Wingate's suggestion is surprising. It contradicted the recently-published Balfour declaration on which Hogarth had expatiated. Sykes who had drafted Hogarth's instructions (and who had had much to do with the Zionist policy of the government) therefore naturally omitted Palestine from the list of countries which, in his draft, were to be given an opportunity for self-determination. In order to support his view he now proceeded to disclose at the meeting another detail of his discussions with Husayn at Jeddah which he had not hitherto revealed:

> Sir Mark Sykes stated [the minutes of the committee record] that he had personally explained to King Hussein at Jeddah the difficulties which would ensue should King Hussein be burdened with the responsibility of the inclusion of Palestine, west of the Jordan, under his suzerainty. He thought that King Hussein fully realized the position in regard to Palestine, but that it was desirable that some definite 'accord' in writing should be effected.

It is impossible, of course, to establish definitely whether Sykes did speak to Husayn in these terms, but it is not inherently improbable. For this was exactly the language which, as has been seen above, he and Picot held to the 'delegates representative of Syrian Moslem feelings' whom they met at Cairo in April 1917. On that occasion, it will be recalled, the 'delegates' agreed – in Sykes's words – that

> for a new and weak state such as the Arab must be, Palestine presented too many international problems to assume responsibility for...

As regards Husayn's request that he should be recognized as king of the Arabs, this went against the established policy which had been adopted in November 1916, and the committee decided that not until his title had been 'recognised as such by the great mass of the Arab peoples and rulers' would Britain acknowledge it. The deliberations concluded with a request that Sykes should draft a telegram to Wingate embodying these decisions.[1] The telegram simply reaffirmed former pledges 'in regard to the freeing of Arab peoples'. But Sykes wanted also once again to make sweeping categorical promises, and the draft had a sentence which read: 'Liberation and not annexation is the policy which HMG have pursued'. Hardinge decided that it was 'safer' to omit 'and not annexation'.[2] Colonel J. R. Bassett, who was deputizing for Wilson at Jeddah, and who transmitted the new declaration to Husayn, pointed out in his report that this latest reaffirmation of the 'pledge' resolved nothing since Husayn

[1] Cab. 27/23, loc. cit.
[2] F.O. 371/3880, 22108/146, telegram to Wingate no. 163, 4 Feb. 1918.

has read into the terms of that 'pledge' very wide territorial boundaries, and professes the most implicit trust in the intention and ability of Great Britain to redeem the 'pledge' as he reads it. Wilson has written so often of the danger underlying this question that I need only say that it is always uppermost in one's mind here in one's daily intercourse with the King. Since his talk with Hogarth on the Palestine question – if not before – I have little doubt that His Highness has realized that he must be prepared to meet certain slight modifications of what he describes as the 'Agreement', and that he will meet them in a reasonable and proper spirit I fully believe, provided they are not too drastic, and full opportunity is given for their discussion with him in detail. He said as much to Hogarth in my presence. On the other hand, anything that would mean for him a rude awakening, I dread.[1]

The 'dread' of disabusing Husayn of his illusions which Bassett felt is, on the face of it, difficult to account for. It is true that Husayn often spoke of abdication or suicide if his own interpretation of what Britain owed him were disputed, but this was hardly a reason for 'dread' to be aroused in the breast of a British official. The proper response to such threats was that of Wilson who ended by finding them tedious and unconvincing. At the end of June 1918 he wrote that he was sure that Husayn had never seriously meant to abdicate,

but at the same time it is somewhat fatiguing and unusual to have a King presenting his resignation and one is tempted to take the matter semi-seriously and ask the King whether Bedlam or St. Helena most appealed to him as a desirable place of residence.[2]

It has to be added, however, that Wilson did not allow his impatience to become apparent to Husayn, and that he continued to humour him with a respectful – not to say indulgent – deference. In the event, we may observe in passing, Husayn did not commit suicide; and if he did abdicate, this was not because of unfulfilled British 'pledges', but because his despotic regime had become insupportable to his subjects, and he was powerless to fend off Sa'udi assaults. But Bassett's feelings of 'dread', which seem to have been widely shared, may perhaps be explained by a particular view of what British interests required. A representative expression of this view is one which occurs in a letter from Wingate to Sykes written at the end of June 1918. In this letter Wingate declares his agreement with Sykes's view that Husayn should have a prominent place in the plans for post-war settlement, and goes on:

He will be content with nothing less: and, failing recognition of his priority may throw in his hand altogether. That would make confusion worse

[1] F.O. 371/3380, 42105/146, extract from Bassett's letter to Wingate of 11 Feb. enclosed with Wingate's letter to Sykes, 19 Feb. 1918.
[2] F.O. 686/39, Wilson to director of Arab Bureau, Jeddah 30 June 1918.

confounded and stultify our decisions and Arab propaganda. We ought to ensure a symbol of Arab political unity – embryonic though that is at present – and I can still see no alternative to our ally King Hussein.[1]

This belief, namely that British interests required that Husayn should be recognized – and advertised – as the symbol of Arab unity, perhaps explains the next declaration in the series – a declaration which Wingate made on his own, without London's prior authority. In a telegram of 16 June 1918, he reported that Husayn had just seen in an Arabic newspaper published in Paris in the French interest the report of the speech – made shortly before the fall of Jerusalem – in which Jemal Pasha had revealed the terms of the Sykes–Picot agreement. Husayn, declared Wingate, had asked his agent to make enquiries about the truth of Jemal's assertions and the scope of the agreement. On the face of it, Husayn's enquiry was peculiar on two counts. In the first place, the agreement had been disclosed to him in May 1917 when Sykes and Picot visited him; in the second place, that very speech of Jemal's had occasioned Abdullah's request the previous January that it should be denied, and had thus elicited the declaration of 4 February. Wingate's reaction to Husayn's move was just as peculiar: he made no reference to the exchanges of the previous January and February, and on the other hand declared baldly to the foreign office that Husayn had not been 'officially' informed of the agreement. He took it upon himself, without asking for instructions, to inform Husayn's agent that what Husayn was referring to was merely 'a record of old conversations and of a provisional understanding (not a formal treaty)' which the Bolsheviks had found in the Petrograd foreign office and which Jemal, 'either from ignorance or malice', had distorted. Presumably in order to make sure that the agent would transmit the message correctly, the text was written down by Hogarth, and the document imprudently given to him. In September 1919, Faysal was to use it in support of his claims in Syria.[2] Wingate's message was untrue, as he – and Husayn – well knew. The purpose of Wingate's move was clearly to expedite a change of British policy which he knew to have been already under way, namely the abandonment of the Asia Minor agreement. As Balfour said with characteristic bluntness at a meeting of the Eastern Com-

[1] F.O. 371/3381, 123868/146, Wingate to Sykes, Cairo 30 June 1918. The policy of recognizing Husayn as 'suzerain' of all the Arabs was advocated by Wilson and Bassett at Jeddah. See Wilson's despatches of 5 June and 23 July 1918 in F.O. 882/13, fos. 60–2, and F.O. 371/3381, 146256/146 respectively.

[2] F.O. 371/4183, 131671/2117, minute by H. W. Young, 20 Sept. 1919.

mittee shortly afterwards: 'Our object apparently now was to destroy the Sykes–Picot Agreement'.[1] But this was impossible without the consent of the French. When, therefore, Wingate asked whether he could also tell Husayn that the agreement was dead for all practical purposes, the Eastern Committee instructed the foreign office to tell him that while his language to Husayn was approved of, yet 'the larger issue could only be decided after consultation with the French Government'.[2]

Wingate's action and its approval by the Eastern Committee marks an epoch in the history of the Husayn–McMahon correspondence. The Sykes–Picot agreement, it will be recalled, was negotiated in order to obtain international recognition for, and confirmation of, McMahon's promises to the Sharif. Now some two years later, the British authorities were encouraging him to regard this agreement as inimical to his claims and ambitions.

These claims Husayn never tired of asserting. In an interview with Wilson at the beginning of June he again claimed that from the beginning of the negotiations he had been indirectly if not directly treated by Britain as the future suzerain of all Arab lands; if he remained merely king of the Hijaz he would stop his work, 'as, to the Moslems, he would appear co-responsible with Great Britain for causing a split in Islam; and Syria and Baghdad were necessary to him'. It was only now, a year or so after he had declared his belief that Husayn was 'opposed to a Caliphate in principle', that Wilson realized the extent of the king's ambitions:

> To our approval of an Arab Caliphate if one is set up the King attaches a far wider meaning than we ever intended, as he includes Temporal as well as Spiritual power in the term Caliphate.[3]

Husayn buttressed his claim by a new argument. One reason why he was entitled to believe that he had been promised rule over the whole Arab world was that

> The National Flag of the King was designed by Sir Mark Sykes and accepted by the King as the National Arab Flag.
> The composition of the Flag was in itself a symbol of King Husein's Overlordship.

Husayn was in fact correct in asserting that Sykes had designed the flag, and that it was meant to symbolize Arab unity. As Sykes

---

[1] Cab. 27/24, Eastern Committee meeting, 11 July 1918.
[2] F.O. 371/3381, 107379/146, Wingate's telegram no. 948, Ramleh 16 June; Cab. 27/24, meeting of the Eastern Committee, 18 June 1918.
[3] F.O. 141/679, file 4088/17, despatch from Wilson, Jeddah 5 June 1918; see also his telegram of 2 June in F.O. 141/792, file 5172/40.

described it, it was 'Black for the Abbassids of Baghdad, white for the Omayyads of Damascus, green for the Alids of Kerbela, and red chevron for Mudhar heredity.'[1]

Husayn's ambitions were shortly afterwards once more asserted in all their amplitude in yet another letter to Wingate. In this letter, dated 28 August 1918, Husayn threatened to abdicate if the British did not confirm their original agreement with himself. According to a memorandum which he enclosed with his letter, Britain had agreed in 1915–16 to

> the formation of an independent Arab Government in every meaning of the word 'independence' internally and externally, the boundaries of the said Government being, on the East, the Persian Gulf; on the West, the Red Sea, the Egyptian Frontier and the Mediterranean; on the North, the Northern boundaries of the 'Vilayat' of Aleppo and Mosul up to the river Euphrates and its junction with the Tigris as far as their mouths in the Persian Gulf but with the exception of the Aden Colony, which is excluded from these boundaries.

Husayn also claimed that Britain had undertaken to 'shield' this vast new state against all interference or encroachment,

> and even in the case of an internal rising caused by enemy intrigues or the jealousy of Emirs, the British Government will give the Arab Government moral and material help in putting down the rising...

The memorandum also made a large new claim, which compels admiration as much for the ingenious interpretation on which it was based as for its cool audacity. In his letter of 24 October 1915, McMahon had stated that his territorial offer was 'without prejudice to our existing treaties with Arab chiefs'. As has been said, McMahon had here in mind chiefly treaties with the Sultan of Muscat and the shaykhs of Kuwait, Bahrayn and the Trucial Coast, but more particularly with the Idrisi. In his reply of 5 November Husayn had attempted to limit this qualification. He wrote that he was ready to respect British agreements with the shaykhs, 'and especially those which are essential'. This McMahon firmly rejected, writing, in his letter of 14 December, that Britain 'cannot repudiate engagements which already exist'. There for the time being matters rested, but Husayn, as has been seen, never gave up his ambition of becoming king of the Arabs, and this qualification must

---

[1] Kedourie, *England and the Middle East*, p. 80. For a discussion of the significance of these colours in the Sharifian flag, and for the possible antecedents of Sykes's design, see Khayriyya Qasimiyya, *al-'Alam al-filastini* (The Palestinian Flag), Beirut, 1970, pp. 9–15. This valuable essay also gives the history of the subsequent use of these four colours in Arab flags.

have irked him considerably to judge by the interpretation which he now gave it. What it meant was that

> [the Arab government] will replace the British Government in seeing that the rights involved in these agreements and contracts are maintained for the benefit of those who are entitled to them.

Husayn, in other words, was to be the residuary legatee of British paramountcy in Arabia and the Persian Gulf.

The reaction to Husayn's letter in Cairo was remarkable. True, the Arab Bureau produced a paper which showed, by copious quotation from the original correspondence, that Husayn's pretensions had no basis in fact. But no one proposed actually to speak to Husayn in this sense. Instead, Clayton, in a memorandum of 8 September (a mere three weeks before Allenby routed the Ottoman fourth army and occupied Damascus), expatiated on Husayn's state of mind which might have 'disastrous effects on our Arab policy'. He went on to retail the catastrophes which might ensue if Husayn were not humoured: he might actually resign, and then

> the whole existence of the Arab movement would be endangered. Disintegration would be the result, followed perhaps by a conflagration in Central Arabia, of which the enemy would take full advantage, and which would seriously affect our military operations, apart from the loss of prestige involved by a collapse of our Arab policy.

Clayton was emphatic that Husayn was 'the only commanding figure in the Arab revolt', and that without him it might relapse into 'spasmodic tribal action'.

> As regards future settlement in the Arabian peninsula, the best that could then be hoped for is the formation of a number of small States under Arab rulers devoid even of the nominal controlling influence formerly exercised by the Turkish Government.

Another reason for 'rectifying' Husayn's 'present attitude of mind' was that

> we have to remember our pledges to King Husein and the moral obligation imposed upon us by his initiation of the Arab revolt and his unswerving loyalty to Great Britain.

But Clayton did not propose that those pledges should be reaffirmed. On the contrary, he suggested making yet another declaration to Husayn which went beyond them. Husayn would be told that the British government 'would welcome the union of all these independent States of Central and Southern Arabia in an Arab alliance, as head of which they would welcome King Hussein with a suitable title to be decided upon hereafter'. As for Syria and Mesopotamia, Husayn would be assured that 'the Allies will uphold the principles of freedom and self-determination of peoples as the basis of settlement'.

The policy of what may be called the 'Clayton declaration' was also advocated by Cornwallis, the director of the Arab Bureau. In a paper of 10 September he put forward arguments which powerfully combined therapy, prophecy and high policy:

> [Husayn] has been reduced to a state of mind which. . .requires most careful treatment; and unless he receives a satisfactory reply to the present letter, he is more than likely definitely to resign, thereby endangering the success of the revolt, adversely affecting our military operations, probably involving Arabia, which would be left without any controlling force in years of internecine warfare and causing us a loss of prestige which would react against us throughout the whole Mohammedan world. It is a matter which will [Cornwallis asseverated] affect India and Mesopotamia equally with Egypt and the bordering countries, and make or mar our reputation for good faith in the East.

Cornwallis did not, however, explain why refusal to accept Husayn's fancies and support his grandiose ambitions (which Britain had not undertaken to support) should mar the British reputation for good faith in the East.

It is clear that both Clayton and Cornwallis were here acting not as advisers, putting forward various alternatives for the consideration of their superiors, but as advocates pushing a particular policy with whatever arguments seemed most convincing. Nor were the government better served by their high commissioner. In a despatch of 21 September, Wingate endorsed Clayton's and Cornwallis's views and urged that Husayn's primacy in the Muslim as well as the Arab world, and particularly in Arabia, should be recognized and supported. Wingate gave yet one more reason why this policy should be adopted. 'Moslems in general', he wrote, 'have hitherto regarded the Hejaz revolt, and our share in it, with suspicion or dislike'. This was an undoubted fact, but it had never before been urged by an official in Cairo; on the contrary, whenever the India office or the government of India had pointed it out, Cairo had denied its truth. But Wingate now used it to argue that Husayn should be protected against failure, which would be 'seriously detrimental' to British prestige in the Muslim world.

By the time Wingate's despatch reached London, the military situation in the Levant had been transformed. Damascus fell to Allenby on 1 October, the Ottoman armies were on the run, and the territories which Husayn was claiming were being occupied by the British, so that Wingate's arguments became somewhat academic. He was told to inform Husayn of the arrangements being made in the occupied territories. These arrangements displeased Husayn who protested in a message sent in October that they were 'fatal to his interests'. Wingate was again frightened that Husayn might abdicate, and in a telegram of 1 November urged that a declaration on the lines he had advocated in his despatch of 21 September be made. The declaration, he now added, should include the statement that France would not annex any part of Arab or Syrian territory.

These exchanges in turn elicited a memorandum written by a new authority on the Middle East in the foreign office, Arnold J. Toynbee. In this memorandum of 5 November 1918, Toynbee solemnly declared that Husayn's letter of 28 August had created a 'very serious situation'. Toynbee recognized that Husayn's version of the promises made to him by McMahon in no way corresponded with the actual facts, but he believed that Husayn was not acting in bad faith in putting forward his version:

> Oriental diplomacy is seldom precise unless compelled to be so, and the method by which the negotiations were conducted in 1915–16 left something to be desired in this respect. It is probable that the King genuinely believes his memorandum to represent the sense of what was tacitly, if not explicitly, agreed to by His Majesty's Government, and there is little reason to doubt that he is in earnest in threatening to abdicate, if his view of what was agreed upon is not adopted by us.[1]

Toynbee was thus supporting in London the arguments being pressed from Cairo. His colleagues at the foreign office probably listened respectfully since Toynbee had just circulated what seemed to be a most authoritative examination of the Anglo-Sharifian negotiations of 1915–16.

[1] F.O. 371/3384, 183342/747. To Toynbee's memorandum are attached Wingate's despatch no. 219, Ramleh 21 Sept., Husayn's letter of 28 Aug., Clayton's note of 8 Sept. and Wingate's telegram no. 1600, Cairo 1 Nov. 1918. Cornwallis's letter of 10 Sept. and the Arab Bureau paper commenting on Husayn's memorandum are in F.O. 882/13, fos. 134–6 and 143–9. Husayn's letter is printed in *Documents on British Foreign Policy 1919–39*, series 1, vol. XIII, 1963, no. 342 appendix.

7. Varieties of Official Historiography I: The Arab Bureau, Nicolson, Toynbee

Toynbee's examination of the McMahon–Husayn correspondence was by no means the first to be undertaken. In fact the first scrutiny in a series which, over the years, made the McMahon–Husayn correspondence even more cloudy and uncertain in its meaning and import, came in April 1916 from the newly-established Arab Bureau. McMahon sent it to the foreign office under cover of a despatch in which he declared, in a significant passage, that

> no guarantees which could give rise to embarrassments in the future between ourselves and the Allies, or ourselves and the Arabs have been given by us to any of the Arab parties...we have made every attempt to avoid definite commitments for the future; and consequently the longer a final programme is postponed the stronger becomes our position as negotiators...[1]

McMahon, then, here advances the view that the negotiations with the Sharif were strictly provisional and preliminary and that no 'definite commitments' had been entered into.

The unsigned memorandum which McMahon enclosed with his despatch did not quite support these assertions. The paper began by giving an account of the exchanges between the high commissioner and the Sharif, and then summed up what had been agreed on both sides:

> We, for our part, have *not* agreed to:
> 1. Do more than approve an Arab Caliphate, if set up by the Arabs themselves.
> 2. Recognize Arab independence in Syria, west of the line Aleppo, Hama, Homs, Damascus or in any other portion of the Arab area in which we are not free to act without detriment to the interests of our Ally, France.
>
> . . . .
>
> What has been agreed to, therefore, on behalf of Great Britain is:–
> 1. To recognize the independence of those portions of the Arab speaking area in which we are free to act without detriment to the interests of France. Subject to these undefined reservations, the said area is understood to be bounded N. by about Lat. 37°, East by the Persian frontier, South by the Persian Gulf and Indian Ocean, West by the Red Sea and the Mediterranean up to about Lat. 33° and beyond by an indefinite line drawn inland West

[1] F.O. 371/2768, 80305/938, McMahon's despatch no. 83, Cairo 19 Apr. 1916.

of Damascus, Homs Hama and Aleppo; all that lies between this last line and the Mediterranean being in any case reserved absolutely for future arrangement with the French and Arabs.

Within the above independent area we have also excepted:–
  1. Aden and district as our Imperial possession
  2. Irak (Vilayets of Basra and Bagdad) as to be in part leased and to be administered by us, and in other part, subject to our control in some degree and manner: We to hold any part of Irak, not by Imperial right, but under concession from the Arabs.

It is difficult to see how this memorandum can be reconciled with McMahon's emphatic assertions in the covering despatch to the effect that definite commitments had been avoided, and no embarrassing guarantees given, and one wonders if McMahon read or understood the paper he was commending to the foreign office.

In any case, the memorandum is a peculiar, not to say incompetent, document. It declares that the British government had not agreed 'to do more than approve an Arab Caliphate, if set up by the Arabs themselves'. In fact, McMahon's letter of 30 August 1915 had gone distinctly beyond this, since it affirmed that 'His Majesty's Government would welcome the resumption of the Khalifate by an Arab of true race'. But if it gave an attenuated version of what the Sharif had been promised over the caliphate, the memorandum went on to describe the territories committed to him with an over-precision which nothing in McMahon's letters justified; its assertions in this respect were so seriously inaccurate as to amount to downright misrepresentation. The memorandum affirmed that the British government had not agreed to recognize Arab independence in Syria 'west of the line Aleppo, Hama, Homs, Damascus'. This way of putting the matter gave yet another twist to Gibbon's original remark. For in his letter of 24 October 1915 McMahon had spoken of 'portions of Syria lying to the west of the districts of Damascus, Homs, Hama and Aleppo'; he had in no way mentioned a 'line Aleppo, Hama, Homs, Damascus'. A line of this kind, drawn on the map, would of course constitute a frontier and, as such, would have to be extended north and south for it to make sense at all. This is in fact what the author of the memorandum, following the logic of his language, now proceeded to do. For he went on to assert that the area of Arab independence recognized by the British, subject to undefined reservations relating to French interests, was bounded on the east by the Persian frontier and the Persian Gulf, south by the Persian Gulf and the Indian Ocean, west by the Red Sea and 'the Mediterranean up to about Lat. 33° and beyond by an indefinite line drawn inland west of Damascus, Homs, Hama and Aleppo'. If the earlier statement was seriously misleading, this latter one was wildly fanciful. For there was absolutely nothing in what McMahon had written to indicate that the Arab state would be bounded on the east by the Persian frontier from latitude 37° north to the Persian Gulf, and on the west by the Mediterranean up to latitude 33° – i.e. Haifa or thereabouts, and thence by 'an indefinite line' – what this expression stood for is not clear – drawn from Haifa and west – how far west was again left vague here – of Damascus, Homs, Hama and Aleppo. Perhaps the most surprising aspect of this memorandum is this sudden introduction of latitude 33° as a boundary of the Arab state. One is quite at a loss to know how it came to figure in the memorandum, since it had never been mentioned either by the Sharif or by McMahon, whether in his exchanges with Mecca or with London. A possible explanation is that Christian tradition held the northern frontier of 'Palestine' to lie at about latitude 33°.[1] Needless to say, Islam did not attach any significance to this particular line, and the Ottomans had never used it as an administrative boundary. Can it be that this was yet another – somewhat oblique – attempt to argue that 'Palestine' ought to be under British control or influence? For, as has been seen, this is what the Cairo authorities favoured when, in July 1915, they had been asked to comment on the various proposals put forward in the Bunsen Report. Another remarkable feature of this summary is that it fails to take into account McMahon's letter of 14 December 1915. In this letter, acting on instructions from London, McMahon, as has been seen, had told the Sharif that the question of boundaries in Syria 'will require careful consideration and a further communication on the subject will be addressed to you in due course'. Likewise, the fate of Baghdad *vilayet* required 'a much fuller and more detailed consideration than the present situation and the urgency of these negotiations permit'. The Arab Bureau memorandum was therefore mistaken in declaring that the British negotiators had in any way agreed that any part of Mesopotamia which Britain held, it would hold 'not by Imperial right, but under concession from the Arabs'.

It is clear that the memorandum concentrates on McMahon's letter of 24 October 1915 as the key document in the series. But there is no reason to think that this particular letter was any more important than any other in the series, or that it enjoyed a privileged

---

[1] See, e.g., article 'Palestine' by R. A. A. Macalister in James Hastings, ed., *Dictionary of the Bible*, 1909, p. 672.

status denied to the other communications. It could be argued, on the contrary, that the letter of 14 December, coming after that of 24 October, qualified and superseded, and (as we know from the exchanges between McMahon, the foreign office and the India office) was intended to qualify and supersede the statements of the earlier letter. In erroneously and tacitly concentrating attention on the letter of 24 October, however, this memorandum inaugurated a lasting tradition in the interpretation of the McMahon–Husayn correspondence.

The memorandum, as has been said, was anonymous, and it is impossible to say with any certainty who was its author. The Arab Bureau who prepared the memorandum had just been set up, and its director, D. G. Hogarth, may no doubt be taken as formally responsible for it. A copy of the memorandum in the Arab Bureau papers[1] is marked: 'by Cdr. Hogarth'. This is a very late attribution since the note seems to have been made with a ball-point pen (contrary to good archival practice), and no evidence is given in support of his authorship. It can also be urged that Hogarth, a careful scholar and always sceptical of Sharifian claims, was hardly likely to indulge in wild interpretations of McMahon's letters. The mystery remains. In any case, the conclusions of the memorandum were included verbatim in the 'Summary of Historical Documents' which, as has been mentioned, the Arab Bureau produced at the end of November 1916.[2] These conclusions were also adopted in full in a paper on 'The Sherif of Mecca and the Arab Movement' produced by the general staff at the war office and dated 1 July 1916.[3]

The account of British policy presented in the 'Historical Summary' is distinguished at one point by an interesting, if eccentric, interpretation which may be noticed here. As was set out in part 1 above, the Cairo authorities issued on 4 December 1914 an 'Official Proclamation' – a copy of which does not seem to have been sent to London – in which the Arabs were informed that Great Britain did not intend 'to possess any part of your country neither in the form of conquest and possession nor in the form of protection or occupation', and guaranteed that her Allies would follow the same policy. This proclamation, as has been argued, may have been the outcome of an exchange of telegrams between Cheetham and Grey; the acting high commissioner, as will be recalled, suggested making a statement to the effect that the British government did not intend to undertake operations in Arabia 'except for the protection of Arab

[1] F.O. 882/2.   [2] F.O. 371/6237, E155/4/91, cited above, p. 142.
[3] Cab. 17/176 contains a print of this paper.

interests or in support of attempts by Arabs to free themselves from Turkish rule'; the foreign secretary agreed, and Reuter, again on Cheetham's suggestion, issued a statement to this effect. In the voluminous exchanges between London and Cairo which were concerned with policy towards the Sharif this Reuter statement and the exchanges in which it originated were never once mentioned or recalled subsequently. It is therefore surprising to see the Arab Bureau 'Summary' begin its account by reproducing Reuter's statement (which, though officially inspired, was not itself an official document) and declare that in Cairo 'the Foreign Office declaration of the 14th November has always been regarded as the governing decision'.[1] For this assertion there is absolutely no evidence, and we may suspect that it does not so much recount past events, as indicate the wishes and predilections then current in the Arab Bureau.

The next interpretation of the McMahon–Husayn correspondence was offered by Harold Nicolson in a memorandum of July 1917 which has already been briefly quoted at the beginning of chapter 4. Nicolson began by reviewing British obligations to European Powers in respect of the Ottoman empire and declared that in respect of these 'we are bound only, in so far as important issues are involved, by treaties which are liable, and indeed destined, to be revised'. He concluded that British obligations were here moral rather than contractual. Nicolson set out in tabular form the desiderata of the Great Powers, which could not be 'ignored without either endangering the unity of the Entente or sacrificing the essential political needs of the future'. These desiderata were as follows:

For Russia	Freedom of the Straits
	Some form of autonomy for Armenia
France	Some form of satisfaction for French aspirations in Syria and the Lebanon
Italy	Sphere of influence in the Adalia region, together with final cession of Libya and the Dodecanese
Great Britain	Mesopotamia
	Independence of Egypt from Turkey
	?Palestine

Against the last entry, 'Palestine', Sir Ronald Graham minuted – rightly, in view of the Sykes–Picot agreement – 'At present we are committed to an internationalized Palestine'.

In describing obligations to the Arabs, Nicolson began with

[1] F.O. 371/6237, E155/4/91, p. 2.

The Fly in the Fly-bottle

McMahon's promise, in his letter of 14 December 1915, that 'Great Britain had no intention of concluding any peace, in the terms of which the freedom of the Arab peoples from German and Turkish domination did not form an essential part', and went on to quote from McMahon's letter of 24 October to show the extent of British commitments in respect of territory. Nicolson did say that McMahon subsequently declared that the position in Mesopotamia would have to be considered more fully later on, but he did not mention that McMahon had also postponed territorial arrangements in Syria to a later communication – which up to then had not been sent. Nicolson referred to the interview at Jeddah with Picot and Sykes in May 1917 when the Sharif

> signified his somewhat grudging acquiescence in French claims in Syria, as well as in our own desiderata in Mesopotamia, but the fact remains [so Nicolson believed] that, apart from these exceptions, we are bound, in so far as the papers in the Foreign Office indicate, to carry out our promise in regard to the liberation of the Arab districts in question.

This assertion was shaky and inaccurate, for if appeal was to be made to 'the papers in the Foreign Office', then what these would establish, as has been shown in part 1 above, is that the British obligation to 'liberate' Arab districts was predicated on an Arab rising and large-scale Arab desertions from the Ottoman army in the Levant.

As has been seen, Nicolson was doubtful whether the papers available at the foreign office enabled him to present a full picture of the negotiations with the Sharif, but this did not prevent him from coming to a conclusion which was unwarranted, if not downright extravagant:

> The extracts given above will...suffice to show that we are bound to the King of the Hedjaz in a far more complex and ineludable manner than we are to our European Allies, and the position is rendered all the more delicate by the fact that our prestige in Arabia and the Middle East will stand or fall by the extent to which we are enabled to act up to our promises.

In this surprising passage Nicolson asserts that the Constantinople agreement with Russia, the treaty of London with Italy, and the Asia Minor agreement were actually less binding on Great Britain than, and inferior in status to, the ambiguous and inconclusive correspondence between McMahon and Husayn. We may suspect that Nicolson came to harbour this error as a result of concentrating on McMahon's letter of 24 October 1915, and of treating it as a unilateral, clear and binding promise of territory, of neglecting the

208

letter of 14 December which took away much of what the earlier letter seemed to concede, and of failing to consider the significance and status of the correspondence as a whole. It is only this which can perhaps explain his solemn admonition that 'our prestige in Arabia and the Middle East will stand or fall by the extent to which we are enabled to act up to our promises', and his even more solemn conclusion, which suggested that

> the opinion of Sir Mark Sykes should be invited, before the matter is pursued further, as he alone will be able to state with authority how far any evasion or modification of our engagements to the Sherif are likely to be resented by Arab opinion.[1]

In referring thus to 'the extent to which we are enabled to act up to our promises', and to possible 'evasion or modification of our engagements to the Sherif', Harold Nicolson was speaking as though Great Britain were some kind of shady promoter liable at any moment to default on his obligations. Unbeknown to himself, he was inaugurating a fashion which many were to follow in discussing Anglo-Arab relations.

The next examination of the McMahon–Husayn correspondence was that found in Toynbee's memorandum on 'British Commitments to King Hussein'. Toynbee had been a member of the intelligence bureau of the propaganda department, which later became the department, and then the ministry, of information. The work of the bureau 'consisted in compiling political summaries of events and trends in important foreign countries, based largely on Foreign Office telegrams and despatches'. At the beginning of 1918 it was decided to transfer the bureau to the foreign office, where it became the political intelligence department. Toynbee joined the department at the end of March 1918.[2]

Toynbee later recalled that six weeks before the armistice he was instructed to report on British 'commitments' regarding the Middle East, and on their compatibility with each other: 'Mountains of files appeared on my desk; and I have never again had to work so desperately hard against time; for, though we could not predict the date of the coming armistice, we did know that hostilities were now nearing their end.'[3] The urgency and the magnitude of the task – for Toynbee had to produce a whole series of memoranda on

[1] F.O. 371/3044, 153075/1173, cited above.
[2] Rothwell, *British War Aims and Peace Diplomacy*, p. 206; Sir James Headham-Morley, *A Memoir of the Paris Peace Conference 1919*, 1972, p. xx. F.O. 366/787, 91660, records Toynbee's transfer from the ministry of information as from 28 Mar. 1918.
[3] Arnold J. Toynbee, *Acquaintances*, 1967, p. 203.

'commitments' in various parts of the Middle East – the fact that
he could not have been very familiar with the files, the extreme
complexity of the issues, and the character of his remit which
positively invited a search for 'commitments', are all perhaps
responsible for the superficiality of the report and the unsoundness
of some of the more important of its conclusions. Toynbee gave an
account of the negotiations with the Sharif which, as his various
references show, leant heavily on the 'Summary of Historical
Documents' which the Arab Bureau had prepared in November
1916. He uncritically assumed that the McMahon–Husayn correspondence constituted a unilateral unconditionally binding 'commitment' on the part of Great Britain, and he also seems to have
assumed that McMahon's letter of 24 October 1915 enjoyed a
privileged position in this correspondence. Thus he wrote:

> The boundaries of Arab independence to which His Majesty's Government
> are committed by Sir H. McMahon's second letter to Sherif Husein (24th
> October 1915), exclude (a) the British territory and Protectorate of Aden;
> and presumably also (b) the British Protectorate of Bahrein, since the
> Sherif's claims take the 'Indian Ocean' as the boundary of the Arabian
> Peninsula, and make no mention of the islands...
> On the other hand, they include (c) Akka-Haifa and (d) Basra...

He was particularly categorical about Palestine:

> With regard to Palestine, His Majesty's Government are committed by Sir
> H. McMahon's letter to the Sherif on the 24th October, 1915, to its inclusion
> in the boundaries of Arab independence.

These are peculiar and erroneous conclusions. Toynbee disregarded
McMahon's explicit proviso in the letter of 24 October that Great
Britain's readiness 'to recognise and support the independence of
the Arabs' was contingent on her freedom to 'act without detriment'
to French interests, and the French were then most undoubtedly
'interested' in Palestine. Toynbee, again, failed to give any weight
to the reservations made in this letter concerning Baghdad and
Basra. He also failed to take into consideration that McMahon's letter
of 14 December left things very much in the air, so far as Baghdad,
Beirut and Aleppo were concerned, and that his letter of 25 January
1916 postponed 'careful consideration' of the future of Baghdad till
'the enemy has been defeated and the time for peaceful settlement
arrives'. The reader of Toynbee's memorandum, if he had no other
knowledge of the subject, would have had no inkling that the so-called
British 'commitments' to Husayn were vague, tentative and conditional promises, rather than hard-and-fast contractual obligations.
As was noted in part I above Toynbee was shortly afterwards to use

in a memorandum directed against French pretensions the argument that Damascus, Hama, Homs and Aleppo had never formed part of the crusader kingdom, and that French claims were therefore historically unsound. But it never occurred to him when writing the 'commitments' memorandum that the obverse of this argument had an important bearing on McMahon's 'pledge'.

As it happens, Toynbee's interpretation was challenged on one particular issue which was to become extremely important in later years. Colonel L. Storr of the war cabinet offices queried his inclusion of Palestine in the territories promised to Husayn. Toynbee's reply is significant in providing a clue to his reading of the McMahon–Husayn correspondence:

> I think [Toynbee minuted on 26 November 1918] our territorial commitments to King Husein depend on his (undated) letter of July 1915 to Sir H. McMahon, the terms of which Sir H. McMahon, acting on instructions from the F.O. accepted, with certain reservations, in his letter of Oct. 24, 1915.

This minute confirms that Toynbee believed McMahon's letter of 24 October to be privileged, and that he considered McMahon's reservation in favour of French interests to be of little or no account. It was also misleading to assert baldly that McMahon accepted Husayn's terms 'on instructions from the F.O.' As has been seen in part I above, matters were not as simple as that. The simplification is understandable in someone writing under pressure, but it did give the impression – so contrary to what in fact took place – that a decision was taken in London, after due deliberation and in full knowledge of its meaning and implication, and communicated to Cairo.

Yet another important clue to Toynbee's thinking lies in another minute of his, in explanation of a map attached to his memorandum which purported to illustrate Anglo-Sharifian negotiations:

> Palestine was implicitly included in King Husein's original demands and was not explicitly excluded in Sir H. McMahon's letter of 24.10.15. We are therefore presumably pledged to King Husein by this letter that Palestine should be 'Arab' and 'independent'.[1]

This minute and the map it accompanied further show that Toynbee had uncritically adopted the interpretation mooted in the Arab Bureau memorandum of April 1916 in which Britain was deemed to have agreed to recognize an area of Arab independence which, on the west was bounded 'by the Red Sea and the Mediterranean up to about Lat. 33° and beyond by an indefinite line drawn

---

[1] F.O. 371/4368, 577/480, for Toynbee's memorandum and his minutes.

inland West of Damascus, Homs, Hama and Aleppo'. But, as has
been seen, there is no warrant in the correspondence for such an
interpretation. This minute of Toynbee's confirms the guess made
by W. J. Childs when he examined the McMahon–Husayn correspondence and its interpretations in 1930, that in including Palestine
within the area promised to Husayn, Toynbee 'felt he was on safe
ground, being conclusively supported by the views of the Arab
Bureau. At all events', Childs rightly added, 'his memorandum
contains no hint of an attempt to examine [McMahon's] pledge
critically'.[1]

V. H. Rothwell, in describing the work and influence of the
political intelligence department, has written that its more out-
standing members 'all had pronounced views on the subjects about
which they wrote as well as the capacity to present their views
persuasively'.[2] For Rothwell it was Namier who best exemplified
these characteristics, but Toynbee's papers and minutes show that
he too shared them. Thus, shortly after writing his memorandum
on commitments to Husayn, Sir Louis Mallet asked him to examine
French and Arab claims in the Middle East in relation to British
interests. The resulting memorandum, dated 19 December 1918, is
divided in two parts, the argument of the second of which is
apparent from its title: 'The Untenability of the Anglo-French
Agreement of 1916'. The agreement was untenable because of the
principle of self-determination, to which the French themselves
were appealing:

> In Syria there is a *de facto* Arab administration, recognised by the Allies,
> and unquestionably competent to express the feelings of the population. On
> the evidence that has reached us from the spot do the French seriously
> believe that the Syrians, through their national representatives, will declare
> for France?
> It is already clear that they will refuse French assistance, and in that event
> the only means left to France for asserting her influence over Syria would
> be to occupy the country militarily. But Sir Mark Sykes, who cannot be
> suspected of lack of sympathy for French aspirations, has telegraphed from
> Syria that the substitution of a French Army of Occupation for the British
> would precipitate a catastrophe.

This plea on behalf of Faysal's regime in Damascus was reinforced
by the argument of the first part, entitled 'The Value of the
Sherifial Arab Movement for British Policy'. Toynbee himself
provided a summary of this part of his paper:

[1] F.O. 371/14495, E6491/427/65, 'Memorandum on the Exclusion of Palestine from the Area
assigned for Arab Independence by the McMahon–Husayn Correspondence of 1915–16',
p. 54.
[2] Rothwell, *British War Aims*, p. 208.

If we support the Arab movement we shall destroy Turkey with much less risk of arousing against us the permanent antagonism of Islam; and we shall knit up our Empire by establishing a link between Egypt and India, without being compelled to take France into partnership, and placing her in a position to break our newly-won territorial continuity. On the other hand, if we allow the Arab movement to fail, and Syria to pass from Turkish to French domination, we shall be playing into the hands of the pro-Turkish faction among our Moslem subjects; we shall incur the resentment of the Arabs, who will consider that we have broken the spirit, if not the letter of our engagements, and we shall place ourselves and France in a position in which our traditional rivalry in the East, which has been removed only with great difficulty, will be bound to arise again in an aggravated form.

In this passage Toynbee, as may be seen, appeals not so much to the principle of self-determination, as to British imperial interests, to strategic considerations, to the long history of Anglo-French rivalry in the Levant, as well as to 'the spirit' and 'the letter' of 'our engagements' to the Arabs. All these varied arguments, of greater or lesser force, are marshalled in order to prove that Britain should support the Arabs, i.e. the Sharifians, and not the French in the Middle East. And British 'commitments' to Husayn take their due place in this advocacy. Indeed the memorandum opens with a striking reference to these 'commitments':

Our commitments to King Husein look formidable on the map; they limit, at least in appearance, our freedom of action in Mesopotamia and Palestine, and in Syria cause difficulties with the French. It is easy to point out that the Arabs have given us little military help in return for all this, and it is a legitimate and necessary question to ask, why we should look upon the Arab movement with favour, or at least why, in cases where our commitments to King Husein clash with those to France or other Arab rulers, we should not let the latter take precedence?

The answer is that the permanent political advantages of the Arab movement for British policy outweigh its comparative military ineffectiveness and the diplomatic embarrassment which it may cause.[1]

This passage is interesting in more than one respect. The categorical certainty about 'commitments' to which Toynbee gave expression in the memorandum he had written so shortly before is here, inexplicably, somewhat attenuated: the commitments to Husayn limit 'at least in appearance' British freedom of action, and in another passage (quoted above) he makes a distinction between 'the letter' and 'the spirit' of British engagements; can it be that he was not as sure of his reading of the McMahon–Husayn correspondence as his earlier paper indicated? Toynbee's view of the correspondence also manages completely to transform the relation between the

---

[1] F.O. 371/3385, 191229/747.

commitments to Husayn and those to France. As will be recalled, McMahon, as he told Grey, had been very careful not to promise anything which might conflict with French interests, and the purpose of the negotiation which issued in the Sykes–Picot agreement was precisely to harmonize the promises to the Sharif with French demands. The British view at the time – as much in Cairo as in London – was that in this at any rate the negotiators had been successful. Toynbee disregards all this and speaks of 'our commitments to King Husein clash[ing] with those to France'. This view of the transactions of 1915–16, which went against all the known evidence, was to have a long and influential career. The passage, finally, shows how difficult it is to disentangle Toynbee's view of what promises had been made in the past from his view of the right policy for the future.

This difficulty emerges even more strikingly from another memorandum of about the same date in which Toynbee strongly took issue with the views and recommendations of Captain A. T. Wilson, the civil commissioner at Baghdad. In a telegram of 11 December 1918 Wilson had begun by referring to a Reuter telegram reporting a series of articles in *The Times* (the anonymous author of which was in fact T. E. Lawerence). The telegram, declared Wilson,

> refers to splendour of early Arabian Empire and...makes the highly controversial assertion that 'a nation that once achieved such brilliance must have root of future greatness within if only circumstances are favourable'. I am not republishing this or similar communiqués which at this juncture do nothing but harm; political arguments based on past glories of decayed nations may go down with British public, but they only serve to excite distrust and misapprehension here among sober men, and swell the heads of the political theorists of Baghdad.

The telegram went on to specify his objections to Sharif Abdullah being made amir of Mesopotamia. Among these objections were that the population of Mesopotamia was almost exclusively Shi'ite, and the likely conflict with Ibn Sa'ud which this appointment would occasion. Toynbee's memorandum – which he seems to have written on his own initiative – strongly attacked Wilson. He brought forward what might be called the standard Arab Bureau arguments that the Arab movements was the antidote to pan-Islamism, and that Abdullah was 'a nominal Sunni with Shia proclivities' (a contention for which there was no evidence whatever) and hence acceptable to the Shi'ites. The memorandum shows no first-hand knowledge of Middle-Eastern conditions, and is only a studious and diligent distillation of Lawrence's, Clayton's and Sykes's familiar views.

Thus, to show how progressive the Arab movement was, Toynbee refers to Faysal's friendly relations with the Zionists, and solemnly declares that the 'leaders of the Arab Movement in Syria have already established an entente with the Armenians'! He also contemptuously dismisses the view of the Shi'ite divines in Mesopotamia on the score that many of them were foreigners and that 'they live apart from the world, and. . .represent very special ecclesiastical interests. Their views about the future of Mesopotamia', the future author of *A Study of History* cuttingly observed, 'should be accepted with the same caution as the view, say, of an Austrian Cardinal in Rome about the future of Italy'. To anyone who knows anything of Shi'ism or Mesopotamia the analogy is as misplaced as it is striking. But it is Toynbee's references to the McMahon–Husayn correspondence which makes this memorandum of particular interest here:

> The fact must be faced that [Wilson's] policy. . .is not consistent, even with the letter, much less with the spirit, of our understanding with King Husein.
>
> We have pledged ourselves to King Husein that Mesopotamia shall be 'Arab' and 'independent', subject to special measures of British administrative control. There is no controversy about this control: it is accepted by King Husein, by the people of Mesopotamia, and by all British Authorities that are concerned in the settlement of the Middle East. But Captain Wilson proposes, in effect, to take advantage of this control to isolate Mesopotamia from the other Arab countries, and deliberately to break up the Arab National Movement.
>
> This would clearly be a breach of faith with King Husein. . .

This reading of what the British were committed to in their undertakings to Husayn was, in part, a repetition of what Toynbee had argued in his 'commitments' memorandum. But, as has been said, McMahon's letters of 24 October and 14 December 1915, and of 25 January 1916, taken as a whole made it very doubtful indeed whether Husayn had been promised anything as definite as that 'Mesopotamia' should be 'Arab' and 'independent'. But in this later memorandum Toynbee went far beyond even these hazardous interpretations. He seemed to think that the 'independence' of the Arabs which McMahon promised to recognize and support in his letter of 24 October 1915 *ipso facto* meant the setting up of a kingdom or a series of kingdoms ruled by the Sharif and his progeny, and that to act otherwise was to 'break up the Arab National Movement', and to break faith with Husayn. This was to forget Husayn's repeated attempts, from the summer of 1916 until the end of the war, to secure recognition of precisely this interpretation, attempts which were as repeatedly rebuffed.

The Fly in the Fly-bottle

Toynbee's memorandum was dealt with in a spirited and forceful reply by Sir Arthur Hirtzel. In particular, he questioned Toynbee's reading of McMahon's promises:

> I can find no evidence that we are committed to King Husain to support the Arab nationalist movement in the sense suggested by the Foreign Office memorandum. We have undertaken that the Arab countries, within certain limits, shall be independent and free: we have not undertaken that they shall be united, still less that they shall be united under King Husain. Moreover [he acutely pointed out], historically the idea of a kind of unity symbolised by setting up members of the Shereefial family as local rulers is of quite recent origin. It did not exist while we were negotiating with King Husain, it came into existence only about a year ago, and it is only since – in the last few months – F.O. and W.O. have passed under the hypnotic influence of Colonel Lawrence that it has gained any currency. It has never had anything to commend it in Mesopotamia, and it has nothing now;...there is all the difference in the world between Husain's ambitions and our commitments, and I demur to the suggestion that what may very likely be a disappointment of the former is in this case a breach of faith.

When Sir Eyre Crowe, the assistant under-secretary of state at the foreign office, saw the exchange between Toynbee and Hirtzel he minuted that it would have been better if Toynbee's memorandum had been shown him before being given to Hirtzel, and that he hoped that it had not been circulated to the Eastern committee. He added: 'I am in agreement with much that Sir A. Hirtzel says'.[1]

This particular memorandum was in fact not circulated. What was circulated – and very widely – was Toynbee's earlier memorandum on 'commitments'.[2] The evidence in the files shows the extent of its influence. Thus, the members of the Eastern Committee received each a copy with the agenda for the meeting of 5 December 1918. The meeting was to discuss, among other subjects, policy in Syria and Palestine and the attitude to be adopted to French, Arab and Zionist claims there. The members heard a long statement by the chairman, Curzon, who began by giving 'the historical facts of the case'. He drew the members' attention to Toynbee's paper, and it is clear that his historical summary was based on it. The 'facts of the case', then, according to Curzon were that

> there was the letter to King Hussein from Sir Henry McMahon, of the 24th October, 1915, in which we gave him the assurance that the Hejaz, the red area which we commonly call Mesopotamia, the brown area or Palestine,

---

[1] F.O. 371/3386, 206913/747, for Toynbee's memorandum, Hirtzel's reply and Crowe's minute.

[2] F.O. 371/3384, 183770/747, contains a distribution list for the memorandum, established by Toynbee himself. Among those who were sent a copy was the foreign secretary, Balfour.

Varieties of Official Historiography I

the Acre–Haifa enclave, the big Arab areas (A) and (B), and the whole of the Arab Peninsula down to Aden, should be Arab and independent.[1]

Curzon's so-called 'facts of the case', needless to say, were totally inaccurate and misleading. He concentrated on McMahon's letter of 24 October 1915, seeming to think it was a kind of treaty. He showed utter disregard of McMahon's other letters, and even as regards this particular letter, he neglected the extensive reservations and qualifications with which McMahon hedged his promises. Curzon also disregarded entirely the exchanges between Husayn and various British officials over a period of two years which, as has been seen, are quite as essential as the original correspondence to a proper understanding of Anglo-Sharifian relations. What Curzon did, in fact, was to endorse – in the privacy of a committee meeting – Husayn's original demands in all their fullness.

Seen in this way, of course, British commitments to Husayn were utterly incompatible with the commitments to France as recorded in the Sykes–Picot agreement. The problem – over which the Eastern Committee spent a great deal of time and ingenuity – then became how to reconcile two contradictory promises or, if they were not to be reconciled, which promise to keep and which to break. It was an unreal problem since the Sykes–Picot agreement was designed precisely to fit in with McMahon's engagements. But since it was then British policy to do away with the Sykes–Picot agreement, this artifical dilemma had its uses in providing British ministers with the convenient argument that a prior set of engagements nullified the engagements to France. But since the French were not to be persuaded, the argument proved worse than useless. Worse, because it spread in British official circles a tenacious feeling of guilt over the supposed bad faith involved in these war-time transactions.

Curzon's 'historical' summary, based on Toynbee's memorandum, also entailed the incompatibility of the Balfour declaration with the promises to Husain. Such incompatibility was as illusory as the incompatibility between the promises to Husayn and those to the French. Since it was then British policy to support Zionism it was very inconvenient for belief in this incompatibility to spread and, as has been seen, Colonel Storr of the war cabinet offices did query, probably on the instructions of Hankey, the secretary of the war cabinet, or possibly on those of Lloyd George himself, Toynbee's assertions in this respect. This presumed incompatibility then

[1] Cab. 27/24.

217

was not insisted upon or publicized. On the contrary. Thus, while he was in Paris as a member of the Turkish section of the British delegation to the peace conference, Toynbee had to compose together with W. G. Ormsby Gore, at the request of Philip Kerr, Lloyd George's private secretary, a memorandum on Palestine for the information of the press. Ironically enough, in this memorandum Toynbee asserted that Palestine, owing to the many international interests there, including Jewish aspirations, was specially excepted from the agreement with France regarding Syria, and that this agreement 'did not conflict with our undertakings to King Hussein'.[1] But as in the case of the Sykes–Picot agreement, the belief that the Balfour declaration was contrary to the promises made to Husayn became prevalent in official circles, and also led to feelings of guilt over the presumed double-dealing.

Sir Louis Mallet, the head of the Turkish section of the British delegation in Paris (who was thus Toynbee's immediate superior), was among those who believed, clearly on the basis of Toynbee's memorandum, that a Zionist policy was incompatible with the promises to Husayn. In a conversation with Herbert Samuel at the end of January 1919, he expressed the view that it was wise for the Zionists to have moderated their demands for a Jewish government in Palestine. He went on:

> H.M.G. were committed, by implication, to the independence of all Arab countries excepting those areas mentioned by Sir H. MacMahon, from which Palestine was excluded. They [the Zionists] must arrange matters with Feisal.

Mallet's minute was initialled, without comment, by both Hardinge and Balfour.[2]

In a memorandum on policy in Syria, written shortly afterwards, Mallet went considerably further. Under the heading 'Our promises to the Arabs', Mallet declared that the acceptance of French proposals to divide the Arab countries between Britain and France

> would be contrary to British undertakings to King Husein as representing the Arabs. On April 14 1915 HMG undertook 'to make it an essential condition in the terms of Peace that the Arab peninsula shall remain in the hands of an independent sovereign state'. This state was afterwards defined as the countries extending roughly from Alexandretta but not including it, to the Indian Ocean excluding a strip of country between the Mediterranean and Damascus, Homs, Hama and Aleppo and Aden [sic; Adana?] leaving these former four towns to an independent Arab State.
>
> The Arabs, however, have never accepted the exclusion of the Coast and have always said that they would resist its occupation by force of arms.

[1] F.O. 608/93, file 360/1/7, paper 3051.
[2] F.O. 608/98, file 375/2/1, paper 1295, Mallet's minute of 30 Jan. 1919.

The memorandum is a surprising production to come from the pen of a senior and experienced diplomat who, by virtue of his office, might have been expected to be familiar with the relevant papers. Not only does Mallet affirm that Husayn was unconditionally and irrevocably promised these extensive territories, but he also buttresses his argument by interpreting Grey's declaration of 4 April 1915 as applying to a state extending from the Mediterranean to the Indian Ocean. In fact, as has been seen in part I above, Grey's declaration related specifically to the Muslim holy places which was all that Husayn was thought then to be concerned with. Mallet sent the paper to Lloyd George and to Balfour. The latter returned it without comment.[1] What makes Mallet's case even more curious is that some four months later he himself signed a despatch in which it was declared that the provisions of the Sykes–Picot agreement 'were entirely compatible with His Majesty's Government's engagements to King Hussein'.[2] If this was the case, then by the same token British promises to Husayn were entirely compatible with the Sykes–Picot agreement, and what Mallet had written the previous February could not be true.

Balfour himself seems in fact to have believed, again most probably on the basis of Toynbee's memorandum of which he had received a copy, that extensive binding promises were made to Husayn and that these were not reconcilable with the Sykes–Picot agreement, or even perhaps with the encouragement of Zionist ambitions in Palestine. A leader in *The Times* of 21 August 1919 complained that the Sykes–Picot agreement was 'not in harmony with engagement contracted by the British Government towards the King of the Hedjaz in the autumn of 1914 [sic]'. In a minute written the following day, E. G. Forbes Adam, Toynbee's colleague in the Turkish section of the British delegation, argued, correctly, that the terms of McMahon's letter of 24 October 1915 had provided in advance for the interests of France and, Forbes Adam went on to point out, again correctly, that 'the territorial form which the Sykes–Picot agreement took, sufficiently show[s] that it was based on our negotiations with King Hussein'. He asked, therefore, whether *The Times* should be spoken to. Balfour turned down the suggestion, and wrote:

[1] F.O. 608/105, 384/1/1, papers 1476 and 1999, Mallet's memorandum, Paris 4 Feb. 1919. Mallet put forward the same version of British promises to Husayn in a memorandum of 17 Feb. 1919 (P.R.O. 30, 30/10 Milner Papers).

[2] F.O. 371/4180, 79981/2117, despatch no. 809 to Curzon (signed by Mallet), Paris 26 May 1919.

The Fly in the Fly-bottle

It is rather dangerous to speak to The Times in this sense, unless we can reconcile our letter to Hussein of 1915 with the Sykes–Picot agreement of 1916. *I cannot.* Can anyone else?[1]

Shortly afterwards, in a memorandum of 15 September 1919 on Syria and Palestine, Balfour set out at greater length his view of the war-time agreements:

> In 1915 we promised the Arabs independence; and the promise was unqualified, except in respect of certain territorial reservations...
>
> ...In 1915 it was the Sherif of Mecca to whom the task of delimitation was to have been confided, nor were any restrictions placed upon his discretion in this matter, except certain reservations intended to protect French interests in Western Syria and Cilicia.
>
> In 1916 all this seems to have been forgotten. The Sykes–Picot Agreement made no reference to the Sherif of Mecca and...he has never been heard of since.[2]

This memorandum shows the foreign secretary to entertain hopelessly fanciful ideas about McMahon's negotiations with Husayn and their outcome. In particular, far from the Sykes–Picot agreement making no reference to the Sherif of Mecca, an appreciable part of it was concerned with setting up an Arab state or confederation of states, and its coming into operation was predicated upon 'the co-operation of the Arabs [being] secured, and...the Arabs fulfil[ling] the conditions and obtain[ing] the towns of Homs, Hama, Damascus and Aleppo'. This memorandum, in short, gives the impression that the foreign secretary was out of his depth, and did not know what he was talking about. Was the reason simply indolence, or was it that Balfour did not much care what exactly had been promised to whom, in the belief that what finally decided the issue was the balance of power? He would of course have been right to believe power decisive. No doubt, great Powers do commit great crimes, but a great Power is not always and necessarily in the wrong; and the canker of imaginary guilt even the greatest Power can ill withstand.

[1] F.O. 608/93, file 360/1/11, paper 5840.
[2] F.O. 608/106, file 384/1/1, paper 18928.

8. The Correspondence in the Peace Settlement: Faysal and Young

While these self-incriminating memoranda were circulating within the foreign office and the British delegation in Paris, their unwitting beneficiaries, the Sharifians, were adopting – through their spokesman – a line of argument which avoided reliance on McMahon's promises. The spokesman was Faysal who had been installed in Damascus, ostensibly as the administrator, under Allenby, of an enemy-occupied territory, and in fact as a British *protégé* who might prove a useful weapon with which to fight the French claims in the Levant.[1] At the suggestion of Colonel Lawrence Faysal was brought to Europe in a British battleship, and exhibited at the peace conference as the representative of his father, the king of the Hijaz. The line which he adopted, no doubt under Lawrence's tuition, avoided any mention of presumed war-time promises. His tactic was to concentrate on Syria – as distinct from Palestine and Mesopotamia – and to fight French claims there. Since this was what the British themselves wanted, he must have thought himself in a very strong position. In a letter to his father written from Paris on 19 January 1919, he said that while in London he had obtained promises of support from British statesmen, 'particularly as concerns the tearing-up of the Sykes–Picot stipulation.'[2] The language he held in London may be gathered from what he said at a meeting with Edwin Montagu, the secretary of state for India on 27 December 1918.

> In Great Britain [Faysal said, with Lawrence interpreting] the Arabs have always felt, and still feel, complete trust. He instanced his own attitude in regard to Mesopotamia, on which subject he had not said and did not intend to say, a single word: he had full confidence that the British Government would do what was right. But he has been greatly disturbed by certain recent developments, and particularly by the terms of the Sykes–Picot Agreement, the tenor of which was not made known to him until long after its conclusion. He had no idea, when engaged in the struggle against the Turks, that any agreement of the kind was in existence, or that Arab rights in Syria

[1] Kedourie, *England and the Middle East*, chs. 5 and 6 *passim*.
[2] Sulayman Musa (ed.), The Great Arab Revolt: Documents and Records, document no. 40, pp. 121–5.

had been bargained away in advance. Syria is the granary of the Hijaz – which in itself is a barren and valueless country – and its possession is absolutely essential to the Arabs.

On being questioned about Palestine, Faysal remarked that

> the Arabs were under deep obligations to Great Britain, and that it would ill become them to make difficulties over a question, of which they regard the British Government as the best judges. The Arabs recognise that many conflicting interests are centred in Palestine. They admit the moral claims of the Zionists. They regard the Jews as kinsmen whose just claims they will be glad to see satisfied. They feel that the interests of the Arab inhabitants may safely be left in the hands of the British Government.[1]

This is the line which Faysal took in his representations to the peace conference. In a memorandum of 1 January 1919, the case which he made for Syrian independence rested not on war-time promises, but on the general principles of national self-determination as stated in Woodrow Wilson's fourteen points. The language of this memorandum regarding Palestine is very close to what Faysal had to say at his interview with Montagu:

> In Palestine the enormous majority of the people are Arabs. The Jews are very close to the Arabs in blood, and there is no conflict of character between the two races. Nevertheless, the Arabs cannot assume the responsibility of holding level the scales in the clash of races and religions that have, in this one province, so often involved the world in difficulties. They would wish for the effective super-position of a great trustee, so long as a representative local administration commended itself by actively promoting the material prosperity of the country.

Again, when he appeared before the supreme council on 6 February 1919, Faysal declared that 'Palestine, in consequence of its universal character, he left on one side for the mutual consideration of all parties concerned.'[2]

Faysal's avoidance at this time of any mention of McMahon's alleged promises is very noticeable. Lawrence's advice, as has been said, was no doubt responsible, but Faysal himself, in his letter of 19 January to his father, mentioned above, justified his silence by a most striking argument. He told Husayn that he could not protest against French claims as he had no documents to prove the prior claims of the Sharifians:

[1] L/P & S/18, memorandum B309 by J. Shuckburgh, 30 Dec. 1918.
[2] D. H. Miller, *My Diary of the Peace Conference*, vol. IV, 1924, pp. 297–9 for the memorandum of 1 Jan., and pp. 227–34 for the record of Faysal's declaration before the supreme council.

The Correspondence in the Peace Settlement

Even your treaty with England is not available, and even if it had been it is of no importance for it is no more than a preliminary and limited contract, (*'ibara 'an muqawala ibtida'iyya wa mahduda*).[1]

This letter clearly shows that Faysal at any rate understood the flimsy character of McMahon's so-called 'commitments' over which Toynbee and others were making such heavy weather at the foreign office.

Whether Husayn understood the position equally well is not as clear. He may well have thought that the installation of his son Faysal in Damascus as the virtual ruler of Syria meant that his ambitions were about to be fulfilled. His newspaper *al-Qibla* published early in October 1918 an exchange of telegrams between his son and him in which Husayn was styled *amir al-mu'minin* and informed of the Syrians' submission to him as their sovereign. In his reply, Husayn accepted the proffered sovereignty and consigned the Syrians to Faysal's care until he himself could attend to their affairs.[2] During the following months Husayn continued to complain that the promises made to him were not being kept. In the course of an interview on 22 November 1918 at Jeddah, Wilson had mentioned Homs and Hama when discussing local government in Syria. Husayn asked him why he did not speak of Alexandretta or Tripoli also: 'These towns were within the agreed boundaries of the Arab Kingdom, and if those boundaries were to be curtailed he could not persevere in the work he had taken up.'[3] On this occasion Wilson replied that Alexandretta and Tripoli lay in an area in which McMahon had 'definitely' stated that Britain could not treat independently of the French, that indeed it had been especially excluded from the area of Arab independence. But he was clearly uneasy at Husayn's continuous complaints of British bad faith. In two despatches of 21 January and 5 February 1919, he expressed his disquiet that Husayn had been allowed 'to remain under the impression that certain of his interpretations are correct'. Wilson considered that Husayn 'has some justification for honestly believing that he has Great Britain's pledged word on certain matters because, although he has frequently stated what his interpretation of the "arrangements" of 1915/16 is, he has never had it challenged to any extent and thus has been left in a "fools paradise"'.[4] Wilson recurred yet

---

[1] Sulayman Musa (ed.), The Great Arab Revolt: Documents and Records, no. 40, cited above.
[2] F.O. 371/3386, 171568/747, Wingate's telegram no. 1506 Urgent, Cairo 13 Oct. 1918.
[3] F.O. 882/13, fo. 187.
[4] F.O. 686/63, Wilson to Cheetham, Jeddah 31 Jan., and F.O. 141/776, file 70/420, Wilson to Cheetham, 5 Feb. 1919.

again to McMahon's letters, the Arabic text of which was still not to be found at the residency, and stressed the importance of dispelling Husayn's illusions with an authoritative and clear pronouncement. Wilson's apprehensions elicited a most revealing despatch from Sir Milne Cheetham who was then in charge of the residency. Cheetham, it will be recalled, had also been in charge of the residency in the interval between Kitchener's departure and McMahon's arrival, and had been thereafter the senior diplomat in Cairo under the high commissioner all through the war. He had therefore been very well placed to follow Anglo-Sharifian relations. Cheetham now informed the foreign office (and this was the first time that the fact was reported to London) that the Arabic copies of McMahon's letters of 14 December 1915 and 25 January 1916[1] were lost, and that only a partial copy of the letter of 24 October was available. He went on:

> This loss, however, will not so much affect the question as Colonel Wilson supposes; for the extreme and erroneous pretensions to which he refers as put forward from time to time by King Hussein seem to be based in reality not on letters of Sir H. McMahon but on certain verbal messages sent with the two letters of October [24] and December [14], 1915. In what form the Arab messengers delivered these, and in what form the sherifial Secretariat may have committed them to writing, it is not possible for us to know.

Cheetham went on to give as an example the monthly subsidy which Husayn affected to regard as rent being paid by Britain to compensate for the temporary occupation of Basra,

> yet, so far as the verbal message entrusted by Sir H. McMahon to the Arab messenger went, it only hinted at the possibility that some proposal for money compensation might ultimately be entertained by His Majesty's Government.

Cheetham's statements constitute the first admission by a highly-placed Cairo official that the methods used in negotiating with the Sharif left something to be desired. But the misunderstandings which these methods engendered did not worry Cheetham unduly. He insisted that Husayn was not 'under much misapprehension about the real scope of our engagements', and doubted 'that he will take very hardly our ultimate interpretation of their letter'. Against all the evidence Cheetham insisted that Husayn had no illusions about the extent of French ambitions in Syria, 'or about the limitations which the consideration of these imposed on our diplomatic engagements to himself'. His reason was the very same that

[1] He erroneously dated them 21 Dec. and 30 Jan. respectively.

had inclined Grey, McMahon and Storrs to make vague and large-sounding promises, namely that the Arabs were childish enough to be impressed by mere words, and that mere words do not in the end matter. Cheetham expressed this attitude as follows:

> He [Husayn] hopes and perhaps believes that we shall prevail against such [French] desires, and his sanguine nature and Constantinopolitan training continue to make him assume and protest that what he desires is, and will be – up to the last moment.

Kidston, of the Eastern department of the foreign office, was not disposed to share Cheetham's complacency. He minuted that Husayn 'has over and over again been allowed to put in writing, without any contradiction from our side, exaggerated statements of what he alleges we have promised him', and he rightly expected this to lead to trouble. But the despatch elicited quite a different reaction within the British delegation in Paris. Mallet recorded that he had consulted Lawrence (who was then simultaneously a member of the British and of the Hijaz delegation) about Wilson's suggestion that Husayn should be informed of 'the real purport of British undertakings', and that Lawrence agreed that such explanations were 'inopportune' then. They would lead to awkward questions and discussions, and 'Feisal understands our position'. Mallet's minute was initialled without comment by Crowe, Hardinge, and Balfour in turn.[1]

During the following months Husayn continued to harp on the extent of British promises and their non-fulfilment. Thus, when H. Goldie, the acting British agent at Jeddah, was moved to tell him that it was perhaps not judicious for his newspaper to call him *amir al-mu'minin*, Husayn in his reply again referred to McMahon's promises:

> I do not like to send you even the numbers of these letters and their dates, let alone the original letters...in which he [McMahon] remarks that Great Britain's intention is to restore the Arab Khaliphate, and Your Excellency now says 'do not write Emir El Moomenine', a matter which I cannot explain...[2]

It was left to another successor of Wilson's at Jeddah, Colonel C. E. Vickery, shortly afterwards to call Husayn's bluff, and at last induce him to show the letters on which had been based the large claims which made Wilson so uneasy. Vickery's attitude to Husayn was clearly not as deferential as Wilson's. He was, writes Sir

---

[1] F.O. 371/4256, 29123/728, Cheetham's despatch no. 66, Cairo 9 Feb. and Kidston's minute, 24 Feb. 1919; F.O. 608/97, file 375/1/3, paper 2921 for Mallet's minute (undated).

[2] F.O. 686/41, Husayn to Goldie, 11 Aug. 1919.

The Fly in the Fly-bottle

Laurence Grafftey-Smith (who served as vice-consul in Jeddah about that time),

> more forthright, and sometimes rather brutal, with our ally. At one interview King Hussein announced, not for the first or last time, that death was better than dishonour, and that he was all but irresistibly tempted to throw himself from the office window. Vickery rose from his chair and walked slowly to the window, where he stood for a moment, as if calculating the exact height from the street. Then he gave one loud, contemptuous sniff, and returned to his desk. His Hashemite Majesty would have had about fourteen feet to travel along the suicides' road.[1]

Vickery's forceful approach succeeded where Wilson's more respectful methods had failed. On 1 October 1919 he reported to Cairo that Husayn had shown him three letters signed by McMahon, one of which, Husayn claimed, proved that McMahon had agreed to all his territorial demands in 1916. Many years later, Vickery described the interview in a letter to *The Times*:

> I was received by the King alone on the top storey of his Jeddah house. For an hour or more I listened to the bitter complaints of King Hussein of the way he had been treated in defiance of pledged and written word; again and again I brought the discussion round to the 1915 letter and tried to provoke the Sherif into showing it to me. It must have been after midday, when I had been with him over three hours, for on looking down from my seat in the bow window there was no shadow in the street and the sun was suspended like some sword over the city, that the King suddenly clapped his hands and bade the slave who came in to bring his portfolio. This was done and unlocked by Hussein himself; he fumbled through some papers and finally threw one at me, 'Read yourself, O light of my eye' he said.[2]

The letter which Husayn at last so triumphantly disclosed was that of 10 March 1916 in which McMahon, clearly referring to Husayn's requests for money, food and ammunition (as listed in his letter of 18 February 1916), had written: 'I am pleased to be able to inform you that His Majesty's Government have approved of meeting your requests'. Husayn argued that this sentence meant that all his territorial demands had been conceded: 'Nothing would persuade the Sherif Hussein', Vickery remarked in his letter, 'that it did not refer to everything that he had asked for in the acquisition of territories to form the Arabian Empire which inspired every waking moment of his life'.

Vickery, of course, hastened to report the disclosure to Cairo.

[1] Grafftey-Smith, *Bright Levant*, p. 146.
[2] *The Times*, 21 Feb. 1939. In this letter Vickery declares the interview to have taken place in 1920. This is clearly a slip of the memory, for the documents show that it took place on 1 Oct. 1919.

The Correspondence in the Peace Settlement

Two days later there was another development. Abdullah showed him the draft of a letter from the Sharif to McMahon dating from the end of December 1915, and claimed that McMahon's letter of 10 March 1916 was an answer to this letter. It is of course the case that the Sharif's letter of 1 January 1916 (which is what Abdullah must have shown Vickery) did reiterate the Sharif's territorial demands in all their fulness. But McMahon had replied to these demands in his letter of 25 January and not, as Abdullah sought to persuade Vickery, in the letter of 10 March. Vickery was asked to verify the text of the letters himself, and he in fact succeeded in making transcripts of McMahon's letters of 30 August, 24 October, 14 December 1915, and of 10 March 1916, which Husayn had jealously kept from Wilson for over two years. But Abdullah still withheld from Vickery the letter of 25 January 1916. Even so, it became clear that when Abdullah first read to Vickery passages from the letters in his possession he had, as Allenby put it in a despatch of 15 December 1919, 'omitted certain passages because he hoped that if he did so they might escape observation'. Abdullah's childish deception availed him nothing, for it was now confirmed that, as Vickery wrote in a telegram of 3 October 1919, McMahon's letters did not commit Britain to much, and that Husayn had 'an exaggerated idea of their importance with very little justification'.[1] Abdullah himself does not seem to have had any illusions about the scope of McMahon's commitments. In March 1920 he told Vickery that he had refused to become Faysal's foreign minister at Damascus

> since he had read the 'McMahon' letters and saw clearly how things must turn out and what the eventual position of Syria would be. It was obvious, he added, that France would put forward claims to Syria, and it was equally obvious from McMahon's letters that England would have to forego any claim to Syria.[2]

Vickery, then, was the first British official to see the Arabic version of McMahon's letters since Storrs and Ruhi had composed them. As has been seen, the fact that hitherto they could not be traced in the residency files had caused no little concern, since it was feared that Storrs and Ruhi had unwittingly committed the British government to more than what the original English text had

---

[1] F.O. 686/42 for correspondence between Vickery and the Arab Bureau 1–31 Oct. 1919, and a table comparing the English text of McMahon's letters with the Arabic version as received by Husayn. Allenby's despatch no. 582, Cairo 15 Dec. 1919, reporting Vickery's researches and their results, is in F.O. 371/4186, 161763/2117.

[2] F.O. 882/22, fo. 228, Vickery to Arab Bureau, Jeddah 6 Mar. 1920.

promised. Only a few days before Vickery succeeded in securing the Arabic text a note written by someone in the residency said that

> it will probably be wisest to say nothing more to F.O. re the original correspondence with King Hussein, otherwise we shall have to draw attention to the fact that copies of the original Arabic versions of letters do not exist in Residency files.[1]

If this note is to be believed, then either Cheetham had erred in declaring (in his despatch of 9 February 1919) that some, at any rate, of the Arabic texts of McMahon's letters were available in Cairo, or these texts had again been mislaid or destroyed.[2] It appears that shortly after Vickery's transcripts were received in Cairo, an official at the residency found the Arabic drafts caught up on the back of a drawer in Storrs's desk.[3] These texts were not sent to London, nor was the fact reported. Neither did Allenby, when he reported Vickery's discoveries in December 1919, send copies of his transcripts to the foreign office. When the Arabic text of McMahon's letters was required during the Palestine conferences in 1939, copies of Vickery's transcripts made in 1937 at the Cairo embassy were supplied to the delegates. This is clear from the fact that these copies did not include McMahon's letter of 25 January 1916 which Abdullah had kept back.[4] Both Vickery's transcripts and Storrs's drafts have since disappeared.

Shortly before Vickery in Jeddah succeeded in obtaining the copies of McMahon's letters the subject of McMahon's promises was once more ventilated, in London, and at the highest level. As is well known, Lloyd George's attempt, in which he had persisted since the opening of the Paris peace conference, to exclude the French

---

[1] F.O. 141/776, file 70/468, note of 28 Sept. 1919 addressed to Owen Tweedy, signature undecipherable.

[2] A minute of 21 June 1936 by the foreign office library (F.O. 371/20807, E3284/22) gives a list of Arab Bureau files which had been destroyed '(whether by accident or design is not stated)' which might have contained these texts.

[3] Grafftey-Smith, *Bright Levant*, p. 155. A minute in F.O. 141/726, file 17, dated 21 Feb. 1931, records that the draft Arabic letters were eventually found by A. Keown Boyd 'among some rubbish left by Sir R. Storrs'. The signature at the bottom of the minute is illegible.

[4] When the Peel commission on Palestine was preparing its report, the cabinet decided (2 June 1937) to allow the inclusion of extracts from the McMahon–Husayn correspondence in the report, and these extracts were the first to be published with official sanction. On the same occasion the cabinet decided that if a demand were to be made for full official publication, this demand should be acceded to without delay. The foreign office began preparing a set of the documents for possible publication. It was then discovered that the Arabic text of McMahon's letters was not available in London and the Cairo embassy was asked to supply these texts. The embassy sent a set of 'certified true copies' but did not indicate of which documents they were copies. The letter of 25 Jan. 1916 was missing from this set. F.O. 371/20807, E3034, 3194, 3284 and 3529/22/31.

from Syria, in the end broke down. He decided in September to cut his losses and concede the French claims. This meant the abandonment of Faysal, who had been the lynch-pin of the earlier policy. He was summoned to London in order to be persuaded to come to terms with the French himself.

Faysal was naturally bitter and indignant at this sudden *volte-face* which left him in the lurch. When he came to London, he protested vehemently; and among his arguments against the new British policy figured McMahon's promises to his father, on the subject of which he had been quite silent on his earlier visit a few months before. He now came armed with a copy of the memorandum which, as has been seen, his father had enclosed with his letter to Wingate of 28 August 1918. Whether he believed it or not, Faysal now claimed that this document was the copy of a treaty between his father and Great Britain, and that by the terms of this treaty Syria was his. But, at a meeting between Faysal and British ministers on 23 September 1919, Curzon, then in charge of the foreign office during Balfour's absence in Paris, had no difficulty in showing that this treaty was purely imaginary. This meeting is notable for the fact that at last and for the first time an official rebuttal was made of the claims which Husayn had never ceased making since 1916. Curzon now stated – and Faysal did not dispute his statement – that no time limit had been agreed for the British occupation of Basra, and that Britain had never undertaken to cut the railway at Mersina or elsewhere prior to the Sharif's rising.[1] Faysal was annoyed with his father for being made to look like a fool and wrote to him a sharp letter declaring that Curzon had emphatically denied the existence of a treaty, and had declared that the letters which had been exchanged required the British government to recognize an Arab government 'only in the four towns (*mudun*), Damascus, Hama, Homs and Aleppo and nothing else'.[2]

Syria, of course, was at the centre of these talks. When Lloyd George decided to give in to the French, he naturally had to consider whether his new policy was compatible with past British engagements. The issue was discussed on 9 September at his house in Trouville, and among those present were Bonar Law and Allenby. The latter, who favoured very much the Sharifian regime in Syria, contended that it was extremely difficult to harmonize the

---

[1] The minutes of the meeting of 23 Sept. 1919 are printed in *Documents on British Foreign Policy 1919–39*, series I, vol. IV, no. 293.

[2] Sudan Archive, Durham University, Sir Sa'id Shuqayr Papers, 493/6, copy of letter from Faysal to Husayn, London 16 Oct. 1919. Shuqayr, a Syrian, was a Sudanese government official whose services had been lent to Faysal.

different pledges which had been made to different people under different circumstances. Lloyd George thought otherwise:

> Our first pledge had been made to the King of the Hejaz. We were to conquer the country and let him establish an Arab State or Confederation of States, with boundaries which should include Damascus, Homs, Hama and Aleppo. We had however at no time promised Syria to the Arabs.[1]

Lloyd George's language shows that he was confusing the provisions of the Sykes–Picot agreement with the terms of McMahon's letter of 24 October 1915. But in spite of this confusion Lloyd George was fundamentally right, for McMahon had never promised to the Sharif outright and without qualification any territory in Syria or elsewhere. The prime minister's argument was no doubt in aid of his policy, but this did not make it any the less correct. With his acute and agile mind he seized on the essence of the matter, which the learned and laborious despatches and memoranda of his officials had only succeeded in obfuscating.

Lloyd George may have been fortified in his views by a memorandum which Grey had shortly before sent to Balfour. The former foreign secretary expressed his surprise 'to see it stated that our engagements to the King of the Hedjaz are incompatible with our engagements to France about Syria'. This was most unfair to those who had negotiated the agreement 'and will do increasing mischief to the reputation of British policy and good faith'. Grey correctly stated that there was nothing in McMahon's promises 'to prevent our agreeing to the demand of France for the Syrian sphere of influence under the Sykes–Picot arrangement'. The dispute with the French which Lloyd George had just settled by his *volte-face* had turned on his insistence that British troops should garrison Syria. Grey's implicit criticism of this stance was justifiable:

> It was perfectly open to us, without any engagement to the King of the Hedjaz, to come out of Syria after the Armistice was signed and let the French take our place...it is important not to allow the engagement to the King of the Hedjaz to be represented as incompatible with the engagement to France without a public contradiction.[2]

At their first meeting, on 19 September, Lloyd George firmly told Faysal that there was no contradiction between the British engagements to his father and the Sykes–Picot arrangement. Husayn had been promised that Damascus, Homs, Hama and Aleppo would be

---

[1] Cab. 21/153.
[2] Lloyd George Papers F12/1/43, memorandum enclosed with Grey's letter to Balfour, 9 Sept., forwarded by Curzon to Lloyd George with his letter of 17 Sept. 1919.

within the Arab state. Exactly the same provision was made in the
Sykes–Picot agreement. This was indeed the case, and if Faysal had
reason to complain it was not because written engagements had
been broken, but because British actions for the past year had –
legitimately – led him to imagine that the British would support him
at all costs against the French. What else was the meaning of
Damascus being delivered to him, of the generous subsidies and the
supplies of arms he had been receiving, of the resolute opposition
to French demands by the British delegation in Paris and by
Allenby in the field? But all these actions by the British, though
they were more eloquent by far than any formal commitment, yet
did not amount to a formal commitment on paper. So, in order to
make out a case for continuing British support against the French,
Faysal, as has been seen, appealed to a non-existent treaty, and also
to the fact that Wingate had told his father in June 1918 that the
Sykes–Picot agreement did not really exist.[1] It was true of course
that Wingate had, without instructions and on his own, disowned
the agreement. But his repudiation had been retrospectively approved, and it was very difficult for the British negotiators convincingly to rebut Faysal's argument in this respect. It had to
be ignored, and the long letter which the foreign office sent in
reply to Faysal's contentions tried to show by means of textual
quotation that the Sykes–Picot agreement and McMahon's promises
were strictly congruent with one another. This was probably the
ablest, most straightforward and most convincing state paper
to be produced in the long history of the McMahon–Husayn
correspondence.[2]

The letter was an answer to Faysal's letter of 21 September. It
was not sent until 9 October. The reason for this delay was the great
care which was taken over its drafting. A first draft was produced
by H. W. Young, Curzon suggested alterations and additions,
Kidston produced an alternative wording for certain passages, and a
composite draft was then sent to the prime minister. He amended
some passages and approved it. Only then was the letter sent to
Faysal, over Curzon's signature. The kernel of its argument is
contained in the following passage:

> From this correspondence two things are clear. First, that the British
> Government are bound by their undertakings to King Hussein to recognise
> the establishment of an independent Arab State comprising within its

[1] *Documents on British Foreign Policy 1919–39*, series I, vol. IV, no. 286, for Faysal's
letter of 21 Sept. 1919.
[2] Printed in *ibid.* no. 309.

borders the four towns of Damascus, Hama, Homs and Aleppo; and second that they made it absolutely clear to your illustrious father before the entry of the Arabs into the war that they regarded France as having special rights in the area west of these four towns. His Majesty's Government would further point out that in 1916 when, for the purposes of the common campaign, it became necessary to arrive at an agreement with France and Russia as to the occupation of Turkish territories in the event of the downfall of Turkey, His Majesty's Government insisted on reserving the independence of the Arabs in the districts which they had promised to reserve to them in their correspondence with King Hussein. They did not communicate this agreement to King Hussein because it was in complete conformity with the undertakings they had already entered into with him.

The attitude of His Majesty's Government, therefore, throughout these negotiations has been entirely consistent and clear. They have entered into obligations to both their Allies, to the French and to the Arabs. These obligations do not conflict but are complementary to one another.

This passage is, on the whole, true to the historical record. But it was not true that Husayn was not told of the Sykes–Picot agreement at the time of its signature because it was 'in complete conformity' with the undertakings which had been given to him. The truth, of course, was that details of the agreement were withheld from him at the urging of the Cairo officials. Nor was it true, as the letter implies, that the agreement was never communicated to him. On the contrary, as has been seen, Sykes and Picot did communicate the provisions of the agreement to Husayn when they visited Jeddah in May 1917. Since the labyrinthine complexity of the foreign office archives made it easy for papers to be lost sight of, it is entirely possible that those who drafted the answer to Faysal were ignorant of these facts, and that this, as much as their desire to make the best case possible for Britain, accounted for their erroneous statement. For if they had known, and made use of, the Jeddah talks, they would have strengthened their brief.

Cogent as the letter was, yet it would have been more cogent and forceful, if certain formulations proposed by Young and Kidston had not been abandoned on the way. Thus where the letter stated that the British government were bound by their undertakings

> to recognise the establishment of an independent Arab State comprising within its borders the four towns of Damascus, Homs, Hama and Aleppo[,]

as Young originally described it, the undertaking was

> to secure to the Arabs the independent control of the four towns of Damascus, Hama, Homs and Aleppo[,]

which was a more exact report of what McMahon had it in mind to promise. A passage which Young drafted, but which was not retained, would also have served to recall more exactly to Faysal's mind the realities of 1915–16 negotiations:

> the British Government have never made the smallest effort to conceal from His Highness Sherif Hussein the fact that they were under obligations to their French allies; that their pledges to His Highness were confined to Arab territories as defined by H. M. High Commissioner at Cairo; and that even in respect of these territories it was expressly stipulated that the assurances of the British Government would only be binding in respect of those portions of the area in which Great Britain was free to act without detriment to French interests.

In his letter Faysal had complained that the policy which Lloyd George was now following was based on the Sykes–Picot arrangement of 1916 and not on McMahon's promises:

> But what [asked Young] was the basis of the arrangement of 1916? It was the encouragement of Arab independence.

Kidston, in turn, suggested a paragraph, also in the end discarded, which pointedly drew attention to the character and extent of McMahon's reservations:

> it will be evident to Your Highness that from the first it was made quite clear that the boundaries suggested by His Highness Your illustrious father could not be accepted by HMG, and that as early as October 1915 HMG explained without the slightest ambiguity that they could not consider certain areas to be purely Arab and made a general reservation that any assurances given must be understood to be without detriment to the interests of their ally, France. I had hoped, therefore, that in Your Highness' reply this reservation would be taken into consideration, but I regret to find that while it is claimed that Arab rights have been dis-regarded, no allowance is made in any part of Your Highness' reply for the interests of France, which HMG so expressly reserved.[1]

Faysal was, thus, abandoned by the British. He attempted to reach agreement with the French on his own, but he was not forceful or authoritative enough to impose such an agreement on his followers who were in a belligerent mood. He gave up the attempt, and abandoned himself to the activism of his supporters. The Syrian Congress, which had been assembled in 1919 in order to impress the King–Crane commission of enquiry, met in March 1920 and proclaimed Faysal king of a united Syria, including Palestine. Faysal acquiesced in this decision. By then, the utter opposition of the Palestinians to Zionism had become crystal clear. Faysal found it profitless, and even harmful, to seem as though he was in any way

---

[1] F.O. 371/4183, 132930/2117 for the various drafts of the letter of 9 Oct. to Faysal.

supporting, or even acquiescing in, such a movement. Also, since the idea of a united Syria under his rule seemed to be supported by the British authorities in Palestine, and even by Allenby himself, Faysal may have actually thought it a good idea to press a claim to Palestine.[1]

This he proceeded to do. The Allies, meeting at San Remo at the end of April 1920, decided to award the mandate for Syria to France, and for Palestine to Britain. When this decision was communicated to Faysal he protested to Allenby that Palestine could not be separated from Syria 'geographically, ethnographically, traditionally, economically and from the point of view and language and national desire'. Moreover, he went on to say,

> There is to be found amongst correspondence between His Majesty Hussein and His Excellency Sir H. MacMahon a letter in name of Great Britain dated October 25th 1915 which recognised Palestine to be within Arab Empire whose limits as therein defined are accepted by British Government.[2]

This was a novel claim on Faysal's part, but he was to recur to it shortly. His relations with the French deteriorated and the French commander in the Levant, Gouraud, determined to deal forcibly with the Sharifian regime in Damascus. Following an ultimatum, he marched on Damascus and evicted Faysal towards the end of July 1920. Faysal went to Europe and spent the summer in Italy. From there he addressed a letter and a long memorandum to Lloyd George in which he set forth anew the Sharifian claims at their most extensive. He now alleged that during the war Britain had promised to establish

> an Arab Kingdom extending from the Persian Gulf to the limits of Cilicia, including Aleppo, Hama, Homs and Damascus, up to the frontiers of Egypt, with a special administration for the vilayets of Baghdad and Basra to be decided upon with the Sharif, my father, at the end of the War.[3]

As may be seen, Faysal's claims were now very different from those he had put forward on his two previous visits to Europe. On the first occasion, he explicitly disclaimed any exclusive rights in

---

[1] Kedourie, *England and the Middle East*, pp. 155–7; *The Chatham House Version*, pp. 57 and 402n15; *Documents on British Foreign Policy 1919–39*, series I, vol. XIII, nos. 216, 219, 223. The King–Crane commission, so called after its two members, Dr Henry C. King and Charles R. Crane, was formally the American Section of an Inter-Allied commission on mandates in Turkey. The British and French governments first agreed to send representatives of their own, but subsequently changed their minds, and the 'American Section' visited the Levant on its own in the summer of 1919.

[2] *Documents on British Foreign Policy, 1919–39*, series I, vol. XIII, no. 248.

[3] F.O. 371/5040, 11500/2, Faysal to Lloyd George, Cernobbio 11 Sept. 1920. The quotation is at p. 12 of the memorandum.

Palestine, and on the second he relied on a non-existent treaty between his father and Great Britain. What he was doing now was to rely on the text of McMahon's letter of 24 October 1915, taken on its own, and to disregard utterly the qualifications in which this text abounded.

He developed this tactic to good effect in talks held at the foreign office at the end of November. He had been officially invited to London in order to discuss a projected Anglo-Hijazi treaty which the British were anxious to conclude, and about which Husayn was proving obstructive. There was also the hope to obtain Husayn's recognition of the mandatory principle in Palestine and Mesopotamia, where Great Britain was the mandatory, and to reach a political settlement in the latter territory where a revolt against British administration (fomented and abetted by Faysal's regime in Damascus) had broken out the previous summer.

This approach to Middle-Eastern problems was very much that of H. W. Young, an Indian army officer who had served during the war in Mesopotamia, Palestine and Syria, and who at the beginning of 1919 joined the newly-formed Eastern department of the foreign office at the recommendation of George Lloyd whom he had known in Mesopotamia.[1] As he says in his memoirs, Young believed in 'the essential unity of the Arab problem'.[2] He also believed that this problem could be settled by negotiation with Husayn, whom he considered to be the spokesman of the Arabs, and by getting him to recognize the mandates in Palestine and Mesopotamia which had been awarded to Britain the previous April. But, as he put it in a long memorandum written on the eve of Faysal's visit,

> this will not be an easy task. Hussein is an obstinate man, and almost unapproachable by ordinary methods of argument...No direct correspondence between London and Jeddah would have the smallest chance of success. The only hope is to convince Feisal first...[3]

Young held the view that Husayn was entitled to have a say in the Middle-Eastern settlement because of McMahon's promises. His view of these promises seemed now very different from those embodied in the letter to Faysal of 9 October 1919 which he in large part had drafted. Young now believed that although no actual agreements were arrived at in 1915–16, yet 'certain definite under-

[1] Hubert Young, *The Independent Arab*, 1933, p. 265.
[2] *Ibid.* p. 282.
[3] F.O. 371/5066, 14959/9, 'Foreign Office Memorandum on Possible Negotiations with the Hedjaz' by H. W. Young, 29 Nov. 1920, para. 3 (the memorandum is printed in *Documents on British Foreign Policy 1919–39*, series I, vol. XIII, no. 342).

The Fly in the Fly-bottle

takings' had been given, and that they were embodied in McMahon's letter of 24 October 1915. Young does not consider in his memorandum the status of this correspondence, how definite these undertakings were, or the bearing on them of McMahon's letters of 14 December 1915 and 25 January 1916, which had left so many issues doubtful and undecided.

What is even more serious, Young does not ask himself how an undertaking relating to territory can be 'definite' in the absence of clearly delineated boundaries. Far from raising this question, Young proceeds to make clear and precise that which McMahon had deliberately left vague and obscure. Thus he argues that in Mesopotamia, the 'literal interpretation' of McMahon's undertaking

> would include all three vilayets of Mosul, Baghdad, and Basra in the areas in which His Majesty's Government were prepared to recognise the 'independence of the Arabs'...

His argument is erroneous since Mosul had not been as such the subject of any discussion or undertaking. He does, it is true, notice that McMahon had warned the Sharif that British interests in Baghdad and Basra necessitated 'special administrative arrangements', but he does not ask how this qualification is to be reconciled with his sweeping assertion that the British had been prepared to recognize the 'independence of the Arabs' in this region. Nor does he take into account that in his letter of 25 January 1916 McMahon had postponed issues affecting Baghdad until 'the enemy has been defeated and the time for peaceful settlement arrives'.

Young, again, takes for granted that in speaking of Syria McMahon had in mind the territory which was known as Syria under the French mandate. But all the evidence indicates that by 'Syria' McMahon meant the territories which after the war came to be known as Syria and Palestine. Young's mistake leads him to ask whether 'Palestine' was included in the area of Arab independence as promised by McMahon. Having asked the question, Young is naturally led to tease out an answer somehow from McMahon's text:

> With regard to Palestine, a literal interpretation of Sir H. McMahon's undertaking would exclude from the areas in which His Majesty's Government were prepared to recognise the 'independence of the Arabs' only that portion of the Palestine mandatory area [which included 'Transjordan'] which lies to the west of the 'district of Damascus'. The western boundary of the 'district of Damascus' before the war was a line bisecting the lakes of Huleh and Tiberias; following the course of the Jordan; bisecting the Dead Sea; and following the Wadi Araba to the Gulf of Akaba.[1]

[1] The relevant passages in Young's memorandum are paras. 9–12.

The Correspondence in the Peace Settlement

Like Toynbee and the author of the Arab Bureau memorandum before him, Young wanted at all costs to transform McMahon's vague and indefinite suggestions into a definite boundary, traced with a map-maker's precision. The boundary that he favoured, however, was different from what had been proposed in the earlier documents. His argument depended on the illegitimate assumption that in speaking of 'the district of Damascus', McMahon meant the *vilayet* of Damascus as this was understood in Ottoman administrative parlance. But this was an untenable argument, as Faysal was quick to point out. During a meeting at the foreign office on 20 January 1921, Faysal claimed that nothing in McMahon's correspondence with his father indicated that Palestine was excluded from Arab independence. Ronald Lindsay argued that Palestine was excluded 'lying as it did west of the vilayet of Damascus'. The relevant passage from McMahon's letter was then read aloud in Arabic (from a text which must have been provided by Faysal himself). Faysal then replied that

> if His Majesty's Government relied upon the strict interpretation of the word 'vilayet' as applied to Damascus, they must also interpret the word to mean the same with regard to Homs and Hama. There was not and never had been a vilayet of Homs and Hama. While he was quite prepared to accept Mr. Lindsay's statement that it had been the original intention of His Majesty's Government to exclude Palestine, he represented that, as the Arabic stood, it would be clearly interpreted by any Arab and had been so interpreted by King Hussein, to refer to the four towns and their immediate surroundings. Palestine did not lie to the West of the four towns and was therefore, in his opinion, included in the area for which His Majesty's Government had given pledges.[1]

Faysal's argument was unanswerable, nor did Lindsay attempt to answer it. But, as will be seen, Young's ingenious reading of McMahon's letter was to receive official sanction, and to become the ground on which the British government publicly justified their Zionist policy.

In the interval between Faysal's arrival in London and his interview with Lindsay, Young made another discovery relating to McMahon's letter of 24 October 1915. In a minute of 25 December 1920 he claimed that the text of this letter had been seriously mistranslated into Arabic in one important passage. The question arises, what was the extent of Young's knowledge of Arabic? He tells us in his memoirs that he began to study the language while he was stationed at Aden in 1907, and that he continued his studies when

[1] F.O. 371/6237, 986/4.

237

The Fly in the Fly-bottle

he was invalided home that year. During his leave in England he was coached by a Baghdadi, Haji Abdul Majid, whose English 'was even more rudimentary than my Arabic'. He was again invalided the following year, and again made use of the Haji's services for some two months, at the end of which he qualified as an Interpreter in Arabic, in July 1908.[1] We may suspect from this record that Young's knowledge of the language was somewhat sketchy. Our suspicion is confirmed by a specimen of his translation which has survived in the foreign office papers. When Faysal was in London in September 1919 he received a telegram in an Arabic cipher from his father. The cipher was broken by the British and the Arabic text sent to Young to translate. The telegram related to Husayn's ambitions to become king of the Arabs, and it asserted that his claim was recognized in many parts of the Arab world. Husayn had written in Arabic:

> awraq al-imam wa ahl al-yaman wa ibn Rashīd wa'l-'Iraq bi'tirafihim bī mawjūda ladayy hatta 'Asīr shakkalna bihā hukūma wa lākin lā sabīl li-wusūlihā ilayka

The passage is straightforward and its literal translation is as follows:

> The papers [i.e. letters] of the Imam [of the Yemen], of the people of Yemen, of Ibn Rashid and Iraq recognizing me, are in my possession; even in Asir we have formed a government; but there is no way of their [i.e. the papers] reaching you.

Husayn's statement about 'Asir requires explanation. As is well known, he had always been at odds with its Idrisi ruler, and at about the time when he sent this telegram, he was supporting a rival of the Idrisi's who had set up a rival government at Ebha.[2] Now Young's translation of this simple passage was as follows:

> Letters from the Imam and the people of the Yemen, Ibn Rashid and Iraq, recognizing me are actually before me – in Asir (the Idrisi). We have framed from them (i.e. the letters) a constitution, but there are no means of transmitting them to you.[3]

As may readily be seen, the end of the first sentence is a nonsense, while the passage, 'We have framed from them (i.e. the letters) a constitution' is gibberish without the remotest relation to the original.

[1] Young, *The Independent Arab*, pp. 1–3.
[2] The situation is made clear by another intercepted telegram from Husayn to Faysal of 2 Dec. 1919 in F.O. 371/4185, 159090/2117.
[3] F.O. 371/4184, 151355/2117.

The Correspondence in the Peace Settlement

The passage which Young now discovered had been mistranslated occurred in the letter of 24 October 1915 in which McMahon reserves the British position as regards territories in which the French were interested:

> As for those regions [McMahon had written] lying within those frontiers [which the Sharif had claimed] wherein Great Britain is free to act without detriment to the interests of her ally, France, I am empowered etc.

Young claimed that the Arabic version of this passage 'literally translated' ran as follows:

> in regard to the areas (or provinces) which those boundaries enclose, where (or whereas) Great Britain is free to act without affecting the interests (or policy) of her ally France, I am empowered etc.

Young is here saying that the Arabic version was ambiguous, that the Arabic word used for McMahon's 'wherein' could equally mean 'where' or 'whereas'. If this were really the case then, the possible meanings to be given to this passage would be substantially different. Was Young right? It is of course true that the translation of McMahon's letters was awkward, loose and weak in places, but as it happens the Arabic passage criticized by Young had correctly conveyed McMahon's meaning. McMahon's 'wherein' the translator had correctly rendered by *hayth*, an adverbial noun of place. It is true that *hayth* can mean 'whereas' or 'because', but for it to do so it has to be followed by the particle *inna*, which was absent from the Arabic text. Whether Young made this discovery by himself, or was bamboozled by Faysal into believing that a mistranslation had occurred is not clear. But the incident neatly illustrates the adage that a little knowledge is a dangerous thing. What makes the episode even more comic is that Young confronted Storrs with the alleged mistranslation, and this other expert in Arabic grammar, Young wrote,

> agrees that the Arabic is an incorrect translation, but can give no explanation of how it came to be passed.

Storrs, it is clear, was most anxious to evade as much responsibility as possible for all that was connected with the Sharifian negotiations of 1914–16. He told Young (what was a plain untruth) that

> he was often away at the time when the letters were written, and may never have seen this one.

Young must also have enquired about the missing Arabic drafts, but Storrs seemed determined to have nothing to do with this affair and, contrary to what he had told Cairo a few years before, now disclaimed responsibility for the filing of Arabic texts, which was the duty of the Chancery, not of the Oriental Secretary, whose functions were limited to ensuring accurate translations. He said also that there had never been any doubt in his own mind of the meaning of the English, since it was well-known at Cairo that reservations must be made to protect French interests in the hinterland as well as the coastal areas.

Storrs, it would seem, was determined to say as little as possible about the translations for which he was responsible. In 1937, when the subject of this correspondence was once more to the fore, the foreign office once more tried to get Storrs to throw light on the subject. Rendel, the head of the Eastern department, saw him many times and in the end concluded that Storrs 'will not be able to throw any light on this', and that there was no advantage in pursuing the matter further.[1]

Young was very shocked indeed by the mistranslation his labours had brought to light. This mistranslation, he declared, was

> clearly responsible for a great deal of the atmosphere of suspicion with which King Hussein now regards us.

This was because from the Arabic text of the letter,

> Hussein and Feisal have always thought that Great Britain was free to act in the *whole* of the restricted area, and that the French advance on Damascus was connived in by us, in spite of our definite pledge.

On the strength of this letter, Husayn and Faysal held the

> justifiable view that we had made *ourselves* responsible for Arab independence in the Syrian hinterland.

But Young was full of admiration for Faysal's forbearance and magnanimity. Faysal, he wrote,

> has no intention of embarrassing us by insisting on this error, but as Hussein's representative he will be perfectly justified in pointing it out.

His attitude was 'perfectly correct', and he had 'repeatedly asked that he might be regarded as a friend, and not as an enemy who came to haggle like a merchant over points of detail'. But Faysal's 'very restraint', admirably generous as it was, 'puts us in a difficult position'.[2]

Young's so-called discovery impressed his superior Lindsay, who began his discussion of British promises with Faysal on 20 January 1921 by referring to the mistranslation which had 'unfortunately

---

[1] F.O. 371/20807, 3284/22, minute by G. W. Rendel, 27 July 1937.
[2] F.O. 371/5067, 16103/9, Young's minutes, 25 and 30 Dec. 1920.

obscured the meaning of one of [McMahon's] reservations'. This preliminary apology naturally cramped the style of the British negotiators who thus gratuitously put themselves in a position of having to make amends for a mistake by which they believed the Sharifians had been misled in all good faith. This could not but promote the 'definitely Sherifian policy in Mesopotamia and Trans-Jordan' which Young had for long been advocating. Faysal of course had no reason on this occasion to correct a misapprehension which was so profitable to his cause. But on the eve of his departure from London at the end of March 1921, after Mesopotamia had been delivered up to him, he admitted in a conversation with Lindsay that from his first interview with Curzon at the beginning of 1919 he had realized what the British attitude was towards the French and the Syrian question, i.e. that the British did not consider themselves responsible for ensuring Arab independence in the Syrian hinterland, as Young had put it:

> an interesting admission this [commented Lindsay], as showing that he was not misled by the misunderstanding arising out of the famous mistranslation.[1]

At the meeting of 20 January, however, Faysal adopted the stance of an injured party which had been defrauded of its just claims. McMahon's letters, in their Arabic version, 'had induced his father to enter the War'. While Faysal realized that Great Britain was not pledged in respect of the Syrian coastal areas, 'they were, however, pledged in respect of Palestine and the four towns. The Arabs had always regarded both Palestine and the hinterland of Syria as being covered by the pledges given by Sir H. McMahon'. The claim to Palestine was new; during his first visit at the end of 1918, Faysal had disclaimed interest in Palestine, and during his second visit he had kept silent about it. Lindsay, as has been seen, now tried to counter Faysal's claim with the lame argument about boundaries which Young had invented, and Faysal had no difficulty in showing up its absurdity. The discussion was on the whole inconclusive and unsatisfactory, or, as Curzon put it in a long minute full of common sense, 'infructuous'. It had, he said, proceeded on entirely wrong lines, being devoted 'to a now belated and rather controversial analysis of the old pledges and the extent to which they have or have not been observed'. After all, it was not Husayn who had conquered Palestine or Mesopotamia: 'we did'. If they went on discussing the situation, the controversy would continue for ever.[2]

[1] F.O. 371/6239, 4075/4, minute by Lindsay, 31 Mar. 1921.
[2] F.O. 371/6237, 986/4.

If the controversy, for a while at any rate, abated, it was not because the issue was ruled out of court, as Curzon would have liked it to be, but rather because, as so often had happened in the past, the Sharifian interpretation of the correspondence was allowed to go unanswered. For Faysal followed up the discussion with Lindsay by a memorandum, dated 24 January, in which he rehearsed yet again the Sharifian version of the British promises. This document elicited a minute by Cornwallis in which he said that, having examined himself the Arabic text of the correspondence,

> I do not blame Feisal for giving it the meaning which he has done, even though one can argue that other passages in other letters should induce him to interpret it differently. We cannot get away from the fact that we did not write or say what we meant to say with sufficient clarity and attempts at explanation now are not convincing to any Arab, though a man like Feisal is quite willing to believe that our intentions were honest. It is better to leave it at that...[1]

And so it was. Once again, therefore, the Sharifian side was allowed to persist in large and unfounded claims, and no attempt was made to put the record straight, to recall to Husayn the origin of the correspondence – its inconclusiveness and its numerous qualifications, his own promises (in his letter of 18 February 1916) to raise a rebellion in Syria, to fall upon the Turks who were attacking the Suez canal, to subdue Medina and occupy the railway line (none of which he fulfilled) – or to insist that Husayn's interpretation of McMahon's letters had no authoritative or privileged status. Cornwallis's minute gives expression to an attitude which was to become the most prevalent one in British official circles. It is one of uneasy suspicion concerning British motives and good faith, an assumption that the onus proving its honesty and good faith lay entirely on the British side, and a barely concealed belief that the onus could never be discharged.

At the meeting on 20 January 1921, Lindsay said at one point that if Husayn succeeded in gaining the consent of all the Arabs within the areas in which the British government were free to act, the government would offer no objection to his rule in these areas. When Sir Herbert Samuel, the high commissioner in Palestine, saw the minutes of this meeting, he wrote that he presumed that Palestine was not in view when this assurance was offered. Cornwallis minuted that it would be as well to make the point clear to Faysal. He also suggested that this should be done verbally, and he offered to do it himself. Lindsay approved of this procedure. Once more,

---

[1] F.O. 371/6237, 1176/4, minute by K. Cornwallis, 25 Jan. 1921.

then, in these Sharifian negotiations, verbal messages were used in preference to a written and permanent record. In view of the claims on Palestine which Faysal had so recently made, it was injudicious to rest content with a private conversation which Faysal could easily deny or misrepresent. In any case, no report of the conversation has survived in the files, and there is no knowing what Cornwallis said, and what Faysal replied.[1] Whether Cornwallis delivered the message with the necessary clarity and firmness is perhaps doubtful. The tenor of his minute on Faysal's memorandum of 24 January quoted above gives a hint of his view of the McMahon–Husayn correspondence. Another significant indication of his attitude occurs in a note, of October 1919, in which he says that 'the people of the East are watching to see whether the promises which they believe we have given will be fulfilled.'[2] Again, many years later Colonel Mackereth, British consul at Damascus reported what he had heard from an employee who had been Cornwallis's interpreter in 1918–19:

> He assures me that General Clayton was most strict in his instructions to Major (as he was then) Cornwallis to make it perfectly clear to the Amir Feisal that the Amir was not to assume any authority [in Syria] other than that of a General under the Commander-in-Chief, Allenby. Teen says, however, that Cornwallis was at times influenced by his personal Arabophil predilections and not always entirely obedient to his instructions.[3]

[1] F.O. 371/6238, 2133/4, Samuel's despatch from Jerusalem, 6 Feb. 1921, and minutes thereon.

[2] F.O. 371/4183, 136602/2117, note of 3 Oct. 1919.

[3] F.O. 371/23239, 5832/6, letter from Gilbert Mackereth, Damascus 10 Aug. 1939, to Lacy Baggallay of the Eastern department.

9. Varieties of Official Historiography II: The Colonial Office, McMahon, Childs

What Cornwallis said to Faysal in London in February 1921, and what Faysal replied, might have been of some significance in future controversies. But with Faysal installed in Baghdad and his brother Abdullah in Amman, the Sharifians largely lost interest in the nature and scope of McMahon's promises. The subject was now taken up by the leaders of the Palestine Arabs. Their interest in the correspondence was confined to one issue, namely to establish that Palestine was included in McMahon's promises, and hence that the British were not at liberty to pursue a Zionist policy there. This belief they must have acquired from Sharifian propaganda disseminated among them during and after the war. Leaflets had been then distributed by the British which exhorted the Arabs of Palestine to join the Sharifians 'so that the Arab kingdom may again become what it was in the time of your fathers'; while after the war Sharifian agents in Jerusalem, tolerated and perhaps abetted by the chief administrator, Bols, and his chief of staff, Waters-Taylor, spread the gospel of Faysal as the king of a united Syria, including Palestine.[1] By 1920 the belief was widespread among the Arabs of Palestine that promises had been made to Husayn by the British government which were incompatible with the encouragement of Zionism, and that these promises were now being broken.[2]

The Palestine Arab leaders could in fact bring forward strong arguments against British pro-Zionist policy: that they had been immemorially settled in the land where they constituted the majority, that the principle of national self-determination had been accepted, and indeed trumpeted by the Allies. Faysal, it is interesting to note, believed that the Palestine Arab case should rest on this

---

[1] Kedourie, *England and the Middle East*, p. 153; *The Chatham House Version*, p. 57.

[2] This was pointed out by the court of enquiry into the 1920 Easter riots at Jerusalem, F.O. 371/5121, 9379/85, paras. 5 and 69.

argument rather than on any pledge made to his father.[1] But the Palestine Arab leaders had convinced themselves that McMahon's letter of 24 October 1915 was a valuable and powerful weapon, and that it should be used against the Zionists and their British patrons. Many of these leaders were able men who had been trained in the law; they came to look upon McMahon's letter as a legal instrument or contract, to be construed or interpreted as ingeniously as possible to the benefit of their cause. Since the mandated territory of Palestine had never been mentioned as such in the McMahon–Husayn correspondence, ingenuity was indeed needful in order to prove – or to disprove – the contention that it had been promised to Husayn. This Palestine Arab strategy resulted in the correspondence being exclusively made to answer a question which the correspondents had never discussed. Attention was therefore concentrated on the letter of 24 October 1915, to the neglect of the other letters, and of the circumstances in which they were exchanged.

A letter from the Palestine Arab delegation which visited London in 1922 was the first to cite officially the correspondence as proof that Palestine had been promised to Husayn. The letter, dated 16 March, and addressed to the colonial secretary, claimed that Husayn had been promised a state the western boundary of which was the Red Sea and the Mediterranean. This contention was answered by a colonial office memorandum dated 3 June, which had been drafted by Samuel in consultation with the department. The memorandum adopted the interpretation which Young (who was now in the Middle-Eastern department of the colonial office) had first put forward in his foreign office memorandum of 29 November 1920. Indeed the draft took Young's argument to its logical conclusion and for 'district' substituted *vilayet*. The draft thus argued that McMahon excluded from the scope of his promise 'the country lying to the west of the vilayet of Damascus'. He reserved

> among other territories the portions of Syria lying to the west of the vilayet of Damascus. This reservation has always been regarded by His Majesty's Government as covering the vilayet of Beirut and the independent Sanjak of Jerusalem. The whole of Palestine was thus excluded from Sir H. McMahon's pledge.

Just as Faysal easily refuted this line of argument, so the Arab delegation had no trouble overthrowing the contention advanced in the memorandum. They pointed out (in a letter of 17 June) that McMahon had spoken of the districts of Damascus, Homs, Hama

[1] C.O. 732/85, 79215, copy of letter from Faysal to Sir Hubert Young, Baghdad 8 Dec. 1929.

9-2

and Aleppo, and that this language excluded the possibility of McMahon having meant the Ottoman *vilayet* of Damascus which, they pointed out – and this was no more than a debating point – had been actually called the *vilayet* of Syria. Since Palestine was not to the west of any of these places, it was 'within the scope of the promise'. The Arab reply contained other, ingenious, debating points, such as the argument that McMahon's general reservation in favour of France was no longer operative since Palestine was now under British occupation. But their main argument was unanswerable: if McMahon's four 'districts' constituted a boundary line, then that boundary line could not possibly be that of the Ottoman *vilayet* of Damascus or Syria; it could only be a line linking those four 'districts'.

But the lame argument advanced in the colonial office memorandum remained the British justification for excluding Palestine from the scope of McMahon's promise. There was little or no attempt to show that, in any case, this narrow exegetical approach to McMahon's letter begged the question of its character or status, to point out that it was not a solemn treaty, or that if it was to be considered a treaty, then Husayn's own promises, in his letter of 18 February 1916, had gone completely unfulfilled. The British government in effect now imprisoned itself within the terms of an argument chosen by its interlocutors. But even the narrow textual issue could have been dealt with more ably and more convincingly. In fact, the foreign office suggested, too late, a modification in the memorandum which would have greatly strengthened it, and would in fact have made it to a large extent faithful to what McMahon had in mind when he wrote his letter. At Forbes Adam's suggestion the foreign office proposed to the colonial office in a letter of 15 June to omit from its reply the last two sentences in the passage quoted above, namely,

> This reservation has always been regarded by His Majesty's Government as covering the vilayet of Beirut and the independent Sanjak of Jerusalem. The whole of Palestine west of the Jordan was thus excluded from Sir H. McMahon's pledge.

The omission would have been of advantage since it removed from the memorandum the untruth that the government had 'always' regarded McMahon's reservation as covering the *vilayet* of Beirut and the *sanjaq* of Jerusalem, since in fact this argument was no older than Young's memorandum of November 1920. The foreign office also proposed that the memorandum, avoiding elaborate arguments about *vilayets* and *sanjaqs*, should simply say that the country west of the district of Damascus 'was regarded by His Majesty's Government at the time as including the whole of Palestine, west of the Jordan'. This, as has been seen, was more or less what McMahon had in mind, though the qualification 'west of the Jordan' would have imparted to his thought a greater precision than it had possessed. This formulation, it is true, might have invited the rejoinder that McMahon's letter by no means indicated that this was what His Majesty's government had in mind. But such a rejoinder really constituted its own refutation: since McMahon's letter spoke, not of 'Palestine', but of 'portions of Syria lying to the west of the districts of Damascus etc.', then its language could, in logic, equally include and exclude 'Palestine', and what the British government declared the phrase to mean had an authority at least equal to that of any other interpretation.[1]

In its need to answer the question whether Palestine had or had not been promised to Husayn, the colonial office called on McMahon himself to explain what he had meant to say in his letter. His explanation (in a letter of 12 March 1922 to Shuckburgh, who had now moved from the India to the colonial office) was curious. He stated that he mentioned specifically Damascus, Hama, Homs and Aleppo because 'these were places to which the Arabs attached vital importance'. McMahon was of course referring here to Faruqi and repeating what Storrs may well have represented as being his irreducible demands. McMahon rightly stated that definitions of frontiers did not seem to be called for then, and that his intention had been to exclude Palestine as well as the more northern coastal tracts of Syria. He also pointed out that he had received nothing from Husayn 'to make me suppose that he did not also understand Palestine to be excluded from independent Arabia'. This statement somewhat misrepresented the position since it implied that Palestine had been the subject of specific declarations from which Husayn did not dissent. McMahon's letter contained two other statements which seem unsupported by any evidence, and which only serve needlessly to make the transactions of 1915–16 even more obscure and complicated. McMahon now declared that he had restricted himself to the

---

[1] The exchanges between the colonial office and the Palestine Arab delegation are printed in Cmd. 1700, *Correspondence with the Palestine Arab Delegation and the Zionist Organisation, 1922, Accounts and Papers*, vol. XXIII, 1922. The draft of the colonial office memorandum is in C.O. 733/34, 25494, and the foreign office letter of 15 June 1922 is in F.O. 371/7773, 5794/65. After the memorandum was shown informally to the Arab delegation, it was decided to substitute 'district' for '*vilayet*', and the memorandum as published therefore speaks of 'districts', while the reply of the Arab delegation in the white paper takes the colonial office to task for speaking of *vilayets*; see C.O. 733/36, 29270.

special mention of the four towns because 'there was no place I could think of at the time of sufficient importance for purposes of definition further South of the above'. This is patently a feeble afterthought. If exact definition had been McMahon's object in 1915, he would have had no difficulty in indicating, somehow or another, what the boundary was to be. One fairly exact boundary, for instance, would have been the course of the river Jordan, but in his letter McMahon claimed that he had not made use of it 'because I thought it might possibly be considered desirable at some later stage of negotiations to endeavour to find some more suitable frontier line East of the Jordan and between that river and the Hedjaz Railway.'[1] There is no evidence that this was a preoccupation of McMahon's in 1915. A possible explanation of this mystifying passage is that it confuses two separate episodes: the negotiations with Husayn, and the discussions which took place in Cairo a short time before over the Bunsen Report. McMahon, it will be remembered, had then argued that 'the Palestine portion of British territory should be included in the dominion of the Sultan of Egypt'. If this was to be, then, of course, the more eastward the frontiers of Palestine extended the better.

This letter of McMahon's, then, far from removing the confusion, actually added to it. The information which would have been helpful McMahon did not volunteer; he did not explain why on more than one occasion, and particularly in his letter of 24 October 1915, his assurances to the Sharif had departed from, and gone beyond, his instructions.

McMahon's letter was never officially published.[2] Sir Herbert Samuel, high commissioner in Palestine, pressed for its publication but Shuckburgh argued that since McMahon put forward a different argument from that officially used in reply to the Palestine Arab delegation, nothing would be gained by publishing his letter. 'I am', he told Samuel, 'rather against making any further public announcement on this troublesome question. I have always felt it to be one of the weakest joints in our armour.'[3]

It is very doubtful whether the publication of McMahon's letter

---

[1] F.O. 371/7797, 2821, copy of McMahon's letter to Shuckburgh, 12 Mar. 1922.

[2] A textually exact report of the letter appeared in P. Graves, *Palestine: Land of Three Faiths*, 1923, pp. 53–4.

[3] Israel State Archives, Samuel Papers, Correspondence for 1922, Shuckburgh to Samuel, 7 Nov. 1922. Some seven years later, Shuckburgh, in a letter to another high commissioner in Palestine, Sir John Chancellor, reported his conviction that the British case over the McMahon pledge was weak. Shuckburgh to Chancellor, 11 Dec. 1929, Chancellor Papers, Rhodes House, Oxford, 16/4.

Varieties of Official Historiography II

to Shuckburgh would have put an end to the claim that Palestine had been promised to Husayn. This claim was by no means answered by the colonial office memorandum of 1922. Supporters of the Palestine Arabs constantly insisted that the McMahon–Husayn correspondence would, if published in its entirety, confirm the Arab case and refute the official view. This argument gained in strength and plausibility by the fact that the government was unwilling to divulge the letters. In February 1923 the colonial office suggested to the foreign office the publication of a white paper which would contain relevant extracts from the correspondence. J. Murray of the Eastern department minuted that publication was not advisable. In the first place, references to the caliphate which showed that Great Britain had encouraged Husayn to obtain the office for himself might make a bad impression on the Indian Muslims.[1] But there was another reason which Murray believed to militate against publication:

> With regard to the question whether Palestine was to be excluded or not from the proposed Arab State, we are not on very sound ground if we interpret the McMahon letters literally, although by implication it seems probable that Palestine *was* excluded. The 'districts of Mersina and Alexandretta and portions of Syria lying to the west of the districts of Damascus, Hama, Homs and Aleppo'... are all well to the north of Palestine.
>
> In Sir H. McMahon's letter of the 14th December 1915...the 'Vilayets of Aleppo and Beyrut' are expressly reserved. I understand that the Turkish vilayet of Beyrut included the Sanjak of Nablus, but not that of Jerusalem which was an independent Sanjak. Thus again Husein can argue that the greater (or southern) part of Palestine (including Jerusalem) was conceded to him by implication.

This passage shows that here was another official who had allowed himself to be trapped by the question which the correspondence was not designed to answer, namely whether Palestine was or was not included in McMahon's promise; and having fallen into the trap, cast about for ways of transforming McMahon's vague descriptions into a definite and precise boundary; and ended by somehow assuming that this boundary was embodied in a strict, contractual, treaty-like obligation. If Murray had looked up in the foreign office files the correspondence which passed between McMahon and Grey in October 1915 he would have discovered what McMahon meant – and what he had been instructed to promise – and he would have

[1] Shuckburgh himself believed that it was inadvisable to publish the passages relating to the caliphate. Hirtzel (still at the India office) agreed with him: 'McMahon as you know...', he wrote on 12 Feb. 1923, 'exceeded his instructions on this subject – a fact which could not of course be publicly avowed'. C.O. 733/55, 9211.

been spared speculation which was as laborious as it was ill-founded. In the event, his reasoning was accepted by his superior, Lindsay, and the foreign secretary, Curzon, initialled the minute without comment.[1]

A few months later, in July, Samuel raised the question of publishing the correspondence before a cabinet committee which had been set up to consider the working of the Palestine mandate. Samuel urged publication, which he believed would put an end to controversy and to the attacks on British good faith. Curzon, obviously repeating Murray's arguments, said that he had 'never been able to satisfy myself, for instance, in spite of what McMahon said afterwards, that he really had excluded Palestine when talking about the areas to the west of the towns.' At a later meeting, Curzon repeated that an objection to making the letters public was that 'McMahon's language was not such as to make it clear to the ordinary reader that it was intended to exclude Palestine'. This and the references to the caliphate made publication inadvisable. The cabinet committee agreed that demands for publication should be resisted.[2]

It so happened that about that time D. G. Hogarth published, in a volume edited by H. W. V. Temperley on the *History of the Peace Conference*, a short description of McMahon's letter of 24 October 1915. It has the distinction of being the most punctiliously accurate account of the so-called pledge to be written; and it was certainly far superior to the ponderous lucubrations of the foreign office clerks. McMahon's letter, wrote Hogarth,

> conveyed the most definite commitment into which, up to that date, Great Britain had entered with Arabs. While it explicitly ruled out of the negotiations all the Turkish speaking districts which Hussein had claimed as Arab, and all Arab societies with whose chiefs we already had treaties – while further, it reserved to French discretion any assurance about the independence of the Syrian littoral, or the freedom from tutelage of the interior, i.e. the districts of the four towns, Damascus, Homs, Hama and Aleppo – while by reserving other Arab regions in which France might have peculiar interests, it left the Mosul district and even, perhaps, Palestine, in doubt – while, finally, it stated expressly that no guarantee for the unconditional delivery of either Lower or Upper Iraq to the Arabs could be given by us; – in spite of all these reservations it recognised an Arab title to almost all the vast territories which Hussein had claimed, including Mesopotamia, subject only to limiting, but not annulling conditions.[3]

[1] F.O. 371/8951, 1751/975, Shuckburgh to Lindsay, 10 Feb., and Murray's minute, 15 Feb. Lindsay answered Shuckburgh in the sense of Murray's minute in a letter of 19 Feb. 1923.
[2] Cab. 27/222, meetings of the Palestine committee, 5 and 24 July 1923.
[3] H. W. V. Temperley (ed.), *History of the Peace Conference*, vol. VI, 1924, p. 126.

Hogarth's ironical summary faithfully conveys McMahon's (or Storrs's) tortuosities. There is no evidence that any notice was taken of it.

The government, then, continued to refuse official publication of the letters on the ground that it was detrimental to the public interest, and this refusal continued to feed the suspicion that it was only trying to hide something unavowable and highly damaging.[1] This suspicion, which in many cases became an unshakeable conviction, obtained not only among publicists and members of parliament who supported the Arab case; it was also entertained by civil servants and diplomats who were concerned with the affairs of Palestine or of the Middle East. A representative expression of their view occurs in a long and important despatch which Sir John Chancellor, the high commissioner in Palestine, sent in the aftermath of the Palestine disturbances of August 1929. In this despatch, Chancellor argued for a fundamental reconsideration of the mandate, and a radical change in the policy of supporting Zionism in Palestine. One argument which Chancellor put forward in support of his views related to McMahon's promises. He declared that the Arab leaders believed that the British government had 'illegitimately' made use of the 'indefiniteness of description' in McMahon's letters 'to evade the fulfilment of pledges previously made to them':

> The distrust that has been engendered by that belief has now become general. It has embittered our relations with the Arabs in our Mandated territories and has gained for the people of Palestine the sympathies of the Arabs in neighbouring territories in their efforts to obtain self-government.

Chancellor, however, was not merely reporting on the beliefs and attitudes of the Arab leaders. The passage which immediately followed shows that he himself was affected by them, and therefore was seized with doubts about the legitimacy of the rule which it was his duty to uphold:

> The doubts which are widely felt as to the completeness of the answers of the British Government to the Arab charges of bad faith have weakened the moral basis on which the Government of Palestine must stand if it is to act with conviction and firmness.
> The consciousness that the moral basis on which it stands is unstable and the knowledge that it would be exposed to attack by either Jews or Arabs for every important administrative act have tended to make the Government of Palestine, in its desire to be credited with an attitude of impartiality, deal

---

[1] A memorandum of 17 Mar. 1925, by W. J. Childs, recounting the various demands for publication and the government's response to them, is in F.O. 371/10820, 2331.

The Fly in the Fly-bottle

with questions which arise not solely upon their merits but not uninfluenced by the consideration that any concession made to one side should be balanced by a concession to the other.[1]

In this passage, Chancellor describes well the sense of guilt that has oppressed so many British officials who have dealt with Arabs after the first world war, and explains how it came to have such a hold upon them. The impersonality of an official document forbade full expression of Chancellor's feelings, but he gave them full rein in the draft of a private letter dating from about the same time:

> I feel we have treated the Arabs infamously, we made promises to them before, as well as after the Balfour Declaration, none of which have been fulfilled. That destroys the moral basis on which the Government must stand if one is to do one's duty with confidence and conviction.[2]

A junior member of the Palestine administration expressed exactly the same sentiment. In a letter to his father, the bishop of Worcester, Stewart Perowne referred to

> the unpleasant truth, which we have always tried to conceal, that the Arabs did not receive the performance of the War pledges given to them.[3]

To believe that one's authority is based on trickery and false pretences is fatal to the exercise of power.

It was the disturbances which swept Palestine in the summer of 1929, and the ensuing public enquiry which brought once more to the fore the issue of McMahon's pledges, and elicited Chancellor's and Perowne's remarks. They also occasioned renewed demands in parliament for the correspondence to be published. This required a decision by the colonial office and the foreign office. It so happened that an extensive enquiry into the McMahon–Husayn correspondence was then taking place at the foreign office. The enquiry resulted in a long memorandum – of some seventy pages – which deals with the exclusion of Palestine from the area assigned to Arab independence by the McMahon–Husayn correspondence.[4] Its author was W. J. Childs, a temporary clerk at the foreign office

[1] C.O. 733/182, 77050A, despatch no. 6022 from Chancellor, Jerusalem 17 Jan. 1930, paras. 4 and 37–8.
[2] Quoted from the Chancellor Papers in P. Ofer, 'The Role of the High Commissioner in British Policy in Palestine: Sir John Chancellor 1928–1931', unpublished Ph.D. dissertation, University of London, 1971, pp. 159–60.
[3] Letter dated 14 Oct. 1929, quoted from the Perowne Papers in *ibid.* p. 336.
[4] F.O. 371/14495, 6491/427, 'Memorandum on the Exclusion of Palestine from the Area assigned for Arab Independence by McMahon–Hussein Correspondence of 1915–16', dated 24 Oct. 1930.

who was engaged in 'doing work in respect of the Near East similar to that of the Historical Adviser [Sir James Headlam-Morley]'.[1]

There is no doubt whatever that Childs's memorandum is the best and most comprehensive historical survey of the McMahon–Husayn correspondence to be produced by a British official. Childs was more painstaking than both Harold Nicolson and Arnold Toynbee. It is of course true that they were working under pressure, and that he had more leisure to produce his report than had been available to them. But he is also much more acute and critical than either they or the writer of the Arab Bureau history had been, and a critical outlook is not essentially a question of leisure. Yet, painstaking and critical as Childs's account was, it was itself not free from serious error.

As the title of the memorandum indicates, Childs was concerned to elicit from the correspondence an answer to a question which neither side had raised at the time, namely whether 'Palestine' was or was not to be part of the Arab state. But he saw that this was by no means easy or straightforward for, as he remarked, neither during the negotiations nor afterwards had any need arisen 'for an immediate, authoritative and final interpretation of the pledge affecting Palestine'.[2] Childs also put his finger on the reason why the Arab Bureau history and Toynbee's 'commitments' memorandum had gone astray. The Arab Bureau writer had offered a 'highly imaginative interpretation' of McMahon's pledge. He had a curious obsession

> in favour of a line – or even of two lines – instead of Sir H. McMahon's definition 'districts'...This authority, not entirely satisfied with the *line* Damascus–Homs–Hama–Aleppo, which...he had gratuitously read into the pledge, must needs invent another line in order to make the inclusion of Palestine in the Arab area perfectly clear. Placing this second line at 'about Latitude 33°' he used it to connect the Damascus end of the imaginary Damascus–Aleppo line with the Mediterranean coast. He thus established for Arab advantage, a southern limit for the territory on the littoral which Sir H. McMahon's pledge excluded from the proposed Arab state.

Childs also pointed out that Toynbee, as various of his references showed, had leant on the Arab Bureau history in his interpretation of McMahon's letter, feeling that

---

[1] F.O. 366/847, X4914/504, minute by Sir H. Montgomery, 22 Mar. 1927. Childs, who had been for some years at the foreign office, and who died shortly after the writing of his memorandum, was also the author of a very readable book of travel, *Across Asia Minor on Foot*, 1918, and of the section on Syria, Palestine and Mesopotamia in Temperley (ed.), *History of the Peace Conference*, vol. VI.

[2] Childs, *loc. cit.*, p. 53.

he was on safe grounds, being conclusively supported by the views of the Arab Bureau. At all events his memorandum contains no hint of an attempt to examine the pledge critically. And although he quotes El Faroki's early declaration that the 'occupation by France of the purely Arab districts of Aleppo, Homs, Hama and Damascus would be opposed by the Arabs by force of arms', he does not trace the connexion of this formula with Sir H. McMahon's subsequent pledge...In short, Mr. Toynbee's memorandum blessed and handed on the perverted reading of the pledge which originated with...the Arab Bureau.

Childs had an explanation to offer for the way in which the Arab Bureau history misinterpreted McMahon's letter. It was merely a supposition, there being no positive evidence to support it, since the history was anonymous; but in view of what we know of the Arab Bureau and of the attitudes of its members, Childs's explanation is plausible, and even probable. Childs rightly pointed out that at the time when the history was written, Zionism was not an issue, and that French claims and Arab claims alone then held the stage:

> The Arab people, the Arab Nationalist design for an Arabian Empire, and every aspect of this bold conception enchanted...the Oriental specialists of the Arab Bureau. They made the policy of the Sherifian family and the Syrian Nationalists their own, and, believing that policy to be one that admirably subserved British Imperial interests, they consistently supported Arab claims as identical with the interests of Great Britain. In their Arab problems, therefore, France figured as the chief opponent of Arab interests, and the claims of France as claims that, within the obvious and decisive limitations imposed by the existence of the *Entente*, were to be circumvented and whittled down as far as possible.
>
> This being so, anything that tended to confirm the Arab claims to territory under Sir H. McMahon's pledges commanded the sympathy of...the Bureau. Therefore, when interpreting the pledge that affected Palestine, [the Bureau] would, in 1915, 1916, when the tide of their Sherifian policy was flowing strongly, accept the meaning which gave Palestine to the Arabs rather than one which did not.[1]

In his account of McMahon's promises Childs emphasized the inclusive and unqualified character of the reservation in favour of French interests. He rightly pointed out that its importance had been overlooked in previous interpretations of the correspondence. He argued – correctly – that when McMahon wrote his letter, the French claim extended to Palestine, and

> the interests of France so reserved in Palestine must be taken as represented by the original French claim to possession of the whole of Palestine. And, therefore, that the general reservation of French interests is sufficient by itself to exclude Palestine from the Arab area.[2]

[1] Childs, *loc. cit.*, pp. 51–4.   [2] Childs, *loc. cit.*, pp. 60–1 and 69.

Childs also stressed the inconclusive character of the correspondence, a feature which had also been overlooked by previous interpretations. The first of the conclusions in which he summed up his findings declared

> That in considering an agreement contained in the loose, inconclusive and incomplete series of letters of which the Correspondence consists, His Majesty's Government are entitled to take their own and Sir H. McMahon's intention into account wherever the meaning of the text is called in question.

The conclusion which Childs drew from the nature of the correspondence is both legitimate and important, but he does not seem to have been aware of the full consequences which the 'loose, inconclusive and incomplete' nature of the letters entailed. Thus, a cabinet memorandum by the colonial secretary, Lord Passfield, had argued that on the strength of the evidence brought forward by Childs, the government had entered into no obligation *vis-à-vis* the Palestine Arabs. Childs agreed with this view, but he added:

> the suggestion that King Hussein's fall liquidated our obligations to him is, I think, open to challenge. It could be argued with a good deal of force that Ibn Saud, as King of the Hejaz, took over whatever residual value these obligations had at the time when he was invited to assume the Kingship of the Hejaz.[1]

Childs's language here assumes that the McMahon–Husayn correspondence is a treaty with a sovereign state concluded in due and proper form, which can give rise to questions about residual rights and obligations. But Husayn had not been a sovereign when the letters were exchanged, and the letters were not a treaty.

Other weaknesses are apparent in Childs's account. They relate mostly to the proper interpretation to be given to the phrase 'portions of Syria lying to the west of the districts of Damascus, Homs, Hama and Aleppo', and arise either from an imperfect acquaintance with the files he had at his disposal, or from his drawing unwarranted conclusions from the evidence before him, or from his ignorance of Arabic. Childs does see – what Toynbee had failed to see – that McMahon's phrase derives from the views which Faruqi was alleged to have expressed, and that its meaning is very much related to these views. But he does not ask himself whether it was likely that Faruqi should have made such curious proposals. Because he assumed without question that the proposal came from Faruqi, Childs goes to ingenious lengths to make sense of it:

---

[1] Childs, *loc. cit.*, p. 69; Cab. 24/214, C.P. 271(30) for Passfield's memorandum; and F.O. 371/14495, 3888, for Childs's minute of 21 July 1930.

The Fly in the Fly-bottle

Now what lay in El Faroki's mind when he used the phrase 'districts of Aleppo, Homs, Hama and Damascus', for which he said the Arabs would fight? He certainly intended no narrow interpretation, and therefore avoided precise definitions. Beyond question he knew that Damascus and Aleppo were capitals of *vilayets* and that Homs and Hama were not. His meaning, I think, is perfectly clear; he meant that the Arabs would fight for the Arab regions of the *vilayets* of Damascus (Syria) and Aleppo; and in order to link together the 'districts' of the two chief cities (Aleppo and Damascus) of Syria beyond possibility of his meaning being misunderstood, he included the 'districts' of Homs and Hama, two intermediate and far less important towns. The minimum so described was the fertile compact Syrian hinterland, extending from, say, Killis (north of Aleppo) southward to the southern confines of the *vilayet* of Damascus (or Syria). So the Syrian Arab State, intersected from north to south by the Pilgrim Railway, would be in geographical contact with Arabia and be assured of unbroken railway communication with Hejaz.[1]

All this was terribly contrived and involved speculation in support of which Childs could not cite the slightest evidence. On the contrary, Faruqi's first letter to the Sharif, written in December 1915 (and quoted in part 1 above) constitutes evidence against his view. But though the letter had been published some six years before Childs came to write his paper, he was unaware of it. Had he been, he would have realized that Faruqi could not so confidently be said to have spoken of 'the districts of Aleppo, Homs, Hama and Damascus'.

Childs also attached much significance to McMahon's own use of the terms 'districts' and 'territories'. As was seen above, the documents show that these terms had crept somehow into McMahon's communications, and that he had offered no explanation of their use or significance. An examination of the exchanges between Clayton, Maxwell, McMahon and the authorities in London shows in fact that these words were vague in their meaning, if not purely redundant, and that for McMahon they were synonymous with 'towns'. But Childs does not seem to have examined in any detail the exchanges of October 1915, and this led him to place an inordinate weight of interpretation on the word 'districts'. In more than one place in his memorandum he drew attention to it and to the word 'territories'; and he believed that by using them McMahon must have intended to promise 'wide areas' to the Sharif:

> ...there can be little doubt that the High Commissioner used the words 'districts of Damascus, Homs, Hama and Aleppo' in precisely the same sense that El Faroki had used them. That they were prefixed by the other words 'portions of Syria west of', is immaterial. What, in effect, the High

[1] Childs, *loc. cit.*, p. 49.

256

Commissioner said to the Sherif in this sentence was: 'You and El Faroki and his Syrian Nationalists demand, as vital to your state, "the Districts of Damascus, Homs, Hama and Aleppo" which assure you continuity of territory from Aleppo to Hejaz. His Majesty's Government accept the demand and assign them to you. But the portions of Syria lying to the west of the "districts" named must be excluded from the Arab State'.[1]

This gloss on McMahon's language, like the interpretation of Faruqi's alleged thoughts, rests on no evidence whatever. It seems to be an attempt not so much to find out what McMahon meant by writing as he did (a properly historical enquiry), as to construe his words (by a legal kind of reasoning) in a way which would provide a neat, coherent and precise answer to a question which McMahon had had no thought of asking.

Childs can be shown to have misread the evidence at his disposal, or neglected it, or gone beyond it, at other points in his argument. Thus he states that Husayn was not informed of the Sykes–Picot agreement because 'If the Allies were defeated, or if the final result was a stalemate and peace by negotiation, the Sykes–Picot Arrangement would become meaningless'.[2] This was not the case, for, as has been seen, the agreement was kept from the Sharif in 1916 at the express request of McMahon, Clayton and Hogarth who somehow felt that it would be embarrassing and inconvenient to divulge its terms to Husayn. Childs, again, states that Husayn's reception of the Hogarth message in January 1918 showed that 'he believed that Palestine had been assigned to the Arabs by Sir H. McMahon's letter of the 24th October 1915, and that whatever the "special regime" there foreshadowed by the message might be, he understood that it would not be in derogation of his sovereignty.'[3] Childs's assertion is contrary to what Hogarth, in fact, had reported. According to his report, it will be remembered, when he broached the subject of Palestine, Hogarth had reminded Husayn of 'proviso in original Agreements safeguarding special interests of our Allies and especially France': not only did Husayn not demur, but he 'agreed enthusiastically' when told of the British desire to favour 'a return of the Jews to Palestine'. The burden of Hogarth's report surely was that details of territories and boundaries did not interest Husayn, that he persisted in his belief that he would become king of the Arabs and that this would come about as a result of the British falling out with their French allies.

Two other features of Childs's account are also worth noticing.

[1] Childs, *loc. cit.*, p. 50; see also pp. 5, 17 and 20.   [2] Childs, *loc. cit.*, p. 33.
[3] Childs, *loc. cit.*, p. 37.

The Fly in the Fly-bottle

In order to show that by the word 'district' McMahon must have had in mind a wide stretch of territory, he drew attention to a sentence in McMahon's despatch of 26 October 1915 (in which the high commissioner explained the terms of his letter of 24 October to Husayn) which declared that the inclusion 'in Arabia' of 'such districts' as Damascus etc. would be insisted on by the Arabs. Childs argued that 'the "district of Damascus" could only be included in Arabia if the "district of Damascus" actually adjoined Arabia – as it does'.[1] It is clear from this language that Childs failed to notice that British officials at the time used the term 'Arabia' very frequently to mean, not the Arabian peninsula, but the prospective Arab state then under discussion. He also does not seem to have been aware that in British official parlance, certainly up to 1914–18, 'Arabia' stretched as far north as the Syrian desert, perhaps to Palmyra and 'Ana on the Euphrates, or that Baghdad and Basra were, until the use of 'Mesopotamia' became established during the war, referred to as 'Turkish Arabia'. In this despatch, McMahon had clearly used the word in some such sense, and the passage was therefore useless in throwing light on the meaning of the word 'district'.

It is also clear, in the second place, that Childs came, albeit by a more laborious and roundabout route, to the same conclusion as that which H. W. Young had reached in 1920. It seems that Childs was confirmed in the soundness of his reasoning by the coincidence of the two conclusions, for he remarked that 'Major Hubert Young, a competent Arabist...examined the Arabic text of Sir H. McMahon's letter of the 24th October, 1915, to the Sherif, and found that the Arabic of "district of Damascus" meant "*vilayet* of Damascus".'[2] Childs's belief in Young's competence as an Arabist goes some way to explain why he was ready to put his trust in the long and precarious chain of reasoning which he devised in order to impart (a wholly imaginary) coherence, precision and congruence to Faruqi's presumed thoughts, and McMahon's loose and misleading language.

Childs's final conclusion was

That from the examination of the history of Sir H. McMahon's pledge of the 24 October, 1915, it is evident that he intended the exclusion of Palestine from the pledge; and therefore that His Majesty's Government's interpretation of the contested passage has been adopted on adequate grounds, and in good faith.[3]

[1] Childs, *loc. cit.*, p. 21.
[2] Childs, *loc. cit.*, p. 67.
[3] Childs, *loc. cit.*, p. 69.

From this conclusion Passfield did not dissent. In a memorandum for the cabinet (cited above), he stated that Childs's argument convinced him that McMahon had not committed the British government to promising Palestine to the Sharif. But, he added,

I have also come to the conclusion that there is much to be said on both sides and that the matter is one for the eventual judgement of the historian, and not one in which a simple plain and convincing statement can be made.

In the light of this memorandum the cabinet decided at its meeting of 30 July 1930 to continue withholding publication of the correspondence. Enquiries from members of parliament were fended off by a reply drafted by Passfield and authorized by the cabinet. This was given in the house of commons on 1 August by the parliamentary under-secretary for the colonies, Dr Drummond Shiels. He stated that there were no 'sufficient grounds' for holding that the British government 'intended to pledge themselves or did in fact pledge themselves to the inclusion of Palestine' in the territories promised to the Sharif. But he added that the 'ambiguous and inconclusive nature of the correspondence may well, however, have left an impression that His Majesty's Government had such an intention'.[1]

II

The language of Passfield's memorandum and of the answer to the parliamentary question which he drafted show that Childs's arguments did not entirely persuade his readers. Passfield was unable to derive from them 'a simple, plain and convincing statement' of the case. To some it seemed, in fact, as though the very complexity of Childs's arguments proved that the British position was weak, and that it could be defended only by means of over-subtle, not to say sophistical, explanations. This certainly was the reaction of Cosmo Parkinson, an assistant secretary at the colonial office, to Childs's memorandum. He seemed to think that there was something faintly fraudulent about it:

It is [he minuted] an ingenious case, but I should be sorry to have to swear that it was ingenuous.[2]

[1] Cab. 24/214, C.P. 271(30), Passfield's memorandum of 25 July; Cab. 23/64, cabinet conclusion, 30 July; *Parliamentary Debates*, House of Commons, 5s, vol. 242, cols. 902–3, 1 Aug. 1930, answer by Dr D. Shiels to a question by S. Cocks. Passfield's wife, Beatrice Webb, on her part, believed that Palestine had in fact been promised to the Arabs: 'The man on the spot gave promises to the Arabs; the British Cabinet gave promises to the Jews'. Margaret Cole (ed.), *Beatrice Webb's Diaries 1924–1932*, 1956, p. 256, entry of 26 Oct. 1930. The whole entry deals with Palestine and is a most curious passage to come from the pen of a Fabian Socialist.

[2] C.O. 733/189, file 77121, minute by Parkinson 21 Nov. 1931.

The Fly in the Fly-bottle

Childs's account aroused much stronger emotions in the breast of another British official. Walter Smart, oriental counsellor at the Cairo residency, was moved by it to express his shame at the way in which Great Britain and France had treated the Arabs.

> It is a pity [he minuted on 9 January 1931] that the story of these pledges cannot be made public. A full disclosure would probably convince the unpartisan public that England, as far as Palestine was concerned, did not *actually* violate her pledges to the Arabs.

But this to Smart was of small comfort. He believed that there was 'little for us to be pround of in the whole story', and went on to recite a catalogue of crimes of which his country together with its ally, France, was guilty:

> The Anglo-French bargaining about other people's property, the deliberate bribery of International Jewry at the expense of the Arabs who were already our allies in the field, the immature political juggleries of amateur Oriental experts, the stultification of Arab independence and unity by the French occupation of the Syrian hinterland and by the splitting up into numerous unpractical States of lands ethnically, linguistically, economically one, not in the interest of the people concerned but to strike a balance between Anglo-French political ambitions – all the immorality and incompetence inevitable in the stress of a great war, could not be exposed to public view without creating a feeling of discomfort in the mind of any but, to steal Balfour's famous quip, 'a trained diplomat'.[1]

Smart, we take it, was himself a 'trained diplomat', and this shrill outburst, with its extravagant moralism and its fanciful evocation of an imaginary world in which vice is Anglo-French and virtue pan-Arab, must therefore be seen as a startling, and disturbing, expression of self-disgust and self-hate.

Like Chancellor's and Perowne's sentiments quoted above, the outburst is disturbing because it comes from officials whose duty it was to uphold and defend the empire of which they were the servants, and is clear evidence of their demoralization. As the documents show, Childs's long and elaborate examination of McMahon's letters and their significance was of no effect at all in doing away with the belief that Great Britain was guilty of double-dealing and trickery in dealing with the Arabs. The belief persisted; it was held most strongly in the foreign office, and particularly in its Eastern department. Thus, in 1936, in a minute occasioned by a request from Lord Lloyd to see the text of the McMahon–Husayn correspondence, M. S. Williams, a member of the Eastern department, stated that the correspondence remained unpublished because

[1] F.O. 141/726, file 17.

of its reference to the caliphate, because it was inconclusive and incomplete, and because

> certain crucial phrases admit of an interpretation different from that put upon them by HMG and entirely favourable to the Arab contention that Palestine should have been included in the area set aside for an independent Arab State.[1]

Williams's statement was by no means the most emphatic expression, within the foreign office, of the belief that McMahon had not excluded Palestine from his pledge to the Sharif. A more senior member of the Eastern department, L. H. Baggallay, went far to convict his government of double-dealing over Palestine. In a minute of 17 August 1937, seen by Oliphant, Vansittart and the foreign secretary, Lord Halifax, he declared:

> However skilfully one may construct an argument in public to show that Sir H. McMahon's pledge did *not* include Palestine, any one coming fresh to the problem and taking his words at their face value would have to be very perspicuous if he found in them any cause to suppose Palestine to be excluded from the area of Arab independence.[2]

In another minute, written a few weeks later, Baggallay affirmed his belief that the British government had said nothing from which Husayn 'might have inferred that they meant to exclude [Palestine].'[3] It is not readily apparent why an official with access to the papers should so categorically assert that McMahon's words, taken 'at their face value', left no doubt that he had promised Palestine to Husayn. At its face value, McMahon's language was so qualified that it meant almost nothing, and from his words it was equally easy to infer the exclusion, as well as the inclusion, of any territory whatever. This, in fact, was McMahon's object, as Baggallay could have easily ascertained from the documents.

Baggallay and Williams echoed, in their minutes the views of the head of their department, G. W. Rendel. What these were emerges with the utmost clarity in a minute of his commenting on a letter to *The Times* of 23 July 1937, in which McMahon had declared it his 'duty to state...that it was not intended by me in giving this pledge to King Hussein to include Palestine in the area in which Arab independence was promised' and affirmed that he also 'had every reason to believe at the time that the fact that Palestine was not included in my pledge was well understood by King Hussein'. As the evidence examined in part I above shows, McMahon's

[1] F.O. 371/20786, 223/65, minute of 22 Dec. 1936.   [2] F.O. 371/20811, E4740/22/31.
[3] F.O. 371/20813, E5306/22/31, Baggallay's minute of 14 Sept. 1937.

The Fly in the Fly-bottle

letter is on the whole consonant with the facts. Where it departs from them is in giving the impression that in their exchanges of 1915, McMahon and Husayn in any way had 'Palestine' in mind. In his minute on this letter, Rendel also erroneously assumed that 'Palestine' was in the negotiators' mind. From this he drew the conclusion that if McMahon had meant to exclude 'Palestine' from his pledge he would have said so. Rendel, in other words, treated McMahon's letter of 24 October 1915 as though it were a contract of sale, to be legitimately criticized for obscurity and imprecision:

> My own impression from reading the correspondence [he wrote on 26 July 1937] has always been that it is stretching the interpretation of our *caveat* almost to breaking point to say that we definitely did not include Palestine, and the short answer is that if we did not want to include Palestine, we might have said so in terms, instead of referring vaguely to areas west of Damascus, and to extremely shadowy arrangements with the French, which in any case ceased to be operative shortly afterwards.

This minute shows that the head of the Eastern department disregarded McMahon's express statement (in his despatch of 26 October 1915) that, being unaware of the details of French claims, he had, to cover himself, made a blanket reservation which would cover these claims, whatever their extent. For a diplomat, Rendel was curiously oblivious of the fact that here was one of these situations where vagueness is deliberate, desirable and indeed necessary. He also seemed singularly impressed by mere debating points: as the last phrase of his minute shows, he took seriously the thesis advanced by the Palestine Arab leaders, that McMahon's reservations of 1915 were of no significance, because in 1918 the French were to give up all claims in Palestine. To Rendel, in fact, the situation admitted of no qualification or ambiguity: it was as clear as daylight that McMahon meant to, and did, promise Palestine to the Sharif. To speak otherwise he considered 'casuistry and special pleading':

> It would be far better [he went on, in a minute of 11 October 1937] to recognise and admit that H.M.G. made a mistake and gave flatly contradictory promises – which is of course the fact.[1]

Such being his views, Rendel entertained not the slightest doubt that publication of the McMahon–Husayn correspondence 'would be in the interests of the Arabs'. He doubted, however, whether it would be published, because (as he wrote in a minute of 23 December 1937) 'Jewish influence – which is very strong, particularly in the House

[1] F.O. 371/20810, E4294/22/31. In his memoirs published in 1957 Sir George Rendel was still of the opinion that Palestine had been the subject of 'conflicting promises' (*The Sword and the Olive*, 1957, p. 119).

of Commons will be exerted to the utmost to prevent its publication.'[1]

Rendel made these comments in the aftermath of the report of the Palestine royal commission,[2] which appeared in July 1937. This report included (in paragraphs 4 and 5) an extract from the Sharif's letters of 14 July and 9 September and the greater part of the text of McMahon's reply of 24 October 1915, the publication of which, as noted above, the cabinet had authorized on 2 June previous. The report also disclosed that McMahon's letter of 24 October 1915 followed lines which McMahon himself had suggested. The report itself made nothing of this genuinely new disclosure, and the uninitiated reader was not well placed to appreciate its significance. The commissioners themselves declared (paragraph 8) that they did not consider that their terms of reference required them 'to undertake the detailed and lengthy research among the documents of 20 years ago' which was necessary in order to establish the extent of McMahon's promises. They contented themselves with reiterating the absurd, and easily rebutted, argument invented by Young and advanced by Churchill in 1922 that Palestine was excluded from McMahon's pledge because it was 'to the west of the district of Damascus'. The commissioners had had access to the whole of the McMahon–Husayn correspondence, as well as to Childs's memorandum, and might have been expected to be somewhat more forthcoming on the subject. The reason for their abstention was disclosed by one commissioner, Professor Reginald Coupland, who, during a visit to the foreign office on 5 May 1937, declared that

> a reason why the Commission did not intend to pronounce upon Sir H. McMahon's pledge was that in everything else their report was unanimous, but that upon this point they would be unlikely to prove unanimous.

Baggallay, who recorded this, eagerly added a gloss of his own:

> This can only mean that some of them at least consider that neither King Hussein nor any intelligent reader could be blamed for supposing that the wording of the pledge contained nothing to show that Palestine was not to be included in the area of Arab independence.[3]

[1] F.O. 371/20823, E7576/22/31. In his memoirs Rendel shows himself still impressed by Jewish power. He refers (p. 120) to 'many circles even in England which could not afford to risk Jewish hostility or even criticism, and which were therefore ready to support the extreme Zionist point of view', and hints darkly (p. 124) at the fate of those who sponsored the policy of the 1939 white paper: 'I do not think that [they] were ever forgiven'. By whom, he does not say.

[2] Cmd. 5479, *Report of the Royal Commission on Palestine*, 1937, *Accounts and Papers*, vol. XIV, 1936–7.

[3] F.O. 371/20806, E2525/22/31, Baggallay's minute of 8 May 1937. Correspondence in F.O. 371/20805, E1760/22/31 indicates that the commissioners saw Childs's memorandum.

Whether Baggallay was right or not in thus interpreting Coupland's remarks, it was perhaps just as well that the commissioners abstained from discussing the meaning of McMahon's language. For the little they had to say about Anglo-Sharifian relations in 1914–16 is inaccurate and misleading. The first paragraph of their report was an abbreviated version of the origins of Arab nationalism as George Antonius – who had given evidence before the commission – was shortly afterwards to present it to the world in *The Arab Awakening*, which was published in 1938. It was hopelessly unsound in tracing the movement back to the 1860s and in exaggerating the extent of Arab nationalist activities after 1908. Again, it took at their face value – and more – Faruqi's assertions, declaring (in paragraph 4) that 'the secret Nationalist Committee in Syria decided to reject the promises of independence offered them by the Turkish and German Governments': there were, so far as is now, and was then, known, no such promises. The commissioners also described (in paragraph 11) the 'McMahon Pledge' as a 'compact': this was to overlook the inconclusive character of McMahon's negotiations and to make the fundamental mistake of giving the letter of 24 October 1915 a privileged status.

One other statement about the war-time negotiations (in paragraph 9 of the report) was also rather misleading. 'It was in the highest degree unfortunate', the commissioners solemnly affirmed, 'that, in the exigencies of war, the British Government was unable to make their intention clear to the Sharif'. This is strong language for a state paper. It manages to give the impression not only that McMahon's letters were a kind of treaty, but also that as a treaty they suffered from a regrettable imprecision of which the British government must assume the guilt, albeit that the 'exigencies of war' constituted extenuating circumstances. This, of course, was to assume that in these negotiations precision would have been a virtue. But precision, as has been seen, was exactly what McMahon was not seeking, and it was wrong to blame him for not achieving it. He may be justly blamed for couching his letter of 24 October 1915 in language that he had no authority to use, but this point the commissioners did not make, and were most probably unaware that it could be made.

By the late 1930s, then, in spite of Childs's labours, the suspicion had become prevalent among the officials at the foreign office, and among others who had to deal with the Arab–Zionist conflict, that Palestine had been promised to Husayn, or at any rate that he had good reason to believe, in all good faith, that it had been so promised. Two expressions of the suspicion, and of the guilt attaching to Britain which it implied, are worth noticing. Malcolm MacDonald, who had just become colonial secretary, told David Ben-Gurion in September 1938 that after studying the McMahon correspondence,

> he has the feeling that the Arabs have not been given a fair deal. The promises contradict one another. It could be said that Palestine was promised to the Arabs.

A month later Ben-Gurion met Lord Lloyd who was to succeed MacDonald at the colonial office. Lloyd was more categorical and emphatic on the subject:

> During the world war they gave the Arabs and the Jews conflicting assurances. *We sold the same horse twice.*[1]

[1] David Ben-Gurion, *Letters to Paula*, 1971, pp. 169 and 200. The colonial office papers seem to have no record of MacDonald's conversation with Ben-Gurion, which took place in a private house.

10. The Foreign Office Wrestles with the Correspondence: Baggallay's Hour

In spite of Rendel's fears, the McMahon–Husayn correspondence was at last made public in a white paper which appeared on 23 March 1939. There is no evidence that Jewish power was exerted to prevent its publication. The power, of course, may have been occult and thus, *ex hypothesi*, intangible. If so, it failed totally of its purpose – a surprising outcome, quite at variance with what is believed to happen when occult power exerts influence.

The correspondence came to be published, following demands made by the Arab delegations to the Palestine conferences of 1939. These conferences – the plural was officially used in deference to Arab objections to sitting together with the Zionists in one conference room – had been convened in order to seek a settlement of the conflict in Palestine, and followed the abandonment of partition which the royal commission had proposed in 1937, and which the British government had initially accepted. At the third meeting of British and Arab delegates which took place on 11 February 1939, MacDonald stated that the British government believed they had fulfilled both the letter and the spirit of their obligations to Husayn, and did not accept the Arab interpretation of the McMahon–Husayn correspondence. The question, he said, was one of intention 'and surely His Majesty's Government as the authors of the pledges must be the last judges of what they had had in mind'. In reply, Jemal al-Husayni, a Palestine Arab delegate, denied that it was a matter of intentions and asked for the disclosure of the correspondence:

> a question of contract was at issue and...such a question could not be discussed on the basis of the intentions of the parties, but the text of the documents.

Following this meeting representatives of the foreign and colonial offices decided 'in principle' that the correspondence should be communicated to the Arab delegations and eventually published in a white paper. At the next meeting, on 13 February, Nuri al-Sa'id of the Iraqi delegation recurred to the point which Jemal al-Husayni had raised:

The Foreign Office Wrestles with the Correspondence

When a dispute between parties over the interpretation of documents arose in an English Court, it was the custom to take the grammatical and literal sense of the words as binding, and intentions were not taken into account unless it was evident that at the time both parties had been using certain words in a special sense.[1]

In response to these claims, a British–Arab committee was also set up to scrutinize the letters and report on their exact signification.[2]

The language held by Jemal al-Husayni and Nuri al-Sa'id shows that the Arab delegations were bent on treating the McMahon–Husayn correspondence as a legal contract to be interpreted as strictly as the courts would interpret a contract drawn up in due form. This, of course, had always been the view of the Palestine Arab leaders, but in 1939 the Arab delegations went so far in this direction that they employed a former chief justice of Palestine, Sir Michael McDonnell, to prepare a statement regarding the proper manner of construing these documents. The statement was crammed full of legal precedents and weighty judgments delivered by lord chancellors and judges of the high court, but leaving entirely unexplored the fundamental question whether the correspondence was at all a contract or like a contract.[3]

This view of the correspondence was in no way questioned or controverted by the foreign office. On the contrary: as part of its preparations for the Palestine conference the Eastern department produced a memorandum, written by J. Z. Mackenzie, which, it is significant to note, purported to deal with the 'Juridical basis of the Arab claim to Palestine'. The memorandum, described by W. C. Baxter, who had succeeded Rendel as head of the Eastern department, as an 'excellent piece of work', rehashed all the views which had previously been current in the foreign and in the colonial office regarding the exact meaning of the word '*vilayet*' and the word 'district'. It repeated Young's reasonings, and Childs's interpretations, and recited the arguments for and against them. But Mackenzie made no attempt to go back to the original exchanges between McMahon and Grey which would have made quite clear the meaning of McMahon's offer. Thus he drew attention (in paragraph 16 of his memorandum) to Faruqi's statement that the Arabs would fight France for the 'districts of Damascus, Homs, Hams and Aleppo.' But the conclusions which he drew from this episode were quite peculiar:

[1] F.O. 371/23223, E1147 and 1148/6/31.
[2] Cmd. 5974, *Report of a Committee set up to consider Certain Correspondence between Sir Henry McMahon [His Majesty's High Commissioner in Egypt] and the Sharif of Mecca in 1915 and 1916*, 1939, Accounts and Papers, vol. XIV, 1938–9.
[3] Cmd. 5974, appendix C, 'Statement by Sir Michael McDonnell on Certain Legal Points'.

Although the Arabs [he averred] are unlikely to admit that anything which El Faroki may have said in the course of these conversations...has any binding effect upon the Arabs generally, no Arab could argue convincingly that, assuming the phrase to have been used at all, El Faroki meant by it no more than the 'immediate surroundings' of Damascus, Homs, Hams and Aleppo...On the contrary, he clearly intended it to convey a broad definition of the Syrian hinterland, as distinct from the Mediterranean coast...and in this sense the 'districts' he named were intended to extend from Aleppo to the Gulf of Akaba.

For this assertion there was, as has been seen, absolutely no evidence in the records, but on it Mackenzie proceeded to erect yet another baseless and gratuitous assertion:

It is thus evident that when Sir H. McMahon gave his pledge of the 24th October 1915 to the Sherif he adopted El Faroki's own phrase in order to assure the Sherif and the Syrian Arabs that the area for which they were prepared to fight was assigned to them, and further that, in using this phrase, he used it in the same comprehensive sense as El Faroki i.e. as one which covered the Syrian hinterland southwards to the Gulf of Akaba.

What in fact is evident from the papers is clean contrary to Mackenzie's reasoning. For, as was set out above, the exchanges between Cairo and the foreign office in October 1915 conclusively show that McMahon had in mind to offer nothing more than the four towns for which he understood Faruqi to be asking, that it is for this offer that he sought and received Grey's approval, and that the actual terms of McMahon's letter to the Sharif where he spoke of 'portions of Syria lying to the west of the districts of Damascus, Homs, Hams and Aleppo' had never been authorized by Grey. None of this appeared in Mackenzie's memorandum which tried, in the by now traditional way, to make sense of the unintelligible by means of a fine-spun and ingenious textual exegesis, which however left things as obscure as ever.

Mackenzie also distinguished himself by making a point which, though not entirely original, was couched in terms of alembicated subtlety. This related to McMahon's so-called 'general' reservation in favour of French claims in Syria. Childs had argued that, whatever may be thought of McMahon's 'specific' reservation about 'portions of Syria lying to the west of Damascus...', this 'general' reservation was in itself sufficient to exclude Palestine from what McMahon had promised to the Sharif. Mackenzie, adopting and embellishing an argument first put forward by the Palestine Arab delegation in 1922, now discovered a serious weakness in Childs's contention:

The Foreign Office Wrestles with the Correspondence

While it is true [he wrote in paragraph 26 of his memorandum] that the French claim to Palestine, or the French claim for an international administration of Palestine, were only withdrawn after the acceptance of the Balfour Declaration by the Allies, this does not alter the fact that it was His Majesty's Government who initiated the Declaration, and thus assumed an obligation which bears no relation to the French claims and which, unless Sir H. McMahon's 'specific' reservation can be held to be entirely valid, was incompatible, and quite unjustifiably so, with their pledge to the Sherif of Mecca. The policy of the Balfour Declaration was not essential to the satisfaction of French claims in this region. On the other hand these claims were not necessarily incompatible with Palestine remaining an Arab State, they were therefore in no way contrary *per se* to Sir H. McMahon's pledge to the Arabs. In short, the 'general' reservation has little, if any, validity apart from the 'specific' reservation.

This reasoning was acute but fanciful since nothing which McMahon wrote to Husayn stipulated that whatever region the French were not interested in, or should cease to be interested in, became automatically the property of the Sharif. In any case, Mackenzie never paused to consider whether a single letter in a long-drawn-out and inconclusive negotiation deserved, or could support the weight of, this kind of hypercritical scrutiny. These far-fetched implications which he discovered in McMahon's language, added to the alleged mistake in the Arabic version which Young had discovered, and which Mackenzie now uncritically rehearsed (in paragraphs 27 and 28 of the memorandum) served to convince him that there were 'points of serious weakness in His Majesty's Government's case'. It is not surprising that his conclusion was quite defeatist. The British case (he wrote in paragraph 46)

is likely to be dependent on a forced line of reasoning, and...the case of H.M.G. in regard to this correspondence lacks that self-evident and decisive clarity, which ought to form the basis of important international acts. Nothing in fact [he bleakly went on] that can be brought forward by way of explanation of Sir H. McMahon's pledge is likely to enable H.M.G. to convince the world at large that the Royal Commission were wrong when they said: 'It was in the highest degree unfortunate that, in the exigencies of war, the British Government was unable to make their intention clear to the Sherif'.

Mackenzie's memorandum was read by W. E. Beckett, the legal adviser of the foreign office, who wrote a long minute (dated 11 January 1939) echoing, endorsing and amplifying its conclusions. As regards Mackenzie's argument about the meaning and extent of McMahon's 'general' reservation in particular, Beckett had this to say:

The Fly in the Fly-bottle

At the time when the McMahon letter was written France was claiming the whole of Syria...Therefore at the time that these words were written H.M.G. did not know whether she would be free to act without detriment to the interests of France in any portion of Syria and, if these words meant anything, they meant that the assurance only applied to areas in Syria with regard to which H.M.G. eventually obtained a free hand as a result of the peace settlement, and it is true that the French claims to Palestine or the French claim for an international administration of Palestine were only withdrawn after the Balfour Declaration had been accepted by the allies, and therefore H.M.G. only got Palestine subject to the Balfour Declaration. But this does not alter the fact that it was H.M.G. who took the initiative as regards the Balfour Declaration and thus secured this fetter on their hands which, unless the interpretation of the first part of the McMahon letter is correct, H.M.G. should never have done...[1]

As a piece of legal reasoning, the minute seems confused. Beckett understands well enough that it was only at the end of the war that the French claims in Palestine were withdrawn, and that the British were in Palestine in pursuance of a mandate of which the Balfour declaration was a part. That, legally, therefore the British government was at no time free to dispose of Palestine, to Husayn or anyone else, is perfectly clear. But Beckett thinks that this legal position is modified, not to say negated, by the other fact that it was 'H.M.G. who took the initiative as regards the Balfour Declaration and thus secured this fetter on their hands'. But this other fact is political and not legal. Since, however, politics is not identical with law it is by no means clear what force Beckett's further assertion, that this 'H.M.G. should never have done', can have. Whatever force the 'should' in this sentence possesses, it cannot amount to a legal prohibition, since there was nothing in law to prevent the British government from engaging in a political negotiation, the outcome of which was that the French gave up their treaty rights in Palestine, and acquiesced in the mandate being entrusted by the League of Nations to Great Britain – one of the conditions of this mandate being to carry out the provisions of the Balfour declaration. Not only does Beckett not consider how cogent his legal argument is, but, more serious, he does not consider at all the legal status of the correspondence. Mackenzie's reasonings and Beckett's glosses impressed Baggallay greatly. In sending a copy of the memorandum to the colonial office, he wrote in a covering letter of 19 January to H. F. Downie:

> I must say that, after going into the whole question of the McMahon–Hussein correspondence again, our position in regard to this correspondence seems to me even weaker than it did before.[2]

[1] F.O. 371/23219, E6/6/31, Mackenzie's memorandum and Beckett's minute.
[2] F.O. 371/23219, E6/6/31.

The Foreign Office Wrestles with the Correspondence

The officials at the foreign office must have been very eager for their views to be made known to the cabinet. On 20 January, one day, that is, after he had sent Mackenzie's memorandum to Downie at the colonial office, Baggallay minuted that Sir Grattan Bushe, the legal adviser at the colonial office, had now read it and had no 'comments of substance' to make. Baggallay concluded that it was therefore unlikely that the colonial office would wish to alter it. This haste is somewhat suspect, and it is made more so by the fact that it was Bushe's views which were specially solicited, and his acquiescence brought forward as evidence that the colonial office officially approved of Mackenzie's composition. Sir Lancelot Oliphant's minute is quite revealing:

> Memo [he wrote in support of Baggallay's views] has been vetted by Mr. Beckett and been seen by the Legal Adviser of the C.O. – who between ourselves is always a power of strength in supporting Mr Baxter and others in championing the cause of the F.O. in meetings at the C.O. Sir Grattan Bushe has before now told me, as an old friend, that he has often been uneasy in the past about the C.O. attitude in regard to Palestine. But this is of course most confidential and not quotable.

As a result of all this hustle, Mackenzie's memorandum was circulated to the cabinet prefaced by a statement in which the foreign secretary was made to tell his colleagues that this document would

> emphasize once more...the difficulty which must confront any Government of this country in attempting to explain the rival promises made to Jews and Arabs during the Great War.[1]

Such language in an official document was quite novel. For as has been seen, the official attitude hitherto was that there were no 'rival promises' to be explained or reconciled, because Palestine was simply not within the ambit of McMahon's pledge. The foreign secretary was now hinting that the opposite was the case, and Mackenzie's memorandum was thus no longer only an examination of arguments likely to be advanced by the Arabs, and of possible refutations of such arguments; it had itself become a plea in favour of the Arab contentions. Beckett's comments on the memorandum, and Baggallay's language in his letter to Downie, both cited above, show this clearly, as does the attitude which the foreign office subsequently took when the correspondence was examined by the British–Arab committee.

And yet, it was not as though Mackenzie's arguments were conclusive. A few days after the memorandum was circulated to the

---

[1] F.O. 371/23221, E764/6/31.

cabinet, Downie answered Baggallay's letter. It then became clear that Bushe's acquiescence was by no means representative of colonial office opinion, and that Mackenzie's was by no means the last word on the McMahon–Husayn correspondence:

> Whatever apparent weaknesses there may be in our case [Downie pointed out in a letter of 1 February], we should not be inclined to take the matter too tragically. The idea that the fundamental issue whether or not Palestine is to be turned into an Arab State can be decided (or even seriously affected) by a legal interpretation of the McMahon correspondence is too ridiculous to need refutation, and we doubt whether any further investigation of the Arabic text is worthwhile.
>
> Surely we need only concern ourselves with refuting the offensive insinuation (which constitutes the sting of the Arab case) that HMG have been guilty of bad faith in the matter. On this point there is no reason why we should condescend to argument with the Arabs. We have always maintained that our intention was to exclude Palestine from the pledges given to the Sharif.

Downie referred to McMahon's recent letter to the *The Times* and argued that on the issue of intentions his evidence was vital. If it were said, as the Peel commission did say, that it was 'in the highest degree unfortunate' that these intentions were not made absolutely clear, then surely the shoulders of the British government were broad enough to bear this criticism. Downie went on to comment on paragraph 26 of the memorandum, which contained, in fact, Mackenzie's only original argument. In this paragraph, it will be recalled, Mackenzie had argued that McMahon's so-called 'general' reservation in favour of French interests lost its significance because it was the British government which had 'initiated' the Balfour declaration. Downie asked whether it was not true that the French had been persuaded by negotiation voluntarily to modify their claims in Palestine; if so, why was so much stress laid on the fact that it was the British who had 'initiated' the declaration?

Downie's arguments were summarily brushed aside and dismissed at the foreign office. Baggallay declared that McMahon's letter to *The Times* was worthless as evidence. He conceded that the British government did consult the French and others before issuing the Balfour declaration but this, he affirmed, 'does not alter the fact that they initiated it.' His legal colleague, Beckett, conceded that the intentions of the British government in 1915–16 were of some importance, but the question remained what McMahon's letters in fact said 'and how the Shariff and the Arabs were entitled to read them.' Clearly, on this point, Mackenzie's explanations were held to be irrefutable. These minutes were seen by Oliphant, Vansittart and Cadogan, by R. A. Butler, the parliamentary under-secretary and Halifax, the secretary of state. Their bare initials indicate eloquently enough acquiescence, if not whole-hearted agreement.[1]

There was more weighty objection to Mackenzie's arguments. The lord chancellor, Lord Maugham, who was to represent the British government on the committee which was to scrutinize the McMahon–Husayn correspondence, complained that the foreign office memorandum did not state the case for the British government as well as it might have been stated. Maugham was entirely a newcomer to the subject and knew little more of the correspondence and its history than what the officials of the foreign office put before him. Even so, being a man of great forensic intelligence, and (as his comments show) possessing some historical imagination, he sketched out a much shrewder line of argument, and one, moreover, which managed to be truer to the historical record. Maugham pointed out that it was impossible to understand what McMahon's letters meant without taking into account the whole surrounding circumstances. Two circumstances were in particular relevant. In the first place, both Great Britain and France attached great importance to controlling ports in the Eastern Mediterranean; it was therefore unthinkable that McMahon should have promised Acre, Haifa and Jaffa to the Sharif. In the second place, it was equally unthinkable that the holy places of Palestine could have been promised to him. As regards the 'general' reservation, so-called, Maugham considered that it was a reservation in favour of French claims as they stood when McMahon sent his letter to the Sharif; his pledge was in no way dependent on what France might do in the future. In short, Maugham believed that McMahon's pledge and the Balfour declaration were fully compatible.

The foreign office minutes uniformly threw cold water on Maugham's arguments. Baggallay did not think that they advanced matters very much. True, the existence of important ports and of the holy places in Palestine 'ought perhaps' to have made the Sharif especially wary about making sure that the British government had no reservations to make in regard to Palestine.

> But this [he objected in a minute of 6 February 1939] does not seem to alter the fundamental principle that when A tells B he wants X and B tells A in reply that he will give him X–Y, the onus of defining Y lies on B, and that if there is any doubt about the meaning and extent of Y it is A who is entitled to the benefit of that doubt and not B.

To this line of argument Sir Alexander Cadogan objected in a minute which stands out as the only demur on record in the foreign office

[1] F.O. 371/23221, E843/6/31.

papers to the view which had now come to prevail within this department:

> No: I can't accept that. 'The onus of defining Y may lie on B, but I don't see why A is 'entitled to the benefit' of any doubt. In a perfect world, if there were any doubt, it should be submitted to arbitration. A is not, in my view, *entitled* to any *benefit* of any doubt. Why should he be?

This minute apart, the judgments of the officials constitute a near-unanimous chorus: there is not the hint of a doubt or a critical scrutiny. The issue is simple, cut-and-dried, open-and-shut, it is a *chose jugée*, settled and done with, ready to be filed away; profitless or even presumptuous for a junior to raise anew, a waste of time for a senior to reconsider. The episode casts the reforms of 1906[1] in a dubious light. These reforms were meant to allow juniors to show their paces, to give scope to critical debate, to discourage the incurious acceptance of dominant orthodoxies. What they seem to have ensured, in this instance at any rate, was the deferential adherence by the juniors to the certainties and predilections of their seniors.

Baggallay also dismissed Maugham's argument about the 'general' reservation in favour of France. It was 'possibly the case' that this applied to French claims as at 24 October 1915:

> But this does not get over the difficulty that it may not have been known to the Sherif that the French claimed Palestine on October 24th 1915. The response...that the Sherif ought to have found out does not seem to have much *legal* force.

Baggallay grudgingly admitted that the points which Maugham had made might help in answering the Arab contention but, he added, 'I doubt if they alter the real situation'. His views were found fully convincing by the superintending deputy secretary, Sir Lancelot Oliphant, and by the parliamentary under-secretary, R. A. Butler. The first wrote that the Sharif

> being a real backwoodsman was not called on to look out for various 'catches' in the McMahon correspondence and in the stress of war cannot be blamed for not taking the pledges *cum grano*.

Butler for his part was equally dismissive of the lord chancellor:

> This opinion [he minuted on 9 February] does not alter my views of the McMahon correspondence. There is no proof that Sir H. McMahon was thinking of the 'Ports' or the Port [i.e. Acre, Haifa and Jaffa].[2]

[1] On which see Zara Steiner, *The Foreign Office and Foreign Policy 1898–1914*, 1969.
[2] F.O. 371/23222, E891/6/31.

The Foreign Office Wrestles with the Correspondence

It is difficult to know what, in such a situation, constitutes proof, but McMahon's observations of July 1915 on the Bunsen Report (reviewed in part 1 above) would have shown, had Baggallay known about them and brought them to the minister's attention, that Maugham's suggestions were not entirely fanciful. These foreign office minutes show how justified was Maugham's *cri de cœur* uttered somewhat later:

> how pleased I should be [he wrote in a letter to Malcolm MacDonald on 28 February 1939] if I could hear of anyone in the F.O. or the C.O. or in the government who could make *one* useful and helpful suggestion in meeting or contesting the Arab claims.[1]

The lord chancellor's anguish will be better appreciated if it is remembered that his two colleagues in the British–Arab committee scrutinizing the McMahon–Husayn correspondence were none other than Sir Grattan Bushe and Lacy Baggallay.

The inclinations, beliefs and policies of these two officials emerge with great clarity from the papers. In a minute attached to a draft report of the committee examining the McMahon–Husayn correspondence, Baggallay wrote that one of the two issues on which the gist of the report turned was:

> The admission that the Arabs really have got a very strong case over the correspondence...

To such an admission, Baggallay went on,

> Sir G. Bushe attaches great importance. I do not know how the Lord Chancellor or Mr MacDonald will regard the proposal, but Sir G. Bushe is most anxious for Foreign Office support. He feels that nothing short of a final admission that the Arab case is really strong will restore their confidence in the good faith of His Majesty's Government. They have said they regard this committee as a sort of test of His Majesty's Government's good faith.

We do not know the exact grounds on which Bushe believed his government guilty of bad faith over Palestine, but he must clearly have regarded the work of the committee of which he was a member, as one of atonement and reparation.

Baggallay went on:

> Personally I agree with Sir G. Bushe. I have drafted the paragraph in question as mildly as possible, but would gladly see it stronger.[2]

[1] C.O. 733/411, 75891.
[2] F.O. 371/23227, E1690/6/31, Baggallay's minute of 3 Mar. 1939.

The Fly in the Fly-bottle

The papers provide a great deal more evidence about his attitude than about Bushe's, and the thrust of this evidence is unmistakeable. Baggallay was utterly determined that the Zionists should not have the best of the argument and adamant in his belief that the British had almost no case over the McMahon–Husayn correspondence. His comment on McMahon's letter of 23 July 1937 to *The Times* has been quoted above. He was equally contemptuous of McMahon's letter to Shuckburgh of 12 March 1922 in which the ex-high commissioner had tried to explain what he had meant by his letter of 24 October 1915. McMahon's explanation, as has been seen, was obfuscatory, but instead of trying with the help of the archives at his disposal to understand what McMahon could possibly have meant by such an explanation, Baggallay dismissed the letter as useless. It might show, he wrote, the intention to exclude Palestine, but it hardly supported the view that McMahon succeeded in doing so. McMahon, Baggallay declared, failed to extend his definition of boundaries to cover Palestine 'for reasons which seem quite insufficient'.[1] For Baggallay then McMahon's intentions were irrelevant, and nothing was admissible as evidence except the bare text of his one letter of 24 October 1915 to Husayn. And how this letter excluded Palestine from the prospective Arab state, Baggallay utterly failed to see. In a minute commenting on some notes which had been prepared for the use of A. C. Trott, the consul at Jeddah, who was to examine for the foreign office the Arabic text of McMahon's letters, Baggallay lamented:

> Our whole case with regard to 'the districts of Damascus etc' is of course hopelessly weak, and I have no real hope that anything Mr Trott may discover will materially strengthen it.[2]

Baggallay evinced the same attitude to later British dealings with the Sharif. A memorandum prepared in the foreign office correctly pointed out that it was not true as George Antonius maintained in his book *The Arab Awakening*, that during his visit to Jeddah in May 1917 Sykes said nothing to Husayn about the Asia Minor agreement. Baggallay feared that the memorandum would not very much aid the British case:

> It is not far from the truth [he gloomily observed] when Mr Antonius says that the Allies kept the Sharif in deliberate ignorance of their real intentions regarding the Arab territories.[3]

[1] F.O. 371/23225, E1420/6/31, Baggallay's minute of 27 Feb. 1939.
[2] F.O. 371/23220, E633/6/31, minute by Baggallay of 25 Jan. 1939.
[3] F.O. 371/23226, E1548/6/31, Baggallay's minute of 22 Feb. 1939.

The Foreign Office Wrestles with the Correspondence

From what has been said above about the complexities of the Jeddah meeting it ought to be clear that Baggallay had no ground whatever for such defeatism, as he could easily have ascertained if he had looked up the foreign office files.

Just as Baggallay was determined that his government must be in the wrong over the promises to Husayn, so he was also determined to ensure that the Zionists should have no ground for arguing otherwise. Thus, the Jewish Agency had asked for a copy of the instructions which had been given to W. G. Ormsby Gore when he accompanied, as liaison officer, the Zionist commission which went to Palestine in April 1918. J. Z. Mackenzie minuted that this should be refused as there was no reason why the foreign office should supply the Jews with material for a propagandist publication. Baggallay agreed with this. But he also added, gratuitously:

> I am not sure that Captain Ormsby Gore's instructions really help the Jewish propagandist point of view. The only important passage in these instructions seems to be that in which it is stated that the commission is proceeding to Palestine so as to be placed in touch with the Arab leaders and representatives of other communities in Palestine, etc, etc. If this does anything, it bears out the view that when the Balfour Declaration stated that HMG viewed with favour the establishment of a national home for the Jews in Palestine, they meant that this home must be established with the acquiescence and approval of the existing population.[1]

The simple fact, of course, was that the Balfour declaration contained nothing about 'the acquiescence and approval of the existing population' and the notion of the British government seeking to obtain such acquiescence and approval from the Palestinians for its policies would have seemed quite absurd to ministers and officials in 1917.

Baggallay was so intent on refuting Zionist arguments that he conducted a zealous one-sided controversy with the Zionists in the privacy of his files. The *Manchester Guardian* of 31 January 1939 published a letter from the Zionist publicist Israel Cohen in which he quoted a speech Churchill had made in the house of commons on 11 July 1922. Churchill had stated that in a conversation at the foreign office in January 1921, Faysal had 'expressed himself as prepared to accept the statement that it had been the intention of His Majesty's Government to exclude Palestine' from the scope of the promises to Husayn. Baggallay was moved to minute on Cohen's letter:

[1] F.O. 371/23237, E4208/6/31, Baggallay's minute of 16 June 1939.

the acceptance by the Emir Feisal of the statement of HMG that they intended to exclude Palestine does not mean that he accepted their argument that they *had* done so.[1]

He went to great lengths to refute Zionist arguments and spokesmen. On 23 March 1939 *The Times* published a letter from Weizmann objecting that only Arabs had been heard on the issue of the McMahon–Husayn correspondence, and the Jewish delegates to the Palestine conference had had no opportunity to comment on the documents put forward, or of producing other documents. In particular, Weizmann complained (and in this he was supported by a leader in *The Times*) that no account had been taken of Faysal's statement at the peace conference excluding Palestine from the territories claimed for the Arabs. Baggallay felt it necessary to refute Weizmann in a minute in which he affirmed that the committee had not been set up to consider discussions between the British and the Arabs during the peace conference and after, but only the McMahon–Husayn correspondence and 'any subsequent declarations which threw light upon the meaning or intention of that correspondence'. Originally, however, the committee had been set up to consider the correspondence alone, but – as its report shows – took upon itself to consider other, subsequent, documents which it considered relevant. It might seem somewhat arbitrary and artificial to hold that documents dating from before the peace conference were relevant, while those dating from after were not relevant. Baggallay hastened to buttress this argument with yet another refutation of Weizmann:

> In any case what Emir Feisal and other Arabs may have said at the Peace Conference cannot [he categorically affirmed] throw any light on the meaning of the pledges given by His Majesty's Government. Moreover, it does not follow that, because the Emir Feisal agreed to exclude Palestine from his demands at certain stages of the post-war negotiations, he did not regard Palestine as probably included in the area of independence promised to the Arabs during the war.

These are no doubt logically sound, and even cogent points. But any force they may have depends not so much on logic as on what actually happened. For it could easily turn out that what Faysal said at the peace conference would have a bearing on the scope and meaning of earlier British promises. In a historical enquiry of this kind, mere ratiocination cannot be a substitute for the evidence. We are therefore quite astonished to see that, at this late stage (when the report of the committee on the McMahon–Husayn correspon-

[1] F.O. 371/23223, E1051/6/31.

dence was already published), Baggallay, who was an important member of the committee – who in fact had borne the brunt of preparing successive drafts of its reports – was still ignorant of these statements of Faysal's about the significance of which he was yet willing to be so fluent. For his minute continued:

> A good deal of information about this part of the Peace Conference will be found in Mr Antonius' book 'The Arab Awakening', pages 298 onwards.
> We must, however, look up ourselves and see what actually did happen. In particular, I should like to see the British aide-mémoire which is said to be given in volume XVI of Mr David Hunter Miller's book 'My Diary of the Conference of Paris', and also the Emir Feisal's statement regarding Palestine which is said to be given on page 230 of volume XIV. In addition, the Emir Feisal is said to have sent a note to the Allies (or possibly to His Majesty's Government) on October 11th 1919. I should like this, and also the papers showing exactly what the Emir Feisal did say to the Council of Five mentioned by Dr Weizmann.[1]

It may perhaps be the case that Baggallay's anxiety to refute any possible objection to the Arab view of McMahon's promises stemmed from his belief – which was current in the foreign office – that Zionism had become a serious embarrassment for British policy in the Middle East, and that everything possible should be done to abate the nuisance. But we may also suspect that he genuinely believed the Arab case. The suspicion derives from the fact that Baggallay manifestly considered Antonius's work *The Arab Awakening* as a definitive authority on Anglo-Arab diplomacy. The minute just cited shows that his authority for the transactions at the peace conference was simply Antonius. The hazy and putative manner in which Baggallay referred to various statements made at that time by Faysal is probably accounted for by the fact that Antonius had not seen fit to discuss, or to quote from these statements in his book, and that Baggallay first came to hear of them when the Zionists started complaining about the proceedings of his committee.

The evidence does show that Baggallay, and the Eastern department of the foreign office, greatly admired *The Arab Awakening* as an authoritative and original work of historical research. As will be seen, it is from this book that they first came to hear of negotiations and documents, details of which had always been available to them in their own files. One may perhaps go further, and say that they came to view not only the Arab nationalist movement, but the whole course of Anglo-Arab relations, exactly

---

[1] F.O. 371/23231, E2230/6/31, Baggallay's minute of 23 Mar. 1939.

The Fly in the Fly-bottle

as Antonius presented it. It is interesting and somewhat suggestive that Mackenzie must have been writing his memorandum on 'The Juridical basis of the Arab claim to Palestine' – which has been discussed above – when he was reading *The Arab Awakening* which had just come out.[1] As has been said, Mackenzie's most original point is his suggestion that, in making the Balfour declaration, Britain had assumed an obligation which bore no relation to French claims, and that the French claim having disappeared, Palestine was therefore included in the territories promised to the Sharif. It is most probable that this argument was inspired by Antonius who wrote:

> If, then, Great Britain were to find herself at the end of the War free to act in respect of any portion of Syria which she had felt bound to reserve in favour of France, the reservation loses its justification and indeed whatever force it may have had when it was originally made; and that portion of Syria which was no longer destined to be included in the sphere of French interests – as was eventually the case with Palestine – must, in default of any specific agreement to the contrary, necessarily remain within the area of Arab independence as proposed by the Sharif and acccepted by Great Britain.[2]

But whether or not this passage is the precise source of the foreign office argument, there can be no doubt of the influence of *The Arab Awakening* within the foreign office. Shortly after its publication, Professor Harold Temperley, the co-editor of *British Documents on the Origins of the War*, wrote to the librarian at the foreign office to complain that Antonius had failed to acknowledge this work as the source for his account of Abdullah's relations with Kitchener, and Aziz Ali al-Misri's quarrel with the Young Turks. Temperley believed that this was because Antonius wanted to suggest that in all important issues his Arab sources were sufficient, 'and to quote us would be to disprove his thesis'. Baggallay had no sympathy with Temperley's complaint:

> However bad Mr Antonius' manners may be [he minuted], there can be no doubt about the value and authority of his book.

He was inclined to believe that in regard to the McMahon–Husayn correspondence 'the Arabs have much better contemporary sources than we have':

> Although therefore [he concluded] Mr Antonius may not have had access to the British side of the MacMahon–Hussein correspondence, he has had access to what is probably just as good and as authoritative material.[3]

[1] A minute by him dated 10 Jan. 1939 in F.O. 370/586, L66/66/407 shows clearly that he was by then familiar with the book.
[2] *The Arab Awakening*, p. 179.
[3] F.O. 370/586, L66/66/407, cited above, Temperley's letter, Cambridge 29 Dec. 1938, and Baggallay's minute, 18 Jan. 1939. In his minute cited above Mackenzie, too, took up the cudgels on Antonius's behalf.

The Foreign Office Wrestles with the Correspondence

In believing that Antonius had access to sources and information denied to the foreign office Baggallay was labouring under an illusion. In his account of Anglo-Sharifian relations Antonius was in fact overwhelmingly indebted to British sources. Temperley's ground for complaint is precisely that Antonius had, prior to its publication, had access to the proofs of volume x, part 2 of the *British Documents* which dealt with the Abdullah–Kitchener conversations and the Misri affair, by permission of Gaselee, the foreign office librarian. Gaselee had also allowed Antonius in 1934 to see the Arab Bulletin.[1] Antonius's records also reveal that he saw Mark Sykes's papers through Storrs's help, that Iltyd Clayton gave him access to the papers of his brother G. F. Clayton, that General Creedy allowed him to see documents in the war office, and that he also consulted D. G. Hogarth's papers. In the United States, Antonius was able to use the archives of the department of state, the Colonel House Collection, and the records of Professor W. L. Westermann.[2] These last, it is interesting to note, contain a copy of Toynbee's 'commitments' memorandum from which Antonius would have been able to glean a great deal of official information which was then still inaccessible to outsiders. Antonius cleverly hid all these sources from his readers. This enabled him to select and suppress according to his convenience, and to give the impression that he was privileged to have access to information contained in Arab archives which were not available to others. This is precisely what the deluded Baggallay came to believe. In a letter to Downie at the colonial office commending Mackenzie's memorandum Baggallay drew his colleague's attention to *The Arab Awakening*:

> you may find it worth while looking at what George Antonius has to say about the MacMahon–Hussein correspondence in Chapter ix of 'The Arab Awakening'. Whatever else may be said about him, he has had unique opportunities of studying this correspondence and its implications.

Downie's response was cool. He had read Antonius 'with interest', but was not impressed:

> His presentation of the case is clever but, to my mind, carries no more and no less conviction than our official defence.[3]

---

[1] F.O. 371/17831, E2456/65, Gaselee's minute of 25 Apr. 1934.

[2] Antonius's notes and his correspondence with the Institute of Current World Affairs, New York (who had appointed him Senior Associate in the Near East); Antonius Papers, Israel State Archives.

[3] F.O. 371/23219, E6/6/31, Baggallay to Downie, 19 Jan.; F.O. 371/23222, E843/6/31, Downie to Baggallay, 1 Feb. 1939, cited above.

The Fly in the Fly-bottle

Downie's scepticism about Antonius, however, seems to have been exceptional in British official circles. According to Antonius himself, it was the British government which asked him to serve as secretary-general to the Arab delegations attending the Palestine conferences. And at the conclusion of these conferences, Antonius described how influential his book had proved to be. In a letter of 6 April 1939 he claimed that *The Arab Awakening* was having a 'visible influence' on the events, that it had been widely used and was constantly consulted during the conference by both Arabs and British.[1] The evidence goes to show that in speaking thus, Antonius was more than merely indulging an author's vanity.

A case in point is the so-called 'Hogarth Message'. This, as will be recalled, was a declaration drafted by Sykes and approved by Hardinge in London, and delivered by D. G. Hogarth to Husayn in Jeddah in January 1918. In *The Arab Awakening* Antonius made great play with it. He claimed that the Hogarth message was a response to a protest by Husayn over the Balfour declaration, and that its terms fundamentally modified and narrowed down the British commitment to the Zionists. The message, he declared,

> was an explicit assurance that 'Jewish settlement in Palestine would only be allowed in so far as would be consistent with *the political and economic freedom of the Arab population*'...The phrase I have italicised represents a fundamental departure from the text of the Balfour Declaration which purports to guarantee only *the civil and religious rights* of the Arab population. In that difference [Antonius solemnly argued] lay the difference between a peaceful and willing Arab–Jew co-operation in Palestine and the abominable duel of the last twenty years.[2]

In the 'Memorandum on Political Pledges to the Arabs' which he presented on behalf of the Arab delegation to the committee considering the McMahon–Husayn correspondence Antonius again drew attention to the Hogarth message. In a forceful and emphatic passage, he affirmed that Husayn had 'always' believed Palestine to have been included in the territories promised to him:

> No sooner was the Balfour Declaration issued than he sent in an immediate protest to the British Government to ask for an explanation. This action and other actions taken by the Sharif in subsequent years may be held to fall outside the scope of the present Committee's investigation...But they are historical facts nevertheless; and in the light of those facts, Sir Henry McMahon's declaration that he had every reason to believe the contrary loses its force and indeed appears meaningless.[3]

[1] Antonius Papers, letters to W. S. Rogers, Institute of Current World Affairs, London 5 Feb. and 6 Apr. 1939.
[2] *The Arab Awakening*, pp. 267–8.   [3] Cmd. 5974, vol. XIV, annex A, para. 18.

Antonius and the Arab delegations must have considered this a very strong argument since the committee's report insisted (in paragraph 20) that the Arab representatives 'rely strongly' on the terms of the Hogarth message.

But Antonius's bold assertions, both in his book and his memorandum, have no basis in fact. As the evidence reviewed above shows, Husayn had not protested against the Balfour declaration, nor was the Hogarth message an answer to such a protest. It was a composition by Sir Mark Sykes (in response to a rival one by Wingate) to which Lord Hardinge had made significant amendments. So far as Husayn was concerned, it had come to him out of the blue, and his reaction shows that had it not contained a single word about Palestine, he would have been neither surprised nor disappointed. As has been seen, his preoccupations lay then elsewhere. It is idle to ask whether Antonius really believed that great issues were involved in the fact that whereas the Balfour declaration spoke of 'civil and religious rights', the Hogarth message spoke of 'the political and economic freedom' of the Arab population in Palestine. His argument here is very much in the style which Palestine Arab leaders liked, namely to search out minute and tenuous verbal distinctions, and erect upon them grandiose arguments. But whether or not Antonius was aware that he was making no more than a clever debating point, the fact remains that, as the documents show, in drafting the Hogarth message, Sykes could not have had in mind any substantive, let alone fundamental, change in the Balfour declaration; for this reason if no other: such a change would have required ministerial authority. Even if we were to assume, *per impossibile*, that Sykes did want substantively to modify without authority the tenor of the Balfour declaration, it is difficult to see how Hardinge would have allowed it. In any case, the paragraph of the Hogarth message to which Antonius was obviously referring was somewhat different in its emphasis from what Husayn had allegedly taken down. Instead of declaring baldly, in Antonius's version, that

> Jewish settlement in Palestine would only be allowed in so far as would be consistent with the political and economic freedom of the Arab population

Hogarth had really said that

> Since the Jewish opinion of the world is in favour of a return of Jews to Palestine, and inasmuch as this opinion must remain a constant factor, and, further as His Majesty's Government view with favour the realisation of this aspiration, His Majesty's Government are determined that in so far as is

compatible with the freedom of the existing population, both economic and political, no obstacle should be put in the way of the realisation of their ideal.

It is amply evident that this paragraph is no more than a reiteration of the Balfour declaration, adds nothing to, and subtracts nothing from, it. We must conclude that the difference on which Antonius seized was merely verbal, and that the imposing argument he based on it was worthless.

All this can easily be ascertained from the record as it is found in the foreign office files. But it seems that before the publication of *The Arab Awakening*, Baggallay had not even heard of the Hogarth message. In a minute of 27 February 1939 he stated that the message 'seems to have been overlooked from January 1918 until Mr Antonius mentioned it in his book'.[1] And when he did come to learn of the message, Baggallay seems to have made no effort to ascertain its true history and significance. Or if he did, there is no evidence that he took any steps to bring the true state of affairs to the notice of ministers who, in the language they held about the message, were both misled and misleading. Thus, in a conversation with Weizmann, MacDonald solemnly affirmed that the Hogarth message 'had very great significance. It had been delivered to the Sharif Hussein at a moment when the Arabs were hesitating about continuing the war, and that message had persuaded them to go on fighting. It was therefore', MacDonald impressed on Weizmann, 'a highly important document'. These assertions were utterly without foundation, as was MacDonald's further assertion that the message 'had received ministerial approval'.[2]

Maugham was also gravely misled. He seems to have accepted Antonius's arguments at their face value and indeed to have made them his own. Thus Bushe recorded him as saying that the Hogarth message was one point in the Arab arguments over which he felt embarrassment and that the Arabs were entitled to interpret the Balfour declaration in the light of the Hogarth message. This language clearly indicated that Maugham believed the message to have modified the Balfour declaration, and thus shows the lord chancellor to have been ignorant of the circumstances in which the message came to be written – in other words, to have been badly briefed. At the second meeting of the committee, on 24 February

[1] F.O. 371/23225, E1484/6/31. In a minute of 21 Feb. Baggallay declares that the significance of the Hogarth message had hitherto escaped him, as had the existence of the Declaration to the Seven. It was the reading of Antonius's book which wakened him to their significance. The documents he considered (and his superior, Baxter concurred) to be 'embarrassing'. F.O. 371/23224, E1357/6/31.

[2] F.O. 371/23230, E2024/6/31.

1939, Maugham mentioned the Hogarth message to the Arab representatives, admitted the force of the assurance it contained, and conceded that it substantially modified the promise made in the Balfour declaration, indeed that it was of the highest importance to an understanding both of the McMahon correspondence and the Balfour declaration. Like MacDonald in his conversation with Weizmann, Maugham said that the Hogarth message 'had the effect at that time of stilling the doubts in the minds of the Arabs and persuaded them to carry on on our side in the War instead of withdrawing from the War'. Maugham went so far as to declare that he was clear in his own mind that as a result of Hogarth's assurance the Jews were not entitled to a Zionist state in Palestine. The effect of this speech on Antonius and the Arab delegates was, a gratified Baggallay reported, 'electrical'. Baggallay put on record the reason for his pleasure:

> I am sure [he minuted] that the right thing was to admit frankly the wording of the Hogarth message...and the fact that we were so frank about this message may go a long way towards convincing the Arabs of our good faith over the question of the Arab pledges generally.[1]

Assuming – what was in fact the case – that the British government were then determined to be rid of embarrassments in Palestine by conceding to the Arabs as much as possible, it still remains true that the attainment of this aim would not necessarily be made easier by the gratuitous admission of non-existent commitments. Baggallay's language in the minute just cited shows that he believed British good faith to be justly impugned, and had somehow to be restored, in the same way in which a suspect regains the confidence of the police, namely by making a clean breast of it. Even assuming that such an abject posture was necessary, it should surely have been adopted only after due deliberation, and in full knowledge of the facts. As it was, the lord chancellor was made to eat, in all innocence, humble pie before the Arab delegates, and to admit that 'frankly' it was their secretary who had unearthed an important statement favouring the Arab cause, which the British government had somehow, inexplicably, overlooked.

The true character of the Hogarth message, and Husayn's reception of it, was also greatly distorted by the way in which the foreign office decided to publish Hogarth's report on his vist to Husayn.

[1] F.O. 371/23225, E1484/6/31, record of second meeting of McMahon–Husayn correspondence committee; minute by Baggallay, 27 Feb., cited above; and minute by Bushe, 25 Feb. 1939. F.O. 371/23230, E2035/6/31, note of certain points made orally by lord chancellor at second meeting.

The Fly in the Fly-bottle

As may be seen from the passage quoted above, Antonius had cited in *The Arab Awakening* only one sentence from the message, which he declared was his own rendering of a note which Husayn had taken at the time. Whether this is true or not is impossible to say. We do, however, know that Hogarth gave Husayn a copy of his message.[1] The British members of the committee made no attempt to draw the attention of the Arab delegates to the difference between what Hogarth actually said and what Antonius declared him to have said. But they decided to make available to the committee the full text of the message, and it was in fact published as an annex to their report. But Antonius and his colleagues now demanded to see Hogarth's report on his interview, as they had no independent evidence that the Hogarth message was delivered in the form intended. Antonius told Baggallay that they considered most of the message to be in their favour

> but some passages in it seemed to be inconsistent with other passages, e.g. the passage in which it was stated that no race should dominate another in Palestine seemed to them inconsistent with the provision for political and economic [freedom] for the existing population. As he said before, the Arabs had no independent information as to the delivery of this message, or King Hussein's reactions. They did not seriously doubt that it had been delivered as intended, but they did feel considerable doubt as to whether King Hussein had swallowed the whole of it without any reservation.
>
> If, in these circumstances, they were to agree to attach the text of His Majesty's Government's instructions to Commander Hogarth as an annex to a report to which they had put their signatures, they would in effect be admitting that these instructions were not merely instructions, but also the terms of an agreement reached between King Hussein and Commander Hogarth.[2]

Antonius's observations were both misconceived and impertinent. Misconceived in speaking of the Hogarth message as 'an agreement' between the British and Husayn, and impertinent in insinuating that the British might be suppressing something which, if revealed, would be to the advantage of the Arabs. But, of course, ample scope had been given to misconception and impertinence by the humble stance which the lord chancellor, misleadingly briefed by Bushe and Baggallay, had found it necessary to adopt. A great deal of discussion in the foreign office followed Antonius's request. In the end it was decided to publish parts of Hogarth's notes on his conversation with Husayn, together with a short fragment of his report to Wingate.

[1] F.O. 371/3383, 25577/675, letter from Husayn to Wingate acknowledging receipt of communication from Hogarth 'written on ordinary paper'.
[2] F.O. 371/23229, E1968/6/31, Baggallay's minute of 10 Mar. 1939.

The Foreign Office Wrestles with the Correspondence

The decision is puzzling. If the Arab delegates wanted to know how Husayn had received the message, they could have been given a copy of his letter to the high commissioner in Cairo which Wingate sent to London together with Hogarth's report. In this letter Husayn acknowledged receipt of the message which, he said, 'was written on ordinary paper', expressed in fulsome terms his gratitude to Britain for her 'noble act which is unprecedented in history', in working for the restoration of the Arab nation, and affirmed the obligation of the Arabs in return to support Britain 'until the end of the world'. Husayn concluded his letter by referring to a letter from the Ottoman commander Jemal Pasha to Faysal. The letter, Husayn wrote, was deceitful and

> already threatens our noble cause by playing on the minds of simple Arabs and other Mohammedans, saying that Great Britain intended to occupy such and such a territory and France intended to occupy such and such a territory etc, which I am sure Your Excellency will refrain from discussing.[1]

Not only was this letter, which would have simply disposed of Antonius's allegations, not given to the Arabs, but also there was omitted (without the fact being disclosed), on R. A. Butler's instructions, from the fragment of Hogarth's report which was made public, three passages, on the score that they had no bearing on the issue of Palestine.[2] Of two of these passages, this was simply not true, while the third gave a somewhat significant detail about Husayn's attitude and outlook which it was the purpose of Hogarth's report to describe. The fragment, as published in the white paper,[3] consisted of three paragraphs, and each one of these suffered an excision. In the first paragraph, Hogarth dealt with the subject of Arab unity and Husayn's actual and possible relation to it. As the white paper recorded, Hogarth wrote on this subject:

> It is obvious that the King regards Arab unity as synonymous with his own Kingship, and (for reasons given above) as a vain phrase unless so regarded. He treats our proclamations and exhortations about it as good intentions but no more, and has no faith in their effect until we support the embodiment of the idea in one single personality – himself.

This paragraph continued with a sentence which the white paper suppressed. It reads:

> 'Arab unity' means very little to King Hussein except as a means to his personal aggrandisement.

[1] F.O. 371/3383, 25577/675, cited above, Husayn's letter enclosed with Wingate's despatch no. 15, Cairo 27 Jan. 1918.
[2] F.O. 371/23232, E2332/6/31.   [3] Cmd. 5964.

The Fly in the Fly-bottle

This sentence was in turn followed by a passage which the white paper also suppressed, and which was of the greatest significance in elucidating Husayn's attitude to Palestine. The passage (which has already been discussed above) is as follows:

> He made this very clear in the matter of the message to Jerusalem Arabs which I was asked to suggest to him, saying that, unless he might sign as 'King of the Arabs' or the 'Arab Nation', the addressee would ask what business it was of his. Even when warned he must not so sign, he drafted the message at first patently on the assumption that he held that position; and I had to get him to redraft it in a different tone.

As has also been shown above, the message which in the end Husayn signed showed that he had no interest whatever in Palestine as a territory. The suppression of this passage altered the significance of the paragraph (and of the published fragments as a whole) to the point of misrepresentation.

The second paragraph published in the white paper dealt with international control of the Palestine holy places. This was certainly Hogarth's own heading. It was, however, made to follow by a sentence which again seriously misrepresented Hogarth. For in the white paper this heading was immediately followed by the sentence:

> The King left me in little doubt that he secretly regards *this* as a point to be reconsidered after the Peace, in spite of my assurance that it was to be a definitive arrangement.

The unsuspecting reader would assume that the 'this' italicized in the above passage could only refer to the international control of the Palestine holy places. There was nothing further from the truth, for in Hogarth's report this sentence ran as follows:

> While the King accepted without demur H.M.G.'s declaration on this matter, as conveyed in Foreign Office telegram No. 6 of November 6 1916 to yourself, he left me in little doubt that he secretly regards *this* as a point to be reconsidered after the Peace, etc.

It should now be clear that the italicized 'this' in the passage above in reality refers not to Palestine or its holy places but to a British declaration of November 1916 which, as set out above, informed Husayn that he could not be recognized as king of the Arabs, but only as 'the titular head of the Arab peoples in the revolt against Turkish misrule'.[1] It is clear that in spite of the heading, Hogarth in this paragraph was continuing the line of thought which he had

[1] F.O. 371/2782, 221869/217652, cited above.

begun in the previous paragraph which dealt with Arab unity. That he should be doing so will appear more natural if it is realized that headings which in the white paper stand at the beginning of each paragraph, do not do so in the original report. There, the headings of the various subjects which Hogarth was proposing to discuss are all grouped together towards the beginning, and are not repeated thereafter. Thus the tampering with Hogarth's sentence in the second paragraph of the white paper may also be said to amount to misrepresentation, or even to outright fabrication.

The third paragraph in the white paper dealt with the settlement of Jews in Palestine and common cause among Arabs, Jews and Armenians in Syria. Here Hogarth shrewdly pointed out that Husayn's ready assent to the settlement of Jews in Palestine which he had described in his formal record was not worth very much: 'But', he added, 'I think he appreciates the financial advantage of Arab co-operation with the Jews'. With this sentence the paragraph as published in the white paper ends. But Hogarth in fact had added: 'The Armenians leave him cold.' This remark, referring to a grandiose idea of Sykes's for Arab–Jewish–Armenian co-operation,[1] was omitted from the white paper presumably so that Husayn might be presented in a benign and favourable light. But this omission did not radically denature Hogarth's report in the way that the mutilations perpetrated on the other two paragraphs had done.

If these omissions seriously distorted the extracts from Hogarth's report which were published in the white paper, an even greater cause of distortion was that the extracts, such as they were, gave a false idea of the burden of Hogarth's report, and placed the emphasis where he by no means wished to place it. Hogarth's purpose in his report was to give 'a summary of the upshot of the conversation as a whole', as well as 'an appreciation of the situation in regard to each matter'. The reader of the full report will get the firm impression that Husayn's over-riding concern was to become king of all the Arabs, and that he feared and hated Ibn Sa'ud as his main adversary, and the stumbling-block on his path. Thus Hogarth wrote:

> He both fears Ibn Saoud as a centre of a religious movement, dangerous to the Hedjaz, and hates him as unreconcilable to his own pretension to be 'King of the Arabs'. This latter title is the King's dearest ambition, partly no doubt, in the interests of Arab Unity, which he constantly says, with some reason, can never be realized until focused on a central personality. He offers to our argument that he cannot be 'King of the Arabs' till the Arabs in general desire

[1] Kedourie, *England and the Middle East*, p. 86.

him to be so, the counter-argument that they will never so desire till he is so called; and he brought forward more than one plea, that, if we destroy the one great Moslem power, Turkey, we are bound in our own interest, to set up another.

Hogarth also had something to say about Husayn's attitude to his neighbours:

> The King despises Idrissi from the bottom of his heart and cannot see why we should support and use him...As far as the Imam Yehia, the King thinks him a virtual nonentity, with no actual hold on the Zeidi tribes.

Regarding territories in which Cairo believed him to be interested, Husayn showed himself indifferent. He

> hardly touched on Mesopotamia and neither said nor asked anything of importance about the future of either Baghdad or Basra.

Hogarth's summing up of Husayn's outlook is particularly striking:

> In conclusion I may say that the King is more assured than ever both of our power to help him and the Arabs, and of our intention to do so, and that he leaves himself confidently in our hands. But he is not easy in his mind either about Central Arabia or about the loyalty of his own Hedjaz people.

And Hogarth's report ended precisely on this note. Husayn, he declared in his last sentence,

> is quite firm in his friendship to us, but none too firm on his throne.[1]

The report as a whole and these words in particular are in startling contrast to what Maugham and MacDonald were made to asseverate concerning the Hogarth message, and its role in persuading the Arabs not to leave the war; notions which Baggallay had uncritically taken over from *The Arab Awakening*, which he made no attempt to verify, and which he fed to the lord high chancellor of England and to His Majesty's principal secretary of state in the colonial department.

The Arab Awakening appealed to yet another document in order to prove the far-reaching character of British promises. This was the so-called 'Declaration to the Seven', to which no one, whether on the Arab or the British side, had hitherto, in this respect, paid any attention. But Antonius now boldly declared that it was 'by far the most important statement of policy made by Great Britain in connection with the Arab Revolt'.[2] The claim impressed Baggallay greatly. The declaration, he minuted, had been unknown to him until he read Antonius's book; it was 'obviously embarrassing', and

---

[1] F.O. 371/3383, 25577/675, cited above.   [2] *The Arab Awakening*, p. 271.

he did not see how it could be 'explained away'.[1] Antonius in fact did not appeal to it in his official submission to the committee considering the McMahon–Husayn correspondence. However, when he asked Baggallay that the declaration should also be officially published along with the Hogarth message,[2] his request was acceded to, the declaration was included as an annex to the committee's report, the British representatives informing their Arab colleagues that 'it has seemed necessary' to make public the terms of this declaration.[3]

The history of this declaration by no means indicates such a necessity. Had Baggallay taken the trouble to acquaint himself with this history, he would have spared himself feeling embarrassed. The terms of the declaration were conveyed to seven Syrians in Cairo in June 1918 by Hogarth in the presence of another member of the Arab Bureau, Osmond Walrond. The latter, in fact, had something to do with the events which led to the declaration. Walrond was a *protégé* of Milner's whose private secretary he had been in South Africa, and through whose intercession Hogarth offered him a post in the Arab Bureau in October 1917.[4] As his activities after the war in Egypt showed, he was devoid of political sagacity, somewhat fanciful, given to ill-judged enthusiasms, and prone to grave mis-understandings.[5] The cast of his mind is indicated by his entry in *Who's Who* where he lists among his recreations 'The problems of the Near East'.

In Cairo, Walrond seems to have taken up some Syrian exiles who were opposed to Husayn's ambitions in Syria and who, in order to oppose these, had formed themselves into a Party of Syrian Unity (*hizb al-ittihad al-suri*). It seems that this grouping was founded in reaction to two developments. In the first place, Husayn's news-paper, *al-Qibla*, published towards the beginning of 1918 a report to the effect that a prisoner in one of Husayn's prisons had attempted to escape, had been caught, and by way of punishment had had a hand and a leg publicly amputated in conformity with Qur'anic prescription. In the second place, the rivalry which had always existed in Faysal's so-called Northern Arab Army between those officers who originated from Mesopotamia and those who originated from Syria became in the early months of 1918 con-siderably more bitter. In consequence, a number of Syrian notables

---

[1] F.O. 371/23224, E1357/6/31, Baggallay's minute of 21 Feb. 1939.
[2] F.O. 371/23229, E1936/6/31.　　　　　　　[3] Cmd. 5974, para. 21 and annex G.
[4] F.O. 371/3061, file 192755 contains the correspondence relating to his appointment.
[5] Kedourie, 'Sa'd Zaghlul and the British', in *The Chatham House Version, passim.*

and exiles in Cairo came together and formed the Party of Syrian Unity in order to detach the Syrian question from the Arab question in general, and to ensure that the Sharifians and their Mesopotamian supporters should not take over Syria and swamp specifically Syrian interests.[1] It is with this group that Walrond seems to have established contact, and he may have looked upon them as an instrument by which to achieve power and prominence in the Arab Bureau, and to impress his patron Milner. When Walrond died in 1927 an old colleague of his stated in an obituary that he 'preferred mysterious work behind the scenes'.[2] William Yale, the special agent of the U.S. department of state in the Near East, in a report of 15 April 1918, reported Walrond as saying to him that he had 'no mission and yet has a mission' and that he was concerned that Faysal should establish an efficient administration in the areas which he controlled 'because he is and will be on trial before the Syrians and before the European powers, which, if it be seen that he is not able to create a liberal and efficient administrative organization may not permit him to become ruler of Syria'. The similarity of these views to those of the Party of Syrian Unity is apparent. Walrond also told Yale that 'on his own initiative and authority' he was making propaganda in the form of a particular solution to the Syrian question:

> In discussing possible solutions to the Syrian and Arab questions [Yale reported] Mr Walrond mentioned the possibility of an independent Arab Empire composed of loosely joined confederated states embracing Irak, Syria and Arabia. He stated that for some time now he had been encouraging the more religious Syrian Moslems in this line and that he had been leading them to think in terms of an Arab State or Confederacy of States. He went on to say that he was supplying them with such materials as the constitution of the United States, of the Federal Republic of Switzerland, and other such documents of which also translations into the Arabic were being prepared.[3]

Very shortly afterwards Wingate received 'by the hand' of Walrond the memorial signed by seven members of the Party of Syrian Unity. The memorial was composed following a visit by Walrond to Shaykh Kamil al-Qassab who had played a leading role in crystallizing Syrian opposition to Husayn and the Mesopotamian officers, and there can

[1] The details are disclosed by Amin Sa'id in his work of 1960, *Secrets of the Great Arab Revolt*, pp. 235–46. It is probable that the author derived most of his information from Shaykh Kamil al-Qassab who had a prominent role to play in these events.
[2] *The Times*, 18 November 1927.
[3] Yale Papers in Yale University Library. Portions of the report are quoted in Kedourie, *England and the Middle East*, p. 114.

be little doubt that it was Walrond who encouraged, not to say instigated, this approach.[1]

The memorial began grandiloquently. The signatories declared themselves to be 'representatives of various Arab Political Societies and, the supporters of the Arab movement', and to 'have been given full power to voice the expression of their tongues'. This claim was repeated and even magnified in the body of the address. The signatories claimed to 'represent four-fifths, and more, of the total inhabitants of Syria' and that their 'different Committees represent all classes of the Nation, especially the enlightened class with the religious leaders of note and well known aristocrats'. This, of course, was loose and glib talk, since in reality the Party of Syrian Unity was only a handful of self-appointed politicians who had no authority or mandate to speak on behalf of any class of Syrians, let alone four-fifths of them. But it is nonetheless of some interest to notice what the signatories had to say about the sentiments of their fellow countrymen. What has prompted the address, they declared, was the doubt which existed in their minds about British policy. Those who felt such doubts

> believe it impossible, as the majority of us who are Moslems feel, to sever their connection with Turkey as their spiritual leader, if their future is to be a matter of uncertainty.

This uncertainty, they argued, was bound to increase as a result of Russia abandoning the war and Ottoman occupation not only of the territories which had been lost to the Russians since 1914, but of parts of the Caucasus as well,

> a fact which will strengthen Turkey and increase the Turkish danger to Arabia.

The memorial then went on to make a point which was of value because it related to public opinion in Egypt, which the memorialists knew at first hand:

> It is worth mentioning that our situation in Egypt has become a difficult one as some Egyptians reproach us with sarcasm saying:
> 'That the Germans, the enemies of Islam, have made conditions in their Peace Terms with the Russians that the people of the Caucasus, who are Moslems, can plan their future themselves and that their relations with their neighbours – especially the Turks – should be free. They have also arranged that Persia and Afghanistan, both Mohammedan kingdoms, should be completely independent. While your Allies, who are the friends of Islam,

[1] F.O. 371/3380, 98499/146, Wingate's despatch no. 90, 7 May 1918; Amin Sa'id, *Secrets*, pp. 244–5.

have concluded amongst themselves an agreement to divide your territory into two zones, the North of which is to be under French influence and the South to be under British'.

These being their preoccupations, the memorialists proceeded to ask a series of questions. They desired to know whether the Arabs were to enjoy 'complete independence in Arabia', by which they meant the Arabian peninsula, Syria, Mesopotamia, Mosul 'and a large part of the province of Diarbekr'. The kernel, however, of the memorial lay in three paragraphs which asserted the claim of Syria to be self-governing, and in no way subordinate to the Hijaz:

> Is it the policy of His Majesty's Government to assist the inhabitants of these countries to attain their complete independence and the composing of an Arab Government decentralized like the United States of America, or other Federal Governments, which suits their social condition; or does it not consider them all equal?
>
> The Syrians, though only too glad to form part of the Arab Federal Government, have, however, for a long time previous to the war, been working to apply the principle of decentralization to Syria, dividing it into provinces, which would have the right to administer their own internal affairs but it would be possible, if Arabia became independent, to apply the same principle to its provinces, including principalities such as Nejd, Yemen and Asir.

The memorial went on to insist on Syria's primacy in the Arab movement:

> Though the source of the Arab revolution appeared in the Hedjaz its corner stone was Syria and it had the greater share in the intellectual movement. The Hedjaz was all along in close touch with it and His Majesty the Great King and his sons the Princes have been in perfect agreement with the Arab Societies there and in Egypt.

To this main theme the memorialists joined a declaration of reliance on Britain and 'her traditional inherited policy that demanded the security and respected the inviolability of the Arab countries as a political necessity', and a promise that the Arabs 'if kept standing at the doors of the East, will be a trusty sentinel and sincere friend to the supporters of their independence'. This paragraph, it is obvious, was a broad hint that if the British prevented the French from establishing themselves in the Levant, they would enjoy the sole privilege of having the Arabs as their *protégés*.

The despatch with which Wingate forwarded the memorial to London was itself a peculiar document. It was not content with providing background information on the memorialists; it also attempted, by hints rather than explicit argument, to forward Wingate's view that the Sykes–Picot scheme should be finally abandoned and Britain become the sole protector of a united Arab state. The signatories (of whom a descriptive list – which is now missing from the file – was attached) Wingate considered representative of Syrian Muslim opinion in Egypt, but he could not say how accurately they reflected attitudes in Syria itself. He realized that the 'far-reaching' guarantees for which they were asking could not be given, and he considered 'inadvisable' 'to give formal engagements to, or to enter into official relations with, the signatories or their Societies'. But when due allowance was made 'for oriental passion for secret association and paper organization for political agitation', it still remained true that such societies could be very influential – witness the role of the C.U.P. in Turkey. If no reply, or an unsatisfactory one, were returned to the memorial, 'the signatories...will feel themselves free to modify their pro-Ally inclinations and ultimately...to enter into communication with the enemy'. Wingate, therefore, felt strongly that it was 'ill-advised' to ignore the 'aspirations towards independence and eventual political union' as described in the address and advantageous 'to supplement, if possible, the very general – and, in native eyes, vague and consequently unsatisfactory – lines of our declared policy in regard to the future of the Arab peoples'. Wingate declared that he was not sufficiently acquainted with British policy or the state of French opinion on Syria to suggest a form of declaration 'but I believe that a sympathetic reference to our desire to see local self-government combined with progress towards political union of the (Asiatic) Arabic-speaking peoples would be opportune and well-received'.[1] It is clear that Wingate ignored the main point which concerned the memorialists, namely the fear of Sharifian domination of Syria, and used the memorial as a pretext for yet another attempt to commit his government to a policy of support for Arab unity, and of opposition to French claims.

The memorial of the seven Syrians was considered in London by Sykes. The papers do not show whether he was aware of Walrond's activities and opinions, but it is clear from the reply which he drafted (and which, after being approved by Hardinge, became the so-called Declaration to the Seven) that he read the memorial wholly in the light of Wingate's despatch, and took account only of the points made in the despatch. The declaration (which was read by Hogarth in Walrond's presence to a representative of the seven, probably Qassab, about 16 June)[2] had nothing to say about Syria.

[1] F.O. 371/3380, 98499/146, cited above.
[2] Milner Papers, New College, Oxford, Walrond to Milner, Cairo 26 June 1918: 'Hogarth (and I was present) read the Secretary of State's communiqué to the Arab Committee, one delegate only being present.'

It was couched in high-sounding generalities which cannot possibly have entailed any new commitments. Thus in respect of areas occupied by Allied forces, the memorialists' attention was drawn to the proclamation issued on the fall of Baghdad and Jerusalem. As has been seen, the Baghdad proclamation had been very chary of specific promises regarding either Mesopotamia or Arab unity. The same was the case with the Jerusalem proclamation which was read at Allenby's official entry on 11 December 1917. The inhabitants of 'Jerusalem the Blessed' were merely told that the city was under martial law and that its holy places would be maintained according to the traditional *status quo*.[1] But to these specific references Sykes tacked on in the same paragraph grandiloquent phrases about 'the wish and desire of His Majesty's Government that the future government of these regions should be based upon the principle of the consent of the governed' etc. If these words had been meant to herald a specific departure from existing policies and commitments, Hardinge would certainly not have authorized them, and they would not have been read in a hole-and-corner fashion to seven Syrians, against giving formal engagements to whom Wingate had clearly warned. If this passage, and a similar one in the following paragraph affirming 'the wish and desire of His Majesty's Government that the oppressed peoples of these areas [still under Turkish control] should obtain their freedom and independence' had any significance more than merely rhetorical, they were probably meant to signal that the British were now hostile to French ambitions in the Levant. If the declaration had any specific political significance, this was in its affirmation that the British government recognized 'the complete and sovereign independence' of the Arabs in territories emancipated from Turkish control by 'the action of the Arabs themselves'. But this point was to acquire importance only somewhat later, when Allenby contrived that Damascus should seem to have been occupied by Faysal's troops.[2]

The history of the declaration to the seven Syrians thus makes clear that Antonius was wildly exaggerating when he wrote that it was 'by far the most important statement of policy made by Great Britain in connection with the Arab Revolt'; he was also patently misleading when he asserted that a 'wave of jubilation swept the Arab world as the contents of the Foreign Office statement became known'.[3] There is absolutely no evidence that the declaration

[1] Text of proclamation in e.g. W. T. Massey, *How Jerusalem Was Won*, 1919, p. 286.
[2] Kedourie, *England and the Middle East*, p. 116; and 'The Capture of Damascus, 1 October 1918', in *The Chatham House Version*.
[3] *The Arab Awakening*, pp. 271 and 273.

became at all widely known in the Arab world, or that it caused a wave of jubilation to sweep over it. The history of the declaration also shows that it had very little to do with Palestine or Zionism. The text of the memorial was enough on its own to show this, but while the British government found it 'necessary' to publish the text of the declaration, the text of the memorial (which would have thrown some light on the meaning of the declaration) Baxter, the head of the Eastern department, deemed to be 'of no importance whatsoever'. If published, it would, he argued, 'overshadow' the Hogarth message and the declaration, 'which are of importance'.[1] When, at MacDonald's request, Weizmann was given the text of the Hogarth message and the declaration to the seven, Butler withheld from him the text of the memorial. He did this on Baggallay's advice, who held that 'at this stage' it was not necessary to disclose the document to Weizmann.[2]

From what has been set out here, it is clear that the publication of the Hogarth's message, of the fragments of Hogarth's report and of the declaration to the seven promoted rather than diminished confusion about the meaning and purport of the McMahon–Husayn correspondence. It is clear that these documents were mentioned in the report of the committee considering the correspondence, largely in order to placate. Largely, but not entirely, since, as has been seen, Baggallay had, with culpable negligence, failed to inform himself about the original significance of these documents, and failed in his duty to put the facts before the lord chancellor, the colonial secretary, the cabinet committee on Palestine, and the cabinet who, at one time or another, had to consider what should be said to the Arabs, or included in the committee's report. This is of course not to say that if the government had been possessed of the full facts, they would have necessarily ruled out placation. But if placation there had to be, its cool, deliberate pursuit would perhaps have been more advantageous than the muddled and profitless manner in which it was, in fact, practised. In the event, the paragraph devoted in the report to these documents (paragraph 22) was a model of confusion, comparable to the lucubrations of McMahon's and Storrs's which had made necessary the committee's labours. It was the last paragraph of the report which dealt with the Hogarth message and other pronouncements subsequent to the McMahon–Husayn correspondence:

[1] F.O. 371/23229, E1968/6/31.
[2] F.O. 371/23228, E1861/6/31, Baggallay's minutes of 9 and 10 Mar. 1939.

The Fly in the Fly-bottle

> It is beyond the scope of the Committee to express an opinion upon the proper interpretation of the various statements mentioned in paragraph 19 and such an opinion could not in any case be properly expressed unless consideration had also been given to a number of other statements made during and after the war.

The paragraph so far is clear and categorical, seeming to rule out further remarks or conjectures. But in spite of this, it continued with some affirmations the obscurity of which was enhanced by their equivocal phrasing.

> In the opinion of the Committee it is, however, evident from these statements that His Majesty's Government were not free to dispose of Palestine without regard for the wishes and interests of the people of Palestine, and that these statements must all be taken into account in any attempt to estimate the responsibilities which – upon any interpretation of the Correspondence – His Majesty's Government have incurred towards those inhabitants as a result of the Correspondence.

At first sight, this passage seems coherent and meaningful. But when scrutinized, it quickly dissolves into gibberish. The passage purports to estimate the responsibilities which the British government have incurred – and it insists, 'upon any interpretation of the Correspondence' – towards the inhabitants of Palestine, 'as a result of the Correspondence'. But four paragraphs before the British signatories had categorically asserted that 'on a proper construction of the Correspondence Palestine was in fact excluded' from McMahon's promises to Husayn. How then could the British be said to have incurred responsibilities to the inhabitants of Palestine, and this 'upon any interpretation of the Correspondence'? Again, how could statements which did not precede, but which succeeded, the correspondence – statements which, except for the Hogarth message, did not purport to deal with Palestine, were not addressed to Husayn, and did not refer to the correspondence – be held to throw any light 'on the responsibilities which – upon any interpretation of the Correspondence – His Majesty's Government have incurred...as a result of the Correspondence'? As for the Hogarth message, what it had to say by no means showed that the British government considered that it had incurred any obligations towards the people of Palestine, or felt any qualms about 'disposing' of Palestine. What, in any case, is the value of all these assertions if, as the first part of the paragraph asserts, it was 'beyond the scope' of the committee to 'express an opinion upon the proper interpretation' of the statements of which so much seems to be made in the second part of the paragraph?

The Foreign Office Wrestles with the Correspondence

The meaning of these riddles is perhaps elucidated by a draft of the report which Baggallay had prepared following the first meeting of the committee on 24 February. The final paragraph of this draft said:

> It is beyond the scope of the Committee to attempt an appreciation of the proper interpretation of the safeguards for the inhabitants of Palestine contained in certain of these documents or statements, but they feel justified in concluding their report by recording the view that:
>
> 1. H.M.G. did not when excluding, or seeking to exclude Palestine from the area of Arab independence at the time of the correspondence, or at any later time, claim to be able to dispose of Palestine without any regard for the wishes and interests of the inhabitants.
>
> 2. The safeguards for the inhabitants of Palestine contained in the Balfour Declaration, the Hogarth message, and the assurances of General Allenby,[1] are complementary to, and explain one another.[2]

As this draft shows, what Baggallay wanted was to commit the British signatories to the admission that, regardless of what McMahon had actually promised, the British government was somehow under an obligation not 'to dispose of Palestine without any regard for the wishes and interests of its inhabitants'. To put the matter in this way was of course to saddle the British government with a commitment for which there was no warrant, and to imply that the British government did in fact default on its obligation. It is not surprising that, as Baggallay recorded, the colonial secretary should have 'disliked' the idea of such a paragraph.[3] In the event, the report as published substituted for these stark declarations the sibylline utterances examined above.

Another feature of Baggallay's draft is worth noting. One of its paragraphs stated that the two sides 'have been unable to reach agreement upon the proper *legal* interpretation of the Correspondence'. That Baggallay should have considered the correspondence susceptible to legal interpretation shows that he believed it to constitute some kind of legally binding contract. That the word did not finally figure in the report (which simply stated – in paragraph 16 – that the two parties had been unable to reach agreement upon the interpretation of the correspondence) was not Baggallay's fault.

[1] This refers to a report by Allenby of 17 Oct. 1918 (an extract from which is reproduced as annex H of the committee's report) in which Allenby declared that he had informed Faysal that measures taken during the period of military administration were provisional and would not prejudice the final settlement, and that 'the Allies were in honour bound to endeavour to reach a settlement in accordance with the wishes of the peoples concerned.'

[2] F.O. 371/23226, E1607/6/31.

[3] F.O. 371/23226, E1607/6/31, first draft of report 27 Feb., and minute by Baggallay, 6 Mar. 1939.

It was Antonius who insisted on its removal, to the clear detriment of the Arab side. Why he should have done so is not clear: it may be that, as Baggallay wrote, Antonius was a 'hard and rather pedantic bargainer', who would suspect a trap if his opponent were to give him a seemingly gratuitous advantage.[1] But it was by no means easy to wean Baggallay from his views. Thus in the report as published, the British representatives are made to admit (in paragraph 13e) that no 'legal weight' could attach to statements by McMahon and Clayton to the effect that it had never been intended to offer Palestine to the Sharif. Again, in a statement which Baggallay drafted, and which Maugham read at the final meeting of the committee, the lord chancellor is made to say that the issues raised there were, 'to a lawyer', of the highest interest.[2]

As has been seen, paragraph 16 of the published report recorded the fact that the two sides had been unable to reach agreement upon an interpretation of the correspondence. The reason for this may be easily gathered from the memoranda exchanged during the first three sessions (on 23, 24 and 28 February 1939), and which were published together with the report. The exchange began with a memorandum by Antonius, the strongest point of which was the argument – really unanswerable – that by the word 'districts', which Ruhi had translated as *wilayat*, McMahon could not possibly have meant *vilayets*, and that therefore the British case as expounded by Young and the Palestine white paper of 1922 was untenable. For the rest it abounded in red herrings, debating points and inaccurate but plausible assertions about the history of British policy. Antonius could easily have been dealt with if the officials had known what their files contained, and if they had not been bemused, on the one hand, by *The Arab Awakening*, and determined, on the other, to get rid of the Zionist embarrassment. As it was, the lord chancellor was very badly briefed, and admiration for his forensic ability in surmounting the handicap of misinformation and in producing a telling memorandum in reply to Antonius is all the greater. Taking the bare text of the correspondence, he succeeded in showing that an interpretation which excluded Palestine from the territories promised to the Sharif was just as plausible as one which affirmed that it had been included. He also drew attention to the fact that the correspondence was incomplete and left many points for later

[1] F.O. 371/23226, E1607/6/31, cited above, paragraph 16 of Baggallay's draft; F.O. 371/23230, E2034/6/31, report of a conversation between Baggallay and Antonius, 10 Mar.; F.O. 371/23232, E2466/6/31, minute by Baggallay, 12 Apr. 1939.

[2] F.O. 371/23230, E2035/6/31.

settlement. He also firmly insisted, in spite of Baggallay's and Beckett's disapproval and deprecation, on the point that McMahon had made a general reservation in favour of French interests and that this in itself must have excluded Palestine. In reply to the lord chancellor, Antonius and Sir Michael McDonnell put in two counter-memoranda with a wealth of ingenious argumentation and a profusion of legal references, which however were either misconceived or irrelevant, and which it would be tedious to review in any detail. To anyone with a knowledge of the transactions of 1915–16 and afterwards, the exchanges look like a curious game of blindman's-buff in which the players did not know that they were blindfolded.

Following the third meeting, the committee adjourned and did not meet until 16 March. In the meantime, its proceedings were considered by the cabinet on 2 March, and on 6 March the cabinet committee on Palestine considered and approved a second draft report which Baggallay had produced. In the cabinet, the lord chancellor explained that, subject to one point, it was very difficult to contend that McMahon's letter of 24 October 1915 had specifically excluded Palestine, but it was

> extremely undesirable to abandon the view which we had maintained consistently for twenty years more especially since the Arabs were suspicious people and appeared to regard all our actions as dishonest.

Maugham then went on to speak of the reservation in favour of France. The Arabs contended that since the French claim to Palestine had not been upheld, it followed that the Arab claim to Palestine held good. But it did not by any means follow, he argued, that if the French relinquished their claim to Palestine, the Arab claim to Palestine was thereby established. Again, the French had relinquished their claim in favour of a mandate in Palestine, and if the mandate were abandoned, the French might claim that they had certain interests in the area which they would want to safeguard.[1]

Following this meeting, Baggallay produced the second version of his draft report. It was first considered by the ministers immediately concerned at a meeting attended by Maugham, MacDonald, Butler, the attorney-general, Sir Donald Somervell, Bushe and Baggallay. It will be recalled that Baggallay's first version had contained a paragraph about the Hogarth message and other documents to which MacDonald had taken exception. The new draft

[1] Copy of cabinet conclusions, 2 Mar. 1939 in F.O. 371/23227, E1686/6/31.

contained an amended version of this paragraph which finally appeared in the published report substantially as it figured in this draft. As he wrote in a convering minute, Baggallay attached great importance to this paragraph. The re-draft, he went on to say,

> attempts to take account of some of Mr Macdonald's criticisms e.g. that if the Committee attempted to express an opinion on matters which could only be thoroughly investigated if many other factors, to which its attention had not been drawn, were taken into account, it would expose itself to criticism, above all from the Jews.
>
> But Mr Macdonald's main objection, I think, was that it would unduly encourage the Arabs. But there is no getting away from the fact that the Hogarth message is very relevant to the questions considered by the Committee and that the Lord Chancellor very rightly, in my opinion, freely admitted this.
>
> In any case I doubt if we shall get a joint report at all without a reference to these later pledges and that [Baggallay opined] would be a pity.

Baggallay was fully supported by his superior, Baxter:

> I think [Baxter forthrightly minuted] we must be honest over this. The Arabs have got a much stronger case than many people have thought. And we shall have to admit this to some extent when explaining the position to Parliament and the public. Most people do not realise [he complained] that the Arabs have a strong case at all.[1]

In Baggallay's eyes, his paragraph, a masterpiece of obfuscation, was 'the most important in the report'. This was so because

> it definitely puts on the map, so to speak, the Hogarth Message and various other declarations made by H.M.G. during the War, which had been forgotten until Mr Antonius resurrected them in his book 'The Arab Awakening'.[2]

Baggallay's second version of the draft report had another crucial passage which, to use his own words, contained

> the admission that the Arabs really have got a very strong case over the correspondence.

It was Bushe who, as has been seen, attached greatest importance to such an admission, for which he was anxious to obtain foreign office support:

> He feels that nothing short of a final admission that the Arab case is really strong will restore their confidence in the good faith of His Majesty's Government. They have said they regard this committee as a sort of test of His Majesty's Government's good faith.

[1] F.O. 371/23227, E1734/6/31, minutes by Baggallay and Baxter, 2 Mar. 1939.
[2] F.O. 371/23231, E2166/6/31, minute by Baggallay, 18 Mar. 1939.

The Foreign Office Wrestles with the Correspondence

Baggallay agreed with these sentiments, and drafted a passage to this effect 'as mildly as possible, but', he added '[I] would gladly see it stronger'. Baggallay's draft declared that the British representative recognized that Husayn had intended to include Palestine in the area of Arab independence and, moreover,

> informed the Arab representatives that the Arab contentions, as explained to the Committee regarding the interpretation of the correspondence, and especially their contentions relating to the meaning of the phrase 'portions of Syria lying to the west of the districts of Damascus, Hama, Homs and Aleppo', have far greater force than has appeared hitherto, and that so far as the words just quoted at any rate are concerned the Sharif could not reasonably have inferred that Palestine was to be excluded from the area of Arab independence.

This paragraph was to appear – in a somewhat attenuated form – as paragraph 17 of the published report. In it, the British representatives admit that the Arab

> contentions relating to the meaning of the phrase 'portions of Syria lying to the west of the districts of Damascus, Hama, Homs and Aleppo' have greater force than has appeared hitherto.

This version of the draft report has other features worthy of notice. One paragraph declared:

> The nearest approach to common ground which [the two sides] have been able to make in relation to the point of legal interpretation is that they agree that the language used in the correspondence is often vague and imprecise and that if one side were to admit that Sir H. McMahon had failed to make it clear to the Sharif of Mecca that Palestine was to be excluded from the area of Arab independence, the other side would have to admit that the Sharif of Mecca had failed to make it clear that Palestine was to be included in that area.

Antonius strongly objected to this passage. The Arab representatives were not willing to admit that both sides were equally vague and imprecise. Baggallay thought Antonius was 'quite right in substance', and that it would be 'only honest to make the admission for which he asks'. In the end he persuaded the British ministers to give way to Antonius's objection. This, as Antonius told Baggallay, would

> turn a report which the Arabs would otherwise frankly regard as disappointing, and which his colleagues might not think worth signing, into a report which they would be likely to welcome. What was more [Antonius persuasively argued] the adoption of a joint report, amended as he had suggested, would, he believed, have a considerable effect on the atmosphere of the

conference, which regarded the attitude of His Majesty's Government towards the correspondence as a pointer to their attitude towards the Arab case generally. If His Majesty's Government could admit after going thoroughly into the whole question once more, they had reached the conclusion that the position of Palestine was not made unmistakeably clear to the Sharif (whatever might have been intended), Arab belief in the good intentions of His Majesty's Government would be immensely fortified.[1]

An emasculated version of the passage thus figured in the published report, which in paragraph 16 stated that the two parties

have tried (as they hope with success) to understand the point of view of the other party, but they have been unable to reach agreement upon an interpretation of the Correspondence, and they feel obliged to report to the conference accordingly.

There was another paragraph in the second draft report to which Antonius strenuously objected. This paragraph would have had the Arab representatives agree that McMahon

intended to exclude Palestine from the area of Arab independence, and that H.M.G. have acted in the belief that Palestine was so excluded until later events began to show that there was some misunderstanding.

Antonius explained that his colleagues were unwilling to subscribe to any declaration about McMahon's intentions. In the first place, they did not believe that McMahon had in fact intended to excluded Palestine, and in the second, intentions were anyway irrelevant.[2] This paragraph was also omitted from the published report.

These paragraphs were included in the draft which had been considered and approved by the cabinet committee on Palestine at its meeting of 6 March. The omissions, however, were authorized by Maugham and MacDonald alone. Following the cabinet committee meeting of 6 March, Maugham asked Baggallay to include another paragraph in the draft report. This dealt with a point which the lord chancellor considered to be crucial to the British case, and on which he laid great stress in his two memoranda of 24 February and 16 March 1939.[3] This was that Palestine formed part of those territories excluded from the promise to Husayn because of French interests. Maugham therefore had a new paragraph included in the draft report which was to be shown to the Arabs, declaring that his

[1] F.O. 371/23228, E1786/6/31, Baggallay's memorandum of conversation with Antonius and minute, 7 Mar. 1939.
[2] F.O. 371/23230, E2034/6/31, report of conversation with Antonius by Baggallay, 10 Mar. 1939.
[3] Cmd. 5974, annex B, paras. 30–3, and annex E, paras. 4–6.

contention that Palestine was a territory in which Britain was not free to act without detriment to French interests –

> a contention which has not, in his opinion, been met by contrary arguments – remains unaffected.[1]

This paragraph, too, did not figure in the published report. The papers do not show whether this omission was also a result of Arab pressure. This was presumably the case, and again Baggallay presumably advised Maugham to give way.

The published report, then, was clearly favourable to the Arab side, in all its three key paragraphs: paragraph 17 which, as has been seen, Bushe ardently desired; the enigmatic paragraph 22, which was the pride of Baggallay's pen; and paragraph 18, which was put together in order to take care of Antonius's objections. The essential passage in this paragraph may be found in its concluding sentences, in which the British representatives

> maintain that on a proper construction of the Correspondence Palestine was in fact excluded [from the territories promised to the Sharif]. But they agree that the language in which its exclusion was expressed was not so specific and unmistakeable as it was thought to be at the time.[2]

A minute in which Baggallay summed up the negotiations which eventuated in the report indicates that he and his colleagues looked upon the report as a vindication of Arab contentions, and that they would have been glad to see it go further in this direction:

> Although the report does not say so in so many words, it is fairly clear to those who read between the lines that the U.K. Representatives abandoned the argument that the words 'district of Damascus' mean 'the administrative area known as the Vilayet of Syria'...which has been the main plank of the British case until now. The Lord Chancellor has called the British case on this point 'straw' and Mr MacDonald has called it 'tricky'. Both adjectives are thoroughly deserved.

Baggallay allowed himself to insinuate a delicate hint of disapproval regarding the lord chancellor's strategy. It was mainly on his advice, Baggallay wrote, that the British side laid great stress on the 'French reservation' argument:

[1] F.O. 371/23228, E1786/6/31, draft report in form approved by lord chancellor after meeting of cabinet committee and as communicated to Antonius.

[2] The successive drafts of the committee's report, and the discussions with Antonius to which they gave rise may be followed in F.O. 371/23227, E1690 and 1734; F.O. 371/23228, 1786; F.O. 371/23230, 2034, 2103, 2104, and 2105; F.O. 371/23231, 2106; and F.O. 371/23232, 2319/6/31. The same paragraph, it should be noted, bears a different number in successive drafts.

The Fly in the Fly-bottle

The Lord Chancellor has called this argument 'cast-iron', although he has also qualified it by saying that it holds good 'on a strictly legal interpretation'. In my own mind I am fairly satisfied that whatever may be the proper legal construction of the language used in regard to French interests (and I rather think that the Attorney General and some other legal experts do not entirely share the Lord Chancellor's convictions) both Sir H. McMahon and the Sharif must have meant that H.M.G. would carry out their promises to the Arabs in any territory in which French claims were found not to have prevailed when a final territorial settlement had been reached.

In saying that 'some other legal experts' disagreed with Maugham, Baggallay no doubt had his colleague Beckett particularly in mind. As has been seen, before the start of the conferences on Palestine Beckett had already affirmed most categorically that his government had no case whatever in Palestine. In a marginal note to Baggallay's minute he now reaffirmed his view. But the passage quoted above contains other statements which are significant in showing Baggallay's carelessness, or else his determination to ignore what did not fit in with his views. Thus he opposes the authority of the attorney-general to that of the lord chancellor on the 'French reservation' argument. But in fact, Sir Donald Somervell's views were not as Baggallay represented them to be. Somervell pointed out the weakness of claiming that in McMahon's letter, 'district' meant '*vilayet*'; he also contended that it was inconsistent to argue (as Maugham did in his memorandum) both that Palestine was unique and thus could not have been promised to the Sharif, and that it was covered by the phrase 'portions of Syria lying to the west of the district of Damascus': no one, Somervell thought, could have believed this to be a reasonable description of Jerusalem, a city which three faiths venerated. But Somervell did agree with the lord chancellor that the reservation in favour of French interests served to exclude Palestine from the lands promised to the Sharif. And he added:

> I feel strongly that there is great force in saying that letters written in the circumstances in which this letter was, cannot be treated as if they were legal contracts, departures from which in unforeseen circumstances amounted to breaches of faith.

The letter in which Somervell developed these views, addressed to MacDonald, was dated 27 February 1939, and a copy of it was in the foreign office files.[1]

Again, Baggallay attributes to Maugham the view that the 'French reservation' argument holds good 'on a strictly legal interpretation'.

---

[1] F.O. 371/23228, E1784/6/31.

But there is no evidence in the papers that the lord chancellor held such a view, and his memoranda annexed to the published report at any rate show that he did not have recourse to this particular argument.

Baggallay hints at another criticism of Maugham when, continuing his minute, he says that it was on the advice of the lord chancellor that the British side laid stress on the circumstances surrounding McMahon's negotiations with the Sharif. In fact, those passages in Maugham's memoranda in which he tried to show that the situation in 1915 did not admit of Palestine being promised to Husayn are perhaps the most telling parts of his argument. And they could have been made even more telling, indeed conclusive, had Baggallay and his colleagues briefed Maugham properly. A last example of the wretched manner in which the lord chancellor was served in this respect may perhaps be given here. At the cabinet committee on Palestine (at which were present the prime minister, the chancellor of the exchequer, the foreign, colonial and home secretaries, the secretary of state for India, and the minister of health, as well as Bushe and Baggallay) the lord chancellor said that from the point of view 'of strict legal interpretation' it might be difficult to maintain that McMahon's language excluded Palestine,

> but there seemed no doubt that it represented the intention at the time of the British negotiators. Sir Henry McMahon had taken the precaution of sending his letter of October 24th in draft to Sir Edward Grey...but no doubt the latter had been too preoccupied with other grave matters to give much attention to drafting niceties.[1]

What the lord chancellor said was the exact contrary of the truth for, as has been seen in part 1 above, McMahon not only did not send the draft of his letter to Grey, but also couched it in language for which he had no authority whatever. And it was precisely because of this that the British government now found themselves the butt of offensive and damaging accusations. Maugham could not possibly know this. But it was the duty of the officials, and of Baggallay above all, to know it. They did not know it. Rather than read their archives, they preferred to draw their information from *The Arab Awakening*.

If Baggallay somewhat deprecated the lord chancellor's strategy, he was, on the other hand, proud with an author's pride of the last paragraph of the report which, in a passage from his minute quoted above, he described as its most important paragraph.

[1] F.O. 371/23228, E1784/6/31.

The Fly in the Fly-bottle

Baggallay ended his minute by saying that the British side gave way to the Arabs on almost every point of detail which they raised. And so far as his own personal feelings were concerned, he declared that he would probably have been willing to go so far even as to concede that the Arab contentions were wholly right. In the margin, Sir Lancelot Oliphant noted: 'And I'.[1]

The Palestine conferences were the last occasion before the documents were officially published on which the meaning of the McMahon–Husayn correspondence was investigated inside the British government. This last enquiry was no more competent than its predecessors. It did not serve to make the issue less obscure or perplexing, and it left the good faith of the British government as suspect as ever.

---

[1] F.O. 371/23231, E2166/6/31, Baggallay's minute of 18 Mar. 1939, cited above.

Epilogue: Knowledge, Power and Guilt

The McMahon–Husayn correspondence and its subsequent inter-pretations in the foreign office raise many grave issues about the conduct of foreign affairs by a country with world-wide interests, about the control exerted by foreign secretaries over their officials, and about the proper use of their archives by the foreign office.

Compared with the other issues which Grey had to deal with after the outbreak of war, negotiations with the Sharif seemed no doubt to be only of marginal importance. But their handling by the foreign secretary was indolent, uncertain and incoherent. The stress under which Grey was then labouring accounts, to a certain extent no doubt, for this unsatisfactory state of affairs. But one cannot help wondering if such mismanagement is not inherent in the very situation of a great power which has to cope with a multitude of problems and emergencies spread over the four quarters of the globe.

The same suspicion arises about the ability of a foreign secretary to control, in such conditions, the activities of his officials, or to make sure that they perform adequately their duties. It is no doubt true that the organization of the foreign office into specialized depart-ments ready and able to provide expert advice to the foreign secretary is meant to help him cope with a heavy burden. But in the case of Anglo-Sharifian relations during the war – whether before or after the Sharif's revolt – the records do not show the officials to have been aware of the unsatisfactory manner in which their Cairo colleagues were dealing with Husayn. The only ones to draw attention to what was happening were Sir Arthur Hirtzel and Sir Thomas Holderness – and they were not in the foreign office.

It is the proceedings of the Cairo authorities, and of their subordinates in the Hijaz, which throw the most unfavourable light on the conduct of British diplomacy. McMahon was not scrupulous in following instructions; he also seems to have been a mere mouth-piece through which Storrs and Clayton uttered. He and Maxwell, in particular, were grievously at fault in allowing Clayton to exercise a veritable monopoly in the collection and interpretation of intelligence, and at the same time to play such a prominent part

Epilogue

in policy-making. McMahon's successor, Wingate, had his eye too exclusively fixed on a scheme of Arab unity under British patronage to consider the possible dangers of leaving unanswered Husayn's claims and allegations. Storrs was careless, flippant, patronizing and complacent; he made a habit of going beyond, or embellishing instructions. Clayton allowed his predilections to influence his reading of the information he collected. The first fatal step into the Anglo-Sharifian quicksand was taken with his astonishing report on the deserter Faruqi. C. E. Wilson in Jeddah was too naive, too respectful and tender-minded to cope with a wily and changeable negotiator like Husayn. Sykes, again, when he came to take a hand in Anglo–Sharifian affairs, was too confident of his abilities as a fixer, and his combinations in the end came unstuck. Only Vickery possessed the requisite scepticism, toughness and shrewdness to acquit himself with credit; but his role was both late and short-lived.

The Anglo-Sharifian transactions generated in time a large quantity of records which accumulated in Cairo and London. Detailed records are indispensable to successful diplomacy. But archives in themselves are useless unless officials master their contents and acquire a precise and detailed knowledge of past transactions. Here, knowledge is indeed power. The evidence reviewed in this book shows that the records of the negotiations with Husayn were imperfectly grasped, and that from first to last faulty and sometimes fanciful conclusions were derived from them. This was the case with the Arab Bureau history, which read into McMahon's letter of 24 October 1915 precise territorial commitments which were simply not there. Its interpretation became influential when Toynbee adopted it in his 'commitments' memorandum, which achieved a wide circulation in the foreign office. Nicolson's summary was also incompetent. Young, in turn, produced an untenable reading of McMahon's language, which yet was adopted as the official and authoritative version of what McMahon had promised, until it was implicitly abandoned in 1939. Childs certainly produced the most competent and intelligent account of what had taken place in 1915–16, but his ignorance of Arabic and of evidence available in Arabic, and his mistaken belief that Young was an authority on Arabic, led him to offer a reconstruction of Faruqi's thoughts which no evidence justified, and to adopt Young's tortured exegesis of McMahon's prose. Notably also, he failed to notice that in his letter of 24 October 1915 McMahon inexplicably departed from what Grey had authorized. As for McMahon and Storrs, who were responsible for the whole muddle, the first subsequently offered incoherent and

310

misleading explanations, while the second clearly considered silence
the better part of valour. Finally, Baggallay, moved as much by his
desire to rid Britain of the Zionist embarrassment as by his uncritical
admiration for *The Arab Awakening*, negligently failed to look at
the actual records, and produced a report which succeeded in
further beclouding the issue, but not in removing the doubts about
British good faith which were by now widespread. The officials,
in their role as historiographers, are thus shown to have been
simply out of their depth, neglecting the evidence in their files,
asking anachronistic questions and coming up with implausible
answers.

Writing in the Chatham House *Survey of International Affairs
for 1938*, H. Beeley declared that the publication of the report of
the McMahon–Husayn committee was, through its effect upon
British public opinion, 'a minor victory for the Arab cause'.[1] This
contemporary judgment was undoubtedly correct. The report contained admissions which British governments had hitherto refused
to make: the admission that Arab contentions had 'greater force than
has appeared hitherto'; the admission that the language in which
Palestine was excluded 'was not so specific and unmistakable as it
was thought to be at the time'; and the admission that the government had not been 'free to dispose of Palestine', having incurred
responsibilities to its inhabitants as a result of the correspondence.
As has been seen, the foreign office and the government considered
these damaging admissions to be expedient, because it was thought
that they would lead to improved relations with the Arabs, and
would help to minimize the trouble caused by the unfortunate
Zionist connexion. The report was, thus, a deliberate political act,
'a concession to the Arab point of view', as MacDonald put it to
the cabinet committee on Palestine – a concession which was made
because, as he also put it, 'the time had come when it might be
politic to state clearly our views in the matter.'[2] But the concession,
though a deliberate act of policy, was not taken in full knowledge
of the facts. This meant that the officials and ministers who had to
do with the wording of the report believed not only that they were
making a political concession, but also that the concession was
justified by previous promises and declarations. To this extent,
therefore, they must have believed that previous governments had
behaved badly towards the Arabs, had in fact been guilty, at the

[1] Arnold J. Toynbee and V. M. Boulter (eds.), *Survey of International Affairs 1938* vol.
I, 1941, p. 454.
[2] F.O. 371/23228, E1784/6/31, cited above.

least, of double-dealing. This in fact is now the received wisdom among officials, and is given wide currency in their published works and memoirs. Thus J. R. Colville who, at the time of the Palestine conferences, was a third secretary at the foreign office, and acted as secretary of the British representatives in the McMahon–Husayn committee, could write in a book published in 1972:

> The Balfour Declaration of 1917 promised the Jews a home alongside the Arabs and the fulfilment of unquenchable yearnings for Zion; the letters exchanged eighteen months previously by Sir Henry MacMahon, British High Commissioner in Egypt, and the King of the Hedjaz had assured the Arabs, whose home Palestine had been for nearly two thousand years, that when they were liberated from the rule of the Turkish Sultan all Arabia, including Palestine, should be theirs to inhabit and to govern.[1]

Other officials, who by reason of their duties had had a more intimate concern with the war-time transactions, were just as full of misconceptions which they authoritatively and confidently imparted to the public. Harold Nicolson was the first to be called upon in the foreign office to review, in July 1917, British commitments in the Middle East. This duty, as has been seen, he did not discharge competently. In a book first published in 1933 and thereafter frequently reprinted, he wrote:

> Our pledges to the Arabs, conflicting as they did with the promises we made to France in the subsequent Sykes–Picot agreement, produced a triangular situation of great embarrassment as between the French, President Wilson and ourselves.

These statements are clean contrary to what took place, as Nicolson, by reason of his official duties in both London and Paris would have been well placed to know. For the Sykes–Picot agreement was worded precisely so as not to conflict – rather so as exactly to fit in – with 'our pledges to the Arabs'. As for the embarrassment which arose in 1918–19, it was occasioned not by conflicting pledges but by Lloyd George's determination to disown the Sykes–Picot agreement. Nicolson went on to say that the letters exchanged between McMahon and Husayn

> were shrouded in the ambiguity inseparable from all oriental correspondence, yet the impresssion left on the mind of King Hussein was that Great Britain had assured him support in the foundation of an united Arab Empire with its capital at Damascus. It is true that in the course of the correspondence the British Government (who were bound by an understanding with France

---

[1] *Man of Valour: The Life of Field-Marshal the Viscount Gort*, 1972, p. 259. The statement that 'Palestine' had been the home of the 'Arabs' for 'nearly two thousand years' is also remarkable.

dating from 1912 to 'disinterest themselves' in Syria) had made some vague reservation about Damascus. This reservation, however, had not been studiously precise and it is significant that the subsequent Sykes–Picot agreement was not communicated by us to the Arabs, even as our pledges to King Hussein were not, until March of 1919, disclosed to the French.[1]

Most of the statements in this passage are, as may be seen from the evidence set out in this book, untrue; and, taken as a whole, the passage contrives falsely to portray Husayn as the victim of British dissimulation and double-dealing. But in writing thus Nicolson was only following the lines of his 1917 memorandum.

The author of another memorandum about 'commitments', Professor Arnold J. Toynbee, likewise remained fixed in his belief that Palestine had been promised to Husayn. He came also to believe that his conclusions had been deliberately suppressed, perhaps by illegitimate means. In 1940, Dr James Parkes who seems to have been then a member of the Foreign Research and Press Service at Chatham House, which Toynbee directed, went to Malcolm MacDonald and said how he

> had been told by Professor Arnold Toynbee that he had prepared a memorandum – presumably for the Foreign Office – before the Peace Conference at Versailles, setting forth the commitments entered into by H.M. Government in the Middle East during the last war. This memorandum clearly indicated that Palestine and Syria were within the area of Arab independence mentioned in the MacMahon–Husain correspondence. At that time the Foreign Office accepted this view of the correspondence, and according to Professor Toynbee it was only later that, as the result of Jewish pressure, H.M. Government changed their attitude and sought for arguments to show that the correspondence had failed to cover Palestine.[2]

The colonial office knew nothing of Toynbee's memorandum and asked Baggallay to investigate. The foreign office library could discover no *prima facie* evidence of Jewish pressure, and Baggallay wrote to Downie on 10 May 1940:

> I am afraid that it would be difficult to establish that the change in outlook of His Majesty's Government which does undoubtedly seem to have taken place between 1918 and 1922, was due to Jewish pressure.

Baggallay thus accepted without question (and without verification) that there had been a change of outlook. But despite the lack of evidence, Baggallay could not forbear to provide his own explanation of the presumed change:

---

[1] *Peacemaking 1919*, [1933], new ed. 1944, pp. 140–1.
[2] F.O. 371/24569, E1897/1897/31, memorandum by Baggallay recording a telephone conversation with H. F. Downie of the colonial office, 18 Apr. 1940.

Epilogue

I doubt whether the change was conscious...What probably happened was that after 1918 the Zionist interpretation of the Balfour Declaration was accepted by His Majesty's Government and ordered to be put into effect by persons who had forgotten or never known about the pledge to the Arabs. Later, when the irreconcilable elements in the situation began to make themselves felt, arguments were sought to show that the pledges did not exclude what was being done for the Zionists.[1]

There is, of course, no evidence whatever that 'the Zionist interpretation of the Balfour Declaration' was ever accepted by any minister or official, let alone that it was 'ordered to be put into effect by persons who had forgotten or never known about the pledge to the Arabs'. As has been seen, the Balfour declaration elicited no protest from Husayn, and it was only in 1920 that Faysal claimed – for the first time – that Palestine had been among the territories promised to his father. It was in order to deal with this new claim that Young put forward the notion that the 'district' of Damascus meant the 'vilayet' of Damascus, and that Palestine was to the west of this 'vilayet'.

Toynbee has never ceased to believe that Palestine was included in McMahon's promises to Husayn. In a book published in 1967, he declared:

> The British undertaking to King Husayn to recognize and uphold the independence of the Arabs within certain territorial limits had expressly excluded the territory to the west of 'the vilayets of Aleppo, Hama, Homs and Damascus' (in whatever way this ambiguous formula is to be interpreted). This strip of territory, however, was small in extent compared to the Arab territory, east of that line, that had also been under Ottoman sovereignty or suzerainty. In respect of this far larger Arab territory, the undertaking [Toynbee baldly asserted] had been unconditional.[2]

Three years later, Isaiah Friedman published an article in which he questioned the line of argument which Toynbee had followed in his 'commitments' memorandum. In a comment on this article, Toynbee justified his interpretation by arguing that the only way of making sense of McMahon's words was to transform his reference to 'the districts of Damascus, Homs, Hama and Aleppo' into a precise boundary-line. As a lawyer's argument, the contention may have some merit; coming from an historian it has none at all. In contrast to his categorical statement of three years before that Britain's undertaking to Husayn had been 'unconditional', Toynbee now argued that even though McMahon's letter had no juridical validity, yet it could be 'morally' valid. Toynbee also attacked

[1]   Loc. cit.   [2]   Acquaintances, p. 196.

Childs's memorandum, Young's earlier interpretation, and Mc-Mahon's letter of 1922 – which had, in different ways, argued that Palestine was not included in the territory promised to Husayn. Toynbee did not do so by showing their argument to be faulty, but by gratuitously impugning their motives: all these documents 'date from after the time at which H.M.G. had become sure that Britain had Palestine in her pocket'.[1] As has been seen, no evidence exists to show that Young or McMahon or Childs were instructed to, or did, tailor their arguments to fit in with a particular policy. The only official who may be suspected of doing this is Baggallay who, on behalf of his department, was eager to placate and pacify the Arab delegates in 1939. And even Baggallay actually believed in the truth and cogency of Antonius's arguments in *The Arab Awakening*, which he genuinely mistook for a piece of historical research.

The idea that the British government had been double-faced and treacherous in its dealings with Husayn was also greatly promoted by T. E. Lawrence's *Seven Pillars of Wisdom*. In a letter published in *The Times* on 11 September 1919 Lawrence had given a summary and inaccurate account of McMahon's letter of 24 October 1915, which considerably magnified what McMahon had promised. But in spite of this, Lawrence declared in this letter that he could see 'no inconsistencies and incompatibilities' – 'and', he added, 'I know nobody who does' – between McMahon's promises and the Sykes–Picot agreement, of which he also gave, in the same letter, a somewhat more accurate account.[2] However, in a passage of *Seven Pillars* which seems to have been written in 1919, Lawrence had quite a different view of the wartime transactions to put before his readers:

> The Arab Revolt had begun on false pretences. To gain the Sherif's help our Cabinet had offered, through Sir Henry McMahon, to support the establishment of native governments in parts of Syria and Mesopotamia, 'saving the interests of our ally, France'. The last modest clause concealed a treaty (kept secret, till too late, from McMahon, and therefore from the Sherif) by which France, England and Russia agreed to annex some of these promised areas, and to establish their respective spheres of influence over all the rest.

Lawrence goes on to say that the Arabs asked him, 'as a free agent', to 'endorse' the promises of the British government. But, 'not being a perfect fool', he realized that in case of British victory the

---

[1] Isaiah Friedman, 'The McMahon–Hussein Correspondence and the Question of Palestine', cited above, and 'The McMahon–Hussein Correspondence: Comments [by Toynbee] and a Reply', *Journal of Contemporary History* 5, nos. 2 and 4 (1970).

[2] David Garnett (ed.), *The Letters of T. E. Lawrence*, 1938, no. 113.

promises to the Arabs were 'dead paper'. One night, a beduin chieftain from the Syrian desert 'brought out a file of documents and asked which British pledge was to be believed'. Lawrence's advice, 'uttered with some agony of mind', was 'to trust the latest in date of the contradictions'. To revenge himself on the British government for making him 'continually and bitterly ashamed', Lawrence tells us that he vowed to lead the Arab Revolt 'so madly in the final victory that expediency should counsel to the Powers a fair settlement of the Arabs' moral claims.'[1] Lawrence's account is inaccurate and mystificatory. It is not true that the Sykes–Picot agreement was kept secret from McMahon until too late; we do not know what documents the beduin chieftain produced in his 'aisled tent', or what authority Lawrence had to make statements about them. But his language is clearly intended to convey that the British government was bound by contradictory engagements, was default-ing on its promises to the Arabs, and that he, Lawrence, was determined to enforce the Arab claims which (the reader is left to surmise) perhaps were strictly legal, or perhaps only 'moral'. But in either case, the reader comes away with the impression that if the British government was not downright fraudulent, its behaviour was at the very least shady and despicable. *Seven Pillars* was privately printed in 1926 in a small subscribers' edition. But after his death in May 1935, his brother allowed it to be published in a trade edition, and by the end of the following September 100,000 copies were in print.[2] Since then, of course, the book has been continuously reprinted, and translated into many languages. And his accusation that the British had acted in bad faith has been given a very wide currency not only by his writings, but also by Terence Rattigan's play *Ross*, and the Panavision technicolor film *Lawrence of Arabia*.

But though Lawrence's and Toynbee's writings have spread wide the idea that the British had defrauded the Arabs, they are by no means the only ones to do so. British officials in their memoirs and other publications have also lent authority to this notion, which has therefore ended by becoming an established and unquestionable truth. Thus Sir Hugh Foot (later Lord Caradon), who spent some fifteen years as a British official in Palestine and in the Middle East, tells us in his memoirs:

[1] *Seven Pillars of Wisdom*, Penguin ed., pp. 282–3. This text is based on a manuscript which Lawrence declares to have written in 1921–2, but a footnote on p. 283 seems to imply that the passage quoted above was written in 1919.

[2] Michael S. Howard, *Jonathan Cape, Publisher*, 1971, p. 156.

Knowledge, Power and Guilt

The failure of British administration in Palestine was inevitable. The double sin had been committed of raising false hopes both with the Arabs and with Jews. The hopes were false because they were conflicting. The Arabs who fought with Great Britain in the first world war to throw off the yoke of the Turkish Empire were led to believe that they were fighting for their freedom...the main responsibility was ours...by prevarication and procrastination and basically by the fundamental dishonesty of our original double dealing we had made disaster certain...In 1915 we supported King Feisal's desert rising. In 1917 we signed the Balfour Declaration.[1]

Sir Hugh Foot's language, though admittedly vague, is very strong. He is not only saying – what is reasonable enough – that British encouragement of a national home in Palestine was unwise, and even unfair to the inhabitants of Palestine. He also charges his government with 'fundamental dishonesty' and 'double dealing': his accusations clearly refer, albeit in an unspecified manner, to the war-time transactions.

Sir Lawrence Grafftey-Smith, a diplomat who spent almost the whole of his career in the Middle East, is also rather censorious. He quotes from Frederick the Great's *Dialogue des morts* a passage to the effect that *il ne faut pas avoir la conscience étroite quand on gouverne le monde* in order to observe: 'The toad beneath the harrow knows, among other things, that this thesis is disputable.' Grafftey-Smith seems to be hinting not only that generally government and a *conscience étroite* are – or ought to be – compatible – a disputable view – but also more precisely, that the behaviour of the British government towards Husayn was simply immoral. He affirms that the Sykes–Picot agreement and the Balfour declaration 'made nonsense' of McMahon's promises. He takes it for granted that the Sykes–Picot agreement was kept secret because it was disreputable, and affirms – as has been seen, clear against the evidence – that 'even our High Commissioner in Cairo, responsible for the political side of the Arab Revolt, only heard of it later, and casually.' Grafftey-Smith also asserts that Hogarth did not believe that Palestine had been excluded from the territories promised to the Sharif. This also, as has been seen, is plain contrary to the evidence which shows that Hogarth, in the interview of January 1918, reminded Husayn, specifically with reference to Palestine, 'of proviso in original Agreements safeguarding special interests of our Allies and especially France.' Grafftey-Smith's assertion is particularly surprising since Hogarth's report had been published in a white paper as early as 1939. But his most astonishing statement is that

---

[1] Hugh Foot, *A Start in Freedom*, 1964, pp. 35–6.

Epilogue

'I grew up with the McMahon letter as the sole background to my thinking about post-war planning in the Arab world'.[1] How a diplomat could look upon the tortured and obscure prose of McMahon's letter as the 'background', let alone 'the sole background', to his 'thinking about post-war planning in the Arab world' is puzzling.

Sir Geoffrey Furlonge also spent the greater part of his career in the Middle East; he was also at one time the head of the Eastern department at the foreign office. In 1969 he published a biography of the Palestinian notable, Musa al-Alami, in which he had some remarks to make on British promises to Husayn. He concurs in Antonius's description of the Sykes–Picot agreement as 'a shocking document', and accuses the lord chancellor of resorting to 'sharp practice' in arguing, in 1939, that Palestine was included in the areas in which Britain was not free to act 'without detriment to the interests of her Ally, France'. Furlonge professes to refer to the original files, though the reference he gives is non-existent and nonsensical. And, as a result of his researches, he accuses Grey of negligence and of 'cutting corners' owing to his 'sense of urgency'. The files, of course, disclose nothing of the kind. What they reveal, as has been seen, is that the 'sense of urgency' was McMahon's and not Grey's; that the foreign secretary authorized the offer to Husayn of 'boundaries...leaving in Arabia purely Arab districts of Aleppo, Damascus, Hama and Homs'; and that McMahon without any authority or any subsequent explanation, altered this phrasing (which he himself had previously suggested), and instead told Husayn that he was excluding from the area of Arab independence 'the portions of Syria lying to the West of Damascus, Homs, Hama and Aleppo'. This patent neglect of the evidence yielded by the records makes all the more misplaced Furlonge's harsh strictures on 'the shifts and evasions to which high-minded Christian statesmen find themselves forced in their efforts to reconcile irreconcilables.'[2]

Some sixty years or so after the exchanges between McMahon and the Sharif, then, there was in Britain a miasm of guilt and self-incrimination, of penitence and breast-beating which hung over relations with the Arab world. It had been chiefly generated by officials hopelessly lost in the labyrinth of their own files. Officials who, to vary the metaphor, were like Wittgenstein's flies, unable to find their way out of the fly-bottle in which their predecessors –

[1] *Bright Levant*, pp. 151–4.
[2] *Palestine Is My Country: The Story of Musa Alami*, 1969, pp. 57–8 and 226–7. Furlonge's reference is to 'P.R.O. file F.O. 317 of 1915'.

Knowledge, Power and Guilt

Clayton, Storrs, McMahon – had, with their eagerness, frivolity and incompetence, entrapped them. And this, perhaps, is the most significant outcome of the McMahon–Husayn correspondence. For the correspondence proved to have little effect over the post-war settlement. As for Palestine, whether or not the Palestinian leaders had succeeded in proving that it was promised to Husayn, this would have made little difference to British policy, and would certainly not have diminished the Zionist threat. But it is not unreasonable to think that the successive interpretations produced in the foreign office – all seemingly complicated, contrived and disingenuous – did in the end demoralize British Middle-Eastern policy, and imbue it with a corrosive feeling of embarrassment, if not of guilt. Its apologetic and placatory tone may now be heard alike on momentous and on insignificant occasions. And the more insignificant the occasion, perhaps, the easier may this tone be detected. It is thus not utterly fanciful to see a connexion between the guilt which the correspondence has induced and two recent incidents which, small in themselves, yet are like the drop of dew in which can be seen the colours of the sun: the advice given in 1969 by a British consul in Tripoli to a group of British women 'to let Libyan soldiers rape them rather than kill them',[1] and the public spectacle two years later in the Cairo whence McMahon had sent his famous missives, of a British foreign secretary, Sir Alec Douglas-Home, mounted on a camel and garbed in beduin dress.

[1] Reported in *The Daily Telegraph*, 1 Dec. 1969.

Works Cited

Place of publication London, unless otherwise indicated

Amin Sa'id, *Asrar al-thawra al-'arabiyya al-kubra wa ma' sat al-sharif Husayn* [Secrets of the Great Arab Revolt and the Tragedy of Sharif Husayn], Beirut, n.d. [c.1960]

    al-Thawra al-'arabiyya al-kubra [The Great Arab Revolt], 3 vols., Cairo, n.d. [1934]

Antonius, George, *The Arab Awakening*, 1938

Arnold, T. W., *The Caliphate*, [1924], 2nd ed., 1965

Arthur, George, *General Sir John Maxwell*, 1932

Ben-Gurion, David, *Letters to Paula*, 1971

Cassar, George H., *The French and the Dardanelles*, 1971

Childs, W. J., *Across Asia Minor on Foot*, 1918

Cole, Margaret, ed., *Beatrice Webb's Diaries 1924–1932*, 1956

Colville, J. R., *Man of Valour: The Life of Field-Marshal the Viscount Gort*, 1972

Foot, Hugh, *A Start in Freedom*, 1964

Friedman, Isaiah, 'The McMahon–Hussein Correspondence and the Question of Palestine', in *Journal of Contemporary History*, vol. v, nos. 2 and 4, 1970

Furlonge, Geoffrey, *Palestine Is My Country: The Story of Musa Alami*, 1969

Garnett, David (ed.), *The Letters of T. E. Lawrence*, 1938

Gilbert, Martin, *Winston Churchill*, vol. iii, 1971

Gooch, G. P., and Temperley, H. W. V. (eds.), *British Documents on the Origins of the War*, vol. x, pt. 2, 1938

Grafftey-Smith, L. *Bright Levant*, 1970

Graves, Philip, *Palestine: Land of Three Faiths*, 1923

Great Britain, Cmd. 1700, *Correspondence with the Palestine Arab Delegation and the Zionist Organisation*, 1922, Accounts and Papers, vol. xxiii, 1922

    Cmd. 5479, *Report of the Royal Commission on Palestine*, 1937, Accounts and Papers, vol. xiv, 1936–7

    Cmd. 5957, *Correspondence between Sir Henry McMahon and the Sherif Hussein of Mecca in 1915 and 1916*, 1939, Accounts and Papers, vol. xxvii, 1938–9

    Cmd. 5964, *Statements made on behalf of His Majesty's Government during the year 1918 in regard to the Future Status of certain parts of the Ottoman Empire*, 1939, Accounts and Papers, vol. xxvii, 1938–9

    Cmd. 5974, *Report of a Committee set up to consider Certain Correspondence between Sir Henry McMahon...and the Sharif of Mecca in 1915 and 1916*, 1939, Accounts and Papers, vol. xiv, 1938–9

    Documents on British Foreign Policy, series i, vol. iv, 1952; vol. xiii, 1963

Grey of Fallodon, Viscount, *Twenty-five Years: 1892–1916*, 2 vols., 1925

Works Cited

Headlam-Morley, Sir James, *A Memoir of the Paris Peace Conference 1919*, 1972
Herbert, Aubrey, *Mons, Anzac and Kut*, 1919
Howard, Michael S., *Jonathan Cape, Publisher*, 1971
Kedourie, Elie, *Arabic Political Memoirs and Other Studies*, 1974
   The Chatham House Version and Other Middle-Eastern Studies, 1970
   England and the Middle East: The Destruction of the Ottoman Empire 1914–1921, 1956
Khayriyya Qasimiyya, *al-'Alam al-filastini* [The Palestinian Flag], Beirut, 1970
Lawrence, T. E., *Secret Despatches from Arabia*, 1939
   Seven Pillars of Wisdom [1935], Penguin Books ed., 1962
Lennox, Lady Algernon Gordon (ed.), *The Diary of Lord Bertie of Thame*, 2 vols., 1924
Loder, J. de V., *The Truth about Mesopotamia, Palestine and Syria*, 1923
Macalister, R. A. A., 'Palestine', in James Hastings (ed.), *Dictionary of the Bible*, 1909
Madelung, W., 'Imama', *Encyclopaedia of Islam*, new ed., 1971
Marmorstein, Emile, 'A Note on "Damascus, Homs, Hama, and Aleppo"', *St Antony's Papers*, no. 11, 1961
Massey, W. T., *How Jerusalem Was Won*, 1919
Miller, D. H., *My Diary of the Peace Conference*, vol. IV, 1924
Muhammad Farid, 'Mudhakkirat' [Memoirs], *al-Katib*, Cairo, July and October 1970
Muhammad Tahir al-'Umari, *Muqaddarat al-'Iraq al-siyasiyya* [Political Destinies of Iraq], 3 vols., Baghdad, 1925
Nicolson, Harold, *Peacemaking 1919* [1933], new ed., 1944
Ofer, P., 'The Role of the High Commissioner in British Policy in Palestine: Sir John Chancellor 1928–1931', unpublished Ph.D. dissertation, University of London, 1971
Rendel, George, *The Sword and the Olive*, 1957
Robbins, Keith, *Sir Edward Grey*, 1971
Rothwell, V. H., *British War Aims and Peace Diplomacy 1914–1918*, 1971
   'Mesopotamia in British War Aims 1914–18', *Historical Journal*, XIII (1970)
Samuel, Viscount, *Memoirs*, 1945
Samuel, Edwin, *A Lifetime in Jerusalem*, 1970.
Steiner, Zara, *The Foreign Office and Foreign Policy 1898–1914*, 1969
Symes, Stewart, *Tour of Duty*, 1946
Storrs, Ronald, *Orientations*, definitive ed., 1943
   'T. E. Lawrence', *Dictionary of National Biography, 1931–40*
Sulayman Musa, *al-Haraka al-'arabiyya* [The Arab Movement], Beirut, 1970
Sulayman Musa (ed.), *al-Murasalat al-tarikhiyya, 1914–1918*, [Historical Correspondence], vol. I, Amman, 1973
   al-Thawra al-'arabiyya al-kubra: watha'iq wa asanid [The Great Arab Revolt: Documents and Records], Amman, 1966
Temperley, H. W. V. (ed.), *History of the Peace Conference*, vol. VI, 1924
Toynbee, Arnold J., *Acquaintances*, 1967
   'The McMahon–Hussein Correspondence: Comments', *Journal of Contemporary History*, vol. V, 1970
Toynbee, Arnold J., and Boulter, V. M. (eds.), *Survey of International Affairs 1938*, vol. I, 1941

Works Cited

Young, Hubert, *The Independent Arab*, 1933

Zeine, Z. N., *al-Sira' al-duwali fi' l-sharq al-awsat wa wiladat dawlatayy Suriya wa Lubnan* [International Conflict in the Middle East and the Birth of the Two States of Syria and Lebanon], Beirut, 1971

The Struggle for Arab Independence, Beirut, 1960

Index

Index

Index

Index

Index

Index

Wilson, Colonel Cyril Edward (*cont.*)
  expresses anxiety over Husayn's being disappointed, 223–4
Wingate, Sir Reginald, 12–13
  promotes Arab unity and Arab caliphate, 42–4, 46–7, 51–2, 71
  suggests answer to Sharif's demands, 95–6
  does not believe that Sharif wanted caliphate, 144
  fails to alert London to Husayn's ambitions about caliphate, 149
  fails to rebut Husayn's claims, 153
  suggests informing Husayn of Sykes–Picot agreement, 161
  his instructions to Sykes, 162–3, 175–6
  wishes French to disclaim annexations in Syria, 186
  suggests disowning Sykes–Picot agreement, 193–4
  denies to Husayn, without authority, existence of Sykes–Picot agreement, 197–8
  fears Husayn's abdication, 201–2
  and memorial from seven Syrians, 294–5

Yale, William, 292
Young, Hubert Winthrop, 231, 232, 245
  his views on Arab policy, 235–6
  his interpretation of McMahon's promises, 236–7
  professes to discover mistake in Arabic text of McMahon's letters, 237–9, 240

Zionism, 233
  Baggallay's attitude to, 277–8

330

Cambridge Studies in the History and Theory of Politics

Editors: MAURICE COWLING, G. R. ELTON, E. KEDOURIE, J. G. A. POCOCK, J. R. POLE *and* WALTER ULLMANN

A series in two parts, studies and original texts. The studies are original works on political history and political philosophy while the texts are modern, critical editions of major texts in political thought. The titles include:

TEXTS

LIBERTY, EQUALITY, FRATERNITY, by James Fitzjames Stephen. Edited with an introduction and notes by R. J. White

VLADIMIR AKIMOV ON THE DILEMMAS OF RUSSIAN MARXISM 1895–1903. An English edition of 'A Short History of the Social Democratic Movement in Russia' and 'The Second Congress of the Russian Social Democratic Labour Party', with an introduction and notes by Jonathan Frankel

TWO ENGLISH REPUBLICAN TRACTS: PLATO REDIVIVUS OR, A DIALOGUE CONCERNING GOVERNMENT (c. 1681), by Henry Neville and AN ESSAY UPON THE CONSTITUTION OF THE ROMAN GOVERNMENT (c. 1699), by Walter Moyle. Edited by Caroline Robbins

J. G. HERDER ON SOCIAL AND POLITICAL CULTURE, translated, edited and with an introduction by F. M. Barnard

THE LIMITS OF STATE ACTION, by Wilhelm von Humboldt. Edited with an introduction and notes by J. W. Burrow

KANT'S POLITICAL WRITINGS, edited with an introduction and notes by Hans Reiss; translated by H. B. Nisbet

KARL MARX'S CRITIQUE OF HEGEL'S 'PHILOSOPHY OF RIGHT', edited with an introduction and notes by Joseph O'Malley; translated by Annette Jolin and Joseph O'Malley

LORD SALISBURY ON POLITICS. A SELECTION FROM HIS ARTICLES IN 'THE QUARTERLY REVIEW' 1860–1883, edited by Paul Smith

FRANCOGALLIA, by François Hotman. Latin text edited by Ralph E. Giesey. English translation by J. H. M. Salmon

THE POLITICAL WRITINGS OF LEIBNIZ. Edited and translated by Patrick Riley

TURGOT ON PROGRESS, SOCIOLOGY AND ECONOMICS: A PHILOSOPHICAL REVIEW OF THE SUCCESSIVE ADVANCES OF THE HUMAN MIND ON UNIVERSAL HISTORY. REFLECTIONS ON THE FORMATION AND DISTRIBUTION OF WEALTH, edited, translated and introduced by Ronald L. Meek

TEXTS CONCERNING THE REVOLT OF THE NETHERLANDS, edited and with an introduction by E. H. Kossmann and A. F. Mellink

GEORG WILHELM FRIEDRICH HEGEL: LECTURES ON THE PHILOSOPHY OF WORLD HISTORY: REASON IN HISTORY, translated from the German edition of Johannes Hoffmeister by H. B. Nisbet and with an introduction by Duncan Forbes

A MACHIAVELLIAN TREATISE BY STEPHEN GARDINER, edited and translated by Peter S. Donaldson

STUDIES

REGICIDE AND REVOLUTION: SPEECHES AT THE TRIAL OF LOUIS XVI, edited with an introduction by Michael Walzer; translated by Marian Rothstein

1867: DISRAELI, GLADSTONE AND REVOLUTION: THE PASSING OF THE SECOND REFORM BILL, by Maurice Cowling

THE CONSCIENCE OF THE STATE IN NORTH AMERICA, by E. R. Norman

THE SOCIAL AND POLITICAL THOUGHT OF KARL MARX, by Shlomo Avineri

MEN AND CITIZENS: A STUDY OF ROUSSEAU'S SOCIAL THEORY, by Judith Shklar

IDEALISM, POLITICS AND HISTORY: SOURCES OF HEGELIAN THOUGHT, by George Armstrong Kelly